Thus plainly, and most truly is declar'd
The needles worke hath still bin in regard,
For it doth ART, so like to NATURE frame,
As if IT were her Sister, or the SAME.
Flowers, Plants and Fishes, Beasts, Birds, Flyes,
    and Bees,
Hils, Dales, Plaines, Pastures, Skies, Seas, Rivers,
    Trees;
There's nothing neere at hand, or farthest sought,
But with the Needle may be shap'd and wrought.
In clothes of Arras I have often seene,
Men's figurd counterfeits so like have beene,
That if the parties selfe had beene in place,
Yet ART would vye with NATURE for the
    grace.
Moreover, Posies rare, and Anagrams,
Signifique searching sentences from names,
True History, or various pleasant fiction,
In sundry colours mixt, with Arts commixion,
All in Dimension, Ovals, Squares, and Rounds,
Arts life included within Natures bounds:
So that Art seemeth meerely naturall,
In forming shapes so Geometricall;
And though our Country everywhere is fild
With Ladies, and with Gentlewomen skild
In this rare Art, yet here they may discerne
Some things to teach them if they list to learne.
And as this booke some cunning workes doth
    teach,
(Too hard for meane capacities to reach)
So for weake learners, other workes here be,
As plaine and easie as are ABC.
Thus skillfull, or unskillfull, each may take
This booke, and of it each goode use may make,
All sortes of workes, almost that can be nam'd,
Here are directions how they may be fram'd:
And for this kingdom's good are hither come,
From the remotest part of Christendome,
Collected with much paines and industry,
From scorching *Spaine* and freezing *Muscovie*,
From fertill *France*, and pleasant *Italy*,
From *Poland*, *Sweden*, *Denmarke*, *Germany*,

And some of th̶̶... ̶̶...̶̶ ̶̶...e set
Beyond the bounds of faithlesse Mahomet.
From spacious *China*, and those Kingdomes East,
And from Great *Mexico*, the Indies West.
Thus are these workes *farre fetcht*, and *dearely
    bought*,
And consequently *good for Ladies thought*.
Nor doe I degrodate (in any case)
Or doe esteeme of other teachings base,
For *Tent-worke*, *Raisd-worke*, *Laid-worke*,
    Frost-worke, *Net-worke*,
Most curious *Purles*, or rare *Italian Cutworke*,
Fine *Ferne-stitch*, *Finny-stitch*, *New-stitch*, and
    Chaine-stitch,
Brave *Bred-stitch*, *Fisher-stitch*, *Irish-stitch*, and
    Queen-stitch,
The *Spanish-stitch*, *Rosemary-stitch*, and
    Mowse-stitch,
The smarting *Whip-stitch*, *Back-stitch*, & the
    Crosse-stitch.
All these are good, and these we must allow,
And these are everywhere in practice now:
And in this Booke, there are of these some store,
With many others, never seene before.
Here Practise and Invention may be free,
And as a *Squirrel* skips from tree to tree,
So maids may (from their Mistresse, or their
    Mother)
Learne to leave one worke, and to learne
    another,
For here they may make choice of which is
    which,
And skip from worke to worke, from stitch to
    stitch,
Until in time, delightfull practice shall
(With profit) make them perfect in them all.
Thus hoping that these workes may have this
    guide,
To serve for ornament, and not for pride.
To cherish vertue, banish idlenesse,
For these ends, may this booke have good
    successe.

John Taylor

The Needleworker's Dictionary

The Needleworker's Dictionary

Pamela Clabburn

American contributing editor
Helene Von Rosenstiel

M

First published 1976 by
Macmillan London Limited
London and Basingstoke
Associated companies in New York, Dublin,
Melbourne, Johannesburg, and Delhi

Produced by Walter Parrish International Limited, London
Designed by Judy A. Tuke
Drawings by Neil McConachie

Printed and bound in Great Britain by
The Pitman Press, Bath, and
Colour Reproductions Limited, Billericay, Essex

ISBN 0 333 18756 3

KLMNOPQRSTUVXY

for Lesley

ABCDEFGHIJKLMN
OPQRSTUVWXYZ

Contents

florentine stitch: detail of a bookbinding worked in wool on linen, English or American, 18th century.

Colour Illustrations

Introduction

Needlework, a craft stretching back to the beginning of the Old Testament, and, if the story of Adam and Eve is to be believed, preceding weaving, is flourishing. Through its long history it has adapted to the requirements of every climate and race, to any fibre which will make thread, and to all materials which can be pierced with a needle. It has taken modern technology in its stride, the sewing-machine is now part of the equipment of everyone who sews, and the uses of man-made fabrics are well understood. Today the craft is as vital and as strong as it has ever been.

It was this very versatility which made this book necessary. It seemed important that a broad survey of part of the vast range of techniques, processes, threads, fabrics and terms which have been used today and in the past should be made, particularly to help those who, working with the new materials, need to understand the old in order to get the best possible results. This survey can only be a compilation from many sources—a distillation of all the knowledge acquired and set down over the centuries, and it can only be selective as the subject is so vast that a complete record would fill many volumes.

As selection was essential it was decided to concentrate on plain sewing which is the basis of all needlework, and embroidery with its superb decorative qualities, and regretfully to ignore dressmaking, tailoring, shoemaking, sailmaking, and leatherwork. These, while technically needlework, are trades in their own right and deserve separate treatment, while needlepoint lace, though also made with needle and thread, belongs more to a discussion of laces.

Embroidery is not confined to one or two countries—it is world-wide, and this is a part of its fascination. Most countries have their own particular techniques and approaches, and each nation makes the artefacts needed for homes, costume and ceremonies, both religious and secular, but when these are analysed it emerges that there are really comparatively few stitches and techniques—the richness and variety comes from their application in many different ways. This means that there are some problems in nomenclature and in the book an attempt has been made, not to eliminate differences, which would be both impertinent and impossible, but to state them clearly, showing how the same things may be called by different names in different countries. There is a similar difficulty as regards spelling, not only as between Britain and America but, for example, in all eastern countries where spelling can vary from village to village and from dialect to dialect. Here alternatives have been given when it was felt that they might help; but in general, English spelling predominates and that of foreign words is generally based on what seems to be the most common English usage.

We have tried, with the aid of the many hundred line drawings and photographs, to give the reader a real understanding of the techniques described; the aim is to give a fairly concise definition, together with a wide-ranging bibliography to enable the interested reader to explore further. When a particular author has been quoted, or a précis made of his or her work, the author's name and the date of publication will be found at the foot of the entry; full details will be found in the bibliography.

Such references indicate the major source of information in an entry, although other points may be taken from other sources. Of course, where a word has a number of meanings, only those relevant to embroidery have been defined. Quotations have been given, where possible, in their original form; where this would not be easily understood, they have been rendered into modern English.

To make the book as readable as possible and at the same time give every help to the serious student, the use of asterisks (which refer to another heading) has been kept for proper names and for words which may be unfamiliar or which are particularly relevant in a certain context. The alternative—asterisking every word which has its own entry— would have made for difficult reading.

For lovers of needlework, as in so many other fields, there is no substitute ultimately for looking at the real thing, and in many parts of the world, wonderful collections of interesting pieces are open to the public. A select list of collections and museums where good embroidery can be seen has therefore been included. While some of these collections may be small they all include pieces of great interest.

Authors and practising needleworkers, amateur and professional, past and present, have provided most of the material for this book, but many colleagues have been, as always, very helpful indeed. That there are not more mistakes is due to them, and where there are mistakes it is probably from neglecting to ask their advice. Particular thanks must be given to all the museums and owners of embroideries who have allowed their work to be photographed and reproduced. For myself I have been buttressed by many people willing to correct my grammar and my spelling, try to read my writing, argue with me, discuss with me and help in every possible way; they include the Associate Editor in America, Helene Von Rosenstiel, the staff of Walter Parrish International, and last but by no means least, Lesley Parker, and to them I owe more than I can ever repay.

Adam and Eve: wool on linen,
American 18th century.

antimacassar: depicting scenes from fairytales, English, early 20th century.

abhla bharat Mirror-work embroidery from Kathiawar (India) in which round pieces of mirror are buttonholed or used in conjunction with stem or close herringbone stitch (Dhamija 1964). See also shisha.

abhla bharat: motif with central mirror, front (top) and back showing stitches (bottom).

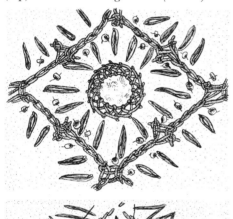

Academy of Armory see Holme, Randle. See also embroidery frame, needle.

Acadian rugs *Yarn sewn rugs on a tow or linen background characterised by a clipped and sculptured pile surface. They were made by French settlers of the Quebec/Nova Scotia region as early as the 18th century and called Acadian from the Indian name for the region. The predominantly formal floral motifs influenced a later type of 19th century hooked rug called a Waldoboro. (Kopp 1974)

acid-free tissue paper Used for storing all textiles because of its neutral content.

Ackermann Rudolph (1764-1834) German lithographer who worked in Saxony, Paris and England as a coach designer. In 1795 he started a print shop in the Strand, London. He used the comparatively new art of lithography in his various publications among which was the *Repository of the Arts, Literature, Fashion, Manufactures etc.* This magazine lasted from 1809 to 1828 and did a great deal to promote interest in fabrics, fashions and needlework.

ackton (acton) see haqueton.

Adam and Eve Favourite subject for needlework pictures especially in the 17th and 18th centuries. Some of these are decidedly naive and most consist of Adam and Eve standing either side of the apple tree in the Garden of Eden, while the serpent writhes itself around the tree, usually with a very human and knowing face.

Adrianople twill see Turkey red.

aër Embroidered veil for the communion vessels in the Greek Orthodox Church. The little aëres were used to cover the chalice and paten separately, and the great aër to cover both together. (Johstone 1967)

aerophane Fine semitransparent fabric resembling thin crape. It was used in the late 18th and early 19th centuries for bonnets, quillings, trimmings on costume, and pictures. In the pictures, which were like the more usual silk-on-taffeta landscape and figure embroideries, parts were worked, covered with aerophane, and then reworked to give varying depths of shading.

Afghanistan Being situated between the USSR, Persia (Iran), and India, the embroideries of Afghanistan have taken something from each culture. The main craft is carpet weaving and the embroidery designs have much in common with those of the carpets. Although the early work on clothes and household articles (using mainly chain, satin, and herringbone stitches) was beautiful, unfortunately modern work has deteriorated in response to the insatiable tourist demand.

Afghanistan: detail of a robe taken at the capture of Kabul in 1839.

agave Botanical name for a genus of fleshy-leaved, semitropical plants, including the century plant or American aloe, which are found in southwest USA, Mexico, and Central and South America. The fibrous leaves are used to make thread and rope. See also aloe thread embroidery.

aglet see aiguillette.

Agnus Dei The Lamb of God—a symbol much used in church embroidery, consisting of a lamb, generally haloed, carrying a staff with a cross or pennant. This was one of the earliest ways of portraying Christ, and refers to John the Baptist saying 'Behold the Lamb of God'.

aiguillette (aglet) Word derived from the French *aiguille*, a needle, of varied usage since medieval times. 1. The metal tag of a lace or point used to secure clothes, especially the doublet to the hose, or shoelaces. 2. Metal ornaments or buttons for dress: 'Aglets or Buttons for Childrens caps' (1582, quoted by Willan 1962). 3. Any metal ornament or *spangle used on dress or in embroidery. 4. Trimming of cords ending in metal tags worn from the shoulder across the breast of various uniforms to denote rank.

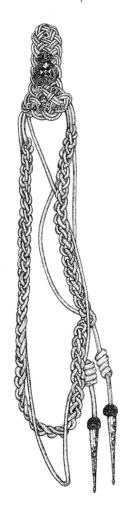

Ainu Tribal people from the island of Hokkaido, Japan. They wear boldly patterned garments for ceremonial and religious use, often decorated with applied work and some surface embroidery.

aksi Type of embroidery worked in Kashmir. The word literally means 'reflections in the mirror'. A very fine needle splits the warp thread of the cloth so that the tiny darning stitches only show on one side. Therefore two different patterns can be worked, one on either side of the fabric, and this double pattern is called dourukha-douranga. (Dhamija 1964) See dourukha.

alb Full-length, sleeved garment of white linen, worn by priests, deacons, and subdeacons at the main church service of the Eucharist. It derives from the long tunic worn by the people of Palestine at the time of Christ. At different periods during the history of the church the alb has been of various colours and rich materials such as *samite and silk, but now it is usually white linen, cotton or synthetic. Today it is absolutely plain but it sometimes has broad embroidered bands called *apparels applied at hem and cuff.

Albania Embroideries of Albania owe a great deal to Turkish influence and are most frequently found on costume, both men's and women's. There is a tendency to use finer silks, muslin, and cloths than is the case in Yugoslavia, north of Albania. Lavish decoration, as in most of the Balkan states, is produced by cords or braids sewn down in beautiful swirling designs as well as by couched gold embroidery and needlepoint. The most common stitches are pulled fabric stitches, tent, satin, and double running. (Start 1939, Jones 1968). See also japangi, jelek.

album quilt (autograph, friendship, or presentation quilt) American quilt which consists of a series of *blocks each of which is designed, made, and signed by a different worker, only the size and type of *patchwork (generally applied) being the same. The blocks are then made up into a quilt which is presented to some member of the community, possibly a minister, as a token of regard. As these quilts were very much treasured and little used, there are quite a number in excellent condition still in existence. See also freedom quilts. (Colour illustration p 17)

Aleut embroidery Characteristic embroidery of two tribes native to the Aleutian Islands off Alaska. Small geometric designs, often worked with single, undyed *caribou hairs which fasten and ornament the appliqué of black or red seal gullet bands, decorate the waterproof coats made of seal intestines. The silvery hairs of old bull walrus beards were also used. (Birket-Smith 1935, Turner 1955) See also Rameleika.

Algerian embroidery For more than three centuries Algeria was dominated by Turkey and this is reflected in the embroidery designs. They are based on flower motifs massed together in large groups, generally cover most of the article, and are frequently found on curtains, *benîqas, and head-kerchiefs. According to Caulfeild and Saward (1882) the craft of embroidery in Algeria was revived about 1840 to help the destitute needlewomen, and a school was founded in Algiers with the work produced being sold in Europe. (*Catalogue of Algerian Embroideries* 1915)

Algerian embroidery: Algerian eye, and punch stitches on etamine linen.

allegory Story or similar in which a spiritual or poetic meaning is conveyed by symbols. The allegories in 16th century needlework, which are very akin to *emblems, generally took the form of a story, probably mythological, embroidered in tent stitch or appliqué. Two of the most famous English sets of allegorical embroideries are still at *Hardwick Hall.

allover Term applied to embroidery, lace, and printed textile patterns which repeat over the whole surface of the fabric and therefore do not include borders, insertions, or edgings.

alms bag The small bag used for collecting the alms of the congregation at a religious service. It generally has an extended top by which it is held, or is attached to a handle of brass or wood, and is embroidered with an appropriate symbol. Sometimes it is known as a collection bag.

alms purse: in silk and couched gold thread from France, c.1340.

alms purse (alner, aumonière, escarcelle, gibecière, gipsire, tasque) Wallet or pouch hanging from the belt which had different names at different dates. Originally worn by rich men to carry small necessities and jewellery, after the Crusades these purses held relics, and were beautifully and often heavily worked with silk, jewels and gold. They were often given as presents and used as containers for gifts of money. In the middle ages the town of Caen (France) became famous for making them, and there they were known as tasques. (Seligman and Hughes n.d.)

aloe thread embroidery Type of work using a thread made from the fibres of the aloe plant. This thread was a pale straw colour and was suitable for satin stitch. The use of aloe fibre in England was a novelty in the late 19th century.

alpaca 1. Domesticated llama-like animal from Peru and neighbouring countries. Its soft, long wool has been spun into yarns for weaving and embroidery since pre-Columbian times. 2. The fabric woven from the wool of the alpaca mixed with other yarns, first introduced into England in the early 19th century. After many difficulties in the spinning and weaving had been overcome, and the wool had been used as the weft with a cotton warp, it became a very popular fabric.

altar carpet see Laudian frontal.

altar frontal (antependium) Piece of rich fabric, generally embroidered, that hangs from a rod or is mounted on a frame in front of the altar. It is defined in Canon 82 of the Church of England as 'a carpet of silk or other decent stuff'. There are two main types: the frontal or antependium, and the *Laudian frontal or altar carpet, also known as the throw-over frontal. Though it may be slightly gathered like a curtain, it is usually straight, and is often finished with a fringe that just touches the ground. As the altar is the focal point of any church, the frontal has always been as richly decorated as the purses and piety of the donors permitted, and it has been the custom for royalty to give the church in which they were crowned part of their coronation robes to be made into frontals. These were often in silk and metal threads. Most churches have more than one frontal, corresponding to the ferial colours, *viz* white for Christmas, Easter, and festivals, red for Whitsun and Saints' Days, purple or ash colour for Lent, plum for Advent, and green for Trinity, but some have only one, and others only an ordinary and a festival frontal.

aluminium twist Modern metal thread which does not tarnish as silver does. It can be bought in 2, 3, or 4 ply, and is used in ecclesiastical embroidery, badges, and collages.

Amager embroidery Cross stitch embroidery on narrow hanging panels from the island of Amager, which lies between Denmark and Sweden. Most of the panels are dated—the earliest so far discovered is 1770 and the latest 1852. They are worked in wool, silk, or cotton threads on heavy linen and the designs consist of isolated motifs of fantastic birds, beasts, fruit, and people. One other type of embroidery found on the island consists of 'plaiting stitch' (flettestingets), a form of long-legged cross stitch worked in vertical rows with black silk on white linen. When finished, the embroidery was dyed dark blue, starched, and made up into christening bibs and hats. There is now a revival of this work using the old motifs made up into many household articles. (Johnson 1955)

Amager embroidery: cross stitch signed and dated 1770.

American cloth   see toile cirée.

American crewel work   Decorative embroidery stitched onto a plain-weave linen background with *crewel wools dyed in a variety of natural dyes, including *indigo. It had its origins in the English 17th century work but, in the 18th century particularly, it developed on its own lines. This was partly due to the fact that wool was not easy to obtain in America, and so the embroiderer developed an economy of stitch not so prevalent in England. Designs were light, leaving a considerable amount of plain ground fabric, and the preferred stitches were those which used as much wool on the surface as possible, with only the minimum underneath. Secondly, indigo grows wild in America and many homes had a tub of the dye outside the back door into which they could dip their wool, with the result that light, medium, and dark blue predominate and some work is done only in these three colours. The third main difference comes in the design.

American crewel work: 18th century bed furniture.

Though the women had access (to a lesser degree) to the same design sources as their English counterparts, they inclined towards drawing and working the flowers and animals around them, giving their work a freshness, homeliness, and vigour which owed little or nothing to its English origins.

American Museum in Britain   see Claverton Manor.

American tapestry   (needle-woven tapestry)   Tapestry process invented by Candace *Wheeler in 1883. It was worked on a silk warp with a needle instead of a shuttle, and embroidery silks were sewn into the warp surface of the fabric. The work was done in the atelier of *Associated Artists after 1883.

amice   Band of white linen worn by priests and others at the service of the Eucharist. It forms a combined filling-in at the neck of the *alb and a collar to fall over the stole and chasuble. The top or collar part is sometimes embroidered with a strip called an *apparel. The amice derives from a secular neckcloth or scarf which in ancient times filled in the gap left when a garment had a wide enough neckline to allow it to be pulled over the head.

Amish quilts   Patchwork quilts made by a group of strict Mennonites, many of whom had emigrated in the early 18th century from Switzerland and areas of the Rhineland to Pennsylvania (in particular Lancaster County), and later to Ohio and Indiana. The strict religious beliefs of these people have encouraged old traditions to be followed, and modes of dress, farming, and transportation have varied little in two centuries. Purely decorative objects were forbidden, but the quilts were a practical necessity, and were beautifully worked in large geometric shapes such as rectangles and stars in muted colour schemes of greys, blues, maroon, browns, and olive green.

'amli   Embroidered shawls from Kashmir. In the traditional Kashmir shawls the designs were woven in on the loom—a slow, and consequently very expensive process. As early as 1803 an Armenian, Khwäja Yüsuf, realised that embroidery would be quicker and cheaper, so embroiderers were trained and the work was made to look as much like weaving as possible. Stem stitch, satin stitch, and darning were most generally used. About 1830, 'amli ceased to be merely cheaper copies of the loom-woven shawls and developed a style of their own, usually illustrating one of the poetical romances of Indo-Persian literature. *Map shawls were also embroidered during the second half of the 19th century. (Irwin 1973)

amphithuron   see iconostasis curtain.

Anglesey Abbey   (near Cambridge, England)   Early 17th century property with a very varied collection of artefacts including several interesting embroideries.

Anglesey Abbey: an Italian 18th century altar frontal.

Among these are an 18th century altar frontal, now framed and glazed; what is said to be the oldest *Garter in existence of that Order of Chivalry; and several heraldic embroideries. It now belongs to the National Trust.

Anglo-Indian embroidery Type of work popular in the 1880s and later, resembling *brocade embroidery. It was done on printed materials from India, especially handkerchiefs, and covered the whole fabric. When finished, it was made into articles such as handbags, sachets, and table centres. (Colour illustration p 18)

angular tear darn see hedge tear darn.

animal furniture Cloth or leather trappings used on animals as protection from heat and flies or purely for decoration. See also bullock furniture and horse furniture.

animals The domestic embroiderer has always delighted in representing the surrounding scenes, and has also found inspiration in *bestiaries, woodcuts, prints etc. Sometimes the animals worked are mythical, or they are taken from books or stories where the writer or teller was as unsure of the subject as the embroiderer. One of the earliest sources was *The Historie of Foure-footed Beastes* by Topsell (1607), which was itself a version of *Historiae Animalium* by Conrad Gesner (1551).

ankh Very old form of the cross called 'ansated' or 'handled', known in Egypt as long ago as 2000 BC. It became a Christian symbol and because of its Egyptian origin is often seen in *Coptic embroideries and textiles.

antependium see altar frontal.

antics (antiques) Fantastic representations of human, animal, and floral forms incongruously running into one another. The heavily embroidered dresses of the 16th century were often worked with antics, and in the list of *The Queen's Wardrobe, 1600* (Elizabeth I) are 'Item, one Frenche gowne of russet stitched cloth . . . embroidered with antiques of gold and silk of sonderie colours' and 'Item, one compasse lappe-clothe of white taphata, embroidered all over with sondrie antiques.' (Nichols 1823)

antimacassar (chair back) Washable cover for the back of a chair or sofa, originally to protect the upholstery from the macassar hair-oil worn by men. In use from about 1840 up to and including the present day, antimacassars were, and are, generally made by the women of the household, and can be in any suitable (and sometimes unsuitable) type of work or embroidery. Modern arm and chair backs are often made to match the chair, while those on trains and planes may be of disposable materials.

antiques see antics.

antique seam Method used in plain sewing of joining two *selvage edges together without overlap so that they lie absolutely flat. It was also used, especially in underwear, where linen of narrow widths had to be joined. The two selvages are laid flat, edge to-edge and, from the right side, a small stitch is taken, first at one edge and then at the other so that they are held close together. This produces a slight fishbone effect. The modern overlock sewing machine makes the equivalent of an antique seam.

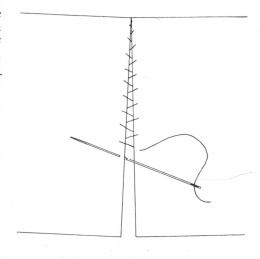

apparel 1. All kinds of clothes. 2. Broad bands of embroidery or lace for decorating certain ecclesiastical garments—the alb, amice, dalmatic, tunic, and cotta. The apparel is frequently embroidered separately and applied to the garment. In the amice it forms a band at the top which turns over to become a collar, but in the other garments it is applied as a block on the front and back of the hem and on the cuffs.

applied lace *Edging or *insertion of lace for decorative purposes. In the 1930s the fashion was for a wide machine-made lace with a design outlined in cord to be applied to the edge of an undergarment by oversewing or french stemming. The underneath material was then cut away leaving the corded outline patterned on the garment.

applied work (appliqué, onlay) The addition of fabrics or embroidered motifs to the surface of a ground material to form a design. In *collage, objects such as buttons, curtain rings, and spangles may be added, but strictly speaking only fabrics may be used in applied work. As an embroidery form, it has been and still is very popular largely because it can be effective whether the design is simple or complicated, and the technique is especially suitable for hangings, curtains, and portières as it can be used to cover a large area both quickly and decoratively.

applied work: leather riding boots with appliqué from northern Nigeria.

It has a very long history, for it was used by the Egyptians and ancient Greeks. In the middle ages the crusaders brought back from the Middle East the idea of wearing a surcoat decorated with appliqué over their armour, both to keep the sun from the metal and to make it possible to identify the wearer. In the late 16th and 17th centuries it was the practice to embroider motifs that were then cut out and applied to other material. In the inventory of Dame Agnes Hungerford (1523) is 'Item . . . a hangyng of red say with a hundert of pyn apples imbrodered with golde to put on the same hangyng.' A great deal of the *raised or stump work of the 17th century was made in this way, and some of the panels with isolated motifs worked in rows, which are so much prized today, were actually meant to be cut out and applied. Many applied work bedspreads of the 18th and 19th centuries were quilted, and in these, the motifs were usually cut from chintzes or printed cottons and sewn on either by blind hemming or with buttonhole stitch. During the present century the emphasis has been on the texture of the material applied, and the technique has been used in large pieces of church embroidery such as copes and altar frontals. Applied work has been and is used all over the world and it is interesting to note how different communities thousands of miles apart have employed the same technique. (Nichols 1859) See also inlay and reverse appliqué.

appliqué Another and more popular name which appeared in the second half of the 19th century for *applied work.

apron (barme-cloth) Article of clothing worn at some period by almost every nation of the world, as the only covering, as a protection for the clothing beneath, and as a decorative costume accessory. It may also be of ritual significance as among freemasons. Aprons have been worn for work from medieval times until the present day, and were made of linen, wool, holland or calico, leather, or sacking, with little or no decoration. In Chaucer's time (1340–1400) an apron with a bib was known as a barme-cloth (from barm, meaning a bosom), and the carpenter's wife in the *Miller's Tale* is described as wearing 'A barme clooth erk, as whit as mornë milk' (Pollard 1965).

In most of the peasant countries of Europe the highly decorated apron has been one of the most noticeable and attractive features of their costume. In western Europe, aprons as a dress accessory began to be decorated in the 16th and 17th centuries but were at the height of their beauty in the middle of the 18th century. Fairholt (1846) suggests that this was part of the French fashion for great ladies, led

apron: Dresden and tambour work on muslin, English, 18th century.

by Marie Antoinette, to play at simple rusticity, the apron being a symbol of the lower classes, but the ornate and expensive variety was in vogue earlier than this. Those of the 18th century are of two main types: one fairly short, of a stiff silk embroidered with silk and metal threads, the other long, of fine muslin embroidered with tambour work, pulled work, or Dresden work. In America the 18th century apron was generally a working garment, and the inventory of Jane Humphries of Dorchester (Massachusetts) lists '2 blew aprons. A white Holland apron with small lace at the bottom. A white Holland Apron with two breathes on it. My best white Apron. My greene Apron.' (Quoted by Earle 1903.) The 19th century aprons, though different, were still an essential part of dress, both smart and not so smart, and in 1840 *Godey's Lady's Book* stated 'Aprons are in very great vogue . . . made in mousseline de laine, a plain ground embroidered in coloured silks with bouquets of flowers.' Towards the end of the century, middle-aged and elderly ladies often wore them made of black satin embroidered either with jet or with bright coloured silk. One in this category, rather smaller than most, was known as the *fig leaf. Aprons of all kinds are still worn today, decorated with cross stitch, ric-rac braid, applied work, patchwork or other techniques.

arabesques Scrolls and curving lines with branches and foliage intertwined. They are derived from Mohammedan art where human representation is not

album quilt: detail of a fine traditional American quilt; each block is made by a different person and is signed and dated 1853.

allowed and pattern is of paramount importance. They reached England in the late 15th and early 16th centuries and aroused the interest in Eastern forms and ideas, which later included India and China as well as the Near and Middle East. The portrait of Queen Elizabeth (wife of Henry VII), who died in 1503, shows her with a carpet on which there is a design of arabesques, and this is the earliest known representation in England.

arabesque: portrait of Elizabeth of York; note the arabesques on the parapet.

Arabian embroidery Elaborate geometric designs worked in silk floss on silk or muslin with couched, chain and satin stitches, especially on garments or towels. A variation is worked with gold and silver threads and silk floss on satin, velvet, or cashmere. According to Caulfeild and Saward (1882) 'it was brought predominately to European notice some forty years ago, when, for the purpose of relieving the destitute Algerian needle-women Madame Lucie of Algiers founded a school in that place and reproduced there from good Arabian patterns this embroidery'.

Arbury Hall see Conyers, Sophia.

ari The hook used in chain stitch embroidery in India, mostly from the Gujerat and Sind provinces. It corresponds to the tambour hook of the West, but the technique is slightly different: no frame is used to hold the material taut, and the design is worked from the front; also the ari can be used on thicker material, including leather. (Irwin and Hanish 1970)

Anglo-Indian embroidery: an example of this 19th century embroidery, worked on a printed fabric.

Armenia Embroidery from Armenia combines elements from three countries: Soviet Russia (of which it is now a republic), and its neighbours Persia (Iran) and Turkey. The fabric used is frequently a handwoven linen, and needleweaving and pulled and drawn fabric stitches are used on cloths, towels, and household articles. Shirts may be embroidered in silk and gold threads in a more naturalistic style. On the whole the colours are paler and less strident than those of central and northern Russia. (*Broderies russes, tartares, arméniennes* 1925)

Armenia: motif in cross stitch.

armilla see stole.

arms see heraldic embroidery.

arrasene embroidery One of the many 'new' types of embroidery of the 1880s, often used for floral designs. It was named after the type of thread employed, which was either of wool or silk, and consisted of only very simple stitches, as the thread had a slight pile, not unlike chenille, and tended to rub.

arrow (arrowhead) Embroidered mark in the shape of an arrow used at the top of pleats, especially in a skirt, to stop the fabric splitting.

art deco Style of ornament of the 1920s and 1930s. The name by which it is now generally known (there are many others) came from the Paris Exhibition of 1925—

L'Exposition Internationale des Arts Décoratifs et Industriels Modernes. If the style can be pinned down (which is difficult) it could be said to be composed of elements from such diverse sources as the Russian Ballet, the opening of Tutankhamun's tomb, and the interest in Egyptian art, American Art, especially that of the Aztecs and Central American Indians, and in the Cubism and Expressionism of 1910 onwards. Art deco was expressed in embroidery by a stylised rendering of the human form, flowers, and other objects, with a strong accent on texture. This involved the use of various thicknesses of thread in one piece of work, coarse ground fabrics, and sharply contrasting and even clashing colours. (Hillier 1968)

art deco: woman's jumper suit.

art embroidery (art needlework) One of the mid to late 19th century products of the *arts and crafts movement in which, as a reaction against Berlin woolwork, there was a return to flowing lines and naturalistic designs. It was taught at centres set up specially, such as the Kensington School (or, as it is now known, the *Royal School of Needlework), the Ladies' Work Society, and the *Leek Embroidery Society. Many eminent architects and artists produced designs for art embroidery, among them William *Morris, Norman Shaw, and

art embroidery: panel by May Morris, English, 19th century.

artificial pearls Manufactured and used in embroidery from the mid 17th century. They can be made in several different ways: one using the silvery scales of small fish; another using a seed pearl, reducing it to paste, and covering a glass mould with the paste; and yet another making a mould of chalk and covering it first with leaf silver and then dipping it into a glue of vellum shavings. (Edwards 1966)

artificial pearls: detail of a green velvet waistcoat, English, mid-19th century.

Art Institute of Chicago Contains a very fine collection of textiles which was begun in the 1890s with a gift of tapestries and vestments from the Antiquarian Society. Now it includes Peruvian, West European, and American samples of embroidery, needlework, and lace.

Art Institute of Chicago: German panel of the 13th century.

John *Sedding. In America it was promoted by Candace *Wheeler after seeing the exhibit from the Kensington School at the Philadelphia Exposition in 1876. As often happens it became too popular, with the result that the needlework magazines at the turn of the century became full of so-called 'new' techniques that were virtually no different from the old, and the standard of workmanship in many cases became deplorably low, typified by the *crinoline lady of the 1920s and 1930s.

art embroidery (machine) see machine embroidery.

artificial flowers The making of three-dimensional flowers, while not strictly embroidery, must be included as an offshoot of the *raised work of the 17th century. Posies and individual flowers were formed from wool, silk, metal threads, wire, and beads, often using a wire outline filled with buttonhole stitch for the leaves. Some of the flowers and leaves made to go under glass domes are beautiful examples of mid 19th century craftsmanship.

Art Journal Extremely influential journal, published in England between 1839 and 1912, which criticised, admired, and condemned the fine and applied arts. Strictly on the side of the establishment, it considered itself the arbiter of conservative good taste. It took a side glance at textiles generally, though not at embroidery in particular, but its influence was felt even in that sphere.

art linen (embroidery linen) Linen or imitation linen of varying weights, woven specially for embroidery. It is generally a tabby weave in natural colour or pastels. See also crash and stamped linen.

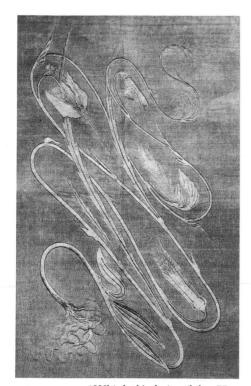

art nouveau: 'Whiplash' designed by Herman Obrist, 1890–1900.

art nouveau Art movement in Europe and America during the second half of the 19th century, particularly between 1890 and 1910. It was a reaction to the fussiness of mid-Victorian craft which was exemplified in the Great Exhibition of 1851. John *Ruskin, William *Morris, and others turned towards the idea of beautiful objects for everyone made by hand, with line rather than decoration predominating. The *arts and crafts movement started the ball rolling and many societies followed. The style they preached was largely derived from oriental art, with a thin, sinuous line and a strange fantasy of invention, and it permeated architecture and every craft, including wrought-iron work, furniture making, glassware and, inevitably, embroidery and textiles.

arts and crafts movement 'The arts and crafts movement means standards, whether of work or life; the protection of standards, whether in the product or the producer; and it means that these things must be taken together.' (Ashbee, quoted by Naylor 1971.) The movement was intended to release men from the bondage of the machine and to help them to find joy in their work through creating by hand, but in the end it became the making of a comparatively small number of beautiful articles for the rich. Though it had its stirrings and beginnings early in the 19th century, it crystallised in the 1880s with the formation of the Century Guild, the Art Workers' Guild, and the Arts and Crafts Exhibition Society. This new approach to design, especially the work of the firm of William *Morris and the various manuals of design and ornament, shaped the development and techniques of embroidery in the late 19th and early 20th centuries.

Assisi embroidery Type of embroidery originating in Assisi, north Italy, which is characterised by the design being left plain and the background filled in. Originally long-armed cross stitch or whipped stitch on drawn threads was used for the background, but now it is more usual to find cross stitch, with double running for the outlines. Because the designs are often heraldic and only one colour is used, usually red or blue, the work has a very formal and dignified look.

Assisi embroidery: detail of an Italian pillow case, 1920–24.

Associated Artists American firm of interior decorators working from 1879 to 1883, whose partners were Louis Tiffany, Lockwood de Forest, Samuel Coleman, and Candace *Wheeler. They designed for industrial mass production as well as private clients, and were responsible for creating a modern American design style. Each partner was in charge of a specific part of the project according to his or her area of expertise, and commissions included theatre interiors, private houses, and the redecoration of the White House. When the formal partnership came to an end in 1883, Candace Wheeler kept the name Associated Artists (1883–1907) for her own design firm where textiles and wallpapers as well as the *American tapestries were created. Other members included Dora Wheeler, Rosine Emmett, and Ida Clark. (Faude 1975)

Aston Hall (near Birmingham, England) Mansion built in the early years of the 17th century, and now a city museum. It belonged to the Holte family for 200 years, and it contains some fine needlework connected with them, particularly the wall hangings in Lady Holte's room. In addition, the embroidered curtains in the 18th century bedroom, the Turkey work chairs in the Long Gallery, and the coverlet in King Charles's bedroom are worth noting. See also Holte, Mary.

astrakhan stitch see plush stitch.

asymmetry Lack of proportion between parts of a whole which may, in the case of design, have a pleasing result.

atelier Literally a workshop or studio, but it can also be used to describe places where fine sewing and embroidery is done, for example, the workrooms of couture houses.

attachments Extra pieces which enable a domestic *sewing machine to perform a number of different operations in addition to straightforward stitching. From the time of the early hand and treadle machines, various attachments, designed to help with the current fashions and of greater or lesser usefulness, have been available, but as the machine itself has become capable of more operations so the number of attachments has diminished. In the late 19th and early 20th century a tucker, which stitched one tuck while simultaneously marking the next, was used extensively, as was an underbraider, which sewed braid on in a pattern working from the wrong side of the fabric. When using a straight stitching machine today it is considered helpful to have a zip, cording, or singlesided foot which stitches close up to metal or a cord; a hemmer which turns a narrow hem and stitches it; a darning and embroidery foot which, when the fabric is put into a frame or held tightly, darns a hole or embroiders, with the fabric being moved to the needle rather than the needle moved over the fabric; and a quilting bar or guide which makes it easy to stitch lines parallel to each other. With swing needle machines a universal foot is considered essential; this copes with buttonholing, blind stitching, overlocking etc. In addition an eyelet plate used with an awl for making and stitching eyelets and a roller foot for sewing stretch fabrics, leather, and vinyl are helpful.

Audubon, J. J. (1785–1851) Artist born in Santo Domingo of French and Creole parentage, and famous for his monumental work *The Birds of America* published between 1827 and 1838. His drawings, which were engraved, printed, and coloured by R. Havell & Son in London, are notable for the beauty of the backgrounds as well as the birds, and they were often used as patterns for embroidery, especially Berlin woolwork.

aumbry veil Curtain, occasionally embroidered, which covers the aumbry, a cupboard on the north side of the chancel used for the reservation of the Holy Sacrament.

aumonière see alms purse.

auriphrygium Fringe or embroidery in gold. The Phrygians were great traders and shipped many Asiatic and Babylonian embroideries to Greece and Italy. For this

reason the Romans called an embroiderer *phrygio* and Eastern embroideries *phrygionae*, thus gold embroidery became known as auriphrygium. The word *orphrey comes from the French *orfroi* (meaning gold bands), which in turn is derived from auriphrygium.

aurum battutum see gold thread.

Austria Austrian arts have been influenced by Italy to the south, Germany to the north, and the Slav countries to the east. As in most of Europe, embroidery was always divided between the church on the one hand, and costume and the home on the other, with the addition of excellent machine embroidery on dress in the late 19th century when Vienna was a very fashion-conscious city. In the late 18th century the Empress Maria Theresa introduced *sericulture to Austria, and traditional ground fabrics are linen, wool, and silk with little or no cotton. Designs are taken from the natural objects of the countryside—flowers, leaves, fruit, birds, and beasts, and the clothes of both men and women including accessories such as scarves, headshawls and aprons, as well as bedspreads and other household articles are all embroidered.

autograph quilt see album quilt.

awl Sharp tool resembling and sometimes synonymous with a *stiletto, but named an awl when required for heavy work especially on leather. It is used for making holes for thread, by saddlers, shoemakers, and all workers in leather, including many Indian tribes who use a slightly curved bone awl for punching holes or piercing skins.

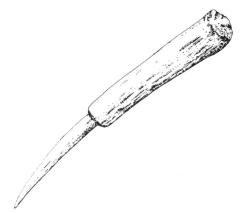

Axbridge Church (Somerset) English church which contains, on a side altar, a remarkable *altar frontal. This was worked entirely in tent stitch between 1713 and 1720 by Mrs Abigail Prowse, wife of the rector and daughter of George Hooper, Bishop of Bath and Wells. The front, two sides, and top are closely fitted. The front

shows an altar of the day, the top the sacred monogram in *splendour and two books bound in leather, the panel on the left side has the arms of her father, the bishop, and that on the right has the arms of her late husband and herself.

Ayrshire embroidery (sewed muslin, Scotch sewed muslin) Type of embroidery on fine muslin characterised by open needlepoint fillings in very fine thread, with the main design in satin and beading stitch. It developed from the *Dresden and *tambour work of the 18th century. These had been worked in Scotland, using Scottish muslin, from about 1790, but in 1814 one of the agents for the embroideries, Mrs *Jamieson of Ayr, was lent a French christening robe inset with lace stitches. She copied these fillings and taught the technique to her workers, and the fashion for this type of sewed muslin spread rapidly. It was used not only for babies' robes and bonnets, but also for women's collars, cuffs, and caps up till the middle of the 19th century. Some of the caps are worked almost like a sampler with every leaf inset with a different patterned filling. (Swain 1955)

Ayrshire embroidery: front panel of christening gown, Scottish, c.1840.

Aztec style Term for a particular style of blouse worn by the Aztec or Nahua women living in the valleys of Mexico, and the Pueblo tribes in power when Cortez conquered Mexico in 1528. It has a square neck bib, is gathered front and back, and is embroidered at the neck, sleeves, and shoulders. Originally the designs of stylised plants, including the maize or toto flower, and animals were cross or back stitched in a single colour, but now most are polychrome.

baby carrier (papoose board, papoose cradle) Bag, often gaily decorated, worn slung on the back of a mother in which to carry her child. They have straps which go over the shoulders and generally cross in front and fasten at the back. Certain tribes have always used these bags and slings, and the custom has spread to other countries where many people find it a convenient method of taking a small child about.

baby carrier: with beaded decoration, Kiowa Indian, Oklahoma.

backing Fabric placed behind another fabric to strengthen the work, either before embroidering, in which case the stitches are worked through both materials, or after. Some fabrics which make beautiful backgrounds are not strong enough to stand the weight and pull of the stitchery and need support, generally a strong linen. Church embroideries, especially where metal threads are used, always need backing.

back rest Article used by the North American Plains Cree Indian in their *tepees. They were very colourful, often made of bright cloth worked with contrasting-coloured beads.

back stitch (stitching) Stitch which goes back and either touches the previous one or leaves a gap between the two equal to the length of the stitch. In the past however, stitching has always meant the kind which touched (as machine stitching does today), while back stitch referred to the kind with a gap. It was worked more exquisitely at the end of the 18th century than at any other time. Then it was generally used as the equivalent of the modern machine top stitching and was so finely worked on seams, cuffs, and collars that it must have been done by stabbing up and down rather than taking a stitch.

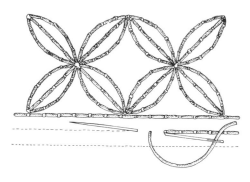

Bacon, Francis (1561–1626) English philosopher, statesman, and essayist. In *Of Adversity* he gives the advice that countless embroiderers have followed: 'We see in needleworks and embroideries, it is more pleasing to have a lively work upon a sad and solemn ground, than to have a dark and melancholy work upon a lightsome ground.'

Baden appliqué Embroidery suitable for large-scale appliqué popular in the 1880s, and used for curtains, portières etc. The design was cut out of a plain fabric and applied to the ground with chain stitch. It was then given its distinctive

Baden appliqué: from supplement to The Queen *October 1881.*

look by working herringbone stitch from the edge of the chain stitch onto the ground fabric.

badge Device by which something or somebody is recognised. In the middle ages, they were used on robes of state and on the caparison of horses, as well as being worn by servants, and during and since the last century, they have been commonly worn on club blazers and school uniforms. Badges such as regimental and divisional signs have always been of military importance. In most cases they are printed or embroidered, nowadays using the Jacquard machine.

badge: handworked by Rumsey Wells & Sons, Norwich, before 1897.

badla Silver or silver-gilt wire, used in Indian metal thread embroidery.

bagh Type of embroidery done in the Punjab, and used for shawls, which are themselves called bagh. The design is evolved by the embroiderer as she goes along, and is worked from the wrong side of the cotton fabric, which is embroidered in silk. (Dhamija 1964) See also phulkari.

baize (bays) Coarse cloth, originally made only of wool but may now be of cotton or a *union, with a short nap which makes it look like felt. The manufacture was introduced into England by the Flemings in 1561, and in the late 18th and 19th centuries it was exported to America as a trade cloth. A fine quality baize is used to cover billiard tables, and the fabric can also be a ground for embroidery. See also bayeta.

balance marks Indications to show where one piece of fabric should match up with another. In dressmaking, they can be notches, chalk marks, or stitches showing the exact spot in a seam where the two marks will meet. In embroidery they are used to match the centre of a piece of work with the centre of the frame.

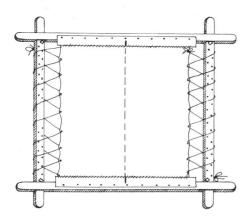

baldrick Band, belt, or sash of leather or fabric, worn over one shoulder diagonally across the chest and under the other arm, to support a sword or bugle. They have been worn with military uniform since its inception, and were originally highly ornamented with embroidery in silk and metal threads, but have gradually become plainer and more utilitarian. They have also been worn by civilians who had to carry something and needed their hands free, such as a huntsman with his horn.

ball button Handmade, ball-shaped button of distinctive type. A small ball of *ravelling is first made, and then a shaped casing of buttonhole stitch is worked over it. Currently they are commercially made of plastic, glass, and other materials.

Baltimore quilts see album quilts.

Baluchistan Now part of Pakistan, between Iran, Afghanistan, and India. Most of the embroidery of this wild, desolate, and sparsely populated area is on costume, and sometimes it is worked on a coloured cotton fabric which is then applied to a white ground for garments such as tunics. There may also be embroidery from shoulder to waist, worked in dark red silk in geometrical satin stitch.

Baluchistan: man's tunic embroidered in coloured cottons.

band Collar of linen or cambric worn in the late 16th and early 17th centuries, especially by men. They could be propped up or allowed to lie flat, the latter being called falling bands, and they developed into the plain Geneva band or rabat worn by some clergymen today. In the 17th century they were often highly ornamented with lace or embroidery and were very expensive. Peacham, in *The Truth of our Times* (1638), says 'he is not a gentleman, or in the fashion, whose band of Italian cutwork standeth him not at the least in three or four pounds, yea, a semester in Holborn told me there are of three score pound price apiece' (quoted by Fairholt 1846).

ball button.

bandoleer bag see shoulder pouch.

bangle Ornamental ring worn on the wrist or ankle; also, in America, a large paillette used for the decoration of clothing, mostly sweaters and accessories, and very popular on the felt skirts of the 1950s.

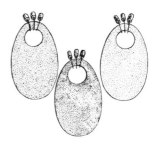

banker Piece of material, plain, embroidered, or tapestry woven which was used to cover a bench or chair before upholstery was introduced.

banner Standard or ensign used by armies as a rallying point, and also used by many modern societies and movements such as trade unions, women's institutes, athletic teams etc. They are generally mounted on one or two poles so that they can be carried. Some, especially those of the 18th and early 19th centuries, have their designs painted on taffeta or some other closely-woven material, but many more are embroidered, the most usual method being appliqué in conjunction with silks and metal threads. There are also smaller examples such as trumpet banners, from which evolved the *banner firescreen, and heraldic banners, such as those over the stalls of the Knights of the Garter in St George's Chapel, Windsor (England). See also Fetternear banner, Pulaski banner.

banner: coloured silks and gold thread, English, 19th century.

banner firescreen: in cross stitch, English, mid-19th century.

banner firescreen Generally square or shield-shaped firescreen, of highly ornamented fabric. It was hung from a rod fastened to the mantelpiece by a screw clamp and could be adjusted to any angle to shield the face from the fire. They were very fashionable from the 1840s to 1870s and were often worked in a mixture of beads and wools on canvas. Both flower and heraldic designs were used, but among those most frequently seen were designs adapted from Thorvaldsen's well-known bas-reliefs, 'Morning' and 'Evening'.

bar 1. In embroidery and needlepoint lace, a stitch (or stitches in the same place) which crosses an empty space and holds the two sides together, giving strength to the work. Also known as brides or ties, they can themselves be strengthened and finished by overcasting or buttonholing over the stitching, and by other means. Bars of this type are used in needlepoint fillings, drawn threadwork, faggoting, Hedebo embroidery, Handanger embroidery, cutwork, Richelieu embroidery, Renaissance embroidery, and broderie anglaise or eyelet embroidery. 2. In making buttonholes, either tailors' or dressmakers', a stitch made at the inside end of the finished buttonhole to hold the material together and stop it from splitting. 3. In dressmaking, a carrier loop in the side seam of a dress to hold the belt. 4. In needleweaving, two adjacent groups of threads joined together by weaving.

bargello stitch see florentine stitch.

Bargello work The most common American generic name for flame and florentine stitch patterns and variations. (Colour illustration p 35) See also florentine embroidery, four-way bargello.

barme-cloth see apron.

baroque Florid extravagant style, specifically of late Renaissance architecture but also applicable to the ornamentation of textiles and embroidery as well as other forms of applied art of the period 1640–1700.

baroque: leaf in crewel work, English, 17th century.

baskets Some baskets made by certain tribes are decorated either partially or completely with bead or shell work, while others, gaily embroidered with raffia or wool, are made as tourist attractions in many parts of the world.

basket: beadwork from Kenyah, New Guinea.

basket weave *Tabby weave, but using two or more threads as one to give a basket-like effect. Basket weave fabric is used for certain types of embroidery. In America, basket weave is the term for the diagonal* tent stitch.

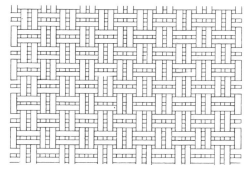

basting Sewing with a long, loose stitch to mark out divisions and also sometimes to outline the design to be worked. Properly, basting is only sewn on one thickness of material, while *tacking is sewn through two or more, but in the US the two words are synonymous. The stitches are removed when the piece is completed.

batting Cotton or polyester fibre in prepared sheets or rolls used for the interlining of *quilts and sometimes of clothes, for added warmth. This could be bought in the US from about the middle of the 19th century, but up till then the cotton for interlining was obtained (usually with seeds) from the southern colonies. After 1793, when Eli Whitney invented the cotton gin, cleaned cotton in many grades became available for quilt filling.

battlemented (crenellated) Shaped like the battlements of a church or castle. This effect is achieved in needlework by cutting the fabric and using an edging stitch, by facing the shape, or by applying braid in this shape.

batuz work Early term for *bete work, used in medieval England and on the continent. It is mentioned in the inventory of Thomas, Duke of Gloucester (1397), as 'iij curtyns de Tartaryn batuz de mesme la suyte' (Dillon and Hope 1897).

baudekin One of the richest fabrics of the middle ages, made of silk interwoven with threads of gold, and used by royalty, nobility, and the church. It appears to have been named from Babylon (originally called Baldeck) where it was first made. In the inventory of Thomas, Duke of Gloucester (1397) it is mentioned as 'two mitres of white baudekin of damask garnished with riband of gold of damask' (Dillon and Hope 1897).

bayeta Spanish word for *baize, a cloth imported into America from Manchester, England. Pueblo and Navajo Indians often *ravelled this cloth and used the yarn in their embroidery and weaving. It has also been used by the Indians of Peru, Colombia, and Bolivia.

Bayeux Tapestry Probably one of the most important pieces of embroidery in the world. Although called a tapestry, it is properly an embroidery, since it was worked with a needle and wool on linen, and is not tapestry woven. It is 231 feet (70.4 metres) long by 19½ inches (50 centimetres) wide, and depicts the events leading up to the battle of Hastings when William the Conqueror defeated Harold of England in 1066, the battle itself, and the death of Harold. Latin inscriptions explain the pictures. The stitches are stem and outline, with laid and couched work,

and in contrast to the rather formal metal thread embroideries typical of this date, it appears very lively. It is generally considered that the tapestry was ordered by Bishop Odo of Bayeux, half-brother of William the Conqueror, and was probably worked in Kent between 10 and 20 years after the Norman Conquest. Much of the information obtained about the dress, armour, ships, and furniture of the period is unique, which is one of the reasons it is so important. It has suffered many moves and vicissitudes, but it is now on permanent exhibition in the former Bishop's Palace, facing the cathedral in Bayeux, France.

beading 1. The outlining and high-lighting of patterned material such as cotton satin with *beads. It was a favourite form of embroidery of the late 19th century. 2. In broderie anglaise (eyelet embroidery) and Ayrshire embroidery, a very fine line of small holes. These are made either with a stiletto or a chenille needle and are then overcast. The result looks like a tiny ladder. 3. Method of joining seams either with *insertion or insertion stitches. See also veining.

beading needle see straw needle.

beads Small, perforated cylinders or balls made of glass, wood, or a variety of other materials, and used strung with others or individually. The beads used in embroidery over the centuries have been made from many different materials, glass being the most common, and could be stained, dyed, or enamelled. In the 19th century the large cylindrical beads were called *OP beads, and the smaller ones, known as pound or seed beads, were sold by weight. Both types, in every imaginable colour, were used in several ways: on canvas, either alone or with silk or wool embroidery; to outline shapes on printed material; tamboured onto fine

material for dresses and accessories; and with a commercial beading machine in the 1890s. In America, as in many other countries, beads were used by the newly-arrived white men as gifts for the natives. Indeed in Virginia, soon after Jamestown was founded in 1607, a glass works was set up which was staffed by Venetian glass workers who manufactured pea-sized coloured glass beads ready for immediate trading with the local Indians. The word comes from bede (Middle English for a prayer) after the rosaries used to count prayers or 'tell your beads'. See also pony beads. (Colour illustration p 36)

beads: case of boxes for beads from France, c.1810.

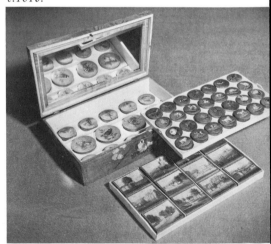

beadwork Properly, the use of *beads in embroidery or in conjunction with knitting, netting, or weaving, but here meaning beads applied to fabric or leather. Beadwork has been used for decoration at some period in the history of practically every country and tribe from the most primitive to the most sophisticated, including Eskimos, Maoris, North American Indians, tribes of Borneo, and Stuart and Victorian ladies.

beadwork: detail of a French dress, c.1927.

There are four main categories of beadwork. 1. Beads sewn down individually. This includes much of the beadwork of the more civilised communities through the ages. In medieval times, beads were used for embroidery, especially in Germany and Spain, sometimes with precious stones or as a substitute for them, and in Stuart England many pictures were either worked entirely in beads, or they were used to highlight embroidery. In the 19th century there was a craze for beadwork of every kind, and it was used, especially in conjunction with Berlin woolwork, for firescreens, cushions, mantel hangings, teacosies etc. There seemed to be nothing either sensible or nonsensical that could

beadwork: collar, Zulu, late 19th century.

not be beaded. Using the same techniques but with a very different result, the North American Indians made garments and accessories of beads, frequently in geometrical designs, dyed in strong, clear colours. 2. Beads strung onto a length of thread, often in pattern, the thread then couched down onto the material. Much tribal beadwork is typical of this class. It is sometimes found on garments, but more often the strings coil round baskets or wire, giving an impression of solid beads with no foundation material. Work of this type can be found in many countries, particularly Zululand, Borneo, and North America. 3. Beads applied onto a fine fabric with a tambour hook. This is the commercial variety done for a sweated living by hundreds of women in the last half of the 19th century when the craze for beading on dresses, capes, and accessories was at its height. 4. Beads sewn onto fabric by machine. Here the dresses of the mid 1920s come to mind. A machine suitable for bead embroidery was invented in 1891 but it was not until the end of the century that the *Cornely or Bonnaz machine was developed sufficiently to make this the practical method of attaching thousands of tiny beads to clothing and accessories. (Colour illustration p 45)

bearing cloth (bearing mantle) Cloth in which a child was customarily carried to baptism. It was oblong and very large, completely covering the infant except for its face, and hung nearly to the ground. They were often red in colour, though 18th century cloths were sometimes of cream satin embroidered to match the christening gown. Their use had died out by the middle of the 19th century. (Colour illustration p 46)

bed curtains   see bed furniture.

bed cushions (bed pillows) Sets of cushions used for sitting up in bed. Also, in the US, small pillows with white or pastel-coloured embroidered covers, used in the bedroom.

bed furniture   Consists of bed curtains, upper and lower valances, decoration on bedposts, and sometimes also the coverlet and pillows. From very early times the bed has been the dominant item in a bedroom, and has been as fine and as well made a piece as could be afforded. Since several people usually slept in the bedrooms, which were cold and draughty, hangings were made for the beds to ensure both warmth and privacy, and these were often heavily embroidered. The furniture generally consisted of three pairs of curtains, three top valances, and three lower valances or pantes, which covered the mattress. Occasionally each pair of curtains would have two sets of top valances so that the curtains could run between them and the mechanism be hidden from inside the bed as well as out. Sometimes all the furniture was embroidered en suite, but in general the curtains wore out before the valances and so new curtains that did not necessarily match in style were added.

Beds and their furniture were a very valuable part of the family possessions and were often left in wills. The inventory of Thomas, Duke of Gloucester (1397) contains many beds, the best being '. . . a great bed of gold, that is to say, a coverlet, a tester, and the entire blue valance of fine blue satin wrought with Garters of gold, and three curtains of tartary beaten to match. Also two long and four square pillows of the set of the bed' (Dillon and Hope 1897). The whole was valued at £182 3s. which at present prices would be no less than £10,000 or $25,000. However, the Duke also had more humble but equally charming beds of worsted embroidered variously with yellow stags, white eagles, crowned lions, and griffins with chaplets of roses. A description of a bed belonging to the Countess of Shewsbury shows what furniture an expensive bed of 1601 would have: 'a bedsted, the Postes being Covered with scarlet laid on with silver lace, bedes head, tester, and single vallans of scarlet imbrodered with gold studes and thissells, stript downe and layde about with golde and silver lace and with gold frenge about, three Curtins of scarlet stript downe with silver lace and with silver and red silk buttons and lowpes' (Boynton 1971). The only known complete set of bed furniture in America is in the collection of the Old Gaol Museum, Yorke, Maine. (Colour illustration p 47)

bed rug: from the Connecticut River Valley, 1790.

bed rugs Heavy needlework bed covering with a pile or smooth face, with or without shaped ends, which is worked in polychrome or, rarely, monochrome wools on a woven foundation. The background was sometimes wool and sometimes linen, and was completely covered with multistrand, looped running stitches (probably worked over a reed or quill), which generally followed the lines of the patterns. They seem to be a specifically New England form of embroidery, and known examples exist dating from 1722 to 1833. Footstool covers and hearth rugs were made in the same technique.

bedspread (counterpane, coverlet) Name to describe top cover for a bed, used for warmth and decoration since earliest times (here excluding those which are quilted). The bed appears in some form all over the world, and interesting examples of bedspreads come from India, the Middle East, and America, as well as Europe. Their size, shape, and flatness today as in the past lend themselves to design, and bedspreads are among the most beautiful embroideries. They can be worked in almost any fabric in many techniques, among them appliqué, patchwork (not always quilted), drawn threadwork, Bokhara embroidery, silk embroidery, crewel work, and metal thread embroidery. It is difficult to understand from inventories the exact difference at any one date between the various names. In the inventory of Dame Agnes Hungerford (1523) we find counterpeyn, counterpoynte, and quylte, and in that of Robert Morton (1488), counterpoynt, coverlyte, and quylte. The Hardwick Hall inventories (1601) contain counterpoynt, covering for the bed, coverletts to hang before a door and a window, a counterpoynt of tapestrie to hang in front of a door, and a coverpane embroidered with gold. From all this nothing very clear emerges except that coverlets are always valued more cheaply than counterpanes. The OED considers that all counterpanes or counterpoints were originally quilted, the words coming from the Latin *culcitra-puncta*, a quilt, and that the only bedspreads not specifically quilted were coverlids or coverlets. This is obviously correct, but it is equally obvious that the words were not always used in their strict sense as it seems unlikely that 'a counterpoynt with a lyon of tapestrie work' in the inventory of Robert Morton would be quilted, and certainly since the 16th century, counterpane has come to mean a bed covering, not quilted.

bed tent Bed curtain used in houses in the Greek Islands which had tapered strips of linen fastened to a wooden ring at the top to form a bell tent. The linen was heavily embroidered on the front, with little or no decoration at the back. (Johnstone 1972)

beeswax Wax used for both strengthening and smoothing sewing thread. Fitted workboxes of the 18th and 19th centuries often had a device en suite for holding a piece of beeswax, which usually had an ornamental top with a spike to stick the wax onto, and sometimes also a base. Often the edges of the wax were serrated so that the thread could be more easily pulled through it.

beeswax: Tunbridge ware container with pin cushion top.

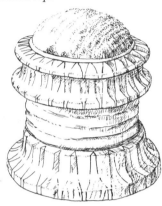

beetle wing Iridescent wing with a minute hole for sewing made at both ends and used in 19th century embroidery in England and America to decorate garments, handbags etc. They were also much used in conjunction with white embroidery in India, on articles such as long scarves.

beetle wing: border of a 19th century Indian stole.

Belgravian embroidery Popular late 19th century work consisting of broad braid cut into shapes (leaves etc) and filled with *bugles. The motif is then applied to garments.

bellows Apparatus for blowing a fire to make it blaze: there is an embroidered example in the *Burrell collection.

bellows: beaded decoration, dated 1673.

bell-pull Long narrow piece of fabric terminating in a decorative handle and attached to a wire, which summoned servants when pulled. They were often dec orated with embroidery ranging from canvas work to crewel work and were used in the 19th century. Nowadays they are a popular item in embroidery *kits, but are for decoration not for use.

Belon, Pierre   French physician and naturalist who wrote several books and treatises including *La Nature et Diversité des Poissons* and *L'Histoire de la Nature des Oyseaux*, both published in 1555. Some of the woodcuts from these books were reproduced in tent stitch by *Mary Queen of Scots on the Oxburgh hangings. (Swain 1973)

belt Article of dress worn around the waist, and frequently embellished with embroidery and beadwork. Among the most decorative are those of the North American Indians worked with quills, wampum, or beads.

benewacka Embroidery on homespun linen worked by the Dutch in America. It is a form of *drawn fabric work which is whipped into a net and on which a geometric pattern is darned with linen thread. It was used as decoration on the ends of pillow cases about 1800.

beniqua: detail showing Algerian eye stitch.

beniqa Combined towel and headkerchief used by Algerian ladies at the public baths. Although similar to the *tenchifa, it is used more as a headdress and less as a towel. It is a long narrow panel of linen worn as a hood, with lappets to wind round the head, and is heavily embroidered, especially on the part that actually covers the head. (Catalogue of Algerian Embroideries, 1915)

Berlin canvas (silk canvas) Kind of canvas manufactured in sizes of 21, 29, 34, and 40 threads to the inch (about 8, 12, 14, and 16 threads to the centimetre), and suitable for the type of Berlin woolwork which did not need a worked background. It could be bought in most colours, but the usual ones were black, white, claret, and primrose. (Lambert 1843)

Berlin wool (German wool, zephyr merino) Type of worsted used for Berlin woolwork. It was a loose untwisted yarn, dyed in very many shades, and it admirably filled the holes in the canvas. In the early 19th century it was produced in Gotha (Germany) and dyed in Berlin; later in the century it was also manufactured in Yorkshire.

Berlin woolwork Embroidery worked on canvas and characterised by the soft wool used (produced in Germany) and by the charts drawn on *point paper where each square represents one stitch. It evolved from the tent stitch embroideries of the 16th, 17th, and 18th centuries. Berlin woolwork was a craze in England and America in the middle of the 19th century and its popularity did not wane until art needlework and the Morris movements became fashionable in their turn. It did not find favour with many teachers, artists, and magazine editors, and in 1886 the *Magazine of Art* wrote: With such signs of improvement [from the Royal School of Needlework] we may feel sure that, whatever betides, so disastrous a crisis as the Berlin wool epidemic is henceforth impossible. It has left in its wake vestiges not even now effaced, in the shape of mats and cushions coarsely worked in strong magentas and violet spinach greens. It also left in its wake chair coverings, cushions, bell-pulls, carpet slippers, braces (suspenders), handbags, pictures, and anything which fancy or ingenuity could consider decorating. See also canvas work, needlepoint.

Berlin woolwork: cross stitch picture, 'Washington Crossing the Delaware', American, 1885-95.

Berlin woolwork patterns: convolvulus and carnation designed by Carl F. W. Wicht, Berlin.

Berlin woolwork patterns Designs of German origin for use in *Berlin woolwork, which were imported into England in the early years of the 19th century by publishers and print sellers such as R. *Ackermann. They were printed on point paper with each square corresponding to a square on the canvas so that the design could be read off from the chart instead of being drawn onto the canvas. Between 1805 and the 1870s many thousands of patterns were imported by firms such as Wilks of Regent Street and Gibbs' French and German Warehouse, from German designers and wholesalers, of which A. Todt, L. W. *Wittich, and Carl Wicht were among the best known.

bermuda faggoting see point turc.

Bess of Hardwick (1520–1608) 16th century noblewoman who outlived four husbands, acquiring large fortunes from each, and is remembered as the builder of *Hardwick Hall in Derbyshire and as the wife of one of the gaolers of *Mary Queen of Scots. She shared a great interest in embroidery with Mary, and several pieces of the Oxburgh hangings were worked jointly and contain both their signatures or monograms. Although many of the pieces at Hardwick from 1570 onwards were worked by the household as well as the mistress, there are some, notably a long cushion powdered with Es and Ss (standing for Elizabeth Shrewsbury), which are her work. Posterity has another reason to be grateful to Bess in that she caused a complete inventory to be written (since published by the Furniture History Society) of the contents of Hardwick Hall in 1601.

bestiary Popular medieval treatise on natural history, generally with a moral angle. After the invention of printing they were illustrated with woodcuts which became very popular as patterns for embroidery.

bete (beten) Obsolete term for gold decoration, embroidered or otherwise, applied to fabric. Earlier this was called *batuz work.

Bethlehem (Israel) The women of Bethlehem wear blue or black bodices with cross stitch embroidery worked on them. The designs have been handed down from mother to daughter and each has a name, and it is interesting that the designs used on American quilts are very similar to some of these. (Erskine 1925)

Bethlehem (Pennsylvania) see Moravian embroidery.

between Sewing needle in the same range of sizes as the *sharp and similar to it, but shorter.

bewpers see bunting.

bias Slanting or oblique line in relation to the warp and weft of a fabric. True bias means an exact diagonal of 45 degrees. See also cross.

bias binding (bias tape) Strip of fabric cut on the true *bias with the edges ironed in, prepared for sewing onto a raw edge. It is used instead of straight tape because it will stretch round curves.

bias cut Term applied to fabric cut on the *bias.

bib 1. Small piece of fabric, plain or embroidered, tied round the neck of an infant to protect its clothes from food and dribbles. Occasionally they were more ornamental than useful, and in the late 17th century were embroidered *en suite with collar, mittens, and other accessories. Today's bibs are made of practical materials, sometimes decorated with applied work. 2. The part of an apron which covers the chest.

big writing see closed square chain stitch.

Binca canvas Multiple-thread canvas popular in the UK since the Second World War for all types of rather coarse canvas work. It is not necessary to cover the ground fabric completely.

birch bark Flexible tree bark used by the North American Indians as a ground for moose-hair, bead and quill embroidery. It was chosen because it held the short hairs firmly, and was sometimes backed with cloth. (Turner 1955)

birch bark: box embroidered with porcupine quills.

birds Mythological or real, flying or on the ground, with wings outstretched or folded, stylised or natural, birds have been represented in both sophisticated and naïve needlework at all times and by all nations. With flowers, foliage, and animals, they form the most general subject matter for embroideries.

birdwork Type of embroidery mentioned in wills and inventories of the 17th century, but so far unidentified. From the will of Joan Sutton of Grimston (1633) is 'one grene coverlet of birdworke', and from the inventory of John Skelton of Norwich (1611) in the Chamber over the Parlour, 'a tapestry coverlet and a bird coverlet'.

Blackfoot Indians (Blackfeet Indians) Influential and important confederation of Plains Indians made up of the Siksika (Blackfoot), Blood, and *Piegan tribes now living in southern Alberta and Montana near the Glacier National Park. Originally nomadic, warlike buffalo hunters, the Blackfoot and *Crow controlled territory from the Mississippi to the Rockies and British Columbia—an area rich in beaver skins and the source of great conflict of interest between the red and the white man. The Blackfoot were willing to trade but fought to keep white fur traders from trapping and developing Indian trade in Montana. They were

Blackfoot Indians: deerskin robe with beaded decoration.

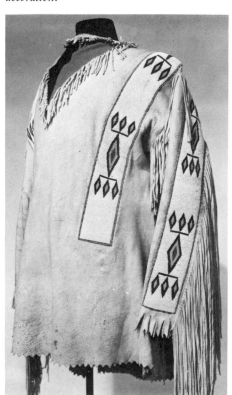

skilled artists and craftsmen, quickly adapting European beads to their old methods of *quillwork on skin clothing, and their beadwork was first mentioned by travellers in 1833. The blue and white *pony beads applied in narrow bands to men and women's clothing did not replace quillwork, but alternated with it. Both came to an end in the 1870s with the adoption of smaller seed beads, especially by the younger women. There is a good collection of Blackfoot Indian artefacts in the Indian Service Museum in Browning, Montana. (Ewers n.d., McCracken 1959) See also Northern Plains Indian Craft Association.

Black Prince, The (1330–1376) Eldest son of Edward I, and hero of the battle of Crécy. He was buried in Canterbury Cathedral, and above his tomb hang his helmet, gauntlets, shield, and surcoat, though the latter has been replaced by a modern replica. A description of the surcoat as it was in 1843 says: '. . . the vest is of one pile velvet, at present of a palish yellow brown colour, probably faded crimson. Its foundation is of fine buckram on calico, stuffed and padded with cotton, stitched and quilted in longitudinal folds, gamboised as the proper term for such work is, and the velvet covering is ornamented with the arms of the Black Prince quarterly France and England embroidered in gold.' (Hartshorne 1848)

Black Prince: reproduction of quilted velvet jupon with gold appliqué.

double running, closed herringbone, stem, and many filling stitches. Frequently only black silk thread was used, but sometimes metal *passing thread was added to relieve the black. The way in which blackwork arrived in England is not easy to trace. It is of Arabic origin and so was very fashionable in Spain, but it was known in England before Katharine of Aragon arrived in 1501, though she may well have been responsible for the renewed interest in the style. One of the earliest apparent references is in the *Miller's Tale* by Chaucer (?1340–1400), describing the dress of the carpenter's wife: 'Whit was her smok, and boyden al bifoore,/And eek bihynde, on hir coler aboute/ Of colblak silk withinne and eek withoute . . .' Coal black silk embroidery on the collar of a smock sounds very like the smocks and shirts of 150 years later. Portraits of the 16th century show blackwork on shirt collars and cuffs, ruffs, and sleeves and it makes an excellent foil to the bright colours of the silks and other embroideries. The *Middleton collection of these embroideries in Nottingham Museum (England) is well worth seeing. During this century there has been a revival of interest in the craft, and some fine pieces have been worked using the same techniques on an evenweave linen and in a modern style.

blackwork: details of a long cover, English, 16th century.

blanket stitch (open buttonhole stitch) Simple loop stitch which resembles the machine-stitched edge of blankets, and consists of a series of buttonhole stitches worked a little apart. It is very useful for edging and can also be used with other types of buttonholing to make decorative borders.

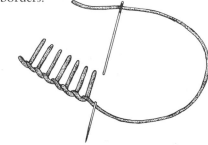

blackwork (Spanish work) Type of embroidery fashionable in England in the 16th century and revived at intervals since then. Many pieces survive from the early date, and it is clear from them that the work consisted of embroidery on fine linen using various stitches including

blind hemming (blind stitch, invisible hemming) Kind of *hemming used especially in applied work where an invisible holding stitch is needed. The stitches are closely spaced and the turned hem and the flat of the fabric are caught together in one movement as for ordinary hemming. It is worked under the fold instead of on the edge, and although the sewing is done on the face of the work the stitches show only on the wrong side.

block Term used in *patchwork to denote the single unit, either of one or of many pieces, which will be repeated to form the entire design. The word is used particularly in conjunction with the American bedcovers that are often made up of a series of blocks and sets.

block: detail of an American patchwork cover 'The Little Schoolhouse'.

blocking see stretching.

block printing In relation to embroidery, block printing has been used in two ways: 1. for stamping the design onto fabric as in *Ayrshire embroidery (Swain 1966), and 2. embroidering over fabric already block printed as in *Anglo-Indian embroidery.

block printing: wooden block with unusual metal scallop, American, c.1840.

blonde Type of bobbin lace made in the 18th and 19th centuries from raw silk, which was usually a pale straw colour but later was also white or black. It was very popular as a dress trimming, especially in the early 19th century, and some embroideries on the dresses of that time are worked in a pale straw coloured silk which resembles blonde.

blouse Garment, usually for women but in some countries also for men, worn between the neck and the hips, with or without sleeves. Under various names it is found in most countries of the world and is often beautifully decorated, especially in southeast Europe.

Blue and White Needlework see Deerfield Society of Blue and White Needlework.

blue cat rug see Caswell carpet.

blunt Type of round-eyed sewing needle which is short, thick, and strong. It is used chiefly by staymakers and tailors.

bobbin 1. Article around which thread or yarn is wound so that it can easily be wound off again when required. They are used in many crafts including weaving and lace, but in embroidery and needlework the relevant bobbins are those used in a sewing machine shuttle, and the cylindrical articles with a broad top and base round which thread is wound, also known as reels and spools. 2. Soft, round cotton cord used as a *piping cord.

bobbin: (left) wooden bobbin for sewing cotton, (right) metal bobbin for sewing machine.

bobbin case see shuttle.

bobbin net (bobbinet) Net made by machine in imitation of handmade net. John Heathcoat of Nottingham and Loughborough patented the first machine capable of doing this in 1808. His invention was the start of an enormous industry involving hundreds of workers who made imitation lace by running the design through the net or by tambouring it. (Halls 1973) See also wash blond.

bobbin net footing Narrow width of *bobbin net with a darned in pattern, used as an edging for garments, cap ruffles, and as insertion.

bodice The part of a woman's dress that clothes the torso from neck to waist. Originally stays or corsets were known as 'a pair of bodies' and bodice is derived from this. The meaning of the word has changed slightly over the centuries from an inner garment (the stays) to an outer garment (the top of a dress), and care is needed when reading old books, inventories, and accounts to get the correct meaning.

bodkin Short, pointed implement. In needlework it can either be a blunt needle with a long eye used for threading cord, tape, or ribbon through holes or a casing; or it can be a sharp pointed implement used for making the holes in broderie anglaise (eyelet embroidery) and other work of that kind—in this sense it is synonymous with *stiletto. The word can also be applied to a dagger (as used by Shakespeare) or to a large hairpin.

Bodley, G. F. (1827–1913) British architect who was keenly interested in embroidery, not only for the churches he himself built, but also as a craft in its own right. He designed ecclesiastical embroideries for various societies such as the *Leek Embroidery Society, the *Ladies Ecclesiastical Embroidery Society, and for the newly-formed *Royal School of Needlework. He also helped to found, and designed for, the ecclesiastical furnishers Watts & Co. Bodley had absorbed the principles of A. W. N. Pugin, but his own work was much more pictorial and not so formal.

Bodmer, Karl (1809–1893) Swiss landscape painter who travelled in America in 1833 with Prince Maximilian von Neuwied. His sketches of the trip were used as illustrations in Maximilian's *Travels*, and his watercolours of Indian costumes and chiefs exhibited in 1836 showed clearly the details of quill and beadwork embroidery, especially of the Plains Indian. (Champlin 1887)

Bokhara (Bukhara) City in Uzbekistan (north of Afghanistan) which has always been known for its embroideries. As might be expected, the designs have a great similarity to Persian (Iranian) ones, and are often of formalised flowers, singly or in bunches, worked in coloured silks on linen.

Bokhara: cover in silk on linen.

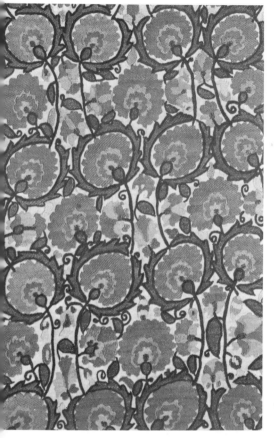

Boler, James see *Needle's Excellency, The.*

bolt Continuous length of fabric 30 to 50 yards (27 to 46 metres) or more long which is rolled on a tube or flat piece of cardboard. It also means a roll of ribbon or tape.

bolting cloth (boulting cloth) Originally a cloth in a fine *gauze or leno weave used for the sifting of flour. However, it is described by Miss Lambert (1843) as 'a very fine description of woollen canvas, principally manufactured in England, but now seldom used except for children's samplers'. Today it can be of linen, cotton, or synthetic thread.

bolton sheeting Coarse type of cotton sheeting in *twill weave. Besides being used for sheets, aprons, dresses, and other articles, it can also be a ground for embroidery.

bolton work The forerunner of *candlewick embroidery, used chiefly for bedcovers in the mid 19th century. It was usually worked on *bolton sheeting with a thick cotton yarn, using the same type of design as for candlewick but not cutting the threads. Bedcovers using this technique, known as Caddow quilts, were originally worked on a hand loom but have been copied in needlework. The term bolten work is not used in America —all work of this type is called *candlewick or tufting.

bombé Term from the French meaning rounded out or puffed up. It is used in embroidery, dressmaking, and upholstery.

bonding Modern aid in different forms of needlework where a plastic adhesive is used which, when heated, joins or bonds together two materials. 1. The adhesive is available already spread onto a non-woven fibre. These are of varying thicknesses and are used in dressmaking as interlinings, in appliqué when it is necessary to stabilise a fabric which frays, and in some modern forms of patchwork. They come under various tradenames such as iron-on Vilene, Pellon, and Stitch witchery. 2. Strips of vinyl, tape, or binding ready prepared with the adhesive can be ironed onto plastic or rubberised raincoats or the backs and edges of carpets both to repair tears or to neaten a raw edge. 3. In the conservation of textiles, net or muslin is sometimes sprayed with the adhesive and ironed on to the fragile fabric to give it strength and body.

Bonnaz machine see Cornely machine.

bonnet Covering for the head worn by babies at most periods from the 17th century onwards, by women in certain occupations, and as fashionable wear at different dates. They were often tied onto the head and were generally soft and light, with the exception of those worn outdoors as street wear in the 19th century. Many, especially infants', were white and embroidered in the style of the time. Sun-bonnets, worn by women working outdoors and by children, have been made of cotton fabrics with a curtain behind to protect the neck, and in an infinite variety of styles with gathering, pleating, bows, and other forms of decoration.

bonnet: linen and Italian cut work, 17th century.

bookbindings: Henshaw's Horae Successivae, *London, 1632.*

bookbindings

Embroidery often used to be incorporated into the binding of a book (as distinct from a *book cover or case which is added to the book to protect the binding). England has a strong tradition of embroidered bindings and there are still a considerable number extant, most being in the British Museum (London), the New York Public Library, the Bodleian Library (Oxford). They were, with a few exceptions, worked on canvas, velvet, or satin, with silk or metal threads. The use of metal threads with fine, light silk was very practical as the metal, being slightly raised, protected the silk and the ground material. Most of these books are religious, and the covers, especially those embroidered on canvas, often reflect this by showing biblical scenes.

Books to be bound in embroidery are made in the same way as those to be bound in leather except that the bands to which the sections of paper are sewn are always flat rather than in relief, thus making it possible to paste the embroidery onto the spine. One of the earliest examples, probably 14th century, is the *Felbrigge Psalter*, which belonged to Anne, daughter of Sir Simon de Felbrigge. Elizabeth I is thought to have embroidered two or more books, the most charming being the one she gave to her stepmother Katharine Parr in 1544, called *Miroir of the Synneful Soul*. Of those bound in velvet the earliest example extant is the

Tres ample description de toute la terre Saincte of about 1540 which belonged to Henry VIII. Another, and probably the most beautiful, is the **Douce Bible* which was given to Elizabeth I in 1583. Embroidered books of the Stuart period were frequently worked on white satin, and are very reminiscent of the embroidered panels of that time. A delightful example is Henshaw's *Horae Successivae*, printed in 1632, which is bound in white satin and most delicately worked with flowers and insects. (Davenport 1899) See also Felbrigge, Anne de.

book cover

(book case) Protection for prized and valued books and, especially in the present century, decoration for plainly bound ones for a special purpose, such as a prayer book at a wedding. In the 17th century, prayer books were often carried in embroidered bags that did not necessarily match the embroidery on the book, but sometimes a matching cover was made at the same time as the book was embroidered. See also slip case.

bookmarker

1. Long piece of thin ribbon embroidered at each end, used in the lectern bible and communion prayer books in churches. They are generally embroidered *en suite. 2. 19th century marker in *card work, often for the family bible or prayer book and generally worked with a rebus such as *The Cross is my anchor*. Secular bookmarks are also often embroidered.

boots

Although not generally considered objects for embroidery, some Eskimo tribes wear boots made of felt which have decorated tops.

Bordados

see net laces.

Bostocke: earliest known dated sampler.

Bostocke, Jane

Known only for having worked what is thought to be the earliest dated *sampler—1598. It has representations of animals at the top and patterns at the bottom. In between, after 'Jane Bostocke' and the date, is worked *Alice Lee was Borne the 23 of November being Tuesday in the afternoone 1596*. Apart from its charm this sampler is invaluable because it shows some of the patterns in vogue at that time. (King 1962)

bargello work: this American pocket book is photographed open to show the inscription 'Judith Morse Her Book 1777 Age 16'.

bourré Term meaning stuffed or wadded, used to describe quilted articles and embroidery.

bourre de soie see filoselle.

box Lidded receptacle of any shape but always stiff which, because of this stiffness, has always been a favourite base for embroidery. Boxes used for showing off canvas work, blackwork, metal thread embroidery, and many other techniques are frequently seen in needlework exhibitions today, while many museums have boxes in the techniques of the past.

boxers The little nude figures seen on either side of a plant on many 16th and 17th century *samplers. There has been much controversy about their meaning, but King (1961) considers that they are a very simplified version of lovers offering gifts to the beloved. This was a favourite theme of the pattern books of this time, and it seems likely that over the years the design, translated onto samplers, lost its meaning and became the two nude figures and plant.

bracelet Ornamental ring or band worn on the wrist or arm. Generally they are of metal and precious or semi-precious stones, but in the 1830s and 1840s there was a fashion for embroidered bracelets. These were from 1½ to 2 inches (4 to 5 centimetres) wide and worked with minute beads, or else embroidered with silks and chenille. With today's fashion for ethnic clothing, embroidered bracelets are once more being worn.

braces (suspenders, gallowses, galluses) Straps passing over the shoulders for keeping trousers up. Until about 1770 breeches had been kept up by being tightened round the waist, but with the advent of a more figure-fitting pantaloon, and later the trouser, it became necessary to use another method, so braces were

beads: a Cherokee woman at an Indian village in North Carolina with her tray of colourful beads.

braces: embroidered in wool and beads, c.1840.

invented. Originally they were called gallowses and also suspenders (as they suspended the trouser from the shoulder) and are still known as gallowses in parts of Scotland, and galluses or, more usually, suspenders in North America. In the 19th century, braces succumbed to the passion for Berlin woolwork and many pairs were embroidered on canvas with wool and small beads by loving hands. It would seem that the beads must have harmed the waistcoat fabric, but this did not prevent their use. Braces worn to be seen are called *bretelles.

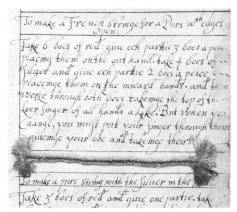

braid: patterns for plaited purse strings from a needlework book dated 1655.

braid Narrow trimming for dress or embroidery. It can be of a plain or fancy weave in cotton, wool, silk, synthetic, gold, or silver thread, in any combination. The more usual kinds are: 1. lacet, a narrow braid with a looped edge; 2. military braid, which is quite flat, and generally nine-plait; 3. ric-rac (rick-rack), a flat braid woven into a chevron or zig-zag shape; 4. russia or soutache, a narrow braid made of two cords woven together in a plait; and 5. stickerei, a braid decorated with embroidery, sometimes having a scalloped edge.

braid: ric-rac and russia lurex.

braiding 1. Embroidery in which decorative *braids are used to form a pattern applied to the fabric either by hand or machine. All through the 19th century, braiding was used extensively for articles such as smoking caps, mantles, dresses, and aprons, both for women and children, and it was also used to decorate articles for household use. 2. See plait (number 2).

braiding: braid sewn down in a pattern.

brandenburgs see frogging.

brassard Armband that carries a badge or some insignia, generally embroidered by hand or machine, to denote the organisation to which the wearer belongs.

brave bred stitch (true marking, two-sided cross stitch, marking stitch) Variation of *cross stitch, used in marking clothes and household linen with names, initials, dates etc. It differs from cross stitch in that the back of the work, which in the case of household linen may well show, consists of crosses as perfect as those on the front. This is achieved by taking the needle back to the first hole after making the first diagonal stitch, putting the needle in at the centre and out at the bottom right, and then taking the second diagonal. Two-sided cross stitch has exactly the same effect but is worked differently.

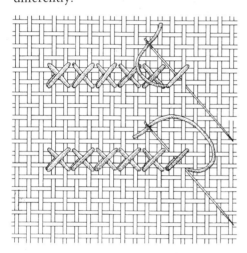

Breed: crewel work bedspread, American, 1770.

breadth The width of a fabric from *selvage to selvage.

brede Obsolete form of *braid.

breechcloth (breechclout, loincloth) Small piece of cloth or leather often worn as the only clothing for men in warm climates, sometimes decorated with *appliqué or *beadwork for ceremonial wear. Those worn by *Pueblo Indian men are usually of handwoven cotton, often fringed at the ends or finished with embroidery or bright cording in geometric patterns. Winnebago (Wisconsin) Indians wear a type consisting of two beaded broadcloth flaps, front and rear. A small triangular or rectangular apron, often beautifully decorated with shell beads, is worn by Greenland and Pacific Eskimos as their only clothing in their hotwinter houses. (Roediger 1941, Skinner 1923 quoted by Radin 1970, Birket-Smith 1935)

breechclout see breechcloth.

Breed, Mary Embroideress from Boston (Massachusetts) known for her beautiful bedspread at the Metropolitan Museum of Art (New York). It was made on homespun in multicoloured *crewels and signed and dated 1770 (when she was nineteen). The stitches are traditional American crewel stitches: buttonhole, herringbone, romanian, couching, surface darning, stem, and outline.

bretelles *Braces worn to be seen rather than hidden. Embroidered bretelles, especially those with a crosspiece over the chest joining the two shoulder straps, are worn in some southeast European

countries by both men and women, and they have been fashionable in West European and American costume at various times.

Breton work (Brittany embroidery) Kind of work done in Brittany (France) on cloth or silk in geometrical or free designs, It was chiefly used for borders to garments, or on tie ends, bookmarkers etc. Caulfeild and Saward (1882) suggest that it is a very old type of embroidery based on chain stitch, but included satin, stem, and dot stitch.

briar stitch see feather stitch.

brick stitch see long and short stitch.

bridal veil see veil.

bride see bar.

bright check purl see purl.

Brighton towelling embroidery Type of work popular in the late 19th century. It consisted of simple stitches such as darning or satin worked on an evenweave linen, and was used chiefly for decorating household linen.

brise-bise Short window curtain made of semitransparent material and frequently ornamented with insertions of handwork and handmade fringes. They were common in the late 19th and early 20th centuries.

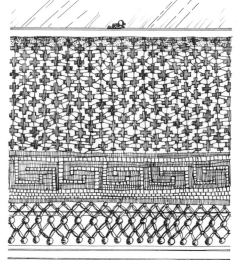

Broderers' Company: the Master's crown, second half of the 16th century.

broach (broche) The wooden spindle onto which metal thread is wound. This ensures that the thread is not touched by hot, sticky hands in working, which would make it liable to tarnish. The broach is one of the 'Embrautherer's tools' mentioned by Randle *Holme in *The Academy of Armory* (1688) and it makes up part of the arms of the *Broderers' Company.

broach: a pair of carved ivory broaches, early 19th century.

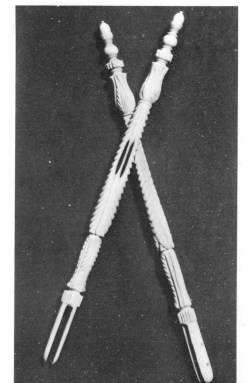

brocade Textile woven with a raised pattern, generally floral or abstract. It was formerly of gold or silver but later silk was added, and now cotton and synthetic brocades are more common.

brocade embroidery Type of embroidery on brocade using the woven pattern of the ground as the design. In the early 18th century parts of the design were sometimes solidly filled in with beads, but in the late 19th century only the outlines and some of the details would be worked. The *Leek Embroidery Society was well known for this kind of work.

brocade embroidery: waistcoat, English, c.1750.

Broderers' Company City of London Livery Company formed to protect the interests of professional embroiderers. Its early history is a little obscure as the minutes were destroyed by fire, first in 1666 and again in 1678, but it is thought to have existed in 1331 and then to have absorbed the Company of Tapissers. In 1561 the Broderers' Company was granted its first charter. Professional embroidery was evidently not a paying concern in the 17th century, for in 1634 the company petitioned Charles I for a licence in mortmain saying: 'The trade is now so much decayed and grown out of use, so that a great part of the Company for want of employment are so much impoverished as they are constrained to become porters, water carriers and the like.' In 1613 James I asked the City of London through its Livery Companies to settle English and Scottish protestants in the six counties of Ulster, Northern Ireland, on the lands forfeited by O'Neill who had rebelled against the Crown. In return for administering the lands, starting schools etc, the companies were to receive the rents. Each of the twelve main companies took some of the smaller companies under their wing and the Broderers, with the Cooks and Masons, were under the Mercers. These four companies worked together until the Irish estates were sold in 1908. The best known warden of the Broderers' Company was Edmund *Harrison. (Holford 1910)

Broderick (Brothericke), William Embroiderer to James I. There is little known of his life but he, with other craftsmen, was busily engaged in preparing for the wedding of the Princess Elizabeth, daughter of James I, in 1612: 'One and twenty pound, ten ounce and a half of coloured naples silk in grain, delivered to William Brothericke our embroiderer by him to be employed upon the embroidery of Hanging and other furniture for the bride chamber.' Also 'Item to William Broderick, our embroiderer for embroidering one whole suit of Hanging upon crimson velvet, richly garnished and brodered all through with cloth of gold and cloth of silver, Lace of gold, part with plates and chain Lace of golde without plates, Venice twists, and gold and silver and coloured naples silk; for embroidering the several parts of a Sparver Bed of crimson velvet, head part, coeler, double Valance. Five very large Curtains, upon crimson satin . . . also one canopy with valance and curtains . . . a very large Cupboard cloth . . . Carpet and screen cloth, Chair, Stools and cushions . . . for thread, fine canvas and many other necessities employed for the same.' (Madden 1835). In 1611 he was paid for embroidering 248 red coats with roses and crowns for the King's, Queen's, and Prince's servants. He died in 1620 and in his will left £100 to the *Broderers' Company to be invested for distribution to the poor and to provide a dinner for the liverymen.

broderie anglaise (eyelet embroidery) Type of *cutwork embroidery which evolved in Britain in about 1850 from the earlier *Ayrshire embroidery, and quickly became very popular. It is always worked

broderie anglaise: boy's dress, English, c.1863.

broderie anglaise: 19th century photograph of a small boy wearing the dress illustrated.

with a soft, white mercerised cotton thread on cambric, and consists of a formalised pattern of a series of round and oval holes. The edges of the holes are tightly overcast and the rest of the design is in padded satin stitch with a very small amount of stem stitch. In addition to the babies' dresses, children's frocks, camisoles, caps etc which were decorated with it, many yards of scalloped edging with a formal design were worked for use round the hems of petticoats, nightgowns, drawers, and anything else ingenuity could suggest. The work was small, simple, and repetitive—just suited to the taste of the mid-Victorian lady. In the 1880s broderie anglaise reached Madeira and was enthusiastically taken up by the local women who made it for sale to tourists in such quantities that it became known as *Madeira work. Apart from slight changes in the designs there is no basic difference between the two.

broderie en lacet Late 19th century embroidery worked on satin with lacet braid and needlepoint or point lace stitches. It was used for mantelpiece and table borders and general household articles. (Caulfeild and Saward 1882)

broderie perse Form of *applied work of the 18th-19th century in which figures, trees, flowers, animals, and objects are cut from cotton material and applied to a plain ground, often with no sense of relationship or scale. Later in the century the same technique was used in a more naturalistic way, with the addition of some stitchery.

broderie perse: counterpane in applied patchwork or broderie perse, American.

broderie suisse Variety of *applied work of the late 19th century. Muslin is first embroidered with chain stitch and is then applied to a silk or satin background using buttonhole stitch.

Brooklyn Museum (New York) Contains a large collection of textiles and embroideries, among which are African, Asian, Peruvian, Near Eastern, American Indian, and West European. Also included are samplers, quilts, and East European embroideries, as well as Paracas textiles and Plains Indian embroideries. See also Nathan Sturgis Jarvis Collection.

Brooklyn Museum: a Paracas mantle from Peru.

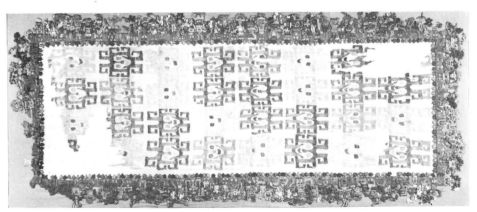

Brothericke, William see Broderick, William.

brussels thrums Fine *thrums used in some needlework rugs. It is similar to *crewel wool but rather tougher and more hairy.

buckler Small shield   The buckler made for Charles IX of France (1560–1574), which can still be seen in the Louvre Museum (Paris), has a lining embroidered in gold on crimson velvet, and shows the work of professional Parisian embroiderers of about 1570.

buckler: crimson velvet lining of Charles IX of France's buckler, 1550–74.

buckram In the middle ages, a fine soft cotton or linen fabric, but now a stiff pasted or gummed cloth used chiefly for interlining household articles, such as pelmets and valences, and for stiffening embroideries.

bugle Small tube-shaped bead of transparent glass. Edwards (1966) discusses a wider definition of the word based on entries in the rate books of the late 16th and early 17th centuries, but generally, and especially in the 19th century, bugles were tube-shaped beads, frequently made of jet. They were much used on mantles, dresses, and accessories from about 1870 to 1910, and again in the 1920s on beaded dresses for evening wear. Among the New Year gifts to Elizabeth I in 1578 was: 'By Mrs Bissels, a partelet and ruffs of lawne wrought with white work, with a blake sipers upon yt, gar' wythe bewgles' (Nichols 1823). See also bugle work.

bugle work: beads massed to give three-dimensional effect, Italian.

bugle work The attaching of *bugles to a fabric by means of a waxed thread and occasionally surface stitchery. This type of work was known from Tudor times and probably earlier, but with the wear from the glass rubbing the thread and the weight of the beads on the

material, it is not in general very long lived. One example can still be seen on a dossal dated 1697 at Weston Favell Church, Northamptonshire, in which the Last Supper is depicted in stitchery with bugles forming the background. In Anglesey Abbey, Cambridgeshire, there is a fine firescreen of Italian workmanship consisting of bugles piled up over padding in a florid design.

Bukhara see Bokhara.

Bulgarian embroidery Derived from Byzantium to the east, and the neighbouring Slav countries, Bulgarian embroidery is worked mainly on blouses and shirts for men and women. Motifs, either geometrical or drawn from plants, are generally outlined with black thread which shows up the strong clear colours used, and these designs are handed down from one generation to the next. Stitches are mostly cross, double running, and a long tent stitch worked in close parallel lines (*La broderie national de Bulgare* 1913). The geometric style of Bulgarian embroidery was popular in the United States in the 1890s. Buttonhole stitch with satin and outline stitch was used, the latter two sometimes being combined to produce a corded effect, and the work, brightly coloured with gold and silver added, was seen as trimming on coats, blouses, and suits.

bullion embroidery Generic name for all types of embroidery worked entirely with metal threads. See also auriphrygium.

bullion embroidery: man's cap embroidered with silver thread, mid–17th century.

bullock furniture Embroidered decorations, including saddle cloths, hump covers, horn covers, and forehead covers, which are worn by bullocks harnessed to a travelling carriage in western India. Traditionally the hump and horn covers have a little bird perched on top, made of stuffed cloth with streamers for its tail.

bunting Woollen fabric of rather open *tabby weave, used for making flags, also known as bewpers and bunting. Bunting (mentioned in the mid 17th century in Samuel Pepys's Diary as bewpers) is always used for the code and identification flags of ships, as it stands up to salt and weather better than other fabrics. It was not manufactured in the USA until after 1865 when tariff regulations made production competitive with British goods. 2. In US *nuns' cloth.

burato embroidery Work resembling one of the *net laces (filet or lacis) but instead of being on a foundation of net it is darned on *gauze or leno fabric, and so is really an embroidery. There are designs for burato work in *Vinciolo's book *Les singuliers et nouveaux pourtraicts . . .* of 1587. A similar technique was used by the *Nazca/Ica cultures of Peru in 900–1400 AD.

Burden, Elizabeth Sister of Jane Morris, and sister-in-law of William *Morris. She was one of the first teachers at the *Royal School of Needlework and re-introduced a variety of cushion stitch, later to be called burden stitch. This had been known and used in the middle ages as a grounding stitch, especially in Italy and Germany, but had not been used since, until it was revived by Miss Burden, partly to work the flesh areas in the large figure embroideries designed by Walter *Crane and William Morris.

burden stitch 1. Couched stitch, used in the past and rediscovered by Elizabeth *Burden. Rounded, slightly thick threads are laid across the design leaving a space between each. These are then tied down by a stitch crossing two threads, leaving a space, crossing two threads, and so on, with the next row filling in the gaps. The top stitches can either be worked close together, showing no laid thread, or wider apart letting the under colour show through. Burden stitch is often used in metal thread and heraldic embroidery where the tying down stitch can be lengths of purl, and it can also be worked with each stitch only crossing one laid thread in which case the under thread will always show through. 2. Miss Burden also taught the use of a type of satin stitch named after her: this crosses an area of any size by means of equal length stitches spaced so as to make a pattern.

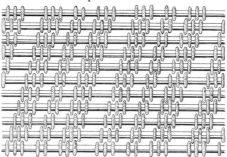

burden strap Strap used by certain North American Indians to carry large loads on their backs. The wider section (about 1½ inches or 4 centimetres) in the middle is decorated and goes round the forehead, while the rest of the length, which is narrower and plain, supports the load.

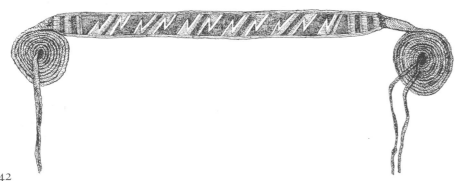

Burgundy: 'The Meeting of Abraham and Melchizedek', silk and gold thread couched on velvet, c.1520.

Burgundy An area of varying size and position, Burgundy in the 15th century was a powerful duchy covering what is now Holland, Belgium, parts of northern France, Luxembourg, Alsace, and Lorraine, and was sandwiched between France and the Holy Roman Empire. The dukes of Burgundy were great patrons of the arts encouraging illumination, painting, tapestry-weaving, and the making of rich embroideries and vestments, and one technique developed to a fine art was that of *or nué. Possibly this had its origins in the new method devised by the painter Jan Van Eyck of superimposing a series of glazes in panel painting, but either way the result was gold embroidery of unparalleled beauty and subtlety of tone. The finest examples of this Burgundian work now to be seen are the Mass Vestments of the Golden Fleece in the Schatzkammer, Vienna.

burlap Coarse canvas made from jute or hemp, generally used for bagging but originally more like *holland. Since the mid 19th century, burlap has been the foundation material for hooked rugs, and in addition it is now a basis for embroidery and collage. The word is seldom heard in England, where burlap is known as 'sacking', but has remained in use in America.

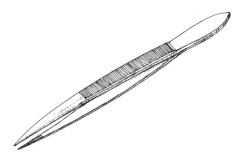

burling irons Tweezers or pincers used in embroidery for pulling out threads and knots when unpicking.

Burrell collection Collection of objets d'art made by Sir William Burrell in the early 20th century, which is particularly rich in embroideries of many countries. A museum to house his enormous collection is now being built in his home town of Glasgow in Scotland.

Burrell collection: detail of a panel with animals, mid-17th century.

burse see corporal case.

buskin High, soft boot worn by all ranks and both men and women in the middle ages, especially for travelling. Nowadays the word applies to a countryman's gaiter rather than a boot. Ceremonial buskins were worn by medieval kings at their coronation and by bishops when celebrating mass, and Fairholt (1846) describes a pair found in a tomb in the Abbey of St Germain des Prés, Paris, as being of 'violet-coloured silk, ornamented with a variety of elegant designs in polygonal shapes, upon which were worked greyhounds and birds in gold'.

buta (buti) Floral motif in Indian textile design derived from Persian sources during the *Mughal period. Traditionally, it is a flowering plant with a curling bud at the top designed within a compact, curvilinear form, variously described as a cone or mango. During the 19th century the naturalistic conception faded and the motifs appeared merely as a cone or mango filled with floral ornament. A buta is a large ornament of this type and a buti is a small one. (Irwin and Hall 1973) See also Paisley pattern.

buta: detail of an embroidered apron.

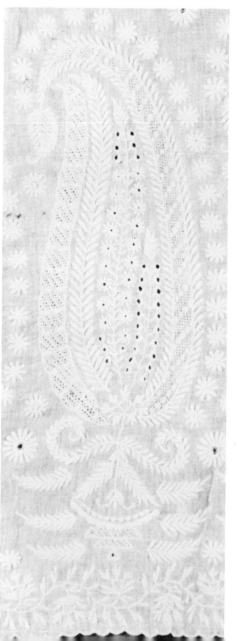

butcher linen Durable and heavy plainweave bleached linen used in America for aprons, dresses, and fancy work. It is called butcher cloth if other fibres besides linen are used.

buti see buta.

Butler-Bowden cope One of the best known and most splendid examples of *opus anglicanum, dating between 1330 and 1350. It belongs to the group of *copes which have zones of arches radiating from the centre back. In this case each arch is filled with the figure of a saint, and the three main scenes down the back show the Coronation of the Virgin, the Adoration of the Kings, and the Annunciation. It can be seen in the Victoria and Albert Museum (London).

butt Join that exactly fits end to end without any overlapping. The word is used in particular with reference to braids.

butter muslin Very openweave muslin originally used for draining butter but now used among other things as the bottom layer of fabric in Italian quilting and trapunto. In America it is known as cheesecloth but this is not the same as English cheesecloth.

button Attachment for fastening a garment or for decoration. They have a long history and can be seen on the costume of both men and women of the middle ages, as depicted on monumental brasses. Often these buttons were decorative rather than useful. They have been made of every conceivable material from wood and horn to diamonds, and where they have been of great value they have been cut off one garment and used on another. *A Tudor Book of Rates* of 1582 (edited by Willan 1962) gives rates of duty to be paid on buttons of 'steel, copper, tin or latten for Jerkins, thread, silk and fine damasked work, when imported'. As well as being fashioned from hard materials they have been worked by professional seamsters and tailors and amateur dressmakers from many different types of fabric, in plain sewing, and with embroidery. The shirt buttons of the 18th and 19th centuries were often homemade *Dorset crosswheel buttons.

In 1674 an Act was passed to help the button makers by prohibiting the importation of foreign buttons, and in 1699 another Act was passed, it having been represented to Parliament that 'many thousands of men, women and children within this kingdom, did depend upon the making of silk, mohair, gimp and thread buttons with the needle, and their business was diminished by the wearing of buttons made of threads of cloth, serge, drugget, frieze, camlet, and other stuffs and materials of which cloths are usually made', and therefore they prayed for relief—which was granted. (Strutt 1842)

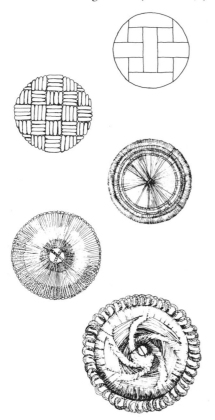

button blankets Characteristic appliqué form of the northwest coast American Indians, used mostly for decorative and ceremonial blankets and shirts. The ground was usually a dark blue woollen blanket from the Hudson's Bay Company, with applied buttons in typical clan patterns of the killer whale and raven outlined with Chinese coins and brass military buttons brought by the traders, as well as iridescent pearl buttons in various sizes. The buttons were sewn on with *sinew, and the number used was very large—a description of one blanket gives 980 for edging the border, 1578 small and 10 large for outlining the killer whale, and another 440 on the motif below. (Gunther 1966)

buttonhole Slit through which a *button can be passed as a method of fastening a garment. There are representations on medieval brasses showing that they have an early origin, though loops and *frogging have also been used. Modern buttonholes may be either bound or worked, and the correct stitch to use is a variation of buttonhole stitch called tailor's buttonhole stitch.

buttonhole cutter Metal tool with a sliding, sharp-pointed knife, used in America in the 18th century for cutting buttonholes and ripping seams. See also seam knife.

buttonhole scissors Type of scissor, adjustable by screw and ratchet, which can be set to start the cut for a *buttonhole any distance up to half an inch (12 millimetres) in from the edge of the cloth.

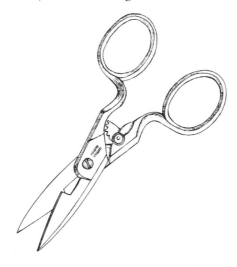

buttonhole twist see silk twist.

button mould (mold) The basis for making handmade buttons. The moulds can either be metal or plastic, which are suitable for covering with material, or they can be wood, which are more generally covered with silk thread. Nowadays wooden moulds are often used in collage.

button rug Kind of rug made from small circles of fabric folded into quarters which are stitched at the apex to a ground fabric of linen, tow, or burlap. When the points are stitched close together the circles stand up in tufts. Few examples of this 19th century rug-making technique exist as the sewing threads easily break or wear away. See also quill patchwork.

Byzantine Word referring to the architecture and arts of the Byzantine Empire which flourished in eastern Europe and parts of Asia, Asia Minor, and Africa roughly from the rebuilding of Constantinople about AD 300 to the 12th century. The dominant characteristics were those of Roman art influenced by the East, and

the greatest achievements were in architecture. However, silk pattern-weaving reached a high peak, and Byzantine silks, designs, and threads had a great influence on the textiles and embroideries of the West from the 4th to the 12th centuries.

Byzantine embroidery Combination of couched outlines, *applied work, and fancy stitches, dating from 1878, and useful for ornamenting thick materials. Shapes traced on the ground fabric are outlined by couching thick threads; other shapes are cut out in various fabrics and applied, again with a couched edge. Any space left in the pattern can be filled in with a variety of stitches.

Byzantium Ancient city of eastern Europe occupying one of the seven hills on which, under Constantine the Great (AD 270–337), Constantinople (now called Istanbul) was built. In the centuries before Christ it was a very important city, conquered in turn by the Persians, Athenians, Spartans, Macedonians, and Romans. In the 6th century it became the first place outside China to produce silk, and during its existence it became the symbol for everything rich and beautiful including textiles and embroideries, and to Western minds it epitomised the fabulous and wealthy 'East'.

(opposite)
beadwork: the corner of a saddle-cloth and a moccasin demonstrating the use of lazy squaw stitch.

(overleaf, p 46)
bearing cloth: a detail of the early 17th century portrait of the Cholmondely sisters; the baby is wrapped in a bearing cloth.

(overleaf, p 47)
bed furniture: the crewel embroidered hangings in the Cecil Bedroom at Winterthur.

cabinets In the 17th century there was a fashion for small cabinets to be made covered with embroidery, often inside as well as out, generally on a ground of white satin. They consisted of a box with a flat or domed lid, a pair of doors in front, and four or six drawers inside. The drawers, the lining to the doors, and the back of the cabinet were usually covered in flat embroidery, with the top and doors in *raised work. These cabinets were frequently the culmination of a girl's training as a needlewoman, and might be termed graduation exercises. In the inventory of Henry Howard (1614) there is an entry, 'Item a riche embroidered Cabinett in coulors' (Shirley 1869).

cabinets: an English 17th century example depicting the Elements, shown open.

cable cord see piping cord.

cabochon foundations Small dome-shaped buckram forms used as centres for flowers or ornaments.

cachemire French spelling of the word *cashmere. It also means a three-ply metal-effect novelty yarn composed of three strands of black wool, each one wound with fine crimped gilt or copper wire.

Calverley: a detail of one of the panels worked c.1717 by Lady Julia Calverley.

caddas (caddis) Generally taken to mean *worsted or *crewel wool, but it may have other, slightly different meanings. The OED considers that primarily it is the yarn, but can also be a cloth woven of the yarn, and a narrow tape of worsted. It is also a coarse, cheap serge, and a kind of stuff. Fairholt (1846) describes caddis as 'worsted, such as is now termed cruell, used for the ornament to the dresses of servants and the lower classes in the 16th century'. This leaves it uncertain as to whether he means thread for embroidery or a tape. Picken (1939) defines it in this way: 'ancient, coarse, simply-woven woollen cloth between flannel and bure. Made in Provence since time immemorial.'

caftan (kaftan) Long outer garment shaped like a coat, with straight, loose sleeves, and generally fastened with a sash. It is worn in many countries including North Africa, India, and the Middle East, and is frequently embroidered, especially from neck to waist.

Caldas da Rainha embroidery see Portugal.

calender To smooth and glaze paper or fabric by passing it through heavy rollers. The trade of calenderer is an old one, and Campbell (1747) says: 'These Tradesmen keep Calendars or Mangles, being heavy Engines moved by Horses, or Men, for pressing chiefly Linnen Cloths of all Sorts.' As well as glazing, the mangles could give a watered or wavy look to fabrics, known as moiré.

calico The name of a cotton cloth, originally that from Calicut on the west coast of India, but now more generally a strong, tabby-woven, cotton cloth. In the US a cheap cotton cloth with a small printed pattern.

calico patch Variety of patch for repairing a plain-coloured cotton fabric. A fresh piece of fabric is laid under the hole and hemmed on, the hole is cut square, and the edges are turned and hemmed to the new material.

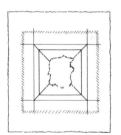 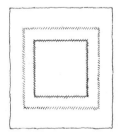

Calverley, Lady Julia (1686–1736) The wife of Sir Walter Calverley of Esholt Hall in Yorkshire, she was a notable needlewoman and, probably with help, embroidered in tent stitch the panels (one dated 1717) which were moved to Wallington Hall (Northumberland) in 1755. These panels can still be seen in the Needle-work Room framed with rococo carving and mounted on the wall. The design, in what might be called crewel work style, has small hills or hummocks at the base, with birds among exotic flowers, fruit, and leaves flowing from a central stem. Lady Calverley worked another screen, also at Wallington, which shows scenes from Hollars' engravings for Virgil's *Georgics* (1633 ed.), and from engravings for his *Eclogues*. (Colour illustration opposite)

calyx-eyed needle (self-threading needle) Type of needle with a very fine slit at the top of the eye through which the thread can be forced.

49

cam Disc of plastic or metal with a specially patterned edge to govern the throw of the needle in a sewing machine adapted for embroidery. (Jones 1965)

cambric Originally a fine linen material made at Cambrai in Flanders, but now applied indiscriminately to linen or cotton or a mixture of these. In the inventory of Dame Agnes Hungerford (1523) is 'Item, lj fyne smoks of cameryke wroght with golde. (Nichols 1859). See also batiste.

camisole (corset cover) Undergarment worn over the corset and often sufficiently decorative to be shown under a thin or low cut dress.

Canadian log patchwork see log cabin patchwork.

candlewick (tufting) Form of embroidery worked on a strong linen or cotton, preferably unshrunk, using a thick, soft thread which is named candlewick, as originally it consisted of several cotton wicks plied together. The pattern is outlined in running stitch leaving a loop of thread between each stitch which is then cut. When washed, the fabric shrinks a little and holds the thread tightly. See also bolton work, roving.

candlewick needle Thick, long needle with an eye big enough to take *candlewick.

cannetille Another name for *purl in gold or silver, and also for a flat, twisted *braid in gold or silver. It was used in the 19th century for making artificial flowers —in Warren and Pullan (1855) is: '. . . with the white floss silk make a chain of 8 stitches; take a piece of cannetille a nail long, and place it under the last chain. Crochet down the chain, working over the wire doubled . . .'

Canterbury Cathedral The seat of the premier Archbishop of England from the 6th century. It contains many beautiful embroideries, the most notable being the surcoat of the *Black Prince (the original is now stored away and a modern replica is on show).

canton crape: detail of a 19th century Chinese scarf.

canton crape Rich and heavy variety of *china crape or crêpe de chine used in the 19th and 20th centuries. From the account books of Grout & Co., Norwich (1825) is: '15 Canton shawls unfinished @ 20/-. 16 Canton shawls finished @ 40/-.'

canvas Originally a strong cloth made from hemp (cannabis) and used primarily for sail-making (sailcloth), but also for tents and as the ground for oil painting. The term gradually widened to include strong unbleached cloth made from jute, hemp, or flax, and generally tabby-woven, which was used for packing goods and as the foundation fabric for large embroideries such as altar frontals (linen canvas), as well as household articles like roller towels. A further widening and more modern use of the word is a fabric made from wool, cotton, linen, hemp, or jute in a lattice-like mesh of various sizes, used mainly for embroidering with silk and wool (canvas work, needlepoint, tapestry work, rug making). These canvases are now available in single, double, and multiple-thread weaves, but it was not until the 1840s that there was anything other than single thread. Since that date the best known single-thread types have been Berlin or silk, English, evenweave, flattened, French (cotton or patent), graph, Ida, locked weave, mono or congress, Moskowa, mosaic, mummy, railroad or net, rug or raffia, thread, and Winchester; double-thread types have been evenweave, Hardanger, Java, jute embroidery, leviathan, penelope or duo,

ponto grado or rug, and rug; and multiple-thread types have been Binca, evenweave, Java or Panama, miracle warp base, and pattern weave or Munster web. (All of these kinds have entries.) See also bolting cloth, scrim, tammy cloth.

canvas lace work Variation of ordinary *Berlin woolwork. It was introduced about 1840 and consisted of a ground imitating that of lace, worked in black silk with the pattern worked in Berlin wool. It typified the Victorian craze for making one fabric imitate another, however improbably.

canvas lace work: reticule, English, mid-19th century.

canvas stitch   see tent stitch.

canvas work   Any type of embroidery worked on canvas. This includes bargello or florentine embroidery, Berlin woolwork, cross stitch embroidery, Hardanger embroidery, and the modern work which uses a variety of different stitches to create textural effects. Tent stitch embroideries of the 17th and 18th centuries were all worked on canvas and the following item from the *Boston News Letter* (USA) of 27 April, 1738 is of interest: 'To be had at Mrs Condy's near the Old North Meeting House; all sorts of beautiful figures on Canvas for Tent Stitch; the Patterns from London, but drawn by her much cheaper than English drawing; All sorts of Canvas without drawing . . .' In the US needlepoint is the generic term for all types of canvas work.

canvas work: tent stitch panel signed Isabella Buxton, English, 1750.

cap   Head covering, usually close fitting, worn by both sexes of all ages. Caps and bonnets for babies have usually been exquisitely embroidered in such techniques as Ayrshire, whitework, and broderie anglaise (eyelet embroidery), as were the women's caps of the 18th and 19th centuries.

cape   Sleeveless garment which originated as an additional short covering to a cloak. The word may still be used in this sense but it later became a garment in its own right, and is now considered interchangeable with cloak. Capes worn by women and children in the 19th century and the carrying capes for babies were often embroidered.

capitonné   Term used for a padded surface drawn in at intervals. It is applied in upholstery to buttoned chairs and sofas and in embroidery to articles such as pincushions.

cap of maintenance: Exeter Guildhall cap, English, 17th century.

cap of maintenance   'Kind of cap or hat formerly worn as a symbol of official dignity or high rank, or carried before a sovereign or high dignitary in procession' (OED). These caps are now rarely seen but there is one in Exeter Guildhall in England of red velvet embroidered in raised silver threads and sequins.

carbonised linen and paper   see transferring designs.

carding   see wool.

card table (gaming table)   Table with a hinged top and frequently with a needlework cover made especially for cardplaying in the 18th century. The needlework often represented a game of cards with money and cards depicted in wool and silk using tent or other canvas stitches. However, it must have been extremely difficult to play on such *trompe l'oeil scenes. Most modern card tables are covered in green baize. See also games board.

card table: with canvas work cover, American, 1730-45.

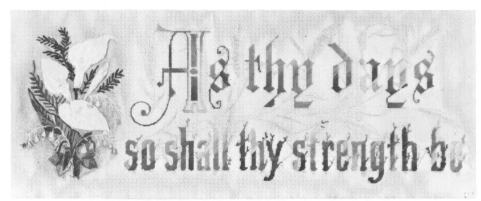

card work: American, late 19th century.

card work 'Embroidery' popular in the mid 19th century and used for small items such as bookmarkers and stamp covers. The card was prepared by being covered with holes in regular lines so that a title or message could be worked, either in wool or silk, and with or without the addition of beads. The message was sometimes contained in a *rebus. In the US this was also called perforated or punctured card work. (Colour illustration p 57)

caribou French Canadian word for the wild reindeer of North America. Caribou skin is frequently used for clothing; it is strong, light, and very warm due to an air-filled cavity in every hair. The hairs for embroidery taken from the ruff round the neck and the spots on both sides of the tail are pure white from root to tip, and are usually used white rather than dyed. The larger, once abundant woodland caribou is now nearly extinct, but the smaller barren ground caribou are found in large herds from Newfoundland to Alaska, and in Greenland. (Birket-Smith 1935, Turner 1955)

carpet 1. Covering for an altar: see Laudian frontal. 2. Covering for a table, cupboard, or floor. In the 16th century, knotted carpets were imported from Turkey and the Middle East, but were considered too precious to put on floors and so were used to cover tables and cupboards. These articles were imitated in tent stitch to provide a cheaper version of the expensive import. Later, in the late 17th and 18th centuries, the idea was taken a step further and rugs and carpets worked on canvas with a large mesh in a greater variety of stitches were made for floors. The designs of the 18th century rugs are generally floral. In the 20th century the making of rugs, carpets, and stair-carpets with the needle has become a favourite occupation, generally using one of a variety of *thrums for the yarn and either a flat or tufted stitch. Though typically English flower designs are still worked, designs from Turkey, Persia (Iran), and the Caucasus are very popular, and in addition to cross stitch and tent stitch, soumak stitch and surrey stitch are much used. One of the most famous needlework carpets is that worked during the Second World War by Queen Mary (wife of George V) in order to raise dollars for Britain; it was eventually sold to Canada. See also needle-made rugs.

carpet slippers Slippers worn by men in the 19th century and originally made out of carpet, but the term has widened to include soft slippers for wear in the house which might be made of any suitable material. They were often embroidered, especially in Berlin woolwork.

carpet: an English table carpet, 16th century.

carpet thread Strong linen thread, generally waxed before reeling, used for all types of sewing requiring strength, as well as for binding carpets.

carpet worsted Coarse, worsted sewing thread which used to be obtainable for repairing carpets, and was sold in carpet colours.

Carrickmacross One of the simulated laces made in Ireland in the 19th century. It consists of motifs drawn onto muslin, outlined with overcasting, cut out, and either applied onto net or else joined with needlepoint bars. The net is sometimes further ornamented with drawn fabric stitches. The designs are based on Brussels and guipure laces as well as on Italian cutwork. Started in the 1820s, Carrickmacross was revived after the famine of 1846 as a means for poor people to earn a pittance, and it flourished, with better designs, during the last twenty years of the century. (Wardle 1968) See also net laces.

Carrickmacross: scarf with applied muslin and drawn fabric stitches, mid-19th century.

cartisane Strip of thin *parchment or vellum covered with silk, gold, or silver thread, which formed the raised pattern in the guipure laces and braids of the 16th century. In the early 19th century, cartisane was used to make motifs for ornamenting dresses.

cartouche In embroidery, term meaning a decorative framework for an inscription or other particular device. Literally, it is a scroll, or the representation of a piece of paper with the corners rolled in.

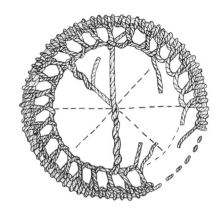

cartwheel button (spider's web button) Originally they were worked with a special zinc ring as a foundation, but a thick linen thread can be used instead. Four threads are laid across the circle to form eight segments. These are then joined with a thread passed over and under each laid thread until the space is completely filled, giving the effect of a cartwheel or spider's web. The *Dorset crosswheel button has the same effect but is worked differently.

Cashmere (cashmere, Kashmir) Word which is difficult to disentangle as it means different things in different contexts. 1. Originally the fabric of which Kashmir shawls were made. Here the word is misleading as the wool (from the mountain goat or from the wild Himalayan sheep) was imported into Kashmir from Central Asia or Tibet. 2. Cloth woven in Europe from any type of wool which approximated as nearly as possible to the original Kashmiri cloth (Cashmere is the older spelling of Kashmir). 3. Wool from which either true cashmere or European cashmere fabric is woven or knitted. It is extremely soft and fine.

cashmere work Embroidery on *cashmere. Originally this meant embroidery on the *'amli shawls from Kashmir, but the term has been widened to include any embroidery on true or simulated cashmere cloth.

cashmere work: detail from the sleeve of a coat from Kashmir, 19th century.

casing Hem or other channel through which a tape, ribbon, or elastic can be threaded.

casket In needlework the word generally refers to a small box covered with embroidery and used for keeping jewels, sewing implements, and other treasures. These were popular in the 17th century and the workmanship was similar to that on *cabinets.

casting see Dorset crosswheel button.

Caswell carpet (blue cat rug, Caswell rug, Guernsey rug) Well-known American tamboured carpet measuring 12 feet by 13 feet 6 inches (3.6 by 4 metres), worked by Zeruah Guernsey, later Mrs Caswell, of Castleton (Vermont) in 1835. Each block was worked in a tambour frame and each pattern is different, and includes flowers, people, cats, and sea shells, in many colours on a black background. According to legend two of the patterns were designed by Francis Baron and a friend, both Potawatami Indians studying at the Castleton Medical College. It can now be seen in the Metropolitan Museum of Art (New York).

catch stitch see herringbone stitch.

caterpillar-braid rug see chenille rug.

catgut The definitions are various and it is difficult to come to an exact conclusion as to what it was. Fairholt (1846) describes it as a 'coarse cloth formed of thick cord, woven widely and used in the last century [18th] for lining and stiffening dress, particularly the skirts and sleeves of a coat'. Fairchild (1967) describes it as 'an open, leno weave fabric made of hardspun yarn and sized . . . Used for embroidery', while in the inventory of the stock of a milliner's shop in 1785 is '12½ yds Catt Gutt and Gauze, 6s 3d'. In the novel *The Vicar of Wakefield* (1766) there are references to it as a ground fabric for embroidery: 'Instead, therefore, of finishing George's shirts, we now had them new-modelling their old gauzes of flourishing upon catgut . . .' However, Harbeson (1938) refers to it as a type of embroidery, quoting from the prospectus (1771) of a school near Boston (Massachusetts) which taught 'Point, Brussels, Dresden, Sprigging embroidery, Catgut, Diaper and all kinds of Darning'. But what is to be made of Mrs Delany's comment in one of her letters in 1731 that 'I have not sent you any catgut for working handkerchiefs' (Llanover 1861)? This implies a very fine fabric or else a thread, and where threads are concerned catgut is usually thick and used for stringing musical instruments, or for whipping cord.

catherine wheel (spider wheel) Filling used in *Ayshire embroidery and other whitework, which consists of spokes of thread partially covered by an intertwined thread.

Catlin, George (1796–1872) First American artist to make a comprehensive pictorial and written documentary record of the North American Indians. From 1830–36 Catlin visited all the important tribes of the still little-explored western plains, accurately painting and sketching their chieftains, medicine men, ceremonials, and daily activities. His detailed journal was published in London in 1841 as *Letters and Notes on the Manners, Customs and Conditions of the North American Indians*. Part of the Catlin collection of decorated garments and artefacts can be seen in the University of Pennsylvania Museum in Philadelphia (McCracken 1959). 470 full-length portraits of Indians and many pictures of their life and customs are in the National Collection of Fine Arts of the Smithsonian Institution in Washington DC. See also Sioux, Crow Indians, Blackfoot Indians.

Catlin: a Sioux village (detail).

Caucasus, The Range of mountains in south Russia between the Black and Caspian Seas which includes the provinces of Georgia and Azerbaijan. The area is known for its carpet-making, and some of the embroidery designs, especially those on bedspreads, bear a strong resemblance to carpet designs. However on collars, sashes, and shirts, as well as on cloths and household articles, light flower and leaf motifs and geometrical and stylised flower patterns are found.

Cecil Higgins Art Gallery (Bedford, England) Museum and art gallery with some interesting pieces of needlework on show, including a portrait of Charles I in tent stitch, dated 1717.

Cecil Higgins Art Gallery: tent stitch portrait of Charles I, signed and dated.

Central School of Arts and Crafts School established in London in 1896 by the county council, with the object of helping British craftsmen and women to maintain their traditions of design and workmanship while using all the modern techniques available.

ceremonial dress Kind of dress made for and worn in official ceremonies of the church and state, and also worn by tribes all over the world for ritual occasions. In general these costumes are meant to impress the onlooker and so are as fine and as lavishly decorated as possible.

chained stitches Group of stitches where the effect is of a series of links, one leading into the next (chain stitch), joined by a connecting stitch (cable stitch), or detached (daisy stitch). They can either be used as line stitches or in rows close together for fillings. The following stitches fall under this heading: basque; braid (gordian knot); cable (cable chain) and variations: broad (reverse), *closed square chain (big writing), crested (spanish coral), detached (daisy, lazy daisy, loop, picot, tail chain, tied loop), double (closed feather), feathered (feather, chained, outline), heavy, magic (checkered), rosette (bead edging), square chain (ladder, *open chain, roman, small writing), singalese, spanish (twisted zigzag, spanish knotted feather, plait), twisted (rope), and zigzag (vandyke, wavy); *chain; long tailed daisy (long tailed lazy daisy); petal; plaited braid; *split; *tambour; tête de boeuf; wheatear (wheat). See also stitches.

chain fork (lucet) Implement of ivory, bone, or wood, with or without a handle, used to make *cords. The cord produced is square rather than round and may be made of any thread from very fine to about the thickness of medium-weight string.

chain stitch One of the oldest and most universal of all stitches which can be used as a line stitch, filling stitch, or on canvas. It forms interlocking flat chains and lends itself to a very large number of variations. It can be worked more quickly by hand by means of a fine hook called an *ari in India, where large embroideries are worked with it, and a tambour hook in Western countries. It was one of the two stitches possible on the early sewing machines.

chain stitch embroidery Probably after cross stitch the most universal type of embroidery. It is found all over the world but appears to have spread originally from India and Persia. Only a keen eye can detect whether it is worked with a needle, a tambour hook, or an ari, as both the latter implements have at times been used to speed up the work.

chair In England, chairs began to be upholstered about the middle of the 16th century, but it was not until the end of the century that the upholstery fabric was decorated with needlework. This took two forms: either the fabric, beautiful in itself, was decorated, or a plain fabric such as canvas was covered entirely in stitchery. In the inventory of Sir Roger Wodehouse (1588) is 'Item a chaire of white satten embroidered with redd velvett'; and from the Hardwick Hall inventories (1601), 'a needlework Chare with yellow silk freng'. These two forms of decoration continued all through the 17th, 18th, and 19th centuries, and even today the seats and backs are sometimes embroidered. The early 18th century was the period when many chairs, especially the wing type, were covered with canvas work, and these are often a monument to the skill and patience of the embroiderer. Sometimes bargello or florentine embroidery was used, in which case the chair would be worked in a zigzag pattern of various coloured wools and/ or silks, or mythological or biblical scenes might be worked in cross and tent stitch surrounded by the ramping flowers so dear to the English needleworker. In the 19th century innumerable chairs were covered with Berlin woolwork, again mostly with designs of flowers. Today, needlepoint and canvas work chair seats, sometimes in matched sets for dining chairs, are a popular needlework form. (Bolingbroke 1904 and Boynton 1971)

chair: an example in Berlin woolwork, English, c.1840.

chakla: Indian, 19th century.

chakla Embroidered square cloth in Kathiawar (India) in which a bride wraps the articles of her dowry. After the marriage the chaklas are hung on the wall of the sleeping-chamber as auspicious emblems. They are generally embroidered in silk or with beadwork or mirrors. (Dhamija 1964, Irwin and Hall 1973)

chalice veil Square of silk or linen, embroidered en suite with the *corporal case and lined, which covers the chalice at the service of Holy Communion.

chalk 1. In pricking and pouncing, chalk is used to mark the outline of a design. See prick and pounce. 2. Tailor's chalk is either white or coloured chalk formed into small blocks, and is used to mark outlines or *balance marks on fabrics. It is slightly greasy and does not easily rub off, so great care must be taken when using it.

Chamba rumal embroidery One of the regional embroidery styles of India, from Chamba in the Himalayas. The cloths or *rumals are worked with representations of past glories, and show figures of men and horses, birds, trees, and animals. The thread used is an un-

Chamba rumal embroidery: detail of hanging, Indian, 18th century.

twisted floss silk, and the main stitch is a fine, even darning stitch, which looks the same on both sides, with double running stitch in black for the outline of the figures. (Dhamija 1964, Irwin and Hall 1973)

chandrawa In Kathiawar (India), a rectangular piece of embroidery hung on the walls of a house to enrich it and give it a festive look. (Dhamija 1964)

chaquira Andean term for ordinary cloth to which has been sewn small discs, bangles, or bells made of copper, gold, or shells.

charcoal Used as a powder or *pounce to rub through the pricked holes of a design onto the fabric to be embroidered.

charlottes see rocailles.

charro costume Mexican costume, usually black, worn by vaquero charros and today adopted by gentlemen as well. Charro was originally a term used to designate the man who cared for and trained horses and the costume is an adaptation of one worn in Zamora, Spain. It consists of long tight trousers, often with rows of small silver buttons along the front pocket and side seam, a short fitted jacket, and a large sombrero frequently decorated with silver and gold embroideries.

chasuble Vestment usually worn by the priest officiating at the Eucharist and sometimes, especially on the continent, also worn by those helping. It derives from the Roman paenula, a circular garment with a hole for the head, worn as a travelling cloak. Because it completely enveloped the body, it was also known as the 'caesula' or 'little house', from which the English word chasuble derives. The Roman paenula was made of plain cloth and was unlined, but when it developed into the garment worn by clergy at the altar, it began to be stiffened, embroidered, and jewelled, and became very heavy. This meant that it was difficult to raise the arms, and so the shape of the chasuble gradually altered to accommodate this need, and while remaining the same length front and back, the material was cut away over the arms until by the 16th century it had reached the very ugly shape known as fiddle back. During the last 50 years, and especially since the Second World War, the chasuble has

chasuble: designed by Henri Matisse, c.1950.

gradually been brought back to a shape nearer the original, and though embroidered, it is once again light and supple. The decoration was generally confined to the *orphreys, which were often Y or T shaped at the back, and pillar-shaped in front. There are a number of medieval orphreys in existence as well as whole garments, and among the most interesting are several in the Victoria and Albert Museum (London) and the Chichester-Constable chasuble (1330–1350) in the Metropolitan Museum (New York).

chatelaine Collection of sewing implements and household necessaries hung on chains or cords and suspended from the waist. The lady of the house, or chatelaine, carried, besides her keys, such things as thimble, scissors, needlecase, tablets, penknife, pencil, and ear spoon, and the objects themselves and their cases were often beautifully made and decorated in steel, ivory, silver, or mother-of-pearl. Chatelaines were used at intervals from very early times to the end of the 19th century.

chatelaine: English, late 19th century.

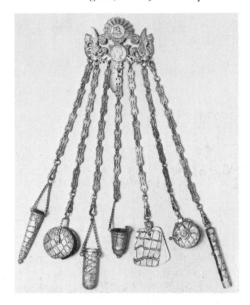

cheesecloth Cheap, tabby - woven, coarse *muslin originally for covering cheeses. Often used for pressing cloths and other utilitarian purposes, cheesecloth was a ground fabric for drawn threadwork in the late 19th century, and there has lately been a vogue for embroidering blouses made of it.

chemise (shift) Under various names, the undergarment worn by women since very early times. At some periods it has been completely hidden, at others the neck and sleeves have been visible and have often been embroidered. In the 16th century this embroidery was generally in black or red thread, often in double running or Holbein stitch, while in the 18th century it was more often edged with a gathered frill at the neck, and might have ruffles attached to the sleeves. In the 19th century the decoration was usually in broderie anglaise (eyelet embroidery). See also smock.

chemisette Underbodice, meant to show under the blouse or dress and not worn for any other reason. It generally consists of a front, back, and collar. The front and back are joined only on the

chemisette: tambour work on net, 19th century.

shoulder and are fastened with tapes at the waist. In the 19th and first half of the 20th centuries, they were much worn purely for decoration, replacing the earlier tucker, and were embroidered in whatever style suited the dress. In the mid 19th century the chemisette sometimes matched the separate sleeves or *engageantes worn under the main sleeves of the dress. See also dickey (number 1).

chenille Round, furry thread, rather like a caterpillar (*chenille* is French for caterpillar). It can be made of wool or cotton but is usually of silk, and when worked it gives a soft, velvety pile. Because of the nap on the thread, chenille is pulled through fabric as little as possible and so is often couched. The date of origin is uncertain, but Saint-Aubin (1770) says that it can be bought from ribbon merchants and that jet is often bordered with it to stop the jet from scratching hands or material, and it was certainly being imported into Virginia in 1771. Mrs Rathell, a shopkeeper of Williamsburg, wrote to John Norton in England on 22 July 1772: 'I must further request youll Send me as I am in Much distress for them, the undernaith Articles without fail . . . 3 Dozn Bunches of Pink Shenell & 3 Dozn Do of Blue Sheneele & No Other Coulars' (Mason 1968). This looks as though it had been known for a considerable time, and perhaps Mrs Delany's remark in 1754 that she is 'working stools of worsted chenille for the Gothic cell' (Llanover 1861) shows that the general use of the thread had started by that date, and does not, as her editor has suggested, mean that she had the threads made to her own specification. Miss Lambert (1843) says that there are two sizes of chenille thread: broder and ordinaire, which was a larger size more suitable for coarse canvas work. See also arasene.

chenille needle Short needle with a large eye and a sharp point suitable for use with *chenille.

chenille rolio Twisted, silk chenille cord stiffened with wire, nicknamed rat tails. It was used to make the chenille fringes and tassels so popular in the second half of the 19th century, and also to outline and edge many objects, especially the glass domes which, with birds, fruit, or flowers under them, were such a feature of the time.

chenille rug (caterpillar - braid rug) Needleworked rug, constructed from long, narrow bias strips folded in half along their length and stitched together along the two cut edges. When these strips are gathered, a fabric 'caterpillar' is formed, which is then stitched onto a base.

chenille work Embroidery with *chenille. This took various forms, and Miss Lambert (1843) considers that the thread was suitable 'for almost any description of embroidery, whether shaded, flat, or raised', but that it looked best on a fabric such as satin, which contrasted with its furriness. Chenille was used on canvas in conjunction with Berlin woolwork, especially for articles which did not get much wear such as pole screens and banner firescreens. As it was a very expensive thread, instructions for its economical use were given, and couching was a favourite method.

chequeté see pinking.

Cherokee rose blanket see rose blanket.

chessboard filling stitch Consists of blocks of three or four satin stitches, each group being crossed by a diagonal cross stitch caught down at the intersection with a tiny straight stitch. The blocks are alternated with spaces in a chessboard effect.

card work: an English example of the 19th century.

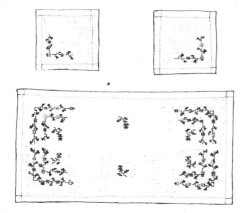

cheval set Set of mats for the dressing-table, generally consisting of one large and two small, which can be round, oval, square, or oblong. They can be of any fabric, often embroidered, as long as they are washable, and if this is not possible they are generally put under glass. They were popular from the middle of the 19th to the middle of the 20th century, and continue today, known as dressing-table sets.

chevening The embroidering of *clocks on hosiery. Cheveners were out-workers to the hosiery trade, especially in the Midlands of England, and their job was to embroider the clocks for the stocking manufacturers. The points of the clocks were designed at the mill, and the sampler given to the worker with a bundle of socks and stockings. Satin stitch was used and each stitch was taken over one or two loops of the knitting. The art has now died out. (Currey 1951)

China: an early 18th century Imperial badge from the robes of a Chinese emperor, embroidered in silk on silk.

chevron Literally, a beam or rafter, or the shape made when two beams meet at an angle at the roof. In needlework the word is used to describe a stitch, a pattern sometimes woven into tweed and other materials, and a shape used in embroidery design.

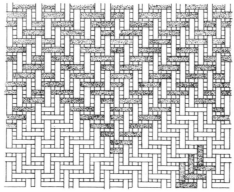

Chiapas embroidery Indigenous Mexican Indian embroidery used on garments in Chiapas, the mountainous southernmost state of Mexico. Although the decoration varies from village to village, it consists mostly of combinations of cross and satin stitch. Indigo-dyed cotton skirts are embroidered on seams and borders, and *huipils on yokes, shoulders, and bands. There is an old tradition in this region that when a woman dies the body is placed on a rush mat with all her existing clothing, and next to her is placed a bag with her comb and her needle and thread so that she can mend the clothes. (Mozzi 1968)

chiffon work Late 19th century form of *patchwork, consisting of stripes of black velvet alternating with stripes of crazy patchwork in silks. The word chiffon is used here in the French sense meaning rags. (Caulfeild and Saward 1882)

chikankari Embroidery from the area round Lucknow (India). It is usually worked 'in white thread upon fine white cotton cloth, the design depending for its effect upon variety of stitchery and the contrast of different grades of thread to form lace-like patterns, opaque fillings,

and delicate or boldly emphasised details and outlines' (Irwin and Hall 1973). The stitches are stem, double back stitch forming shadow work, fine french knots massed closely together, buttonhole, and satin, with areas of pulled fabric. Chikankari as a craft did not develop until the 19th century.

Chile Under the rule of the Spanish until 1810, most Chilean embroideries show Spain's influence in design. However in recent years there has been a revival of folk embroidery in various villages including Ninhue, and on the Isla Negra.

China Early records in China show that embroidery existed there by at least 2000 BC and that it was already of a high standard. The art of silk production (*sericulture) originated in China and was practised for many hundreds of years before the secret was learnt by the West, and many Chinese embroideries, especially those to do with high officials and the court, are worked in silk threads on silk. Peasant work is often in cotton thread on cotton, generally in cross stitch. The designs are highly stylised and very early ones are similar to those found on bronzes, inscriptions, and later on porcelain. They frequently tell a story, or show the favourite Chinese flowers (the peony, chrysanthemum, and rose) and animals (of which the dragon is the most common). Metal thread is much used, the tone of the gold thread being paler and cooler than that of Japanese gold. The most usual stitches are couching, laid work, satin, pekinese, and the pekin knot. This last one is often considered the same as the french knot, but in fact it is worked differently and does not have the same appearance. Very little good Chinese embroidery is obtainable today, but there is a lot of cheap, quick commercial work available. (Lovelock 1952, Whymant 1935, Schuster 1935) See also Noin Ula, Han silk, mandarin square. (Colour illustration opposite)

china crape (crêpe) The earlier phrase for what is now more generally known as crêpe de chine. This was a heavy pure silk used mainly for dresses, shawls, and underwear, which lent itself to beautiful, fine embroidery.

chinai embroidery The name given to the work done by the Chinese embroiderers who settled in Surat (India) in the 19th and early 20th centuries. The work was Chinese in conception and technique but was adapted to local use, and it consisted mainly of garment pieces for women and children. (Irwin and Hall 1973)

china ribbon Very narrow ribbon no wider than $\frac{1}{16}$ inch (1.5 millimetres), either in plain colours or shaded. It is used for threading underwear and children's dresses, for bookmarkers, but especially for *china ribbon embroidery.

china ribbon embroidery Type of embroidery using the narrow *china ribbon as the thread. This kind of work was very fashionable in the period 1820–40 when it was used to decorate men's waistcoats, among other things. However when it was revived in the late 19th century it was used more for domestic furnishings such as mats and sachets, and was then generally called *rococo work.

china sewing silk Fine, strong sewing silk sold only in white. It is used in plain sewing where strength is required, and by glovers and staymakers.

china taffeta An early reference to fabrics imported from China appears in the inventory of Henry Howard (1614): 'one Tester with head and double valance frindged, and 7 curtains, whereof fowre are made upp, and 3 unmade, the stuffs of China taffata white embroidered with birdes and flowers' (Shirely 1869).

chiné Word from the French meaning mottled or variegated, and applied to thread that is dyed in different colours along its length. In woven fabrics, warp threads may be dyed or stained before weaving to give a mottled effect. Many fabrics of the middle and end of the 19th century were chiné. See also long and short shades, ombré.

chinese knot (pekin knot) Stitch resembling *french knots and often mistaken for them, but the chinese knot is flatter, more shapely, and not so twisted. In Chinese embroideries it is seldom used as an isolated stitch but is generally massed together, often covering large areas. It is important to pull the thread fairly tightly round the needle.

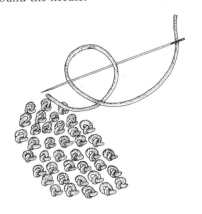

chinese stitch see pekinese stitch.

chinoiserie: detail of an applied patchwork bedspread dated 1828.

chinoiserie Foreigner's exercise in the Chinese style or manner, which very seldom bears any real relationship to the original. Chinese goods first trickled and then flowed into Europe from the 16th century and the styles and motifs were adapted to suit European tastes. In embroidery the fashion started in the 17th century in nightcaps and other small items, and in crewel work pieces such as the Ullswater hangings at Belstead House, Ipswich, and carried on into the 18th century in delicate and charming designs on articles like aprons and bedcovers.

chintz 'Originally a name for the painted or stained calicoes imported from India; now a name for cotton cloths fast printed with designs of flowers, etc in a number of colours, and usually glazed' (OED). Indian chintz was very popular for bed furniture and curtains as well as for dresses, especially in the 18th century. The fabrics were being imported from India directly into the USA by 1790 but had reached England considerably earlier than that. In many of the applied patchwork quilts of the late 18th and early 19th centuries the pieces applied were motifs cut from chintz.

chi-rho The first two letters of the Greek word for Christ, XPISTOS. These two letters made into a monogram were used by the early Christians as a symbol

of their religion as they easily formed a cross, and could also be interpreted as *pax*, the Latin for peace. The sign was adopted by Constantine in AD 313 and placed by his command on the imperial standard of Rome. It is now frequently used in ecclesiastical embroidery.

choga Long-sleeved garment, like a dressing gown (a purpose for which Europeans often make use of it). It is properly an Afghan form of dress and is generally made of some soft woollen material and embroidered on the sleeves and shoulders. In Bokhara the word is used for a furred robe. (Yule and Burnell 1903)

christening gown The ceremony of baptising or christening a child in the Western church has always been a festive occasion for which the infant wears a beautiful gown which may have been handed down in the family from generation to generation, and there are still many 18th century examples in use today. These are often made in a deep cream satin, sometimes with a matching petticoat and trimmed either with the fringe fashionable in the early 18th century or with fine embroidery. In the 19th century, gowns of Ayrshire work or broderie anglaise (eyelet embroidery) were popular.

christening gown: north German, c.1700.

christening sets Sets of accessories for babies dating from the late 17th and early 18th centuries found in most museums with collections of costume, but whether they were used only for christenings is not known. They are delightful examples of needlework, being made of fine white lawn embroidered or couched with white thread and they generally comprise a bib, collar, apron, mittens, and what may be a pincushion top or else a muckinder. That so many sets have been saved indicates they were little used.

Christie, Grace (Mrs A. H.) One of the most influential teachers of embroidery in the early 20th century. An aloof personality entirely devoted to the study and perfect working of embroidery, she was the first teacher of the subject at the *Royal College of Art (London). She turned away from the large appliqué hangings and naturalistic designs of the *Morris/Burne-Jones era, and advocated design that evolved from the stitches used. She also recommended the use of embroidery notebooks to help students with ideas from the past. Her research into the history of embroidery culminated in the classic *English Mediaeval Embroidery*, and her *Samplers and Stitches* and *Embroidery and Tapestry Weaving* became the text books for generations of students. She also edited the magazine *Needle and Thread*.

chromo embroidery Type of work of the late 19th century used by the inexperienced or diffident embroiderer who doubted her capacity to shade or colour correctly. Thin paper of the required colour was tacked to the fabric and was worked over in satin stitch with a matching thread. The finished article was not washable as the paper was left in.

chuddar Sheet or square piece of cloth of any kind; also the ample sheet commonly worn by women in India as a mantle. In 1832 it is described as ' . . . a large piece of cloth or sheet, of 1½ or 2 breadths thrown over the head so as to cover the whole body. Men usually sleep rolled up in it.' In 1665, in *Some Yeares Travels into Divers Parts of Asia and Afrique*, Herbert said: 'The habit of these water-nymphs was fine shudders of lawn embroidered on the neck, waist and shirt with a border of several coloured silks or threads of gold.' (Yule and Burnell 1903)

church embroidery see ecclesiastical embroidery.

church kneelers (hassocks) Until after the First World War the kneelers in most small churches were either of rush or covered in a material such as baize,

church kneelers: an American example in canvas work, 20th century.

leatherette, or serge. In the 1930s, inspired by the example of Louisa *Pesel at Winchester Cathedral, the fashion for embroidering church hassocks started, but it was not until after the Second World War that the movement spread so that now there are only a few churches that have not at least some of their hassocks worked. The designs have been drawn from many sources. Sometimes, as in Chelsea Parish Church, London, the motifs refer to former parishioners; sometimes, as in Guildford Cathedral, Surrey, they refer to events in the diocese; and sometimes, as in St Peter Mancroft, Norwich, they show scenes of city life. (Colour illustration p 75)

ciré Term used for certain fabrics, especially ribbons, treated to give them a hard, shiny surface. Literally it means waxed.

Clandon Park (near Guildford, Surrey) National Trust property whose most noteworthy embroidery is on a late 17th century state bed in the style of Daniel Marot. Clandon Park also contains the *Gubbay collection which is particularly rich in 18th century needlemade rugs and carpets.

Clare chasuble Famous *chasuble in *opus anglicanum which can be seen in the Victoria and Albert Museum (London). It was probably worked between 1272 and 1294, and was commissioned by or for Margaret de Clare, wife of Edmund Plantagenet, Earl of Cornwall, nephew to Henry III. It consists of lions and griffins within foliate scrolls, and on the back there is a vertical band with four backed quatrefoils, which show Christ crucified, with the Virgin and St John; the Virgin and Child; St Peter and St Paul; and the stoning of St Stephen. (King 1963)

Claverton Manor (near Bath, Somerset) The American Museum in England. Its purpose is to show the story of the de-

velopment of American craftsmanship and art against a living background of domestic life on the North American continent. The textile room contains a superb collection of quilts showing all the various American styles, and there are also other embroideries in their appropriate rooms.

clavus Originally a purple band on a toga, as worn by Roman senators. Later they were embroidered in gold and became known as auri clavi, and eventually they developed into the *apparel seen on the cuffs and hems of albs and dalmatics and the *orphreys of copes and chasubles.

clavus: fragment from an Egyptian tunic, late 8th or early 9th century.

Cleveland Museum of Art (Ohio) Contains a large representative collection of textiles, many of which are embroidered. Some of the most outstanding pieces are examples from Russia, China, Czechoslovakia, and from the Hungarian provinces of Matayo, Ivásos, Bizsaki, and Torockoi.

clew Ball of thread or yarn. In Greek mythology it was the ball of thread Theseus used to mark his route through the Cretan labyrinth.

clinquant Flat gold ribbon used in embroidery in the last quarter of the 19th century. (Howe 1973)

cloak Sleeveless outer garment, of great antiquity, found in one form or another all over the world.

clocks The embroidered decoration on socks or stockings from the instep up for five or six inches (about 14 centimetres). They were worked by cheveners, but today can also be done by machine. See also chevening.

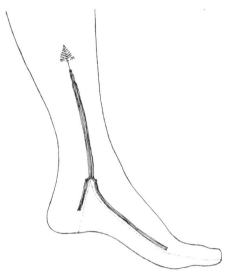

cloisonné thread Modern embroidery thread of gold or silver metallic thread and polyester, tarnish proof, and capable of being washed and dry cleaned.

cloister cloth Rather coarse American fabric in basket-weave which may be used as a ground for some types of embroidery. It is similar to monks cloth.

closed square chain stitch (big writing) Stitch used extensively in Hungary to form broad, heavy areas of design, sometimes with two rows worked close together. It is worked like open chain but is even wider, and each stitch lies close to

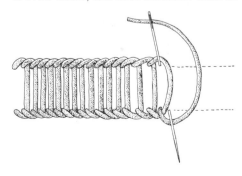

the last. Generally it is done on homespun linen which is then washed and beaten with a mallet to loosen the textures of the fabric while slightly shrinking the tightly twisted embroidery yarn—the result is a very dense, tight stitch on an attractively rippled linen. The name big writing comes from the wide traced or 'written' line over which the stitch is worked.

cloth 'Piece of pliable woven or felted stuff, suitable for wrapping or winding round, spreading or folding over, drying, wiping or other purpose' (OED). The original plural of cloth was clothes, but about 1600, cloth was being used for the fabric of which clothes or garments were made. During the 18th century, the word cloaths was used as the plural for either the fabric or the garment, and it was not until the 19th century that there was a complete break between the two words, the plural of cloth becoming cloths, and clothes being used only in the plural sense of garments.

cloth appliqué Late 19th century adaptation of types of Eastern embroidery. Pieces of coloured cloth were applied to a ground of the same fabric and sewn down with various ornamental stitches.

cloth embroidery 1. Late 19th century adaptation of a type of Indian embroidery where pieces of cloth are joined together and then various stitches worked over. It is a type of *inlay. 2. At the same date a 3-dimensional form of embroidery where fabric shapes were loosely applied to a cloth or silk ground, forming flowers, birds, and so on.

cloth measure Originally cloth in Britain was not measured in yards, feet, and inches, but in ells, quarters, and nails. *The Finchley Manual of Industry*, No 4, 1860, gives the measurement of cloth as: '2¼ Inches make 1 Nail. 4 Nails make 1 Quarter. 3 Quarters make 1 Flemish Ell. 4 Quarters make 1 Yard. 5 Quarters make 1 English Ell. 6 Quarters make 1 French Ell.' Recently the metric system has been introduced into Britain to conform to general European measurement, but in America, yards, feet, and inches are still used.

cloth of gold Fabric, generally of silk, with some gold threads woven in. Of very ancient origin, it is one of the richest ever made and was used both for garments and hangings when a great display of wealth or status was needed. The meeting place of Henry VIII of England and Francis I of France in 1520 was named the Field of the Cloth of Gold because of the amount of fabric woven with gold thread that was used.

cloth of gold embroidery Late 19th century embroidery in which gold braid is laid over *Berlin canvas and stitched down with gobelin stitch over each strand of the braid, using coloured filoselle silks. (Caulfeild and Saward 1882)

cloth of silver Fabric woven of silk using some silver thread, sometimes in conjunction with gold thread.

cloth plate see footplate.

coat Sleeved outer garment of varying lengths, but longer than hip length, worn in many countries of the world. In England they were worn by men in the 15th century, and from then onwards until the present day they come in various styles and shapes. The word coat can also mean skirt, and as such is used in 'petticoat' and in the phrase 'putting a child into short coats', but in the modern sense, coats for women did not appear before the last half of the 19th century.

coat:
by Worth of Paris,
early 20th century.

coatee Short coat with tails. They were part of the uniform of a soldier during the latter part of the 18th and the 19th centuries, and those for officers were heavily decorated with braid in various patterns. In the 1920s and 1930s the word was also used for a short coat made of some light fabric for wearing indoors in chilly houses, and was generally called a bridge coatee.

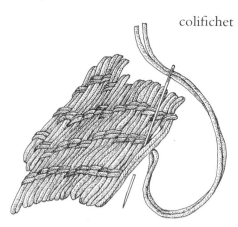

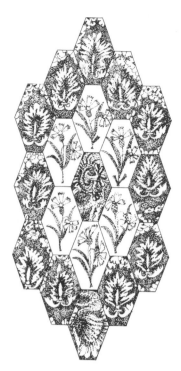

coffin The name of a shape used in *patchwork. It is a hexagon whose top and bottom sides are equal but whose other four sides are considerably longer, giving a coffin shape.

Coggleshall embroidery Type of *tambour embroidery on muslin practised in and around the village of Coggleshall in Essex. The industry flourished in the mid 19th century and the main characteristic distinguishing it from other tambour work was that the designs were generally of wild flowers with trailing cow parsley and honeysuckle and other hedgerow flowers worked over the garment. (Moore 1956)

coif (quoif) Close-fitting cap for the head, worn in the middle ages by both men and women. Elderly men wore them through the 16th century, and they became part of the dress of a lawyer. As such they were first worn tied under the chin, and later, when wigs became fashionable, as a skull cap worn under the wig until the middle of the 19th century. Coifs for women were at their most beautiful at the end of the 16th century when they were decorated either in black work or polychrome silk embroidery enriched with spangles and metal threads. Usually called caps, they were worn under hats in the 18th and 19th centuries, and in various forms have been a feature of women's dress in many countries up till the present day.

colbert embroidery Type of embroidery described by de Dillmont (n.d.), which appears to be a late 19th century adaptation of the needlework laces of the 18th century. It is worked on an even-weave tammy cloth and the main design is outlined in cord and filled with various stitches, while the background is worked with a pulled fabric stitch.

colcha Spanish term for quilt or bedspread, and also used to define embroidered hangings and covers made by the Spanish colonial settlers in New Mexico. These embroideries were usually worked on wool with woollen threads in a laid or couched stitch which entirely covered the surface. The word colcha was in use as early as 1745 when Fray Pedro Montaño of Santa Cruz wrote, 'I, Frai Pedro Montaño, in 1745 placed a curtain before the picture of Lady St Anne which is a colcha from Tlascalteca' (Boyd 1974). They decorated the walls of churches and were sometimes used as carpets in both houses and churches.

colcha: New Mexico, 19th century.

colcha stitch Resembles romanian couching and is used in New Mexico for working the *colchas of that country. It is worked with two threads of wool at various angles according to the design, and has a rough, woven effect. Colcha stitch is used either for filling large areas or for free-standing separate figures.

colifichet Embroidery worked in silk floss through thick paper or parchment and reversible. Thus it is seen to best advantage when framed with glass both sides and placed in a window. The art appears to have come from China in the 17th century and was practised in convents, particularly *Ursuline, in the 17th, 18th, and early 19th centuries. The designs are portraits, vases of flowers, and religious subjects. (Saint-Aubin 1770, de Farcy 1914, Swain 1965)

colifichet: portrait with a painted face, English, early 18th century.

collage Art form in which the design is built up from assembled objects which may bear no relation to one another. For the past twenty years it has become very popular in embroidery. Because the objects used, such as buttons, beads, curtain rings, string etc, make the work three-dimensional, it has little practical application and is generally used for panels and wall hangings, though in the US it may also decorate clothing.

collar The part of a coat, cloak, or dress which encircles the neck or is nearest the chin. Those on women's dresses may or may not be an integral part of the garment, and where they are added they are frequently embroidered in any fashionable style. In the late 19th century it became the custom for the uniform of certain groups such as the Salvation Army or Post Office workers, to wear tunics with standing collars, and these generally had a badge worked on them.

collar: detail of a dress by Fox, American, c.1896.

colletto see koleto.

Colonial American period between the first European settlements and independence in 1776. In embroidery and needlework, techniques and patterns brought from the old world slowly blended with the new. Decoration is usually fairly simple, the use of open designs characteristic. Native plants and animals are helpful in identification. Basic patterns are usually European, but less restricted than their originals.

colours Flags bearing the insignia of regiments. In the British Army they are always in pairs—a Queen's (or King's) and a regimental—and they are always hand embroidered. The Queen's colour consists of the Union Flag with the regimental badge in the centre of the St George's cross, the royal crown above, and the battle honours inscribed on the two horizontal arms. The regimental colour is always the same colour as the uniform facings and has the badge and royal crown in the centre surrounded by the Union Wreath of roses, thistles, and

colours: the insignia of a regiment in the British Army.

shamrocks, and outside this a wreath of laurel with the battle honours superimposed. In the US colours were first authorized in 1780, two per regiment, following the British custom.

comforter (comfort, comfortable) Bedcover, wadded or filled with cotton, wool, down, or polyester batting, which usually is tufted or tied rather than quilted.

commercial embroidery Term referring to machine embroidery which is quickly but not necessarily very well done. It is produced in large quantities for the dress and domestic furnishing trades.

communion cloth (houseling cloth) Long cloth or napkin that used to be held along the communion rail so that none of the consecrated bread fell on the floor. It was sometimes lightly embroidered.

composite stitches Combinations of two (or more) stitches often with the second worked in a different colour. They generally look richer and more decorative than single stitches and are used for border patterns and fillings. Nearly every simple stitch can be turned into a composite one by whipping, threading, interlacing, or tying it in some way, and so the

number of permutations is enormous. A few of the more frequently used stitch variations are: cloud filling (mexican), guilloche, interlaced band, interlaced herringbone, overcast running, *pekinese (chinese), portuguese border, raised band, raised chain band, raised lattice band, sheaf, tied herringbone, threaded back, twisted lattice band, twisted running, whipped back, whipped chain, woven band. See also stitches.

congress canvas (mono canvas) Evenly woven single-thread canvas called congress in the UK and mono in the US. It comes in various mesh sizes and is the most generally used for needlepoint and canvas work.

conservation The stabilisation of textiles to preserve them from further decay and damage. Textiles are among the most vulnerable of all artefacts and are attacked by humidity, light, fungoid growths, and insects, as well as by careless handling, and it is vital that the comparatively few remaining examples of the work of past generations should be preserved for the enjoyment and study of future generations. Broadly speaking the term conservation implies mending obvious tears and rents and strengthening fragile fabrics by backing, and it is now

conservation: detail of an Italian pall belonging to the Parish Clerks Company.

generally considered that while all repairs should be as unobtrusive as possible there should be no attempt to hide the fact that at some date they were done.

continental stitch see tent stitch.

convent influence The influence of religious orders on embroidery through the centuries cannot be overestimated. In the dark ages, learning and slow patient craftsmanship were kept alive in the convents of the then known world, which in effect meant Europe. When through piety or status seeking, rich embroideries were required by church and state, it was usually from the convents that they were ordered, though there were secular embroiderers and even secular schools of embroidery. In the middle ages and later, convents were often a refuge for high-born or gentle ladies either from spinsterhood, or during widowhood, or sometimes because they were just not wanted at home. Children would be sent at an early age to learn how to behave in polite society and to learn the polite arts, which included needlework. Having received a good training themselves, the nuns were excellent teachers and so the art was spread. Later when exploration had opened up more of the world, the religious orders were among the first to go and work among the natives and, believing as they did that European arts were the examples to be followed, they attempted to teach their skills and techniques to the natives, with varying success. When small religious communities emigrated many hundreds of miles from home it was difficult for them to get supplies of fabric and thread, and so they often grafted their techniques onto native materials, generally with very happy results—the *moose-hair embroideries of Canada and North America and the piña embroideries from the Philippines being cases in point. The result of this interchange of materials and techniques over the world is that innumerable types of embroidery and allied crafts are known as convent work or nuns' work.

convent stitch see couching stitch.

conversation pieces Name applied to American embroideries of about 1930, usually in crewel or canvas stitches, which relate episodes of family history or details from the life of one of its members. A variation of this form may show historical events of the day.

Conyers, Sophia First wife of Sir Roger Newdigate of Arbury Hall, Warwickshire. According to tradition she was incurably untidy and her husband made her embroider all the possessions she left lying about onto a set of twelve stools. She must have been a good artist as well as an excellent needlewoman as all the objects, including a hat, scarf, fan, and books, are faithfully and accurately represented. An almanac is dated 1757. (Jones 1954)

co-operative embroidery Large pieces of needlework done by more than one person. In medieval and Tudor times the lady of a large house would generally be helped by her ladies and/or her servants to make hangings, bed furniture, quilts, and carpets. The best-known example of this is in the household of *Mary Queen of Scots, where it is known that her ladies worked with her. In America in the late 18th and 19th centuries, after a quilt had been pieced, friends would gather together at a *quilting bee to finish off the work; while in the 20th century, groups have worked on co-operative projects for their

co-operative embroidery: bedspread made in 1973.

churches, in England co-operative groups such as women's institutes and townswomen's guilds have become commonplace, and the needlework produced has generally been excellent.

Cooper-Hewitt Museum of Decorative Arts and Design, Smithsonian Institution Museum with an extensive collection of designs and decorative arts from all over the world, as well as textiles and costumes. It was founded in 1897 by the Hewitt sisters, grand-daughters of Peter Cooper, one of the manufacturer-philanthropists of New York. The collection was first housed at Cooper Union and now, associated with the Smithsonian Institution, is located in the 1901 mansion of Andrew Carnegie in New York.

Cooper Hewitt Museum of Decorative Arts and Design, Smithsonian Institution: man's waistcoat from France, late 18th century.

cope Ecclesiastical outergarment or cloak, derived from the ordinary protective garment of the Greeks and Romans. Though it is often thought of as a richly decorated processional vestment, the ordinary cloaks with hoods worn by most religious orders are, in fact, copes. In general they are cut as semicircles with a 4 to 6 inch (10 to 16 centimetre) band, the *orphrey, along the straight side, falling from the neck to the feet. Most of them still have a vestigial or shield-shaped hood, which shows their derivation from the original protective garment. They are fastened at the neck by a *morse. Because of the shape and the fact that it is so often worn by high dignitaries of the church on festal occasions, the cope has generally been the most highly and beautifully decorated of all ecclesiastical garments, and many from the middle ages have been preserved.

Coptic embroidery Christianity came to Egypt in the 1st century AD and the Egyptian Christians were known as Copts (from the Greek *Aigyptos*). From their habit of burying their dead in the clothes they normally wore, and the fact that the textiles were preserved with natron (a kind of salt drawn from the Nile), it has been possible to excavate pieces of Coptic weaving dating from the 2nd to the 8th centuries. Embroidery was not a separate art but an integral part of weaving, and was used to highlight parts of the tapestry-woven designs or to put in a small point or motif which was impossible to achieve with weaving. In fact it needs close examination of a piece to see where the weaving stops and embroidery starts. (Kybelova 1967) See also Egypt.

coral stitch Knotted stitch which can be used for edgings, lines, or veining. It changes its shape slightly according to the angle of the needle when crossing the main thread.

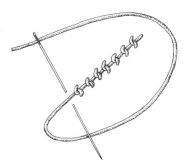

cord Thin rope or thick string, either plain or decorative. If decorative, it may be made of coloured silk or rayon thread, or of any fancy thread of the period. In needlework it can be used in several ways: 1. in *cord quilting; 2. to outline a design in conjunction with other stitches; 3. to form a design by couching down very fine cord; 4. to edge various articles such as teacosies and cushion covers; 5. to give required effects in collage; and 6. as *piping cord.

cording foot see attachments.

cord-making machine *Cords have been used for innumerable purposes for many hundreds of years, not least for the fastening of garments, and they have of necessity often been made by hand at home. Sometimes the *chain fork or lucet was used, but in the 18th and 19th centuries cords were often made on small machines. These consisted of a board with three hooks at one end, and a metal pillar with a large wheel geared to three smaller wheels at the other. When yarn was fastened between the three small wheels and the hooks, and the large wheel turned, it began to twist, and as it shortened, the

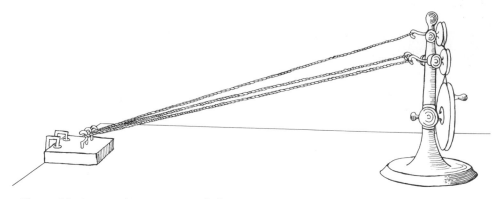

pillar with its attachments moved forward. After sufficient twist was obtained, the end was unhooked and the wheel turned in the reverse direction so that a three-ply cord was formed. There were many variations on this theme, and a number of 19th century reel holders and pincushions which clamped onto a table carried a hook as well for the making of cords.

cord quilting Quilting which uses a *cord sewn into the back of the fabric to define the pattern. There are two methods of working. The first uses only one layer of fabric, under which the cord is held with one hand while the other works two parallel rows of back stitch, each one taken alternately either side of the cord so that it is encased in herringbone stitch. The result gives a much more strongly defined design than does the other method, which is popularly known as *Italian quilting.

cord quilting: corset embroidered and made by Sadelia Sweet, American, c.1835.

cord seam Join sometimes used in underwear of fine quality fabric. One of the pieces to be sewn together is laid flat on the table, and the second piece is

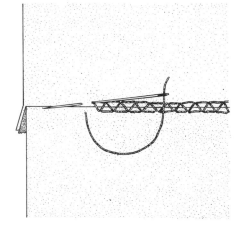

placed over it with its raw edge folded under so that the two raw edges are together. The folded edge is stitched to the underpiece with french stemming or point turc, and the raw edges cut away.

cord work 1. Small *rosettes made with a needle in buttonhole stitch joined together with crochet. 2. Small hexagons made by twisting fine *cord round three bodkins lying diametrically across one another. The thread in the eye of the bodkin is then pulled through, and the resulting hexagons joined one to another with this bodkin thread. Both these types of cord work were popular in the late 19th century and could be used for any flat article such as a runner or antimacassar or even to cover a teacosy. (Caulfeild and Saward 1882)

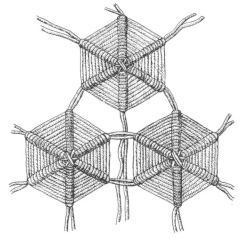

Cornely machine Sewing machine for embroidery, invented in 1865 by a Frenchman named Bonnaz and manufactured by Ercole Cornely. The early ones could work both chain and moss stitch and could sew in any direction, and by 1900 models were produced which could make raised cords, double zigzag lines, and do two-needle braiding. As the Cornely machines were no bigger than an ordinary domestic treadle machine they were excellent for outworkers and did not have to be used only in factories. The principle used was that of the hooked needle and universal feed, with the reel of thread below the machine. In America, it is known as the Bonnaz machine. (Risley 1961)

cornucopia One of the shapes associated with quilting design, representing the horn of plenty.

coronation robes The robes worn by royalty at their coronation have always combined highly decorative qualities with a very conservative tradition. These garments are never 'fashionable', for only splendid fabrics together with impeccable craftsmanship are considered suitable for such an occasion. As a result they have either lasted well or have been made into

vestments and frontals for the church. In England, between the coronations of Edward I (1272) and Charles I (1625), the actual robes of St Edward the Confessor (king from 1004–1010) were worn during part of the ceremony, but after the execution of Charles the robes and other appointments were sold and dispersed. From the coronation of Charles II to that of Victoria a new set of robes was made for each monarch, which were then handed to the Dean of Westminster and made into a *cope or put to other suitable use. At the Weltliche Schatzkammer in Vienna, are the coronation robes of the Holy Roman Empire. This set, made between 1133 and 1220 in the Royal Workshop at Palermo, Sicily, consists of the mantle (dated 1133–4), dalmatic, alb, and gloves. The mantle is semicircular and divided down the centre back by an embroidered palm tree. In each of the two halves are representations of a lion attacking a camel. (Halls 1973, Schuette and Müller-Christensen 1964)

corporal Linen cloth on which the consecrated elements are placed at Holy Communion, and which covers the remains of the bread after the service. Some churches use two corporals, the second to cover the chalice, but others use a *pall instead. When not in use, it is folded in nine and kept in a *corporal case or burse. It has an embroidered cross on the centre bottom square. This generally hangs over the edge of the altar.

corporal case (burse) Stiff pocket in which the *corporal is kept when not in use. It is made of two squares of stiff material generally covered on the outside with a silk fabric of the set to which it belongs, and on the inside with linen. The squares are joined at the bottom and have a gusset up the sides, and open just sufficiently to insert the corporal or the pall.

costryng (costering) Carpet or hanging used in medieval houses.

costume embroidery Decoration of dress for both sexes by means of embroidery. For women it reached its peak in the two periods 1540–1600 and 1870–1914, while for men it was the 16th and 17th centuries. The craft was usually practised by professionals and at times fabrics were sent abroad to be worked, notably muslin for *ruffles (for both sexes) in the 18th century. In 1767 Lady Mary Coke says in her diary that she 'bought some muslin to send to Germany to be worked', and that she 'received some ruffles from Hanover that I had sent to be worked there' (Home 1970). In the 19th century the dresses, mantles, and coats encrusted with beadwork and embroidery were the product of an industry that showed the worst characteristics of sweated labour, and it can have been of little pleasure to the workers to use such superb fabrics and materials. Today both hand and machine embroidery on costume and accessories is still fashionable, especially on sweaters, evening clothes, children's wear etc, worked by home dressmakers, haute couture, and in places with low labour costs such as Hong Kong and India.

costume embroidery: detail of the embroidery on a black silk coat, late 19th century.

cot cover (crib quilt) Miniature bedcover for a child's cot. They are generally embroidered in the same techniques as ordinary-sized bedcovers, but as they are for children there is more often variety and fun in the designs. Embroiderers wanting to make a patchwork or quilted bedcover often start with a smaller cot cover.

coronation robes: mantle of the Holy Roman Empire, Sicilian, 1133–34.

Cotehele House: detail of the crewel embroidered bed hangings.

Cotehele House (near Plymouth, England) Medieval house which contains many fine English and Flemish tapestries and much excellent and unusual needlework. One suite of furniture is upholstered in *knotting. The wool between the knots was stitched to the ground fabric in a floral design, so that no stitchery is visible on the hard-wearing surface of tightly-packed, many-coloured knots. Another interesting item is a set of linen bed hangings of c 1680, embroidered in red wool. The effect is very light, unlike the more usual heavy crewel work of that date. There are also some beautiful quilts and bedcovers. The house belongs to the National Trust and is well worth a visit.

coton à broder see soft embroidery cotton.

coton perlé (perle cotton) Thread much used for general upholstery in the 19th and 20th centuries, also known in England as star sylko and in America as jewel embroidery. It is a two-ply rayon thread available in two thicknesses, though there used to be more.

cotta Knee-length white linen robe resembling a surplice, which may be worn at any time in place of one, but is neither so long nor so full. It may have an apparel of lace or embroidery.

cotton The generic name for a wide variety of different fabrics and sewing threads all made from the cotton plant. The plant grows in sub-tropical climates and the fibres, which are eventually spun into yarn, are attached to the seeds of the fruit. It comes from different parts of the world and its type and quality varies, but the finest are Egyptian and Sea Island (grown in Georgia, USA). Though Indian cotton can be woven very fine, it is not of such good quality as the other two. To prepare the yarn the cotton is first freed from the seeds, cleaned, loosened, and carded. Next it is drawn out into slubbing or roving, and is then spun. According to the spinning and weaving it can be made into the finest muslin or the heaviest canvas.

cotton barrel Small barrel shape turned of wood, ivory, or bone, which contains little balls of cotton thread. Near the bottom there is a small hole through which the thread passes—thus it is kept clean and unknotted. These barrels are frequently found in fitted workboxes.

cotton canvas see French canvas.

couched and laid stitches Group in which threads are laid on the ground fabric and tied down by an extension of the same thread or by others. In *couching a single thread is held, while in *laidwork many threads are laid across the ground and are held by couched threads passing over them. There is a plethora of names for the couching stitches where the same thread ties down a laid thread on the return journey, mostly indicative of where it is commonly done. In romanian stitch a single thread crosses slightly obliquely, while in romanian couching the thread is crossed several times at a very oblique angle. Bokhara couching has the crossing stitch at right angles to the laid stitch at regular intervals, giving a diaper effect, and roman stitch also has the crossed stitches at right angles, but they are pulled rather tight and follow each other in a straight line. In colcha stitch the crossing thread is slightly oblique and at irregular intervals, while new england (deerfield) stitch has an oblique crossing stitch nearly as long as the first laid thread. The couching stitches are: bokhara stitch, *burden stitch, *colcha stitch, *couching stitch (convent, kloster), crewel stitch (deerfield, new england laid, self couching),

*or nué (glaze embroidery, lasurstickerei), roman stitch, *romanian stitch (antique couching, figure, janina, oriental couching), satin couching (trailing), thorn stitch, trellis couching, *underside couching (point couchée rentré ou retiré). See also stitches.

couching Technique in which a thread of any thickness is sewn onto the ground material by means of a different and generally finer thread visible as a pattern. It is used when the main thread would be damaged if pulled through the ground material, when it is too thick to pull through, or when it is too expensive to waste by being underneath. In church embroidery, where metal threads are common, two methods can be used—surface or underside. In surface couching the metal thread, usually doubled, is sewn down at intervals with a fine strong, waxed thread called horsetail or Maltese silk, and the couching stitches may be so arranged that they come alternately or in pattern, forming part of the design. *Underside couching is the method frequently used in opus anglicanum. There are also other methods for metal threads, such as *or nué and burden stitch. In modern embroidery, couching is used, especially in collage, where the threads employed are often so unwieldy that it would be impractical to secure them by any other method.

couching stitch (convent stitch, kloster stitch) Basic stitch in *couching, which has been traced back to Scythian embroideries of the 1st century BC. One thread is laid along the top of the work and is held down by another thread crossing it regularly at right angles or obliquely. It is used to outline designs or as a filling stitch, and was much used in German and Swiss embroideries worked in the convents from the 15th to the 17th centuries.

count The number of *warp and *weft threads to the inch (or equivalent metric measure) in a woven fabric, or the number of hanks or skeins to the pound in yarn.

counted thread Term used for any type of embroidery based on an even-weave fabric and worked by counting the threads of the ground fabric. This

counted thread: detail of a Persian cover in needleweaving and cross stitch, 19th century.

includes all types of canvas work or needlepoint, darning, blackwork—in fact all formal as opposed to free embroidery.

counted thread stitches The main division in the use of embroidery stitches is between those worked freehand, varying in angle, shape, size, and direction according to the pattern, and those worked evenly by the counted thread. In attempting to classify them two difficulties arise: first, that a number of stitches can be worked in both ways, and second that every smallest variation in direction, size, or method has been given a different name. The permutations of the basic counted thread stitches are endless and nearly impossible to tabulate, and so only those most generally used are given here, and are divided into the following categories: those based on a cross, those based on a half cross, those based on horizontal or vertical stitches, those with a pile, those based on a square, and those which are couched.

1. *Based on a cross.* This group are all cross stitch, generally diagonal but sometimes vertical, and sometimes in combination: *cross (gros point, sampler) and variations: brave bred (marking, true marking, two-sided cross), double cross (*smyrna cross, *star), *long armed cross (long legged cross, plaited slav, portuguese), oblong cross (czar, economic long cross), and persian cross (rep); double leviathan; greek; leviathan (railway);

montenegrin; plait (spanish); *rice (crossed corners cross); triple leviathan; two-sided italian cross (two-sided cross); web stitch. 2. *Based on a half cross.* These are all worked diagonally covering one or more threads in different combinations (where the effect is the same even if the manner of working is different they are counted as synonymous): aubusson (rep); byzantine; cashmere; checkerboard; chequer; diagonal; german; *gobelin (oblique gobelin, gros point) and variations: encroaching, plaited, straight (upright), and wide; jacquard; milanese; moorish; mosaic; oriental, perspective; scottish; soumak (kelim, kalem, knitting, reverse tent); *tent (canvas, continental cushion, half cross, needlepoint, petitpoint). 3. *Based on horizontal or vertical stitches.* These include the group known in America as the bargello family, more often called florentine in England; basket filling; brick; *double running (holbein); *florentine; (bargello, cushion, flame, hungary, irish); *hungarian; parisian; old florentine; willow (basket). 4. *With a pile:* *plush (astrakhan, raised, rug, tassel, velvet); *surrey. 5. *Based on a square:* brighton; checkerboard; diamond; flat; norwich; southern cross; triangle. 6. *Couched.* At whatever angle, these are all held down by a cross thread as in couching; french; knotted; *rococo. See also stitches.

counterchange The transposing of design and ground. It is very effective in *inlay where light and dark, ground and pattern, exchange roles, and there is consequently no waste of material. It was also used in applied work with two different fabrics such as silk and velvet and with the edges outlined in cord, and in American Indian ribbon embroidery. (Day 1900)

counterchange: detail of velvet hangings, Italian, 17th century.

counterpane (coverlet) see bedspread.

cover plate (throat plate, feed cover plate) Round metal plate which can be clipped over the teeth of a domestic sewing machine thus adapting it for free embroidery. By covering the feed, fabric is no longer evenly carried under the needle and so the length and direction of the stitch can be controlled by hand.

Crane, Walter (1845–1915) English painter and illustrator whose ideas had a great influence on embroidery design at the turn of the century. He was principal of the Royal College of Art (London) from 1898 to 1899 and he designed many embroideries which were worked at the *Royal School of Needlework. His subjects were often figures, generally worked in outline with long and short stitch, and his designs were in the Pre-Raphaelite tradition where the subject is of more importance than the technique employed.

Crane: a swan from a screen designed by Crane for the Royal School of Needlework in 1879.

crape (crêpe) Fabric woven in tightly spun yarn with mechanically-added ripples on its surface. The word is from the French and means crisp or frizzled, and the English spelling is generally confined to the crape made in Norwich since the 16th century. This was originally of silk warp and wool weft, and by the intervention of Sir Robert Walpole, Prime Minister to George I, it became the fabric used for court mourning. Thus this spelling is used for all crapes connected with mourning. Crape lesse or crêpe lisse is plain crape without the ripples. Crêpe de chine is generally spelt in the French manner though it was often translated in the early 19th century as canton or china crape. The pastel-coloured crêpe de chine of the 1920s and 1930s was a favourite fabric for the making of beautiful underwear, generally exquisitely embroidered.

crash Fabric which may be fine or coarse, with a rough, irregular surface woven with uneven yarns, usually cotton or linen. It is available in various weights which can be used for clothing, table linens, or as a background for embroidery. See also Russia crash.

Craske, John (d 1944) Fisherman from Sheringham in Norfolk (England), known for his embroideries. Because his life was dogged by illness, with no formal training and working in the tradition of the mid-19th century *ship pictures and the *needle painting of the early part of that century, he set about producing panoramic embroideries as well as small pieces, all worked in rough, cheap threads on calico. His bird's-eye view of the north Norfolk coast is in the Shell Museum at Glandford (Norfolk), and his reconstruction of the evacuation of Dunkirk, still unfinished at his death, is in Strangers Hall Museum, Norwich. (Colour illustration p 76)

crazy lace Type of *patchwork using assorted lace scraps, which was an American handicraft fad during the early 1900s. Three methods of construction were used: the lace was applied onto a black or coloured silk background as in *crazy patchwork; it was applied onto net, then placed over a background fabric; or the pieces were joined with needlework bars or pieces of fabric.

crazy patchwork (puzzle patchwork) Pieces of fabric of different shapes, types, and colours joined together to make a pleasing whole. As far as is known it has not got a very long history, but it had a great vogue towards the end of the 19th century when small scraps of the rich fabrics then in fashion (silks, satins, velvets, and brocades) were hemmed together to

crazy patchwork: late 19th century American quilt.

make a kaleidoscope of rich jewel colours. The joins were then covered with an embroidery stitch, usually feather. It was very popular in America as shown by the following advertisement by J. L. Patten of New York City in *Godey's Lady's Book* of 1885: 'Crazy patchwork. We send ten sample pieces of elegant silk, all different and cut out so as to make a diagram showing how to put them together, and a variety of new stitches, for 35 cents. We send a set of thirty-five perforated patterns, working size, of birds, butterflies, bugs, beetles, spiders web, reptiles, Kate Greenaway figures, flowers, etc with material for transferring to the silk for 60 cents.' The disadvantage of this type of work was that, because of the nature of the fabrics used, it was not washable, but it was made into lambrequins, table runners, teacosies, and household articles of that sort, and also occasionally into dressing gowns. Nowadays it can of course be dry cleaned, and is also simulated in printed cotton, wallpaper, etc.

crazy quilt (crazy quilt throw) Type of late 19th century American quilt, made from *crazy patchwork and embroidery stitches. Usually they were smaller than the traditional pieced or applied quilts and were tufted or tied instead of quilted. See tufting 2.

credence cloth The white linen cloth used on the credence table at the service of Holy Communion. The cruets are placed on it and therefore it is not embroidered in the middle, but usually at each end.

crêpe see crape, china crape.

crêpe work Described in McCall's *Needlework* as the forming of imitation flowers and leaves of crêpe, which are then sewn onto silk or satin backgrounds, or made up on wire foundations as detached sprays. The craft was also taught at the Moravian schools in Bethlehem (Pennsylvania) about 1800–1825.

Crete An island in the Mediterranean, Crete has one of the longest histories of civilisation. It is known that there was embroidery there at least from the time of the Odyssey, which was probably written about the 11th century BC. In Greek mythology, Ariadne gives Theseus a clew of thread to lead him out of the labyrinth, and a workbasket with a ball of thread, and metal needles with a sandstone for cleaning and sharpening them has been found in an Egyptian tomb dating from about the same time as Theseus is supposed to have gone to Crete. Designs from frescoes in the palace of Minos at Knossus, which dates from about 500 BC, are commonly seen on the

Crete: detail of a skirt border, 19th century.

skirts and jackets worn in Crete, but these must have been handed down by tradition as the palace was not excavated until the end of the 19th century. The best embroideries are seen on skirts, and cretan stitch is much used. (Pilcher 1965, Johnstone 1972) See also koleto.

cretonne Printed fabric, often with rather blurred edges to the design, made originally from hemp and linen, but later from cotton. It had a thick warp and a fine weft, was very strong, and was used chiefly for loose covers, cushions, and curtains in England and America from about 1880 to 1940. It was first introduced in 1825 by M. Cretonne, a French linen manufacturer, and has since been woven with various textures of surface, sometimes resembling chintz.

cretonne work Form of *applied work and *broderie perse popular in the 1880s. The shapes of birds, flowers, and leaves were cut out of *cretonne and applied to a ground fabric. Any extra details were then put in with embroidery threads.

crewel needle Needle in the same size range as *sharp, but with a long narrow eye for taking a thicker thread.

crewel stitch see stem stitch.

crewel wool (cruel wool, crewels) Lightly-twisted, two-ply, worsted yarn which has been used by embroiderers for at least 600 years and is still widely used today. It is strong, not too thick, and well suited to work on canvas as well as other fabrics. The name of the wool has been given to the embroidery, hence *crewel work or crewel embroidery. It is mentioned in the inventory of the Earl of Shrewsbury (1582) as 'It' shorte carpetts of needeworke, Crewell lyned with black buckeron', and in the Hardwick Hall inventories (1601) as 'An other long quition of nedleworke, silk and Cruel'. (Tucker 1875, Boynton 1971) See also tapestry wool. .

crewel work (crewel embroidery) Literally, any embroidery worked with *crewel wool. Although crewel embroidery in some form or other has been worked since the middle ages and possibly earlier, the term is particularly associated with the wrongly-named Jacobean work of the 17th and 20th centuries and with the revival of crewel work as a reaction against Berlin woolwork in the 1860s. There is a difference, not always clearly understood, between worked in (or with) crewels, and crewel work. The first implies that in the embroidery, of whatever type, the thread used is crewel wool, while the second refers specifically to the free type of embroidery on linen practised in the 17th, 18th, and late 19th centuries.

During the 17th century there was a vogue for bed furniture and window curtains to be embroidered at home in crewel work on a twill fabric, generally a mixture of linen and cotton. The designs often consisted of large leaves and flowers springing from a tree trunk, generally with small hills or hummocks at the base on which might be stags, rabbits, squirrels etc. For a long time it was considered that these designs reflected the interest in the Indian goods which were then coming into Britain, but it is now known that, far from having an Eastern origin, these patterns were a direct descendant of the verdure tapestries of an earlier date. In fact this type of English design was sent to India for the Indian draughtsmen to copy as an example of what would be likely to sell in England.

The charm of crewel work, which was revived in the 1920s and 1930s under the title of Jacobean embroidery, was that though the stitches used were many and various, the crewel wool made them very

crewel work: English wall hanging, c.1675.

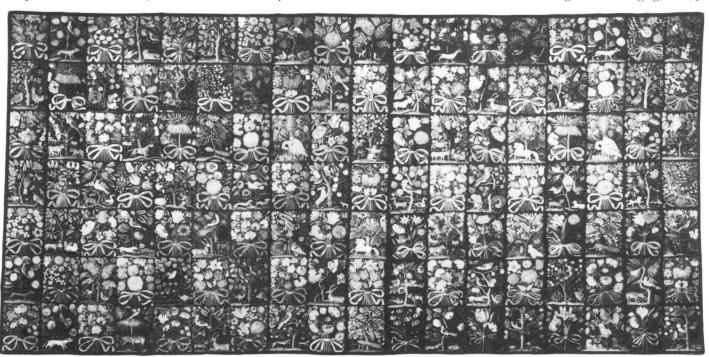

easy to work on linen, and strong effects could be quickly produced. The stitches were mostly stem, long and short, brick, couching, and a series of filling stitches. In the crewel embroidery of the 1860s to the end of the century there was no design connection with the 17th century work. A strong Japanese influence prevailed on the one hand and a vogue for allegorical figures on the other. These large panels, screens, and hangings were worked in crewel wool and silk in simple stitches, the design rather than the technique being considered all-important. The 20th century revival of the 17th century style failed artistically because the same large designs were mutilated to make small objects such as firescreens and cushions for which they were totally unsuited. See also American crewel work.

crib quilt   see cot cover.

crimped gimp   One of the metal threads used in ecclesiastical embroidery. It is stiff and can only be used on the surface of the work, couched down with a fine silk.

crinoline lady   Favourite design of the 1920s and 1930s. It consisted of a lady in a crinoline dress and bonnet, often with a parasol, in a flower garden. Her face was always hidden by the bonnet. This rather over-used design was worked in stranded cottons on cheap linen and was made up into a multitude of teacosies, mats, quilts and cloths. In the US a similar design was the sunbonnet baby.

cross   1. Of a fabric, across the grain or parallel with the weft. This is sometimes called crosswise. 2. In England, on the cross can mean something which is neither the true *bias, nor straight with the thread, but in between the two. 3. The symbol of the Christian religion, signifying the cross on which Jesus Christ was crucified. This symbol has taken many forms in ecclesiastical art which have all been translated into embroidery. The Greek cross of four equal sides was used in various forms in heraldry as well as Christian art.

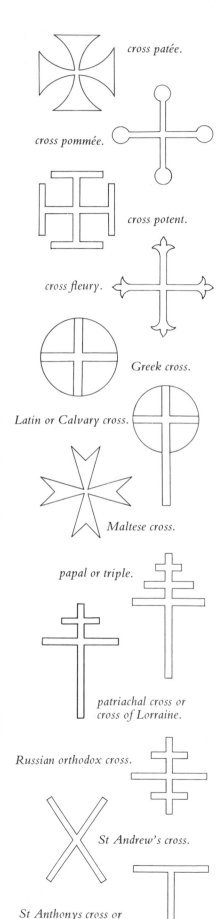

cross patée.

cross pommée.

cross potent.

cross fleury.

Greek cross.

Latin or Calvary cross.

Maltese cross.

papal or triple.

patriachal cross or cross of Lorraine.

Russian orthodox cross.

St Andrew's cross.

St Anthonys cross or Egyptian cross or tau cross.

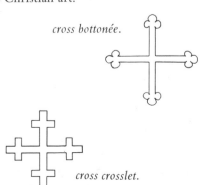

cross bottonée.

cross crosslet.

cross-cloth   see forehead cloth.

crossed corners cross stitch   see rice stitch.

cross stitch (gros point, sampler stitch) Probably the oldest decorative stitch in the world and used by every ethnic group in some way or other. It is worked by the counted thread, usually diagonally, but may also be upright or oblique, and has many variations. In its simplest form it is worked diagonally from left to right and crossed back diagonally from right to left. Alternatively all the first half crosses along a row can be completed, with the second halves added coming back along the same row. This method is more economical with thread. See long-armed stitch.

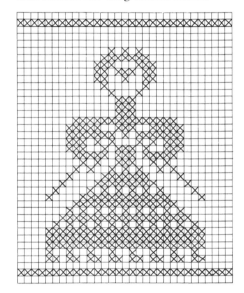

cross stitch embroidery   Counted thread embroidery worked in cross stitch on any suitable fabric, generally linen. It has appeared in practically every country in the world, and its origins are too far back to be known exactly. However it seems logical to believe that handwoven linen lent itself to the counting of threads and that embroidery of this type started

cross stitch embroidery: seat cushion worked by Martha Washington.

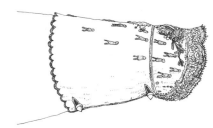

almost as early as the linen itself. These embroideries have been particularly associated with peasant communities, and those of southeast Europe have provided excellent examples of the work, as have India, Persia, and the Near East. The stitches can either make a pattern, with the linen as part of the design, or the embroidery can be worked on a loosely-woven linen or a canvas, with the stitches completely covering the ground and no fabric showing. Some of the early church embroideries were worked like this, for example the early 14th century corporal case in long-legged cross stitch belonging to Wymondham Abbey (Norfolk). Cross stitch on canvas always has been and probably always will be used because of its hard-wearing qualities, making it eminently suitable for upholstery and church hassocks and kneelers.

crosswise see cross.

Crow Indians American Indian tribe of the northern plains well known for their *quillwork and *beadwork. Laroque, an explorer of the first decade of the 1800s wrote, 'They are fond of small blue glass beads that they get from the Spanish but by the second or third hand.' During the 18th century, horses were introduced and this made the Plains Indians more mobile, necessitating *horse furniture such as bridles, saddlebags, cruppers, and martingales which could be elaborately decorated with beadwork. A complete set is in the collection of the Denver Art Museum. Another decorative item of the Crow were the milk teeth of the elk, drilled and sewn to ceremonial clothing. However, these were only for the wealthy since milk teeth were rare—only two per elk. A girl's dress of red flannel decorated with semicircles of these teeth is in the collection of the University of Pennsylvania Museum (Philadelphia). See also tepee.

Crow Indians: buckskin jacket with quill-work embroidery, 19th century.

crown The headwear, usually of embroidered velvet, worn by Masters of the City Livery Companies at the ceremonies of the Livery Companies of London. 2. Crowns are associated with the marking of underwear, handkerchiefs, stockings etc belonging to royalty. 3. Crowns are also frequently incorporated into embroideries, including samplers.

crown: detail of a handkerchief.

crow's foot Embroidered decoration put on a garment where excessive pull might break the machine stitching, for example at the top of a skirt pleat. It is a more elaborate version of an *arrow.

cryppen work Probably a form of net work or *lacis of the 16th century. A crepine, or crespin, was either 'a net or caul for the hair', or 'a fringe of lace or net work for a dais' (OED).

cuff The lower part of a *sleeve, either attached to the garment or made separately and tacked on as required. They have often been an important part of the sleeved garment and have generally been enriched with embroidery. The cuffs of men's coats and sleeved waistcoats in the first half of the 18th century were attached, were very large, and were fre-

quently embroidered to match the main part of the garment. Embroidered women's cuffs have generally been worked separately, often as a set with a collar and on a different fabric, and tacked on as required.

Cuna Indian embroidery (San Blas embroidery) Form of *reverse appliqué made into *molas or blouses, and worked by the Indian women of the San Blas area of the Caribbean Islands off the eastern coast of Panama. The fabrics used are plain cottons in strong colours. See also Sappi Karta tree.

Cuna Indian embroidery: women from San Blas, Panama, wearing molas, 20th century.

cupboard carpets (cloths) see carpets.

curtain strap Strap or holder to keep a window curtain in place when drawn back. They are either of metal fixed to the wall, of brass chain, or of fabric embroidered to match the curtain. In the 19th century there were often two if not three sets of curtains to each window, and sometimes the outer set was never drawn, but held back in draped folds by the strap.

curved needle Needle with a normal-sized eye, curved almost into a semicircle. They are of varying thickness and are used for upholstery and for awkward sewing jobs such as lampshades where a straight needle would be inadequate.

cushion: canvas embroidered in silk, Cretan, 19th century.

cushion (quition, quysshon etc) Soft, resilient pad used from earliest times for comfort and decoration for hard benches or stools. They also have a second, ceremonial use, and may support a missal on the altar, hold objects presented to royalty, and also support a child at its christening. As they have a more or less flat surface they are very suitable for embroidery and there is scarcely a technique which has not been used on them at some period or other. In the 16th and 17th centuries, when furniture was heavy and dark, and upholstered seats few and far between, cushions must have provided a welcome amount of colour and comfort, and from early inventories it is clear that all homes, great and small, had their quota. They ranged from 'velvet of divers colours, imbrodered with golde with C and A' and 'tawny sarcenet imbrodered with

branchis' listed in the inventory (1523) of Dame Agnes Hungerford (Nichols 1859), to a 'wrought cushion' in the probably not very grand parlour of an Essex yeoman in 1689 (Steer 1950).

cushion canvas Coarse linen canvas used as the ground fabric for cushions in the 16th and 17th centuries. It was generally woven 21 to 22 inches (53 to 56 centimetres) wide and this determined the width of the long cushions of the period.

cushion work (opus pulvinarium) In 13th and 14th century inventories there are references to a type of embroidery on canvas or coarse linen, then known as opus pulvinarium but which is usually translated as cushion work or *cushion stitch. It is uncertain exactly what this was, and different writers have given different opinions. Higgin (1880) writes of the 'ancient opus pulvinarium of the middle ages likewise called cross stitch', but also suggests that the work included long armed cross, tent, and two kinds of satin stitches. According to Christie (1906) the term is synonymous with canvas work.

cut canvas work see raised work.

cut-cloth flower embroidery Embroidery of the mid 19th century, considered by Caulfeild and Saward (1882) to be 'now out of date'. It consisted of forming naturalistic flowers by cutting petals and leaves from fabric of the correct colours and applying them to the ground material. Parts of the flowers too small to cut out were put in with stitchery.

cutting gauge see scissor cutting gauge.

cuttlefish When ground to a fine powder, dried cuttlefish bones are used as *pounce to rub through the holes made in a pricked design. This powder has the advantage of not being greasy and of being easily brushed off the fabric. See also prick.

cutwork (opus scissum) Embroidery on fabric, common in the 16th and 17th centuries, which was the forerunner of all the needlemade laces. Part of the ground fabric is cut away and the resulting space is crossed by threads, which are button-

cutwork: detail of a border, Italian, late 16th century.

church kneeler: one of the modern kneelers from Coventry Cathedral, England.

cutwork: alternate squares of cutwork and darned net, Italian, 16th century.

holed over and then joined to each other in pattern. The art appears to have been imported from Flanders and Italy in the 16th century, and can be seen on most of the whitework samplers of the 17th century. Parchment was tacked to the back of the fabric in order to keep the work rigid when the threads had been cut, and it also ensured that the embroiderer's needle slipped over its smooth surface. Ruffs of the period were often made of cutwork and the New Year gift presented to Elizabeth I in 1588 by the Baroness Dudley was 'Two ruffs with rabatines of lawn cut-work made, and one ruff of lawne cutt-work unmade' (Nichols 1823).

Cyprus Island in the eastern Mediterranean which has been conquered and ruled by many nations including Phoenicians, Greeks, Persians, Turks, Arabs, Venetians, and British. In consequence the embroidery has affinities with many cultures, most especially Italian and Turkish. Cross stitch is much used, and also whitework. (Johnstone 1972)

Cyprus gold (sipers gold) Gold thread not made in but imported from Cyprus in the middle ages. It is mentioned not only in descriptions of embroideries in wills and inventories, but also in the laws of the 15th century. There was a regrettable tendency to mix inferior metal with the best gold, and in 1423 the Commons had to petition Henry VI in respect of these injurious practices. It was stated that the wardens of the guilds were to impound any embroideries they discovered

Craske: a detail of his embroidered reconstruction of the evacuation of Dunkirk, worked in cheap thread on calico.

in which the gold and silver thread of Cyprus had been mixed with 'laton de Spayne' (alloy from Spain). Later, gold thread was imported from Venice.

Czechoslovakia Modern state made up of Bohemia, Moravia, and other parts of the Austro-Hungarian Empire. As in so many European countries the embroidery can be divided into two groups: that worked for the church and nobility, and that worked by the people for their own use on their clothes and in their houses. The whole area has always had a very strong tradition of needlework and has absorbed influences from Byzantium and China in the East as well as from the Adriatic; French trends came to the country with Blanche de Valois in the 14th century. In most of medieval Europe, the convents were to the fore in promoting the arts, and the Benedictine convent at Prague was a notable centre for both weaving and embroidery. Many of the early works still in existence are of appliqué, and *pearl embroidery was also practised—a frontal dating from 1300 in Musée Municipal at Cheb consists of figures of saints each standing in an arcade and is worked entirely in pearls. The 15th century became very 3-dimensional with forms built up in card, paper, or leather covered with fabric, and faces and hands were worked in split stitch, there called english stitch. The church embroidery of the 17th and 18th centuries was rich and rather heavy in style but of very fine workmanship. Embroidery on national costume (seldom worn nowadays) included geometrical patterns worked by the counted thread, combined with drawn threadwork, appliqué, needleweaving, and cutwork. See also Moravian embroidery.

Czechoslovakia: bell pull worked by nuns, c.1870.

Dacca silk (soie ovale) Untwisted silk floss originally imported from Dacca, India. It was in general use in the 18th and early 19th centuries and was considered suitable for copying Berlin woolwork patterns in silk, and for flat embroidery. (Miss Lambert 1843)

dacron filling see terylene filling.

dagge (dag) The ornamental cutting of the edges of garments. In the 14th and 15th centuries it became the practice for men's clothes, especially the long hanging sleeves, to be cut jaggedly as a form of decoration, and this was known as dagging. (Fairholt 1846)

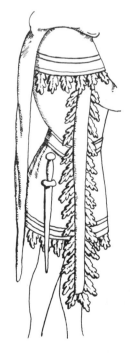

Dahcotas see Sioux.

dalmatic Vestment worn by a deacon assisting at the Eucharist and other solemn services. In the 2nd century it was an overtunic with wide straight sleeves, as worn in Dalmatia, and it was generally decorated with two vertical stripes from shoulder to hem, or *clavi, which later developed into the more modern orphrey. The dalmatic has always been an important garment, and it is still one of the

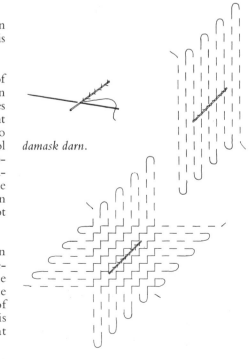

dalmatic: showing the Angel appearing to Joachim, 14th–15th century.

coronation robes of an English sovereign and is also worn by a bishop under his chasuble.

damask Reversible fabric, originally of silk, woven with an ornamental and often self-coloured design. Over the centuries the style of weave has remained constant but the choice of yarn has widened, and so there is linen damask used in napery, wool damask used in the 18th century for upholstery and curtains, as well as combinations of cotton, rayon, and man-made fibres. In old inventories, damask can mean 'made in Damascus' and need not refer to fabric at all.

damask darn (cross-cut darn) Used in the repairing of damask-weave tablelinen, where the tear is usually on the cross of the fabric. The two edges of the slit are drawn together, the first block of darning on the straight of the thread is worked and then the second block at right-angles to the first is worked.

damask darn.

damask gold Gold thread imported from Damascus. In the wardrobe account of Henry VIII (1533) is 'It'm for making of a shamewe of blacke printed satten embrowdered with damask golde . . .' (Caley 1789)

damask hem see napery hem.

damask patch Type of repair for holes in table-linen. A well-washed piece of similar fabric is tacked underneath the hole, and the edges of the tear are darned down onto the patch which is then cut away on the wrong side.

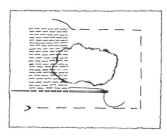

damask work Described in *Godey's Lady's Book* of 1860 as a novelty in needlework for curtains, couches, chairs, and table covers. It was worked in overlapping appliqué stitched with matching silks and then outlined with different coloured beads.

dance aprons Ceremonial garment worn by the shamans or medicine men of the *northwest coast Indian tribes during secret rituals and ceremonies. Decoration of applied fabric, buttons, dentalium sewn on with sinew, bands of quillwork, beads, and fringes edged with thimbles and bullet shells was variously used. An example with a wolf figure appliquéd in beads with a thimble and bullet shell fringe is in the collection of the Museum of Anthropology at the University of British Columbia, Vancouver. See also Hope embroidery, kilt, Pueblo Indians.

dance apron: from New Vancouver Village.

Danish National Museum (Copenhagen) Founded in 1841 with ethnographical objects belonging to the Royal Cabinet of Curiosities. This was begun in the middle of the 17th century by King Frederick III who later added the comprehensive collection of Ole Worm, professor of Copenhagen University in 1654. Specimens in the museum include examples from Greenland, the American Indians, and the Eskimos.

darn 1. Repair in a fabric made by filling the hole with an appropriate thread. Parallel threads are laid across the hole and cross threads are woven alternately over and under. 2. Darning may also be ornamental. In America in the late 18th century, coloured samplers were used to illustrate fine darning for clothes and socks where the pattern of the fabric was

darned embroidery: Picture, English, early 19th century.

reproduced in a space cut out of the sampler. In England this type of darning is mostly found in 19th century instruction books. 3. In the late 18th century there was also a vogue for samplers and pictures worked entirely in darning stitch. See darning samplers.

darned embroidery Darning is one of the simplest embroidery stitches and in one form or another it has been used by many countries at different periods—sometimes as the main stitch but also working the background to other stitches. India has always made a speciality of darning as has Portugal and a number of countries in eastern Europe. In England it was very popular in the 18th century, and had a revival in a different form in the late 19th, when designs of flowers and leaves were outlined and the ground filled in with darning stitches.

darned muslin Popular late 19th century embroidery on a firm muslin in darning stitch with the addition of other suitable stitches such as herringbone and satin. It is important that all the stitches in the design are worked so that the embroidery is reversible. (Caulfeild and Saward 1882)

darned net The technique employed in the simulated laces of the 19th century, especially those of Nottingham and *Limerick. Generally a machine-made net was used and the design was worked by darning in and out of the ground holes. Many beautiful articles were made by this method, including bonnet and wedding veils, shawls and flounces. See also net laces.

darned net: bonnet veil, English, mid-19th century.

darning cotton Loosely twisted and generally mercerised cotton, sold either in balls or on cards for darning stockings.

darning egg (darning ball) Egg-shaped or round ball of wood, bone, ivory, or glass which was dropped inside a sock or stocking in order to make a firm foundation for darning a hole. In America dried gourds were sometimes used. In the 20th century, darning balls were superseded by the darning mushroom, a mushroom-shaped piece of wood or plastic with a handle to make it easier to hold.

darning foot see attachments.

darning mushroom see darning egg.

darning needle (darner) Long needle with an eye large enough to take sock wool, used for darning socks and stockings. For ornamental darning a crewel needle or a sharp is more suitable.

darning samplers Type of *sampler popular in England from about 1770 to 1820. It was a method of teaching children fine darning in a variety of weaves, generally worked on a fine, even linen scrim in light pleasant colours, but sometimes in thread exactly matching the ground fabric. Most of these samplers have four large crosses in the corners, each worked in a different pattern and perhaps with a small motif in the centre, but some are far more ambitious and have an overall design of trees or flowers, each part worked in a different stitch pattern. In America they were not so prevalent, being worked mainly by German immigrants who had learnt the craft in Europe.

darning stick: English, Tunbridge ware, early 19th century.

darning stick Wooden stick with a shaped knob of different size at either end, used for poking up the fingers of gloves before darning them. In the 19th century they could be very decorative.

Daughters of the American Revolution Museum (Washington DC) Founded in 1890, this museum contains collections of American samplers, mourning embroideries, whitework, trapunto (stuffed quilting), candlewicking, costumes, and accessories. Also included are 28 period rooms with many needle-worked accessories.

Daughters of the American Revolution Museum: a signed and dated sampler.

David and Bathsheba: raised work panel, English, c.1700.

David and Bathsheba Old Testament story (2 Samuel 11), very popular in the 17th century, episodes of which are frequently seen in the *raised work on caskets and cabinets of the time and in tent stitch panels. The story tells of King David seeing Bathsheba, the wife of Uriah the Hittite, washing herself on the roof of her house. David commits adultery with her, engineers the death of Uriah, and eventually marries Bathsheba.

De Antiquitate Ecclesiae Britannicae Book written in 1572 by Matthew Parker, Archbishop of Canterbury. He not only wrote it but as he had his own private printing press it was probably printed by John Day under his supervision. He also had in his household 'Boke-binders', and so it is likely tha the copy of the book he gave to Elizabeth I was also embroidered under his supervision. This copy, now in the British Museum (London), has for its design a *rebus on the name Parker, with the park fence drawn flat, as a border, and flowers and animals inside. (Davenport 1899) See also bookbindings.

Dearle, J. H. (1860–1932) Designer who joined the firm of Morris & Co in 1878. He became assistant to William *Morris and followed his ideas. When Morris died in 1896, Dearle became art director of the firm and took over the designing of most of the wallpapers and textiles. (*Catalogue of the Morris Collection* 1969)

death's head button Type of button made by covering a dome-shaped wooden mould with thread, which was usually silk but could be metal. The thread was laced so that the finished design made a pattern of four quarters.

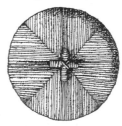

découpé   see reverse appliqué.

Deerfield Society of Blue and White Needlework Founded in 1895 by Margaret Whiting and Ellen Miller in Deerfield, Massachusetts, with the aim of reviving old colonial design in embroideries and raising the quality of embroidery through a home industry for local women. Though old methods of production were not strictly adhered to (linen and indigo were imported), the designs were taken entirely from original blue and white New England embroideries. The letter D in a spinning wheel became the mark of all Deerfield reproduction pieces, and the traditional characteristics of colonial crewel work were retained, even when other colours were gradually added and the form was adapted to modern use.

Deerfield Society of Blue and White Needlework: linen head curtain from Massachusetts, c.1895.

Delany, Mrs (née Mary Granville, 1700–1788) *The Autobiography and Correspondence of Mrs Delany* was edited by Lady Llanover in 1866, and it gives a picture of a woman who was famous in her day, not only as an embroiderer, but as a worker in many crafts. Mary Granville married first Mr Pendarves, who died in 1724, and then in 1743 Dr Patrick Delany, who died in 1768. During her widowhood of 20 years she lived in London and at Windsor, where she was a friend not only of the king and queen, but of various notabilities of the day, including Fanny Burney. In her letters to her sister Ann Dewes, Mrs Delany describes all the different pieces of embroidery she has undertaken and their progress, and she gives a clear picture of what was or was not in fashion at the time: 'The work I design sending you is some I have ready drawn, but it must not be traced—traced work is very ugly and quite out of fashion. You that have a knowledge of shading cannot be at a loss, and if you spoil a bit of canvas, what does it signify.' (16 Feb 1733–4.) Her chief claim to fame rests on her cutpaper botanical drawings which are now in the British Museum (London).

denim Heavy-twilled cotton fabric used for working clothes, dungarees, jeans etc, and as a base for various forms of fancy work or art embroidery. See also jean.

denim: jacket with satin appliqué designed by Wendy Stitt.

Denmark While the best-known type of embroidery found in Denmark is undoubtedly *Hedebo, there is also a tradition of cross stitch from *Amager, a small island not far from Copenhagen. These designs are of a peasant-like simplicity and the isolated motifs are charming and often naive, incorporating crowns, birds, and mythical beasts, as well as stylised plants. The modern tradition in Denmark, fostered by the Society for Women's Handwork, is strong on naturalistic motifs in cross stitch made into articles of household linen.

Denmark: sampler dated 1810.

dentalium Genus of tooth shells or tusk shells which are tapered and slightly curved, used as appliqué decoration by the American Plains Indians.

Denver Art Museum: Chinese Imperial hanging, Ch'ing dynasty.

Denver Art Museum (Colorado) One of the comprehensive collections of Plains Indian art, including bead and quillwork examples, and a complete set of Crow Indian horse trappings. The textile department has a widely varied collection from India and China, Portugal and Mexico, America and England, including samplers, quilts, and embroideries.

diamond see lozenge.

diaper Linen or *union fabric woven with a small geometric design. In the inventory of Dame Agnes Hungerford (1523) is 'a tabylcloth of dyapure' (Nichols 1859). The word can also be used for the small geometric pattern which can best be described as formed in staggered horizontal rows to give the distinguishing overall effect of diagonal lines, sometimes called bird's-eye diaper. The same pattern is often found in gold couching.

dickey 1. Detachable insert of fabric worn under a man's jacket or in a dress neckline to give the appearance of a shirt or blouse. It is sometimes used in addition to a shirt, especially in clerical garments. 2. Hooded coat of sealskin or duffle worn by the Nain Labrador Eskimos. See also dickey beads.

dickey beads (dickey ornaments) Uniform, pear-shaped pieces of ivory or walrus tooth sewn about an inch (2.5 centimetres) apart round the bottom of the hooded coat or *dickey of the Labrador Eskimos to weigh down the garment and prevent it from blowing up in the wind. They were used mostly on festival or formal dress, and were ornamental, made a pleasant, clicking noise, and were high in trade value. (Speck 1940)

dimity Cotton fabric, generally with a raised line in the weave. The word probably comes from Damietta where it was originally made. It is a very serviceable fabric and was used for bed hangings and curtains, usually undyed. In the 18th and 19th centuries it was also used for petticoats and sometimes children's dresses, and it was often the basis for embroidery.

dissolution of the monasteries The Dissolution of the Monasteries by Henry VIII in 1537 had a profound effect on the art of embroidery in England. Although it is known from inventories that in the middle ages there was a large amount of secular embroidery, especially in noble households, most embroidery was worked for the churches and religious houses, and it was for this that England was famous. With the Reformation, the advent of Protestantism, and the loss of monasteries and monastic life, the whole pattern of embroidery changed. Numbers of vestments were cut up to make household furnishings but, more important, there ceased to be any work done for the church, and so the talents of embroiderers turned exclusively to secular objects. The outcome was the ebullient and exciting embroideries of the Elizabethan age—in fact it was not until the 19th century that embroidery for the church was again attempted on any scale.

djellaba (jellâba) Loose, ankle-length garment worn in Morocco and Algeria which goes over the head, and has a hood and long sleeves.

djillayeh (jillayeh) Literally 'decorated', used of the coats worn by Arab women in various districts of Palestine. These were frequently beautifully adorned both with applied work and embroidery, the designs varying according to the locality. (Weir 1969)

djillayeh: detail, from Beit-Dajan, Jordan.

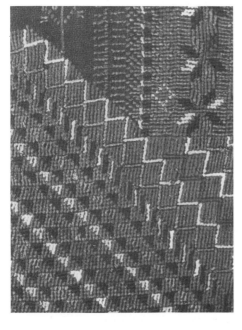

domed button Simple form of home-made button able to go through a mangle without breaking, and used for household linen. For each button two circles of linen were cut, a gathering thread run round their edges, and a small quantity of ravelling placed in the middle of each circle. After these were drawn up and finished off, the two little bags were flattened, placed together with the drawn up parts to the inside, and buttonholed together. (Armes 1939)

domett Type of baize or flannel invented by Josiah Domett, a cotton manufacturer from Manchester (England), which was woven of wool and cotton, and used as an interlining in various forms of embroidery. It was often the warm lining in dresses and petticoats in the 18th century, and was also used for shrouds. In America, outing flannel has a slightly shorter nap, but is an interchangeable term.

Dorset crosswheel button The surviving type of handmade button from the many which formed the staple industry of east Dorset, England from c 1700 to 1860. The crosswheel button is made in four stages. 1. Casting: a curtain ring is closely buttonholed. 2. Slicking: the buttonholing is turned with the ridge of the stitch inside the ring. 3. Laying: six threads are laid across the ring making twelve spokes radiating from the centre. 4. Rounding: the thread is woven in and out of the spokes, making a back stitch round each one, until the whole wheel is filled. (Pass 1957)

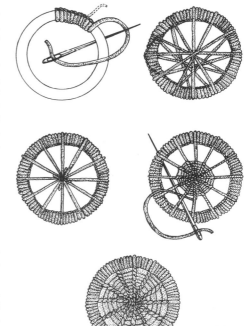

Dorset crosswheel button.

Dorset feather stitchery Embroidery started in the 1950s by the women's institutes of Dorset, England. It is based on feather stitch together with traditional patterns from smocks and continental peasant embroideries, and ric-rac braid is also a feature. The work has great charm, is comparatively simple, and is still very popular. (Pass 1957)

dossal Curtain or cloth hung behind an altar or round the walls of a chapel. It may be of plain or patterned fabric, or embroidered.

dossal: from the Mass Vestments of the Order of the Golden Fleece, Netherlands, mid-15th century.

dot stitch Stitch consisting of two back stitches worked over one another, which can be used in a line or be powdered over the ground.

dotting The embroidering of small dots on muslin, generally in conjunction with small tamboured sprigs, and used on dresses and accessories. Together with tambouring, it made an appreciable difference to the economics of Ayrshire and Perthshire in the late 18th century, and was a considerable source of income to the women and girls of southern Scotland. (Swain 1955)

double cross stitch see smyrna stitch.

double darning (pessante) Technique akin to double running (Holbein) stitch, much used in the 16th century. Double darning is worked in the same way but in close rows, so that blocks of colour are formed which are reversible. This type of embroidery is found in the Near East, Persia (Iran), and the Greek Islands.

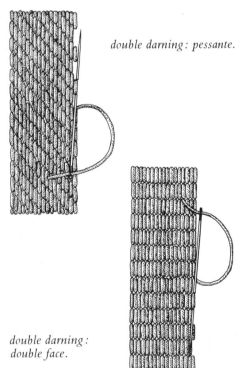

double darning: pessante.

double darning: double face.

double running embroidery (Holbein work) Type of embroidery worked in double running or Holbein stitch. The reason it is also called Holbein work is because it appears on so many of the garments worn by those members of Henry VIII's court (both men and women) who sat for the portrait painter Hans Holbein (1497–1543). Generally it is worked in black or sometimes red thread on the white linen shirts, chemises, sleeves, and ruffs frequently seen in the portraits.

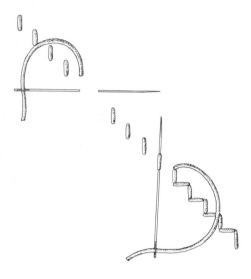

double running stitch (Holbein stitch, line stitch, square stitch, stroke stitch, two-sided line stitch, two-sided stroke stitch) One of the oldest, simplest, and most effective counted thread stitches. It is the basis of blackwork, and can be made to follow any outline except curves. Equally spaced running stitches are made, and the space between them is filled on the return journey to make a thin line, but it is important that these second stitches go into the same holes as the first, otherwise the line will not be clear. See also double running embroidery.

doublet Close-fitting jacket of the 15th to 17th centuries, worn chiefly by men but also by women, which varied in length at different dates, was with or without sleeves, or had sleeves which tied in.

doublet: with matching coif, English, 1575–1610.

Douce Bible Printed in 1583, one of the Douce Bibles was bound for Elizabeth I and is now in the Bodleian Library, Oxford. The embroidered design is magnificent yet not heavy, consisting of intertwining sprays of Tudor roses with birds and leaves springing from a central rose. It is the same on both sides and is carried out in silk thread, silver gimp, gold cord, silver twist, and pearls. The ground is crimson velvet. See also bookbindings.

dourukha Embroidery done by men in Kashmir. Dourukha, which means double-side embroidery, is worked in stem, satin, and darning stitches and is completely reversible. On the other hand in dourukha-douranga, which uses the same stitches, such a minute thread of the weft is picked up that it is possible to work a completely different design and colour combination on each side of the fabric. (Dhamija 1964)

dove The symbol of the Holy Ghost. Doves have always been prominent in Christian symbolism and are often embroidered, either by themselves on articles such as burses and veils or in conjunction with the Father and Son to represent the Trinity.

dove: from the Genesis Hanging, Catalonia, 11th century.

dower chest Large, lidded wooden box, usually carved or painted, which was traditionally made by a father for his daughter when she was very young to store the quilt tops and other handworked household items made in anticipation for the time when she would marry.

Elizabethan: a needlework firescreen in the Blue Room at Hardwick Hall, Derbyshire.

overleaf (p 86)
embroidered picture: worked freehand in wool on canvas by Miss Letitia Neill, c.1910.

dowlas Strong coarse linen, originally used for shirts for poor people, but now generally used as the backing fabric for large pieces of heavy embroidery such as altar frontals.

down The finest, softest bird feathers, which have practically no hard centre. It is the best (and most expensive) filling for cushions, eiderdowns, quilts, teacosies etc, and also frequently appears in the form of swansdown trimming in the late 18th and 19th centuries.

downproof fabric Specially-treated fabric, such as ticking or sateen, which prevents down working through its covering. Originally a closely-woven material was rubbed with damp soap on the inside to make it completely downproof but now the fabric is prepared commercially.

d'oyley frame (shawl frame) Square or rectangular wooden frame into which brass pins are fixed at regular intervals for use in *frame work. An old picture frame also makes a suitable base.

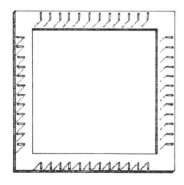

draft Plan, chart, drawing, or sketch. In quiltmaking in America, drafting means something a little different: Ickis (1959) describes drafting a pattern as cutting out the pieces of fabric to a template design and preparing them for attaching to the ground materials. In England the draft would be the original design from which the embroiderer worked. The word is also used in connection with dressmaking when a pattern is drafted from the measurements of the person for whom the garment is being made.

draper Originally, a maker of cloth; later, a dealer in cloth; but for the last 150 years or so, a shopkeeper selling cloth

overleaf (p 87)
fan: a late 18th century Chinese ceremonial fan, κ'o ssu, with birds among pine trees and plum blossom.

florentine stitch: detail of a bookbinding worked in wool on linen, English or American, 1725–80.

among other articles of haberdashery and clothes, more nearly approaching the old milliner.

drapery 1. Firm, opaque, decorative fabrics usually hung in carefully-arranged folds at windows, sometimes in combination with other curtains, and often with added embellishment such as tambour, applied, or flat embroidery. They are also called drapes and window drapery. 2. Goods sold by a draper, including curtain fabric.

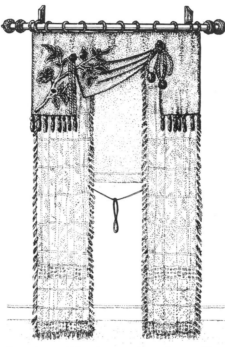

drawing Word meaning the pulling together or drawing up of gathers made by running stitches. From this comes the term drawstring.

drawn fabric stitches Group which, by pulling the threads of fabric aside, leave holes that form the pattern. A number of these are also suitable for use as surface filling stitches when worked on firm fabric, and they can be combined with other forms of needlework such as whitework or quilting. Stitches in this group are: algerian filling stitch, back stitch, ringed filling, chained border, chequer filling, diagonal chevron stitch, diagonal drawn filling, diagonal raised band, double stitch filling, eyelet stitch, faggot stitch, greek stitch filling (greek four-sided stitch), honeycomb filling (net passing stitch), indian drawn ground, lozenge filling, net filling, open trellis filling, *pin stitch (point de paris, paris point), *point turc (bermuda faggoting, lace stitch, three-sided stitch, turkish stitch), *punch stitch (four-sided stitch, open groundwork, openwork stitch, single faggot stitch), rosette filling, squared ground stitch, wave stitch filling, window filling (straight line stitch).

drawn fabric work (pulled fabric work) Embroidery worked with a thick needle and a fine thread in which the stitches are pulled tight, drawing the fabric together and leaving a hole. It is these holes made in a variety of sizes and patterns which give the work its unique style. A number of filling stitches can be adapted to use as drawn fabric stitches merely by drawing them tightly together. This type of embroidery has been known for several centuries but was probably at its best in the Dresden work developed in Germany in the 18th century. Sometimes drawn fabric work is combined with quilting.

drawn fabric work: baby's cap, English, early 18th century.

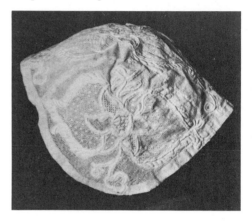

drawn thread stitches Group which includes all the stitches where threads have been pulled out of the fabric. This makes the fabric weak, so strength must be put back in the form of decorative threads. Especially where hems are concerned it is important not to pull more threads than necessary. This group of stitches can be divided as follows. Bars: buttonholed, overcast, woven. Fillings: russian drawn, russian overcast, weaving. *Hem stitch and variations: antique, combination, interlaced, italian (double, double-rowed openwork, romanian, shadow), ladder, serpentine, warp, woven (*needleweaving, openwork insertion).

drawn threadwork: child's cheesecloth dress, early 20th century.

drawn threadwork: detail of a cover, 1900–10.

drawn threadwork (opus tiratum) Basis of many types of embroidery in which some threads of the ground fabric are drawn out. However, unless the remaining threads are strengthened by binding and extra stitches, the ground is very much weakened. In early 20th century work, washing and ironing and general wear have often torn the weak threads away but the main fabric remains in very good condition. Sometimes drawn threadwork is shortened to drawn work, but this is unfortunate as it is then not clear whether drawn threadwork or *drawn fabric work is meant. See also cutwork, Hardanger embroidery, Hedebo embroidery, hemstitching, needle-weaving, Sicilian embroidery, tele tirata.

drawstring One or two cords or laces which, when threaded through a casing, hem, or rings, can be pulled to tighten. They can be used to fasten a bag or to make a garment smaller at the waist or neck.

drawstring: crewel embroidered linen bag, American, 18th century.

Dresden work (point de saxe) Type of embroidery which reached its peak in the middle of the 18th century in Dresden, Hanover, and the surrounding areas. It was drawn fabric work on fine muslin and was intended to take the place of the popular but expensive bobbin laces, and was used principally for ruffles, aprons, kerchiefs, and all light muslin accessories. Although it was imported into England, ladies also sent their muslin to Hanover to be worked there. Dresden work was copied in Britain as well as in other countries, and in the 1750s prizes for good imitations were awarded by the Art-Gallican Society in England, the Edinburgh Society, and various Irish societies. It also found a place in the curriculum of some schools. In 1849 the *American Ladies' Memorial* said 'Muslin worked with glazed cotton was formerly called Dresden-work, but is now known by the name of Moravian, from its production having formed the principal employment of a religious sect, called the Moravian Sisters, which originated in Germany, and some of those establishments exist in England.' See also Moravian embroidery.

Dresden work: English muslin kerchief, 18th century.

dress 1. Word synonymous with costume and applying to the complete outfit of men, women, and children at all times. 2. The name first used in the 17th century for the outer garment worn by women and children, and known at various periods as a robe or gown. 3. To prepare or array. The most usual use of the word in this sense is in the phrase 'to dress a frame', which means the preparation of an embroidery frame ready for working.

dressing The stiffening found in some fabrics. Sometimes it is an integral part of the fabric, as in chintz, but often it is put in to hide poor quality and leaves a very limp fabric after the first wash. It is either starch, gum, china clay, or size.

dressing table sets see cheval sets.

dressmaker's carbon see tracing paper.

dressmaker's cord see piping cord.

drizzling (parfilage, ravelling) Strange craze of the 18th century which consisted of unpicking the metal from metal threads and laces and selling it. This pastime, which started in France at the court of Marie Antoinette, was pursued by the wealthiest ladies as well as by those who needed the money, and gentlemen of the army or navy who wore a considerable amount of gold lace and braid on their uniforms often found themselves without it when they left a dinner party or assembly. The craze was brought to England by the French who had fled from the Revolution and who used drizzling as a method of making a little money. It was taken up by some English ladies who carried bags with small scissors and stilettos whenever they went out in case they might acquire some lace to unpick.

drizzling: tool for pulling the metal from threads.

drum-major's sash Belt worn over the shoulder and across the chest by a regimental drum major. It is embroidered with the Battle Honours and has two pockets for spare drum sticks.

dry goods American term for fabrics and related articles such as yard goods, ribbons, shawls, thread, carpets, upholstery, yarn, and bedding. However, according to Cole (1900), the first recorded use of the term to describe fabrics collectively occurred in a report to the English House of Commons in 1745. The nearest English equivalent is drapery.

duo canvas see penelope canvas.

dupion Modern fabric of French origin with a slightly rough weave and a silky finish. It is suitable for some types of free embroidery among them Dorset feather stitchery.

Durham quilting see wadded quilting.

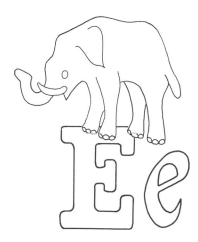

Eanswitha Embroideress from Hereford (England) who in the year 802 was granted by Denbert, Bishop of Worcester, a lease for life of a farm of 200 acres on condition that she was to renew and wash and from time to time add to the garments of the priests and ministers who served in the cathedral church. (Lambert 1843)

ease see full.

Eastern Woodland Indians (Forest tribes) Numerous tribes of Indians that inhabited the seaboard from the Mississippi River Valley to the Atlantic and from north of the Great Lakes to Florida. They belonged to two nations, the Iroquois and the Algonquin. The Iroquois included the Mohawks, Onondaga, Oneida, Cayuga, and Huron, while the Algonquin included the Penobscot, Lenni, Lenape or Delaware, Ojibwa or Cherokee, and Mohicans. Most of these tribes were permanent and peace-loving, in-

Eastern Woodlands Indians: fringed buckskin apron incorporating double curve motif characteristic of these tribes' embroidery.

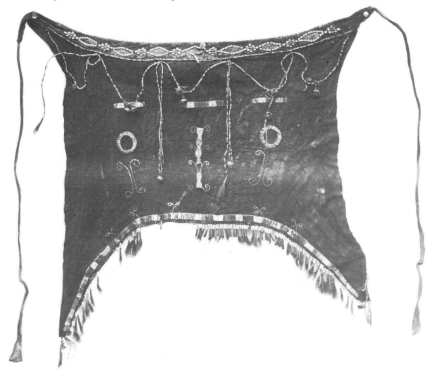

volved in agriculture and hunting, and readily adopted the methods of the European settlers. Early embroideries worked on quills sewn on buckskin with sinew were replaced by red, blue, and black tradecloth and white seed beads sewn in symmetrical, lacy designs, and later by the floral and leaf patterns of the French Canadian nuns. These tribes were also a major source of *wampum.

East India Company English company founded in 1600 for the purpose of trade with India, China, and the East generally. While the main object was to acquire spices for England, embroideries were both exported and eventually imported. In a letter of 1618 to the directors in England, Sir Thomas Roe, King James's Ambassador, says '. . . gloves, hangers, scarfs, by these only they picke out the workes. Instead of sweet baggs, rownde cushions gathered like cloke bags, to leane upon. Any of this in needleworke or inbroderie being fallen in value, for they have learned by ours to do as well. Boxes inbrodered will sell to profitt and great glasses . . .'

Eastlake, Charles L. (1836–1906) All-round English artist who trained but did not practise as an architect. Three years travelling as a young man stimulated his love of medieval building and decoration, and he spent most of his working life designing furniture, wallpapers, metalwork, and jewellery. His *Hints on Household Taste in Furniture, Upholstery and other Details* was published in 1868.

ecaille Imitation of *nacre work, and should more properly be called stamped quillwork. Quills of birds were opened, softened, and flattened and were then cut into shapes and sewn onto a ground fabric such as velvet. The process is described by Miss Lambert (1843).

ecclesiastical embroidery (church embroidery) Embroidery worked on the vestments of ministers and church furnishings. Its history is as long as the history of churches and in fact goes back to the early chapters of the Bible. It is natural that where religion is the most important force in people's lives the enriching of places of worship to the glory of God should be important. In the middle ages there was also the added thought that gifts to the church on earth might lay up rewards in heaven. The result is that in most countries, especially those which have Christianity as their main religion, ecclesiastical embroidery has always been very rich, sometimes spectacular, and generally beautiful. In the middle ages, *opus anglicanum or English work was known and admired all over the civilised world, but whitework in the form of opus teutonicum was also being worked in Germany, and Sicily too was a great centre. In countries which became Protestant at the time of the Reformation, ecclesiastical embroidery practically ceased, and in cases of extreme Protestantism has never restarted. Embroidery for the Anglican church began again in the 19th century, and in the second half of the 20th century the beautifying of churches with embroidery for kneelers, altar frontals, and vestments has caught the imagination of many people who find in it a most satisfying outlet for their creative ability.

Ecclesiologist, The High Church Anglican magazine started in 1841 by the Cambridge Camden Society to promote the ideals of Gothic architecture and furnishings for churches. It not only advised on such things as stained glass and pews, but also on vestments and fabric furnishing, and was largely responsible for the return of vestments for the seasons of the church and the resurgence of ecclesiastical embroidery.

ecru Word from the French, literally meaning raw or unbleached, used to denote a pale beige or natural colour, especially of lace.

ecru lace 1. Type of embroidered lace, made in the last quarter of the 19th century. It was very like Renaissance lace and consisted of two different kinds of braid joined with buttonhole bars, picots, and wheels. 2. Machine-made lace of the 20th century, especially the 1930s, which was beige or coffee coloured and much used for trimming petticoats and underwear.

edgings Narrow laces or braids used to decorate the edges of garments, especially children's, and undergarments. Edgings of lace used to be handmade and so sometimes were the braids, but nowadays they are practically all machine made.

Edlin, Martha (b 1660) Embroideress known only by the fact that a collection of her needlework done between the ages of 8 and 13 has survived intact. The collection has been handed down the female line of her family and is now in the Victoria and Albert Museum (London). Her important pieces of work consist of a polychrome sampler dated 1668, a cutwork sampler of 1669, a casket of 1671, and a beadwork box of 1673. This sequence gives a good indication of the needlework education of a girl of her age in the 17th century. (Ashton 1928)

Egypt Two periods of Egyptian history in particular produced very fine embroideries: that of the Fatimid dynasty (909–1171) and the Mamluk (1250–1517). During the Fatimid period, weaving of velvets and brocade reached a very high standard and for people who could not afford these, embroideries were worked copying the designs of the sumptuous fabrics. Many of the embroideries were inscribed giving a firm date, and most of the stitches known to present day embroiderers were used. An Arab historian, Makrizi, made an inventory of the treasures belonging to the Caliph Mustansir (AD 1050), among which were silks embroidered with the history of the dynasties of the East, portraits of famous men with their dates and deeds, and a tent covered with embroidered designs which took 50 artists 9 years to make, and which was so large that it needed 100 camels to transport it and its furniture. Egyptian embroidery of this century has mainly been confined to reviving ancient techniques such as the Coptic tissues and copying the old wall paintings in applied work, sold mostly to tourists. No strong native tradition has yet developed in modern Egypt. (Newberry 1940) See also Coptic embroidery.

Edlin: embroidery 1668–73.

elastic 1. Term meaning springy or flexible; also, capable of returning to its original position after being stretched out. It applies to needlework techniques such as shirring, and smocking. 2. Rubber thread woven with cotton, silk, or synthetic thread to form a material of varying widths, used where it is necessary for an article or garment to expand and contract.

Elizabeth I of England (1533–1603) Although remembered mostly for the political and economic policies she pursued during her long reign, her patronage and interest in the arts, especially that of needlework, should not be forgotten. Elizabeth was a notable embroideress and while her output was nothing like that of her cousin *Mary Queen of Scots, her work was as good. Among the pieces worked by her as a young girl are bookbindings for her own manuscript of the *Miroir or Glasse of the Synneful Soul* and the *Prayers* of Queen Katharine Parr. It was partly due to Elizabeth's love of finery and display and her example in dress that embroidery flourished so well in her reign, as is shown by the gifts given to her at New Year as listed in *Progresses of Queen Elizabeth* (Nichols 1823).

Elizabethan The age of Elizabeth I (1558–1603) produced the finest embroideries ever worked in England. This was partly due to the introduction of fine steel needles, but also to the spirit of the Renaissance, the love of finery and rich fabrics of the court and nobility, the emergence of pattern books and aids for the home embroiderer, and the rise in power and wealth of the trading classes. (Colour illustration p 83)

Elizabethan: linen cover embroidered in black silk using closed herringbone stitch, English, c.1600.

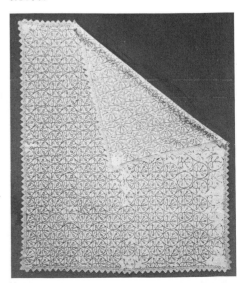

Elizabeth Day McCormick Collection: fragment of a crewel embroidered hanging, English, late 17th century.

Elizabeth Day McCormick collection (Boston, Massachusetts) Now in the Museum of Fine Arts, it contains an extensive collection of English and continental textiles and embroideries, and also fine examples of Greek Island embroideries.

elk tooth ceremonial dress see Crow Indians.

ell Measure of length varying in different countries, but all deriving from the length of the arm from the shoulder to either the wrist or the finger tips. The ell was superseded by the yard in Britain and America and by the metre on the continent, but the original measurements were as follows: England, 45 inches; Scotland, 37 inches; France, 54 inches; Flanders, 27 inches.

elysée work Embroidery of the late 19th century in which a running spray of leaves and tendrils is cut out of one fabric and pasted onto another. When dry, stems, veins, stamens etc are embroidered. It is stated by Caulfeild and Saward (1882) to be 'an arrangement of two coloured cotton materials after the manner of appliqué, and an easy and inexpensive kind of Embroidery'.

emblems Allegorical mottoes in pictorial form popular in the 16th century. The Elizabethans enjoyed intellectual allusions, riddles, and conceits which were prevalent in drama, pageants, and speeches and which conjured up pictures in the minds of the listeners, and emblems were also popular in embroidery. Emblem books were published in Italy and France in the first half of the 16th century and in England rather later. Embroiderers used the books of design, especially *Devises Héroiques* by Paradin written in 1557 and translated into English in 1591, and Whitney's *A Choice of Emblems* (1586). Sometimes royalty took an emblem as a badge for their personal use, and this was known as an *impresa. Probably the most famous embroidered emblems are those worked by *Mary Queen of Scots on what are now called the Oxburgh hangings at *Oxburgh Hall, where many of the small panels contain mottoes with pictures.

emboss 1. Term used more in America than in England which implies needlework in relief. The relief can be formed either by padding or by making layers of stitches underneath the motif, such as chain stitch underneath satin stitch, or satin stitch worked in the opposite direction underneath satin stitch. 2. Method of stitchery used in Romanian embroideries in which the material is puckered or raised and is more like smocking than an embroidery design in relief. The embossing is usually worked in either white or off-white silk threads. (Harkness 1959)

embossed velvet work Described by Caulfeild and Saward (1882) as the outlining of a design on embossed velvet with gold cord or other suitable stitchery.

embroidered centres American term used to describe pre-worked designs on needlepoint canvases, especially those imported from Europe.

embroidered pictures These have been used to decorate rooms since the 17th century and are now enjoying a revival. In the 17th century the pictures were generally of biblical subjects and were worked either in tent stitch or in the prevailing techniques of raised or stump work. In the late 18th century, they were often worked on silk taffeta in fine spun silk with the faces, hands, and sometimes skies painted. New England schools and the Moravian schools in Bethlehem (Pennsylvania) were renowned for picture embroideries using biblical, romantic, or historical themes, often copied exactly from existing prints. There was also a vogue for printwork and mourning pictures, and for the type which Mary *Linwood embroidered so successfully, where exact representations of portraits were worked in straight stitches in a multitude of shades. Pictures of the 19th century were often of Berlin woolwork, sometimes again copying painting as in the *Descent from the Cross* by Rubens, paintings by Morland and *Landseer, and prints by *Baxter. In the 20th century framed pictures are often collages, machine embroidered, or built up

embroidered picture: pheasant worked in silk on satin, English, late 18th century.

stitchery, sometimes of abstract design. Since the 1960s in America there has been a vogue for crewel and needlepoint pictures, especially of animals and flowers. (Colour illustration p 86) See mourning pictures, Ninhue embroidery.

embroidered pile cloth (Kasai velvet) High-pile *raffia embroidery on woven raffia cloth made by the tribes of the Kasai region of Zaire. Traditionally the cloth is woven by the men and then embroidered by the women in brown, yellow, pink, and mauve, in stem and cut pile stitch.

embroidered ribbon (liston bordado) Woven strip of red cotton about 8 feet (2.5 metres) long by $4\frac{3}{4}$ inches (12 centimetres) wide with elaborate embroidery in the centre and for 18 inches (45 centimetres) at either end. Spanish-Mexican women '. . . place the central design over the nape of the neck, part their hair in the middle and plait it together with the two ends of the strip. The embroidered ends are then made into a bow tied with the hair.' (Mozzi 1968)

embroidered rugs see needlemade rugs.

embroidered tapestries In early Peru, popular and extraordinarily well-made embroidery was done with a needle-like implement in cotton or wool yarn, generally on loosely-woven cotton fabric. The stitches always followed the weft line, for free embroidery with stitches at various angles was virtually unknown. The earliest and finest pieces are from Paracas Cavernas, and known as *Paracas embroidery. As the art declined in popularity and quality, embroidery on a cotton-base fabric with a double warp became the forerunner of tapestry-weaving techniques, and the two became so similar in appearance that it is hard to tell them apart. Embroidered tapestry, in which the secondary pattern was worked with a needle after the web had been taken from the loom, can be distinguished by the knots and loose ends on the back. Brocade, whose pattern is made by an auxiliary weft inserted into the web while still on the loom, has floats at the back, and the auxiliary weft lies more firmly on the base fabric. (Means 1932)

embroiderers By far the greatest number of embroiderers in the world, men and women, are unknown. They may have worked in a professional workroom, or in a school of embroidery, or been among the thousands who have worked in their own homes for relaxation and to create beautiful objects. As a professional class, embroiderers have never been very highly considered, as this entry in *The London Tradesman* (1747) makes clear: 'Embroiderers may be reckoned among the Dependents of the Lace-Man; as in his shop the greatest part of their rich Work is vended, and he furnishes them with all Materials for their Business. It is chiefly performed by Women; is an ingenious Art, requires a nice Taste in Drawing, a bold Fancy to invent new Patterns, and a clean Hand to save their Work from Tarnishing. Few of the Workers at present can Draw, they have their Patterns from the Pattern-Drawer, who must likewise draw the Work itself, which they only fill up, with Gold and Silver, Silks or Worsteds, according to its use and Nature. We are far from excelling in this Branch of Business in England: the Nuns in Foreign Countries far exceed anything we can perform. We make some good Work; but fall short of the bold Fancy in French and Italian Embroidery.

Unfortunately we know the names of very few embroiderers as they seldom signed their work, except in the case of samplers; but occasionally a name can be

embroiderers: 'Girl Embroidering' by G. F. Kersting, c.1814.

found in some of the royal accounts, or a family can give some illuminating details about an ancestor who was also an embroiderer. Following is a list of some of them about whom we know something, even if only a very little, and that little will be found in the text under their names: Bess of Hardwick, William Broderick, Lady Calverley, Mrs A. H. Christie, Mary Delany, Eanswitha, Martha Edlin, Anne de Felbrigge, Edmund Harrison, Mary Holte, Mary Jones, Mary Knowles, Mary Linwood, Mabel of Bury St Edmunds, Ann Macbeth, Mary Queen of Scots, Mrs J. R. Newberry, Pierre Oudry, Louisa Frances Pesel, Betsy Ross, Mrs St Osyth Wood.

embroiderers: from Diderot's Pictorial Encyclopedia of Trade and Industries.

fig. 1.

Embroiderers' Guild One of the forces behind present day needlework, the Embroiderers' Guild was formed in 1906 as 'The Society of Certificated Embroideresses'. The members were all past students of the *Royal School of Needlework who held the teacher's diploma, but in 1907 other members were elected having submitted work for judgement. In 1920 the society was widened still further and became the Embroiderers' Guild, serving the needs and interests of anyone who cared for embroidery. After the Second World War its numbers increased enormously and branches were started all over England and in countries abroad. The Guild, at present at 73 Wimpole Street, London, has a comprehensive library, lends portfolios of embroidery technique to its members, has a good collection of historical embroideries, publishes a quarterly journal, *Embroidery*, and runs classes and schools in London and the provinces.

Embroiderers' Guild of America, Inc Branch of the *Embroiderers' Guild (England), founded in 1958. In 1970 the American guild became a separate organisation concerned with establishing and maintaining high standards of design, colour, and workmanship in all kinds of needlework. It publishes *Needle Arts*.

Embroideress, The English magazine which from 1922 to 1939 was a source of wisdom, help, and inspiration to those interested in embroidery. It was edited first by Mrs J. D. Rolleston and then by Mrs K. Harris, and was noted for the high standard of its articles. The magazine was published quarterly by Pearsalls and the Old Bleach Linen Co of Northern Ireland, who manufactured linen and various embroidery threads.

embroidery The art of ornamenting material with needlework. The basis of embroidery has always been plain sewing, but nowadays more emphasis is put on the decorative qualities of different threads and materials than on the underlying skills and techniques which earlier, and especially before the advent of the sewing machine, were considered essential. Embroidery undoubtedly followed soon after man learnt to weave, and in Scandinavia, simply embroidered woollen garments have been found dating from the bronze age, while Chinese embroideries of the 5th century BC can still be seen whose style shows that the craft must have started much earlier in order to have reached such a high level of sophistication by that time. Until the 19th century there were only a few well-

embroidery: 'The Petit-point Cupid' by J. B. Mallet.

defined techniques, named for their style and usage rather than for the materials on which they were worked. However by the end of the 19th century many new names and types had appeared with the development of the art needlework movement, the art needlework departments in department stores, and the big firms selling threads, transfers, and materials. In many cases these new names of embroideries were just old friends freshened up, but their numbers have made for confusion.

Embroidery Journal of the Embroiderers' Guild, a publication which since its inception in December 1932 has had a great influence on the study and working of embroidery in England. Originally edited by two well-known teachers and embroiderers, Mrs Rolleston and Mrs K. Harris, and then by Mrs Harris alone, it contains articles on historical pieces as well as modern stitches, design, and anything considered to be of interest to the average needleworker. It is now edited by a small committee, and is published quarterly.

embroidery cotton Soft, mercerised cotton thread, thin and tightly twisted, which has the appearance of silk. It makes a firm, even line.

embroidery designs 1. Designs taken from virtually any source and made suitable for embroidery. This may be done by the worker, by professional artists made into pattern books, or by *pattern drawers. 2. Title given to the only existing copy of a manuscript notebook containing about 300 embroidery designs found in Abbeville, South Carolina, and now in the Valentine Museum. The patterns are drawn on English paper, manufacturered by Joseph Coles after 1801, but the name and nationality of the author are unknown. Handerchief and dress borders are carefully indicated, and numerous designs for general embroidery are included, four of which are hand-coloured. (Davis 1971)

embroidery floss In America a soft, loosely-twisted, six-strand thread of mercerised cotton.

embroidery foot see attachments.

embroidery frame (tent, tenter, or slate frame) Frame used to stretch out the ground fabric before embroidering. Some techniques, especially metal thread embroidery and quilting, cannot be worked until this is done, and so from earliest times frames have been used. These have varied enormously in size, from 11 or 12 feet long to only about 1 foot, but in every case the principle is the same. The frame consists of two long bars or beams (from the inventory of Hardwick Hall in 1601 is 'nyne payre of beames for imbroderies') which have webbing tacked on along their length. This pair of beams is joined at the ends by two cross pieces which are put through horizontal holes in the beams. The fabric to be framed is sewn to the webbing on each beam, and is then rolled round one of them until a comfortable working width is obtained. Then the cross pieces are slipped in and pegs dropped into holes giving a well-stretched oblong of ground fabric on which to work. The frames can rest either on the backs of chairs or on trestles, or some of the smaller kinds have

their own stands which are put on the floor or the lap. Frames were often called tent frames from the resemblance to the woven cloth stretched on the tenter hooks in the fields during the process of making linen. Randle *Holme in *The Academy of Armory* (1688) says that among the embrautherer's tools is the 'Working Tent' and 'in the Working Tent or Straining Frame there are these parts. The Frame or straining Tent. The Mortised pieces, which have square holes cut thro' at each end. The Running pieces, which go thro' the Mortices, to make the Frame wider and closer together. The Holes and Pins, they hold it at its distance. The Pack Thread by which it is strained.' See also embroidery hoop, fanny frame, and tambour 1.

embroidery hoop Two rings or hoops of wood, metal, or plastic used for stretching small pieces of work, and especially useful for tambour work. It is often called a tambour hoop from its resemblance to a drum, for the two rings fit together, keeping the fabric taut between them. The hoops can either be held in the hand or mounted on a stand. See also tambour 1, fanny frame.

embroidery kits see kits.

embroidery linen see art linen.

embroidery on the stamp see raised work.

embroidery paste Special paste which can be applied to the back of a finished embroidery, partly to stiffen it and partly to hold loose threads. Recipes for pastes

vary from worker to worker but generally they are made by melting resin or cabinet-maker's glue and adding to it a flour and water paste. One reliable method is as follows. A piece of best cabinet-maker's glue, about the size of a small nut, is put into a saucepan with a quarter pint of cold water, and brought to the boil. Three teaspoons of plain flour are mixed to a smooth paste with cold water, and when the glue is quite melted, the glue water is added to the flour, stirring to avoid lumps. This is poured back into the saucepan and cooked for three minutes until the paste is thick. When cold, it is rubbed thinly into the back of the work.

embroidery stamps Wooden blocks used for stamping a pattern onto fabric ready for embroidery. In England they were made of sycamore, in America of rock maple. The paper pattern was glued onto the base of the block, the design was scored into the wood, and pewter or copper strips were then let into the scored lines.

embroidery stamps: a selection of 19th century American stamps.

embroidery stitch see long and short stitch.

embroidery stitches see stitches, and also under their individual names.

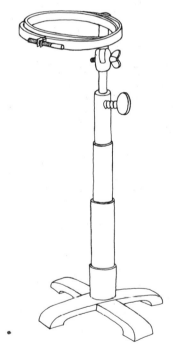

embroidery design: poppies from an etched embroidery design published in Leipzig in 1798.

France: an embroidered book cover dated 1740.

embroidery threads The more usual threads for embroidery are made of silk, wool, flax, cotton, metals and synthetics, but embroiderers have always used what comes most readily to hand. The North American Indians used moosehair and porcupine quills, nomadic tribes of North Europe and Asia use reindeer sinews, in Southeast Asia the fibres of the pineapple plant make thread, while in Africa raffia has often been used. In the 19th century advances in technology made it possible to produce many varieties of thread, and manufacturers were not slow to exploit this possibility. The situation then arose where a manufacturer produced a new thread and developed a type of embroidery which was named after it, for example lustrinc, manufactured by the firm of Vicars, and lustrine work which was developed by the London Guild of Needlework in 1903. Human hair has been used for embroidery at different times, notably in the printwork pictures of the late 18th century, and it is still used in some repairing techniques where invisibility is essential. See also Berlin wool (German wool, zephyr merino), chenille, cloisonné thread, coton perlé (star sylko, jewel embroidery), crewel wool (cruel, crewels), dacca silk (soie ovale), embroidery cotton, embroidery floss, filo floss (filo silk), filoselle, fleecy, floss silk (slave silk, sleave silk, sleided silk), flourishing thread (flax thread, lin floche), Guatemalan silk, Japanese gold, linen thread, lurex, lustrine work (for lustrine), Maltese silk (horsetail silk), mitorse silk, ONT, passing thread (passé thread, uni thread), plate, purl, purse silk (netting silk), sewing cotton, skanny, soft embroidery cotton, stranded cotton (art thread in US), tambour thread, tapestry wool (paternayan yarns in US).

emery cushion (emery bag, emery ball, strawberry) Small pincushion, often in the shape of a strawberry, which is filled with emery powder and usually kept in the workbox. If needles become damp and rusty they are run through the cushion to make them shiny and smooth again.

grenadier cap: an 18th century officer's cap belonging to the Honourable Artillery Company of London.

emery powder Form of carborundum, one of the hardest minerals known, which for needlework is ground into a fine powder and firmly packed into small *emery cushions for use in the sewing box.

endyti Greek Orthodox Church equivalent of the *altar frontal of the Western church. As the altar is free standing, the endyti covers the top and all four sides of the Holy Table. The cloth is of rich fabric and decorated, generally with an abstract design. (Johnstone 1967)

engageants In the 17th and 18th centuries deep ruffles on women's sleeves, and in the middle of the 19th century the white detachable undersleeves often worn under the big sleeves of dresses. These engageants were sometimes embroidered en suite with the collar in styles such as broderie anglaise (eyelet embroidery), darned net, and whitework.

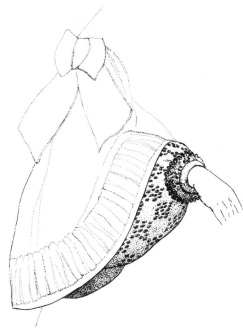

Engelbrecht, Martin (1684–1756) German publisher from Augsburg of patterns for small embroideries, especially those intended for chair seats. The designs included the Four Continents, vases of flowers, birds, and other scenes.

England The beginnings of English embroidery are lost in the past, but that good quality work was done from earliest times is known from references in deeds and other writings. The first style we know of today was the world-famous opus anglicanum, worked mostly for the church between 900 and 1500 on vestments, frontals, and hangings. It is characterised by a great sense of drama and vigorous drawing, and excellent use of space. During the 13th and 14th centuries it was exported to most of the countries of Europe, but during the 15th century the quality declined, and the Reformation in 1538 effectually stopped all embroidery for the church. Though there must have been domestic embroidery during the middle ages, none of it has come down to us and little is known about it.

The 16th century was a period of expansion, adventuring, and a new middle class, all reflected in embroidery. One type was blackwork, made popular by the Spanish-born Queen Katharine of Aragon and used throughout the century on clothes, accessories, and household articles. Other embroideries were often on satin worked with coloured silks and gold threads in designs with coiling stems enclosing garden flowers, with all spaces carefully filled in. In this century too the fashion for hangings and panels in tent stitch started, a fashion which has never lost its popularity right up till today. Worked on an openweave linen where stitches could be counted, these hangings were the domestic needlewoman's answer to the very expensive foreign tapestries for covering walls and making bed hangings.

The 17th century is notable for two styles of embroidery—*crewel work for hangings and raised or stump work for all kinds of decoration (on mirrors, cushions, cabinets, and caskets), and also for the number of samplers generally showing cutwork and lacis as well as geometrical satin stitch, double running, and other stitches. The crewel work of the 17th century was rather crude and heavy but in the 18th century it gradually became lighter in keeping with furniture and decoration, and also showed the influence of the East, especially of China. It was often worked in silk, sometimes combined with quilting. Towards the end of the 18th century whitework on muslin became fashionable for dresses and accessories such as aprons, kerchiefs, ruffles, and caps. It was often a combination of drawn fabric work with flat stitches, and the vogue for whitework, taking many different forms, lasted all through the 19th century. It was complementary to the other contemporary technique, Berlin woolwork, which probably had a wider acceptance than any style before or since, but in the last quarter of the century even it had at last to give way to the Morris-style crewel work and the many techniques and variations thought up by the thread and fabric manufacturers.

The early 20th century saw some excellent teachers who taught the use of stitches as the basis of design and fitness for purpose, a precept which had rather been forgotten, and with that in mind the use of linen as ground fabric for many different techniques became widespread almost to the point of monotony. Since the Second World War there has been a great revival of embroidery for the church and for the use of strong colour, different fabrics, and a great variety of threads. Partly because there is little place in the modern house for domestic embroideries, and even less in dress, there is a very experimental atmosphere, all things being tried with varying success, frequently made up into panels to hang on walls.

english canvas Modern single-thread canvas made from man-made fibres. Though strong, the roundness of the threads makes it rather difficult to work.

Englishwomen's Domestic Magazine Publication devoted to articles, stories, fashion, some craft work, and embroidery, which first came out in 1852. In 1880 it became the *Illustrated Household Journal and Englishwoman's Domestic Magazine,* and in 1881 it was merged with *The Milliner.*

enlarging There are occasions when it becomes necessary either to enlarge or to reduce the size of a design for embroidery. In order to keep the proportions correct, the design is first enclosed in a rectangle, the line AB is lengthened or shortened to the required length AE, and a line is drawn diagonally through AC and extended until it meets a line from E drawn parallel to BC. The new rectangle will be AEFG. Then both rectangles are squared up, using the same number of squares in each, and the design is redrawn in each corresponding square. Alternatively mechanical or photostat enlargers may be used.

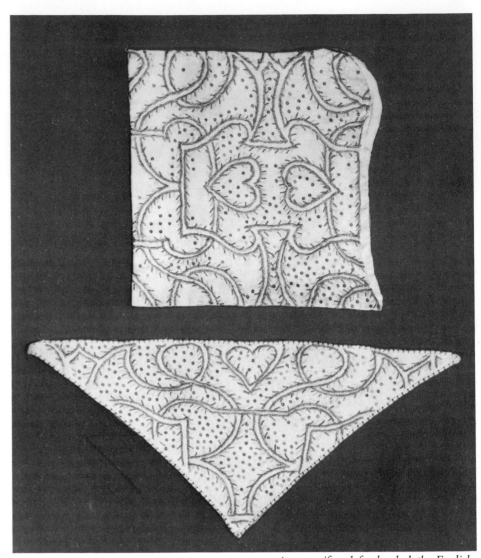

en suite: a coif and forehead cloth, English, c.1600.

en suite Phrase meaning in agreement or harmony, and used to describe a matching set. For example, a set comprising a chasuble, burse, veil, stole, and maniple, or a sofa and chairs, or a collar and cuffs are said to be embroidered en suite when the design is adapted to each shape, with the colouring, stitchery, and materials constant.

entomological pins Pins usually sold for pinning out dead butterfles and beetles, but which are ideal for embroidery as they are long and very very fine.

entre deux Phrase, literally meaning between two, used to describe a narrow insertion of embroidery or lace which has a sewing edge on both sides.

epaulettes Form of decoration or trimming on the shoulder of a dress, uniform, or livery, from the French *épaule* meaning shoulder. Originally the word referred to

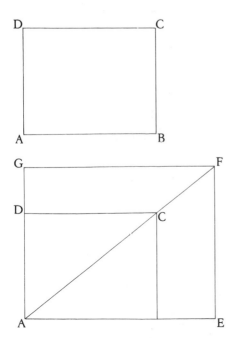

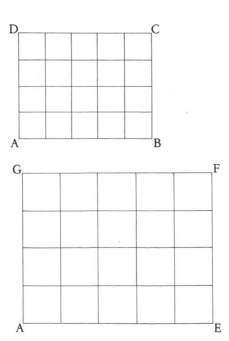

the plate which protected the shoulder in armour, and thence to the insignia of rank worn on the shoulder, but the term now has a much wider use.

epigonation Stiffened square suspended from the girdle by one corner, worn by bishops in the Greek Orthodox church. It derived from the ceremonial cloth or handkerchief which in the West developed into the maniple, and it is usually embroidered. (Johnstone 1967)

epigonation: a Byzantine representation of the Washing of the Feet.

epimanikia Cuffs worn by bishops in the Greek Orthodox church, derived from the ornament or apparel on the wrists of the *sticharion or alb. (Johnstone 1967)

epitaphios: Slavonic, late 18th century.

epitaphios In the Greek Orthodox church, a veil which covers the chalice and paten (*aër), or a large veil decorated with the Body of the Crucified Christ which is carried in procession in Good Friday services. (Johnstone 1967)

epitrachilion The *stole worn by all priests and bishops in the Greek Orthodox church. Unlike the stoles of the West, the two halves of the epitrachilion are joined down their length with only enough left undone to allow the garment to be slipped over the head of the priest. Its whole length is heavily embroidered.

epitrachilion: a Serbian example, 17th century.

ermine stitch Detached filling stitch made up of a straight stitch with a diagonal cross stitch superimposed, the whole being supposed to resemble the tail of an ermine.

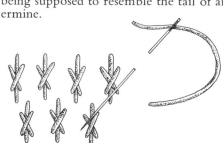

Eskimo Group of peoples of nothern Canada, Alaska, Greenland, and eastern Siberia. As protection from the intense cold, most Eskimo clothing is loose fitting with an insulating layer of air, has a hood, and is made of fur or birdskins.

Eskimo beadwork Decoration used mostly on the soft, warm, inner, Eskimo garments made of birdskin and worn under the outer fur clothing. Among the known examples from the Hudson Bay area is one embroidered with a profusion of beads in geometric designs borrowed from the Indians. There is also a west Greenland eiderskin garment with a high collar worn covered by a silk or cotton jumper over which the large beaded collar falls loosely, and a Bering Straits wedding dress of caribou hide with the fur inside ·which is solidly decorated with beadwork, fringes, and teeth, and has three wooden amulets suspended from the neck. See also dickey beads.

Eskimo fur work Loose fitting Eskimo garments made of fur and often decorated. They are usually well made, and are sewn in small regular stitches with split sinew thread in running stitch, overcasting, and blind stitch in which the needle is taken only halfway through the skin. Eskimo women wear thick, skin thimbles on their index finger and sew from right to left. They are not allowed to sew deer skins during the seal-hunting season, nor do any sewing during the caribou-hunting season, as the *caribou is considered to be sensitive to women. Styles, techniques, and designs vary with the region, as do the skins used: sealskin is strong, reasonably waterproof, but in the very cold weather not warm enough; bearskin is very warm, waterproof, but heavy when wet; fox skin is warm and light, but fragile; and caribou and deerskin are liked for their suppleness, warmth, and sturdiness. Some fur garments are now being replaced by duffle cloth. (Birket-Smith 1935)

Eskimo laced edge stitch Variation of the running stitch used by the Eskimos and Aleuts to bind together the seams of the sealgut and fishskin parkas or anoraks, making them waterproof. Caribou and walrus sinew was used as thread.

Eskimo pieced fur work Designs formed by inserts, appliqúe, or mosaic in furs of contrasting colours, sometimes embellished with embroidery, that were devised by the Eskimos to achieve a decorative effect in their fur clothing. Style, technique, and design vary with the region: the Caribou and Central Eskimos obtain a cheerful impression with white insertion and fringes on the velvety-

brown summer skin of reindeer; the Pacific join horizontal bands made from skins of small seabirds or marmots into a long parka with a yoke covering the shoulder and a high, stiff collar edging the neck; the Aleuts apply bands of seal gullet with hair embroidery; and in west Greenland, skin mosaics are made out of skins cut into narrow stripes and squares and sewn to a foundation to form variegated patterns. There is a collection of different kinds of pieced fur work in the National Museum in Copenhagen. (Birket-Smith 1935) See also dickey beads, Eskimo fur work.

etamine Loosely-woven fabric originally used as *bolting cloth. It is frequently the ground fabric for the embroideries of Algeria, and in America it is used for dress goods and curtains.

etching embroidery When *printwork was revived in the late 19th century it was known as etching embroidery. It was very similar, using mostly landscape subjects, but with the grounds often filled with fine french knots to simulate the stippling in engraving. There was another revival in the 1930s when rather different subjects, which might be called 'tourists' England', were used. They were usually buildings such as cathedrals, Shakespeare's birthplace, or the Tower of London, and a kit was sold with the subjects traced on linen and a skein of black thread with which to follow the lines of the etching. This was an early example of the embroidery kit.

etching silk see silk twist.

etui Ornamental case designed to hold necessary feminine articles such as thimble, scissors, bodkins, and toothpick. The word seems to have been first used in the early 17th century.

evangelists The four evangelists, authors of the four gospels, Matthew, Mark, Luke, and John, have been represented many times in embroidery. They have been shown as apostles in human form and also by their symbols: St Matthew the Man, St Mark the Lion, St Luke the Ox, and St John the Eagle (Ezekial 1.10, Revelations 4.7).

evenweave canvas (evenweave linen) Linen or other fibre woven with single, double, or multiple threads, which has a mesh sufficiently clearly defined to make the counting of the threads possible. Evenweave linens are most frequently used for household articles (such as place mats and tablecloths) worked in cross stitch, double running, Assisi embroidery, and other techniques where threads must be counted.

exchanges for woman's work American charitable organisations founded in the late 19th century to enable women to help themselves financially. The New York Exchange for Woman's Work was founded in 1878 by Candace *Wheeler and provided an outlet for homemade foods and handicraft items: quilts, children's clothes and toys, needlework items, jams, cakes etc. The exchanges, located throughout the US, are still active.

eye and eyelet stitches Stitches radiating out from a centre. They can either be large, or very small as in the eyelet stitch so popular in the 18th and 19th century samplers, often used for marking linen. They may be worked by the counted thread or simply oversewn or buttonholed round a single mesh or, in the case of tightly-woven fabric, round a hole made by a stiletto.

eyelet 1. The hole made in material for passing a lace or point through. These are strengthened by overcasting the edge with thread or by inserting a metal grommet. 2. Hole made purely for decorative purposes in embroidery and finished either by overcasting or blanket stitching the edge. The type of embroidery in which eyelet holes chiefly figure is broderie anglaise (eyelet embroidery) and Madeira work.

eyelet embroidery see broderie anglaise.

eyelet plate see attachments.

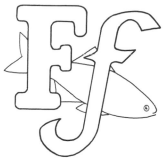

fabric That which is manufactured from thread interlaced to form a continuous web. This includes fabrics produced by weaving, knitting, netting, lacemaking etc. Also included, though not webs, are non-woven stuffs such as felt and bonded interlinings. Any type of thread or fibre can form a fabric, so leathers and hides have to be classed here as materials. The history of fabrics starts in remotest antiquity with very primitive weaving, and it has continued unbroken with the emphasis at the present time on those manufactured from man-made rather than from natural yarns.

facing The part of a garment or article which is stitched onto an edge and turned back onto the wrong side in order to finish and neaten the edge. Where a decorative edge is required a facing is sewn onto the wrong side, turned over onto the right side, and stitched down in a shape such as a scallop with a decorative stitch (*Italian or *Portuguese hem). Facings are particularly used round the necks and armholes of dresses, and on articles such as tray mats when for some reason a hem is not considered a suitable finish. With uniforms and liveries the facing at cuff and neck is frequently of a different colour and fabric from the garment. See also false hem.

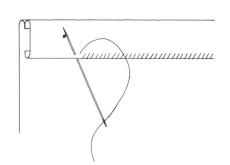

faggoting 1. 'The process by which a number of threads in the material are drawn out and a few of the cross threads tied together in the middle, hence the work done in this manner' (OED). 2. Name given to a number of insertion stitches used to make *openwork seams. They are all based on plain faggoting or twisted insertion stitch. This must not be confused with faggot stitch which is both a drawn fabric stitch and a drawn thread stitch.

faggotting 1.

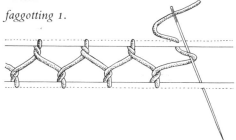

fair linen cloth In the Anglican church, the cloth which covers the table at the service of Holy Communion. In the rubric for the service are the words 'The Table at the Communion-time having a fair white linen cloth upon it . . .' This cloth is always the exact width of the table and hangs nearly to the ground at the sides. It has a narrow hem along its

fair linen cloth: lacis border, English, 1632.

length and a wide hem at the hanging ends. On the cloth, corresponding to the exact centre and the four corners of the table, five small crosses are embroidered, and there may or may not be an embroidered border at either end. The work is always done with a white embroidery cotton.

falconry Probably introduced into Britain by the Romans, falconry remained the sport of the nobility until the middle of the 17th century when, with the advent of sporting guns, it gradually declined in popularity. The furniture associated with it is the glove, pouch, hood, and lure, and many of these are beautifully embroidered.

falconry: hawking furniture from Wroxton Abbey, 1603–19.

faldstool (prayer desk, litany stool) Literally a movable folding stool with no arms, but in the ecclesiastical sense it is a small prayer desk with a kneeling bench which can be moved to the appropriate place in the church. It is often used for reciting the litany and is therefore known as a litany stool. They sometimes have a fall or hanging in front which may be embroidered en suite with the pulpit fall.

fall 1. The hanging, which may be embroidered, in front of the reading desk on the pulpit or in front of the faldstool. 2. Cascade of lace or embroidered muslin, especially from the neck or wrist in some costumes (both male and female). 3. Curtain or veil hanging from a bonnet. 4. Flat collar worn in the 17th century, sometimes called a falling band. See also band.

falling band see band.

false embroidery Technique practised by some tribes of North American Indians of ornamenting textiles by wrapping a separate decorative material, usually moosehair, round the exposed part of a weft in the process of twined weaving. As each weft thread is brought forward in the weaving to cross over the warp, a moosehair is wound tightly round it several times. The length of hair remaining then passes on to the next crossing of weft over warp, and this gives a pattern on the right side, with all the ends of the moosehair left on the wrong side.

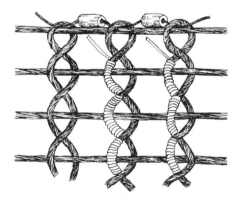

false hem see facing.

false quilting (flat quilting, Queen Anne quilting) Entirely unpadded quilting, formerly always worked on linen, which may or may not have a layer of butter muslin underneath. In the late 17th and early 18th centuries the silk thread was generally yellow, but later various colours and *chinoiserie designs were used. The stitch is a firm back stitch. Although this type of quilting takes longer to work than wadded or Italian, it is very rewarding and is still used for articles such as tea and coffee cosies.

fan: English, early 19th century.

fan Accessory used either to make a cooling current of air or as a decorative adjunct to an outfit. Although they were and are frequently used by women, they were also used by men in Europe in the 18th century, and in the East. As a dress accessory the fan has taken several forms. In the 16th and again in the late 19th and 20th centuries it might be a feather mounted on a stick. More common is a folding leaf shape fastened to sticks with guards either end. The leaf can be made of any suitable material such as silk, paper, or chicken skin, and when made of a silk fabric it is often embroidered. However the constant opening and shutting makes these embroidered fans easily damaged and few have lasted in good condition. (Colour illustration p 87)

fancy goods Late 19th and 20th century term describing items made specifically for show and decoration, such as collars, tidies, cushion covers, aprons, and other handmade needlework. It also refers to such items, whether hand or machine made, when sold at fêtes and sales of work.

fancy work Term describing embroidery and allied domestic crafts done by women at home. At different periods it has been either polite or derogatory. An advertisement of 23 June 1804 in the *Norwich Mercury* reads: 'To the Ladies/ Fancy Works/In Silk, Crewel, Lambs Wool, Printwork, Crape and Indian Wafer/Henry Sass/Begs leave to acquaint Ladies and his Friends in general that he has a large assortment of subjects drawn for the different Fancy Works and also all kinds of Ornaments with proper material to finish them, ready for their inspection.'

fanny frame Frame mounted on a metal plate which slides under the seated embroiderer, whose weight holds the

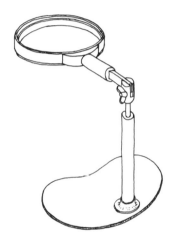

frame steady at a convenient height above the lap. See also embroidery frame, embroidery hoop.

fanon see maniple.

fashion plates Idealised images of fashionable clothes, mostly for women but also for men and children, published from the 18th century onwards in magazines, almanacs, and pocket books. The plates give accurate details of the garments but they always show women as they would like to look, not as they will look. The first publication devoted entirely to fashion was *Le Cabinet des Modes* in 1785, but other magazines with some fashion plates were *The Lady's Magazine* (1770), Heideloff's *The Gallery of Fashion* (1794), Graham's *American Monthly Magazine of Literature, Art, and Fashion* (1841), *Englishwoman's Domestic Magazine* (1853), and *Godey's Lady's Book* (1830). Fashion plates generally clearly show whether a garment is embroidered, and many needlework details such as the rouleau so fashionable in the early 19th century can be studied in them. (Moore 1971)

fastentuch see hungertuch.

Faulkner Family consisting of Charles, Kate, and Lucy, associated with the firm of Morris, Marshall, Faulkner & Co, in Red Lion Square, London in 1861. Charles was one of the partners and Kate and Lucy worked as artists, designers, and craftswomen on tiles, wallpapers, and embroideries. (*Catalogue of the Morris Collection* 1969) See also Morris, William.

feather One of the shapes most commonly used in quilting. It is found on both English and American quilts in all sorts of ways—straight, curved, running, and in a circle. In quilting it is important that the design used should be fairly small and compact so that the ground can be evenly covered, and a feather with its fronds lends itself to these requirements.

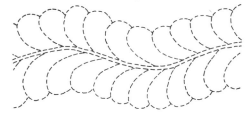

feather cape (feather robe, feather mantle) Ceremonial garment worked in elaborate *featherwork, usually in areas with an abundance of bright-plumaged birds, notably Hawaii, Polynesia, Mexico, New Zealand, and pre-Columbian South America. In Hawaii, the great circular capes worn by the chiefs were tailored from a small-mesh, net fabric covered with brilliant feathers, which was cut into segments to form the circle. They were usually made from the red feathers of the iwii and apapani, and decorated with the yellow of the o-o and mamo birds (green was rare). Feathers were graded so that small ones could be placed over large ones, and were worked so delicately that the final product was like velvet or plush. In Mexico, not only did chieftains wear feather robes, but warriors wore a cotton shirt to which feathers were applied, and carried a feather mosaic war shield on their backs as an emblem, with designs of

gods, animals, and secular and religious objects. In pre-Columbian South America, brilliant iridescent feathers were applied to fine cotton in layered, horizontal rows. Every feather quill was bent double and fastened by means of a string, then fastened to the cloth with a second string so that the feather tips were even. Sometimes featherwork was applied to garments pre-woven to exact size, sometimes to large mantles in rectangles of only two colours, and sometimes to hats and ponchos in mosaics of brilliant colour and design. (Keleman 1969, Bushnell 1963)

feather stitch (briar stitch, single coral stitch) The basic stitch of a large group of looped stitches. It is a line stitch and is worked by making a blanket stitch alternately either side of a line, in each case the needle coming out on the line.

featherwork 1. The application of feathers in a recognisable pattern by gluing, knotting, weaving, or sewing to a base of different material—cloth, wood, paper, leather, or bark—to form decoration for tools, arms, religious articles, and clothing. It has been found in southern and eastern Asia, Indonesia, Oceania, and the two Americas, but reached a high point in Polynesia and Central and South America. Feathers are glued or sewn singly or in bunches to a smooth base, and are positioned close together in overlapping rows like roof slates to conceal the quills of the row below. The craft is still practised with great skill by some South American Indians, and colour combinations and technique identify the area of origin. The contemporary Tupinamba Indian ceremonial feather capes of red ibis follow a long tradition of workmanship and colour, and they were favourite souvenirs of the 16th century sailors who took many of them home to Europe. In

the 18th and 19th centuries in UK and US, feather muffs, capes, and hats were very popular and were made in the same techniques as those practised by the tribes of the southern hemisphere, using either imported or local feathers, while in the late 19th and early 20th century they were also made into articles such as valances, brackets, and screens. Today some poultry farms, especially those which breed and sell birds with exotic plumage, have a sideline of featherwork, and delightfully decorative objects are made. Two other names for featherwork are feather mosaic, feather embroidery. See feather cape, New Zealand, quetzel. 2. See long and short stitch.

Federal American post-revolutionary period c 1790-1830, of strong central government, westward expansion, and classical influences in dress, architecture and the decorative arts. It was an era of Moravian embroideries and mourning embroideries to the memory of George Washington, samplers, pieced and broderie perse quilts, bed rugs, white embroidered apparel and accessories, darned net and tambour work.

feed The part of a domestic sewing machine which moves the fabric along from stitch to stitch. It consists of parallel rows of bent metal teeth, between which the needle passes.

feed cover plate see cover plate.

Felbrigge, Anne de The owner of the *Felbrigge Psalter* and probably the embroiderer who worked the binding. This psalter was written in the 13th century and the binding dates from the 14th century. Anne de Felbrigge was the daughter of Sir Simon de Felbrigge KG, standard bearer to Richard II. She was a nun at the convent of Minoresses at Bruisyard in Suffolk and it is very likely that she worked the cover there. It has a representation of the Annunciation on the front and of the Crucifixion on the back. The figures are worked in split stitch and the ground is in gold underside couching. (Davenport 1899) See also bookbindings.

fell To stitch down the wider of the two edges left after trimming a seam so that it lies flat over the other edge and leaves a smooth surface on the underside.

felling see hemming.

fell seam see run and fell seam.

felt Non-woven material formed by the close compression of woollen fibres. It has the advantage that it can be cut without fraying and therefore is eminently suitable for all forms of applied work. As it is easy to work it is frequently used for teaching embroidery to children. Another form of felt can be made by knitting and then soaking and shrinking the knitting so that the fibres of the wool become so densely matted that the article is impervious to rain. This method was used for men's caps in Tudor England. Some Eskimo tribes wear felt stockings under their sealskin leggings with a turnover top embroidered in brightly coloured designs.

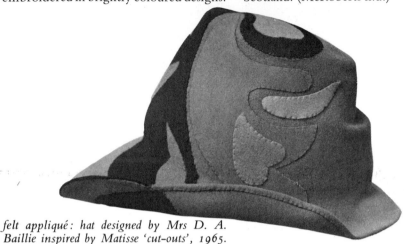

felt appliqué: hat designed by Mrs D. A. Baillie inspired by Matisse 'cut-outs', 1965.

felt appliqué The decoration of felt by the addition of variously coloured fabrics, including felt, in pattern. This has been a popular technique from very early times until the present day, and was particularly used by the nomadic tribes which roamed Russia from the Balkans to the Gobi Desert from about 200 BC to AD 220. Felt, which was extensively worn by all wandering cattle-breeding tribes, was used by them for religious and ceremonial practices even after silk became available. Genghis Khan and his successors were crowned with felt, and in the burial grounds of *Noin Ula a large applied felt carpet had the place of honour under the coffin. A collection of native felt products was excavated from the *Pizirik burial site, among them a wall hanging and ten saddle covers outstanding for their appliqué. (Salmony 1942)

ferret Narrow binding or tape. When made of silk it is known as Italian ferret, but it is more often made of cotton and sometimes of worsted. The phrase 'green ferret' has much the same meaning as 'red tape'.

Fetternear banner Unique religious banner of the 16th century. Embroidered on linen it shows the Homage of Pity—Christ wounded with the *Instruments of the Passion. The central image is surrounded by a border representing the beads of a rosary, and then by another border based on a cordelière or friar's girdle. From the heraldry it can be deduced that the banner was worked between 1515 and 1522 and that it was intended for the collegiate church of St Giles, Edinburgh, for the use of the Holy Blood Confraternity. This banner is, by half a century, the earliest piece of known Scottish embroidery, and is also the only known pre-Reformation ecclesiastical banner in Great Britain. It is now on loan to the National Museum of Antiquities of Scotland. (McRoberts n.d.)

fibre The thread or filament which is spun and then woven to make textiles. It may be animal, vegetable, mineral, or synthetic. Animal threads are represented by alpaca, mohair, wool, and silk; vegetable by cotton, flax, pineapple, jute, hemp, and leaf fibre; mineral by asbestos, glass, gold, silver, and aluminium; and synthetic by lurex, rayon, nylon, and others.

fibre silk (fibersilk) In America a term meaning artificial or imitation silk, formerly used to designate rayon.

fichu Neck covering worn in the 19th century. They were light half-handkerchiefs of net, lace, or muslin, often decorated with embroidery.

fig leaf Small black satin apron worn over dresses between 1860 and 1870. Usually embroidered and edged with black lace, they were worn at home over morning dress, and were purely decorative with no utility value at all.

figure stitch see romanian stitch.

filé see ply.

filet see net laces, lacis.

filé thread see tambour (number 3).

filling stitches Group of stitches used either singly or together to fill a space. They are all worked on the surface and may be light or heavy in appearance. In 17th century crewel work they were frequently used as filling for the large leaves and flowers so popular then which have never really gone out of fashion. Often the same stitches can be adapted as drawn fabric stitches. There are two groups. Single stitches: dot; ermine filling; fly filling; sheaf filling; star filling. Ground cover stitches: darning and variations: damask darning, pattern darning; diamond filling; honeycomb filling; open buttonhole filling and variations: fancy buttonhole filling, knotted buttonhole filling, paced buttonhole filling; plaid filling; trellis couching; wave filling.

filo floss (filo silk) Pure silk, two-ply thread which is loosely twisted and fairly thick. It is not easy to use as the thread is quickly roughened by any minute snag, but it is excellent for blending shades of colour in long and short stitch and was much used in ecclesiastical embroidery.

filoselle (bourre de soie) Thread made from the waste products of the silk worm and therefore cheaper than filo floss. It is stranded, easy to use, and can be described as the silk version of *stranded cotton.

fine-drawing 'Fine drawing is sowing two pieces of cloth together so curiously that it shall not be seen where the sowing is' (Holme 1688). This kind of repairing was known as fine-drawing until the 20th when it became called invisible mending.

finger Measure of length equal to $4\frac{1}{2}$ inches (11.4 centimetres). It was in use until the end of the 19th century among needleworkers and anyone connected with the textile trade.

finger shield Shield worn on the first finger of the left hand to protect it from being pricked. It resembles a thimble with one half cut away. It is also known as a finger guard.

firescreen Generally taken to mean a movable screen used for keeping the heat of the fire from the face. They can stand (*pole screen), hang (*banner firescreen), or be held in the hand (*handscreen). However some firescreens were embroidered, glazed, and framed, and in the first half of the 20th century were meant to stand in the cold fireplace during the summer and other times when the fire was not lit.

firescreen: 'The Sicilian' in Berlin woolwork, English, 19th century.

Fisherton-de-la-Mere: detail of a coverlet, English, early 20th century.

Fisherton-de-la-Mere Group of Wiltshire embroiderers, trained by Mrs Arthur Newall, who made and sold embroideries between about 1890 and 1923. Mrs Newall was a talented embroiderer who became interested in and studied the counted threadwork which had long been done in Italy. She evolved a style of embroidery based on the Italian which was adapted to English tastes, and taught it to workers who lived near her home at Fisherton-de-la-Mere in Wiltshire. She taught her pupils the basic stitches, gave them linen and thread, and then left them to arrange the patterns and decide the stitches. If the finished work reached her very high standard it was sold. This industry, which employed about forty people, continued until her death in 1923. See also Home Arts and Industries Association.

fishing lady embroideries American needlework pictures, probably mid 18th century, worked near Boston. Little is known of the picture source for these works. There are twelve known examples: five are chimney pieces with a fishing lady and her escort as well as other small figures, trees, and animals; the other seven are smaller with only the lady and her escort. One of the best known is in the Museum of Fine Arts in Boston.

fishscale embroidery Popular late 19th century embroidery. The scales of fish such as carp, perch, and goldfish were prepared by steeping in cold water, making two holes in the base of the scale, and tinting them if necessary. They were stitched to a ground of silk, satin, or velvet in overlapping patterns to make reproductions of butterflies, birds, or flowers. Details were added with silk embroidery.

Fitzwilliam Museum (Cambridge, England) Contains an excellent collection of embroideries, especially rich in samplers and in work from the Greek Islands.

Fitzwilliam Museum: an English cutwork sampler, 17th century.

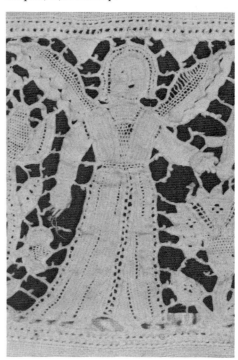

flame stitch see florentine stitch.

flannel Loosely-woven napped fabric, generally made from wool but sometimes from cotton or a union of wool and cotton. The softness of the fabric makes it easy to embroider with a fairly thick thread and so attractive effects can be simply and quickly made.

flannel seam Join used when making garments in flannel, especially for babies and small children. As flannel is rather thick and does not easily fray, the seam is made by joining two edges with running stitch, cutting one edge down to half the width of the other, flattening the seam, and then fastening the wide edge to the garment with herringbone stitch. No turning is necessary.

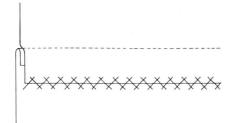

flat-covered buttons Small linen buttons suitable for children's clothing etc. Six thicknesses of linen are cut into a circle and then tacked into a pile. A hole is made through the centre, and radiating from this, tailor's buttonhole stitch is worked. A small buttonhole loop at the back forms a shank. (Armes 1939)

flat embroidery see machine embroidery.

flat fell seam Resembles run and fell seam and can be worked either by hand or machine. To work it a plain seam is run with the wrong sides of the fabric together, one turning is cut down to half the width of the other, the turnings are

flat fell seam: used on the original Star Spangled Banner.

pressed to one side, and the raw edge turned under and hemmed. It is generally used in the making of flags, men's shirts, and other items where strength is required.

flat quilting see false quilting.

flat stitches Group used as outline or filling stitches which have a flat appearance, though they may be interlaced in working. The stitches are algerian eye (star eyelet); arrowhead; basket; basket filling; bosnian (zigzag); brick; *burden; cable outline; chevron; *darning and variation: *double darning (pessante); dot (rice grain, seeding, single seed, speckling); eyelet; fern; fishbone and variations: open fishbone, overlapping herringbone, raised fishbone; flat (croatian flat); *herringbone (catch, mossoul, russian cross, witch) and variations: *closed (double back, oriental, shadow), double (indian herringbone); japanese; leaf; *long and short (brick, embroidery 'feather', half-work, Irish, plumage, opus plumarium, shading, surface, tapestry shading); persian; portuguese stem; *satin and variation: sham satin (surface); straight (single satin, spoke); *stem (stalk, kensington) and variations: *crewel (outline), cable stem; zigzag.

flattened canvas Embroidery canvas which had its round threads flattened by passing it through a roller. This made it easier to draw directly onto the canvas, but according to Miss Lambert (1843) it is a process 'rendering the work more expensive, and which does not appear to be productive of any beneficial result'.

flax The plant *Linum usitatissimum* from which linen is made. After the stalks have been cut, they are laid in bundles in water until the outer fibres have rotted away. This is known as retting. The fine fibres left are then spun and woven into linen. In colonial America it took 18 months from the planting of the seed to the finished homespun.

flax thread see flourishing thread.

fleecy Type of wool thread used mainly for darning and knitting in the 19th century. Miss Lambert (1843) describes fleecy as being of any ply from 2 to 12, and considers it a good and useful wool, but Caulfeild & Saward (1882) say that it is less expensive than Berlin wool, but rough and unsuitable for embroidery, so perhaps by then the quality had deteriorated.

fleur-de-lis The flower of the iris plant, and the royal emblem of France. As well as being used in heraldry, it has always been a popular motif in embroidery.

flock Coarse tufts and waste of wool and cotton. It is sometimes used as the wadding in quilted armour, and as the interlining in very cheap quilts.

florentine embroidery (bargello work, hungarian point) Type of embroidery worked on canvas, which is characterised by a wavy or flame-shaped design. This is one of the cases where the type of embroidery and the name of the stitch are inextricably mixed. Florentine embroidery has a universal appeal and it is found chiefly in Hungary, North Italy, and Great Britain. Its origins are still rather obscure but it is supposed to be the result of a 15th century Hungarian king marrying an Italian princess. Italian Renaissance craftsmen were invited to the Court of Hungary, and there was a fusion of Hungarian motifs and Italian silks and interpretations. It is worked on fine or coarse canvas in mercerised cotton, silk, or wool. It is eminently suitable for chair seats, stools, handbags, and many other articles, as it is hardwearing when worked in wool, and its contrasting but shaded bands of colour are extremely decorative. This, with the comparative simplicity of technique, probably explains its popularity in so many countries for so many years. (Colour illustration p 88) See also fourway bargello.

florentine embroidery: an American hand screen, late 18th century.

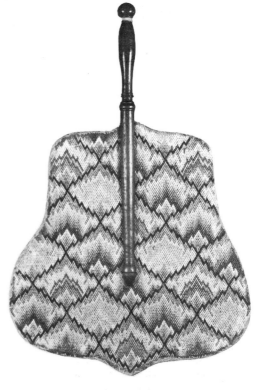

florentine stitch (bargello stitch, flame stitch, cushion stitch, irish stitch, hungary stitch) The stitch used in florentine embroidery or, as it is sometimes called, bargello work. It consists of an upright straight stitch, generally taken up over four threads and down two threads a certain number of times according to the pattern, when it drops again. Many variations can be made by altering the length of the stitch, the steepness of the drop, and the shading of the colours used.

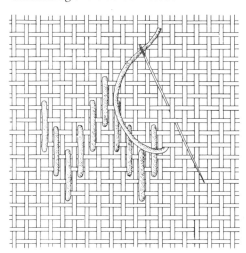

floss embroidery Form of work using *floss silk, the thread employed in some of the embroideries of India and China, some ecclesiastical embroidery, and any household embroidery where the article will not get hard wear and where delicate shading is required.

floss silk (slave silk, sleave silk, sleided silk) Raw and untwisted silk thread which can be split down into very fine filaments. It is made from the soft external covering of the silkworm's cocoon. As it is untwisted the threads lie closely and evenly together, making it very suitable for laid work and long and short stitch where shades must blend in evenly. Though now generally known as floss silk it was called sleided or sleave silk in the 16th century, and the best known quotation mentioning it comes from *Macbeth* (act II, scene 1): 'Sleep that knits up the ravell'd sleave of care'.

flourish To adorn, decorate, or embellish. Among the New Year gifts to Elizabeth I (1578) is 'vale of networke florisshed with gold' (Nichols 1823).

flourishing thread (flax thread, lin floche) Soft silky thread of flax made in different weights and colours, and used since the 18th century for mending linen and damask as well as for embroidery. Work done in this thread was taught in Boston (Massachusetts) as early as 1716.

Flowerers: all the fillings on this bonnet differ, Scottish, 19th century.

Flowerers, The The name given to Scottish, and sometimes Irish, girls and women who embroidered or 'flowered' muslin in the late 18th and the first half of the 19th centuries. This term includes work done with a hook on a tambour frame as well as pulled fabric work and Ayrshire work. (Swain 1955)

flowers While flowers appear as designs and motifs for embroidery all over the world, generally in a stylised or conventional form, the English, well known for their love of gardening, have used them more frequently and in a more naturalistic style than most other countries. In every generation flowers have been worked in some technique or other.

Never was this more true than in Tudor England, when all the plants then known were used as designs, with coiling stems and leaves, or as slips in shaped frames or lozenges. Vegetables and fruit were as popular as flowers, especially the pea which is found in Elizabethan as well as Stuart embroideries, and from the Hardwick Hall inventories (1601) is 'imbrodered with silver, gold and pearls with sivines [raspberries] and woodbines' (Boynton 1971). Portraits of the 16th and 17th centuries show many garments embroidered with flowers, both formal and informal. They were rampant in the large crewel work hangings of the 17th century as well as in the raised work embroideries. In the 18th century they were

flowers: an American embroidered picture of a vase of flowers.

worked in tambour stitch on muslin as well as in silk on bedcovers and other household effects, and in canvas work on chairs and sofas. The 19th century Berlin woolwork often had large, overblown bunches of flowers, especially in the middle of the century; more formalised flowers were worked in darned net, Limerick, Carritkmacross, and Ayrshire embroidery. The latter part of the present century has seen a return of interest in plant forms as much as in the flowers themselves, and there are no signs that their use as the basis of design in embroidery will ever cease. See American crewel work.

fly-fringe Knots and bunches of floss silk attached in pattern to a gimp cord. It was a favourite decoration on 18th century dresses and christening gowns and was used on the garment rather than hanging from the edge of it.

fly running Method of working running stitch by hand where several stitches are picked up by the point of the needle before the thread is pulled through. Its advantage is in its speed.

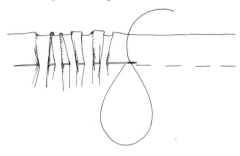

foot 1. The part of a sewing machine which holds the fabric down onto the *footplate and through which the needle works. It is sometimes called the presser foot. 2. Measure of length equal to one-third of a yard or 12 inches. Its metric equivalent is 30.48 centimetres.

footing Folded edging of plain net. The raw edges are often decoratively joined to the garment with insertions or entre deux.

footplate The metal plate over the bobbin which surrounds the feed on a domestic sewing machine. It is also called a throat plate or cover plate.

footstool Although still used today, footstools were most popular last century. They were useful for raising the feet from the draughty floors of the large, badly-heated Victorian houses, and were often the recipients of Berlin woolwork covers, as well as covers in crewel work and other suitable techniques of the 19th century.

forehead cloth (cross-cloth) Tri-angular piece of fabric worn in conjunction with the *coif in the 16th and early 17th centuries. Its exact use is uncertain, but the number still in existence, both for women and small children, show that they were often embroidered en suite with the coif and were definitely considered a requisite part of dress.

forehead cloth: embroidered in silk and metal threads on linen, English, early 17th century.

forepart Panel of embroidered fabric mounted on a petticoat which showed when the skirt parted in front. It was used in the 16th century, was interchangeable, and sometimes formed a set with the sleeves and *partlet. As they were separate pieces they could be and often were given as presents, and one of the New Year gifts to Elizabeth I (1588) is 'By Sir Roberte Southwell, foareparte of lawne cutwork, florished with squares with owes' (Nichols 1823).

forepart: shown on the lady's dress in this embroidered picture.

foundation The coloured threads laid across a motif or shape ready to be tied or couched down. This is the basic technique of *laidwork.

foundation fabric The fabric, generally stretched on a frame, onto which other materials and threads are applied, laid, couched, or otherwise fastened. It may or may not not be visible when the work is finished.

fourchette Narrow piece of material which, in a glove, runs down each side of the finger from tip to base.

four-way bargello: an American 20th century example.

four-sided stitch see punch stitch.

four-way bargello (mitered bargello) Type of *florentine embroidery revived in the mid-20th century which was originally popular in the 18th century, especially in America, for working on rug borders and book covers. It uses the 18th century stitches and techniques but instead of being worked horizontally and vertically it radiates in four directions from a central point.

frame see embroidery frame, embroidery hoop, fanny frame.

frame work (travail au métier) Type of work in which wool or silk is wound round pegs and across a frame and, where the threads cross, they are tied together with needle and thread. Sometimes embroidered decoration is added. Although it can scarcely be classed as embroidery or plain sewing, it is included because it involves a certain amount of tying down with silk threads. It is worked on a d'oyley or shawl frame, and was a popular pastime in the 19th century for making mats, doilies etc.

France Country probably more generally thought of in connection with the finest tapestries, woven fabrics (especially silks), and clothes, rather than embroideries. French work is noted for its sense of style and design combined with meticulous workmanship. In part this comes from a long tradition of royal patronage with the setting up of schools at an early date—Anne of Brittany (1477–1514) established one, as did Catherine de' Medici in 1551, and also *Mary Queen of Scots when she was Dauphine of France—and partly from the close association with Italy and its painters and craftsmen. France possibly interpreted the Chinese style (*chinoiserie) better than any other European country, and French rococo embroideries of the 18th century have a lightness and gaiety unequalled elsewhere.

Most costume collections contain men's waistcoats of the 18th century professionally worked in France, and these, often on a pearl grey satin with floss silk embroidery in delicate colourings, are delightful things. In the 19th and 20th centuries France has been best known for household linens, children's and babies' dresses, and lingerie, all in fine whitework with hemstitching and drawn thread stitches, while French couture embroideries are among the best in the world. (Colour illustration p 97)

fray (frazzle) To wear out by rubbing. As such it is applicable to the loose threads which appear when a hole is made in cloth. The word is also used of a loosely-woven fabric in which the weft comes away from the warp when cut, but this is more properly called *ravelling.

frazzle see fray.

freedom quilt The only type of quilt made specifically for men. It was pieced by the friends and family of a young man in America to celebrate either his coming of age or the end of his indenture as an apprentice, and he put it away ready for his marriage. The custom died out about 1825 but was briefly revived in the 1870s. (Finley 1929)

free hand and free motion embroidery see machine embroidery.

french and overcast seam Join used in fine lingerie. The two pieces of fabric are run together on the right side as in a *french seam, the fabric is turned, but instead of another line of running on the wrong side, a line of fine close overcast stitches, sometimes in a coloured or embroidery silk, is worked on the right side.

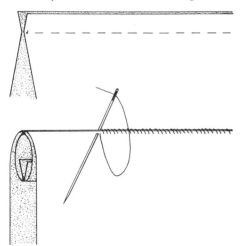

french canvas (patent canvas, cotton canvas) Cotton canvas made in France, England, and Germany in the 19th century. Miss Lambert (1843) considers that

from France to be the best, and the German, with each tenth thread yellow, the most limp and difficult to use but she recommends it for its evenness of mesh. The modern canvas called french is excellent quality, unstarched, single-thread, brown linen.

french chalk Kind of talc, sometimes used for removing grease spots from light fabrics, and also used for pouncing through the pricked holes in a design. See also prick, pounce.

french dot see french knot.

French embroidery Type of *whitework popular in France in the 1850s, and revived in America about 1900. The designs were similar to those of broderie anglaise (eyelet embroidery) but instead of cutting out petals these were filled in with padded satin stitch. (Levey 1971)

french fell seam see overhanded seam.

french gathering The gathering of fabric with an uneven stitch, long on top and short below, so that when the fabric is pulled up the fullness appears to be less on top and more underneath. (Picken 1939).

french knot (french dot, knotted stitch, twisted knot stitch, wound stitch) Useful stitch consisting of small isolated knots, which can also be closely grouped. It is frequently used to represent the centres of flowers. The needle is brought up, the thread is twisted twice around it, holding it taut, and the needle is taken back into the fabric as close as possible to where it emerged.

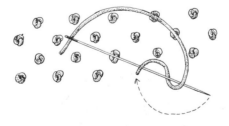

french raised work (raised Berlin work, velvet woolwork) Three-dimensional embroidery based on the methods of working the Savonnerie tapestries. Some of these 18th century tapestries had a cut-pile surface which gave a more realistic look to portraits, animals, fruit etc. In the 19th century the technique used was transferred to Berlin woolwork designs, with the result that a number of pieces on a tent stitch or cross stitch ground have parts of the design worked in plush stitch over a mesh, which were then cut, giving a smooth, raised, sculptured appearance. The technique employed and

french raised work: a banner firescreen, English, mid-19th century.

the cutting gauge used are described by Miss Lambert (1843). In mid 19th century America this was called worsted work on canvas. (Groves 1969)

french seam Join in which the two pieces are run or machined together on the right side, the fabric is pressed and turned, and another row of running is worked on the wrong side, enclosing the raw edges. It is used on thin fabrics, underwear, and children's garments. See french and overcast seam.

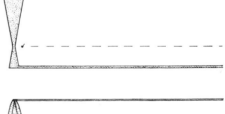

french stemming Method of attaching lace to a closely-woven fabric. The lace is laid over the main fabric about $\frac{3}{8}$ inch (1 centimetre) in from the raw edge and closely oversewn. The raw edge of the fabric is then cut away close to the lace.

fretts Ornamental and interlaced designs in decorative art, which were used in needlework, expecially in the 16th century. They are described in the glossary to the Hardwick Hall inventories (1601) as strap work patterns, often cut out and applied to a second material, 'long quition of golde and silver fretted with greene velvet' (Boynton 1971). See also strap work.

friendship bag   see shoulder pouch.

friendship quilt   see album quilt.

frieze   1. Narrow strip of embroidery or beadwork hung round a room or over a door or window on festive occasions in Kathiawar, India, known as a pachhitpati. When these friezes have square embroidered cloths hanging from them they are known as bhitayas, when they edge a shelf they are called pattas, and when they are placed over a door with two long strips hanging down the sides of the door frame they are called sakh-torans. (Irwin and Hall 1973) 2. Heavy napped woollen cloth, almost impervious to weather and so made into rough outer clothes in all cold climates.

fringe   Ornamental bordering to many embroidered objects, and sometimes the only decoration to plain material. They are made of any thread, or even of threaded beads, hanging loose from the edge. In their simplest form they consist of the warp threads of the fabric left loose, but more generally a made or bought fringe is added to the overall design of the article. Fringed leather was a favourite form of decoration among American Indians. See also fly-fringe, knotting, prince albert.

fringe: a kerchief from the Greek Islands, 19th century.

frizé   Type of *purl formed by winding *tinsel onto a square mould. It is then cut into short lengths and sewn on like a bead.

frog   Fastening for a coat or cloak which consists of a button or toggle, and a loop of braid or other material. The ornamentation round these fastenings, which generally consists of silk braids,

cords, or metal threads sewn down in a pattern of loops and swirls, is known as frogging, or, from its association with Prussian military uniform, as brandenburgs. Originally frogs were used only on military uniform, but later they were put on women's costume, and how they are the usual fastening for a duffle coat.

frontal   see altar frontal.

fukusa   Embroidered cover for throwing over a lacquered box conveying a ceremonial present in Japan.

fukusa: detail showing storks embroidered in metal thread, 19th century.

full   1. To put slight gathering or ease in a seam in order to give freedom of movement. Sometimes this may only involve a small amount of fabric as in the fullness required in a sleeve for the elbow, or it may mean several widths of fabric as in the fullness required for smocking. 2. Fulling is the process by which cloth, when woven, is shrunk and made thick.

fuller's earth   Kind of clay which when dried and powdered is used for removing grease from fabrics.

Furber, Robert   English nurseryman from Kensington (London) who in 1732 wrote a book running into several editions called *The Flower Garden Displayed*. He described it as a work 'very useful, not only for the Curious in Gardening, but the Prints likewise for Painters, Carvers, Jappaners etc, also for Ladies as Patterns for working and Painting in Water Colours.' The prints consisted of vases of massed flowers which could be copied or adapted for embroidery.

fusing   Method of joining two pieces of nylon fabric by running a hot piece of metal such as a steel knitting needle along the seam. The nylon melts slightly and the two pieces become fused together. See also bonding.

fustian   Coarse twilled cotton cloth, sometimes made with a linen warp and cotton weft, woven in the same way as velvet, with a sheared surface. It was made in Italy, Spain, Germany, and Holland, and was first mentioned in England in 1114, though it was not made there until the 14th century when it was woven in wool, copying the imported cloth in the local thread. Velveteen and corduroy are included among the different types of fustian. (Beck 1882)

fylfot   see gammadion.

Gale, Walter 18th century schoolmaster from Sussex, England, who added to his income by drawing patterns for ladies to work. From his fragmentary diary he seems to have been one of those people who can turn their hand to anything, for as well as being a village schoolmaster he was a land-measurer, a practical mathematician, an engraver of tombstones, a painter of public house signs, a pattern drawer, and a maker of wills: '1751. Jan 8. I waited on Miss Anne Baker of whom I received a neckerchief to draw. Sunday. Finished drawing Miss Anne's handkerchief and carried it home to her, receiving 1s for my labour.' (Blencowe 1857)

galloon (galon) Trimming for liveries or dress of three sorts: 1. silk, woollen, or union tape used for binding and braiding; 2. embroidered trimming made in narrow widths of silk or cotton; 3. narrow lace made of gold, silver, or other metal threads, employed in edging and trimming uniforms, also called orris. Galon is often used in the same sense as galloon, but strictly speaking it is a narrow silk or gold braid for the hair. (Murphy n.d.)

gamboised Word meaning quilted or padded which was used in the middle ages to describe some of the padding necessary under armour. The word gambeson, which has the same derivation, means a padded and quilted tunic worn with or without additional armour. The surcoat of the *Black Prince at Canterbury Cathedral is gamboised.

game boards Fashionable needlework project in the mid 1970s, game-boards particularly for backgammon and chess are available as complete kits, as painted canvas only, and as graphs. They are most frequently worked with flat stitches to provide the smoothest possible playing surface.

gaming tables see card tables.

gammadion (fylfot, swastika) Device consisting of a cross with equal arms, each ending with a stroke at right angles to the arm, and each stroke pointing in the same direction, usually clockwise. It is called a gammadion because it is made up of four representations of the Greek letter gamma. It is believed to be the oldest Aryan symbol, the cross standing for the Supreme God and the flanges indicating the heavens revolving round the Pole Star. Later it became a sign of good luck and good will, and later still was taken by the Christian church as a symbol of the Crucifixion. For American Indians the sign represents the four winds. According to the OED, the word fylfot is probably a nonce-word only found in the Lansdowne manuscript of the 9th century. The word swastika, the symbol of the National Socialist party in Germany, comes from a Sanskrit word meaning good luck. To complicate the matter still further, this symbol is used in heraldry where it is known as a cross potent.

Gardiner, George 19th century shopkeeper in Allenheads, Northumberland, who was well known as a designer of wadded or Durham quilts. His designs were rich and full, and usually contained feather patterns and scrolling. (Colby 1972) See also wadded quilting.

garnished Adorned or decked. One of the New Year gifts of Elizabeth I (1577-8) is 'By the Lady Ratclif, five creppins of lawne, garnished with gold and silver purle' (Nichols 1823).

garter 1. Binding of the hose or stocking from earliest times to the present day. Garters have been long tapes wound round the leg or above the knee and tied;

garter: of The Order of the Garter, 1489

in later years, circles of elastic worn above or below the knee; or in America the fastening known in England as a suspender. At different periods they have been decorative or strictly utilitarian,

and sometimes they have had a design woven in, been embroidered, or even made in beadwork. 2. The Order of the Garter is the oldest order of Chivalry in England, having been founded by Edward III in c 1346.

gathering Process by which the fullness of fabric is controlled. Gathering by hand is achieved by making even running stitches in the fabric and then pulling the thread so that the fabric is reduced to the desired length. Gathering can also be done on the sewing machine by means of a gathering foot or ruffler which gathers as it stitches, or by making the machine stitch as long as possible. When the length has been sewn it will be found that on pulling the under thread the fabric gathers evenly.

gauge 1. Any piece of wood, ivory, bone, metal, or other material, either flat or rounded, which can be used to ensure that loops or spaces are the same size. Two other names for gauge are spacer and reed. See also mesh. 2. See gauging.

gauging Parallel rows of gathers, with each stitch exactly under the one above, drawn up to make a block of gathered fabric. It is used as a preliminary to *smocking and also, when machined, as a yoke or bodice for children's dresses. If elastic thread is put into the bobbin of the machine, gauging can be used at waist and cuff as it will expand when stretched. See also shirring.

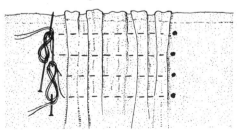

handkerchief: cotton embroidered with silk in double darning with double running and satin stitches; the ends are trimmed with bobbin lace; Turkish, 19th century.

gauntlet: English, early 17th century.

gauntlet Originally a glove worn with medieval armour, but later that part of a glove which flared out from the wrist. These were known as gauntlet gloves. In the 16th and 17th centuries especially, gauntlets were magnificently embroidered in silk and metal thread and were often decorated with ribbon, lace, sequins etc.

gauze (leno) Very thin fabric woven by twisting warp threads round each other, the weft being shot through to bind the crossed threads. Gauze is the finest and most transparent of fabrics partly because of this manner of weaving which leaves spaces between the warp threads, and partly because of the fineness of the thread used. Originally a silk fabric from Gaza in the Near East, it can also be made of cotton or other yarn. It is used as a base fabric for Italian *buratto and *Nazca/Ica embroidery.

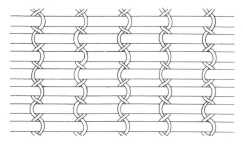

hat: conical-shaped, beaded hat worn by the women of the Penobscot North American Indian tribe.

Gawthorpe Hall (Lancashire, England) Jacobean house now owned by the National Trust. It was once the home of Lord Shuttleworth, and houses the excellent collection of embroideries, lace, textiles, costumes, and accessories collected by the Hon Rachel Kay-Shuttleworth. This collection is used to foster the love and knowledge of textile crafts, and students either individually or in groups are particularly welcome.

Gawthorpe Hall: detail of the embroidery on a Queen Anne apron.

Geneva embroidery Popular late 19th century embroidery in which strips of velvet ribbon were sewn down onto chessboard or Java canvas with decorative stitches. The squares of canvas so formed could be filled with stars or rosettes in chenille or other decorative motifs. (Caulfeild & Saward 1882)

Genoese embroidery Form of whitework popular in the late 19th century and supposedly resembling Genoese lace. In effect it is like *Madeira work, the main difference being that in Genoese embroidery the cut edges are outlined in cord which at intervals is formed into small loops, and the cord is then closely buttonholed over.

geometrical satin stitch see satin stitch.

Georgian Period in English history between 1714 and 1830 when the four Georges were on the throne. However in needlework, as in many crafts, the period

Georgian: a pair of 18th century embroidered shoes.

is taken to end just after the turn of the century, the years 1811–1830 being called Regency. The general trends of Georgian embroidery were lighter in design and tone than the heavy 17th century work, following the fashion in furnishing and woodwork. There was a far wider use of silk thread, with wool used mainly for the canvas work upholstery on furniture. Plain sewing became fashionable and its techniques were made decorative and beautiful, as in the darning samplers at the end of the century. Because cotton was easily obtainable, whitework also grew fashionable, mostly Dresden and tambour work.

German wool see Berlin wool.

Germany In such a large country it is obvious that there must be numerous different styles of embroidery. The Rhine was one of the earliest highways of Europe and many outside influences penetrated to the interior from the river; the south of the country absorbed ideas from Italy, while the east was nearer to the Slav cultures. In the middle ages, Germany produced a particular form of whitework (opus teutonicum) used for cloths and covers in the churches and also probably for domestic use, though the latter has not survived. In contrast to the opus anglicanum of England, this made no attempt to produce realistic draperies, but filled the spaces left by the outlines of the garments with flat diaper patterns. Relief from monotony was obtained by the variety of stitches used and by the changing forms where a solid figure could be placed next to a finely curving plant or stem. The 16th century saw the beginning of the heaviness of design which has since been a characteristic of German work. Large woollen table-cloths and hangings told stories which were embellished with scrolls and lettering.

The best known embroidery in the 18th century was called *Dresden work, though it came from other areas as well. It

Germany: a cushion from Westphalia, 14th–15th century.

was done on fine muslin in different drawn fabric and surface stitches and was a cheaper alternative to the very expensive French laces of the time. German embroidery of the 19th century will always be remembered as it was there that the ubiquitous Berlin woolwork was started which swept most of Europe and America. The country also became very aware of, and was one of the chief innovators of, art nouveau. In embroidery this probably reached its peak in the 1880s with the work of Hermann Obrist, whose thin sinuous line is as far removed from the florid bunchiness of Berlin woolwork as it is possible to get.

Gesner, Conrad Swiss who in 1551 published (in Latin) the first of four folios on birds, fishes, and mammals. In 1560 these were produced in a one-volume edition. He also wrote *Historia Animalium,* one of the first popular works on natural history, combining sound knowledge with a certain amount of fantasy. These books, which ran into several editions, provided the 16th century needlewoman with an attractive variety of themes and patterns for embroidery and they were much used, in particular by *Mary Queen of Scots.

ghagra The skirt worn by the Jat women of Sikar and Jhu-Jhunu in Rajasthan (India). They have embroidery worked in a deep red cotton on the hem, belt, and part of the side. The patterns are drawn freehand by the embroiderers. (Dhamija 1964)

gibecière see alms purse.

gilet Mock waistcoat for women much in vogue in the late 19th and early 20th centuries. They were often embroidered to match the dress with which they were worn.

gilet: English, 20th century.

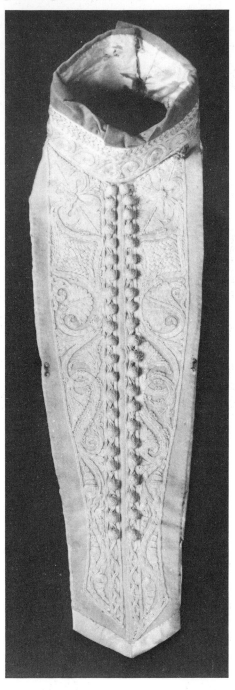

gimp Wire or stiff cord covered with silk. From this basic meaning the use of the word has widened to include braids made with a stiff base (often used in upholstery), as well as cords used to outline the patterns of some laces, notably Bedfordshire, and dress trimmings. It also means a neckerchief or stomacher worn by a nun.

gipon see jupon.

gipsire see alms purse.

girdle Belt worn by either sex round the waist to hold in garments. Girdles can be of many types from those worn by a schoolgirl on her tunic, made of wool braid, to the twisted cords worn round the alb by a priest and round the habits of monks and nuns. They can also be decorative, and some ecclesiastical girdles in the middle ages were not only embroidered but also studded with jewels. Among Elizabeth I's New Year gifts in 1588 is 'By Mrs Owen, a girdle of white sipres, imbrodered at bothe ends with leaves of faire cullored silke of needle work, friendged with Venis gold, silver and silke' (Nichols 1823).

girdle: English, 20th century.

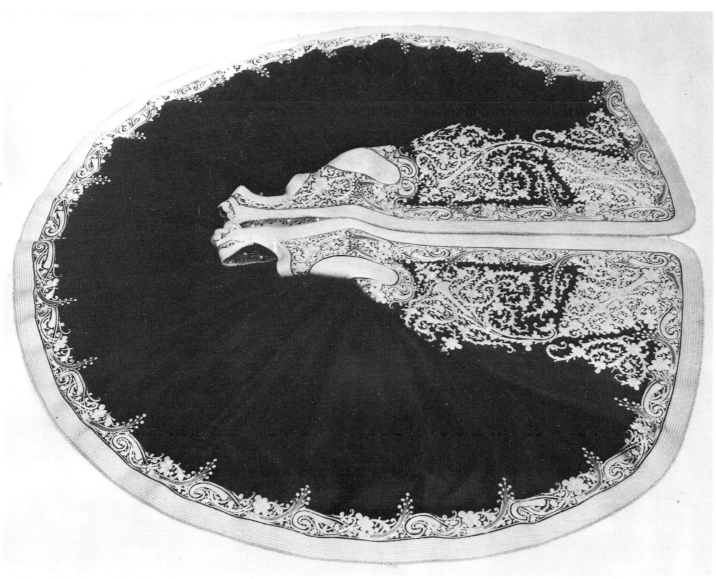

guibba: Albanian, mid-19th century.

giubba Sleeveless coat worn by the women and girls of the Middle East over shirt and full trousers or trousered skirt. They fall straight in front but the back is cut with a very big flare. The front, back, and hem are frequently decorated with a scrolling design in fine braid. (Start 1939)

Glasgow School of Art Pioneering force in the teaching and practice of embroidery from the appointment of Francis Newbery as principal in 1885. His wife Jessie *Newbery, with Ann *Macbeth, started classes in embroidery, relating it to other decorative arts and taking the building up of patterns from stitches as their basis. By loaning collections of specimens to schools throughout the British Isles the influence of the Glasgow School on teaching and designing embroidery was spread and the approach they suggested soon became the accepted form of training.

glastra Term literally meaning flower pot, which is used to describe an element in the embroidery designs of the Dodecanese Islands off Greece. These elements are fairly large, isolated motifs in the design and can resemble a star, a 'blob', or even a compact version of the *Tree of Life. In the island of Astypalaia a similar pattern found in the sleeves of underdresses is called dixos. (Johnstone 1972)

globe sampler Variation of the early 19th century *map samplers. These silk-covered balls were embroidered with couched lines of latitude and longitude, with the countries edged in outline stitch. Additional details such as people, ships, and names were sometimes painted on. Most of them were made at the Westown School, Chester county (Pennsylvania), to help in teaching geography.

globe sampler: from America.

119

glover's needle Stiff, short needle used in glove-making, which is three-cornered and so easily penetrates the leather.

gloves Articles of clothing, nowadays worn primarily for keeping the hands warm. They were considered an integral part of dress and sometimes, as in the case of ecclesiastics, could almost be considered a vestment. Gloves have a separate division for each finger thus distinguishing them from mittens (also called mitts), which may end at the knuckle or else cover the hand with a single division for the thumb. In the middle ages gloves were used as tokens to be given by a lady to her knight, as pledges of intent in transactions of land or property, and as part of the ceremony of investiture of lands or dignities. They have always been used in single combat, whether in the middle ages or later duelling, to offer provocation or a challenge. For several hundred years they were given to mourners at a funeral, the type being nicely graded to the status of the mourner; to the guests at a wedding; and a pair of white gloves is still presented to a judge at assizes when there are no cases for him to try. With all this background it is natural that gloves should have been made in many types of material, frequently decorated and sometimes jewelled. Probably the most beautiful were those of the early 17th century with their gauntlets embroidered in silk and metal threads with added sequins and jewels.

gloves: English kid gloves, c. 1860.

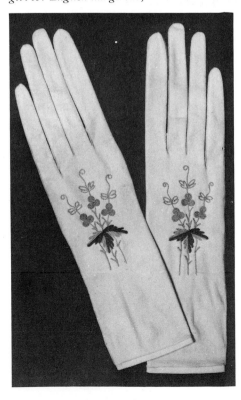

gobelin stitch Counted thread stitch invented to imitate tapestry. Levey (1971) says 'As early as 1840 an elongated tent stitch known as Gobelin stitch had been introduced to imitate the effect of a woven tapestry, but because the Berlin patterns were based on a square mesh they were distorted by the technique and the old method of drawing the design directly onto the canvas had to be used. Although the original Berlin method remained more popular, the term tapestry work came to be applied to all forms of woollen embroidery, creating a confusion with the proper woven technique which has survived to the present day.' The stitch is worked diagonally over two threads in height and one wide and has many variations.

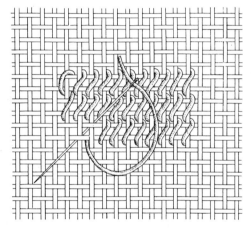

godet Triangular piece of fabric set into a garment, generally in the skirt or sleeve, for added fullness. They were popular in the 1930s in the skirts of bias-cut long dresses.

Godey, Louis Antoine (1804-1878) Philadelphia publisher and founder in 1830 of *Godey's Lady's Book*, the first popular American monthly magazine devoted exclusively to women's interests with works by American authors. He was also an innovator in other areas of the magazine world, for he was the first to pay American authors liberally (previously payment was uncertain or non-existent), and the first to use a copyright statute, established in 1790, to protect the material in the *Lady's Book*. (Finley 1931)

Godey's Lady's Book One of the most influential magazines dedicated entirely to women in 19th-century America. In each issue from 1830 to 1898 it included serial novels, recipes, comment on behaviour and manners, patterns and instructions for all the latest embroidery and handwork items, fashion descriptions and hand-coloured fashion plates. It was founded by Louis Antoine Godey (1804-78), in Philadelphia; he is also remembered for being

Godey's Lady's Book: a fashion plate from the February 1840 edition.

the first publisher to pay American authors liberally (previous payment was uncertain or non-existent), and the first to use a copyright statute, established in 1790, to protect the material in the *Lady's Book* (Finley 1931).

gold embroidery see metal thread embroidery.

gold thread Generally a fine strip of gold wrapped round a silk thread. In the middle ages this strip was cut from fine quality gold sheet, beaten very thin (aurum battutum). In the later middle ages silver gilt thread was used, or else gilt membrane. With the latter, gold leaf was stuck to thin animal membrane, cut into strips, and wound round a silk core. These threads are often found named in Tudor inventories as Venice, Cypress or Damascene gold, but it is likely that these were the places from which gold thread was exported rather than where the thread was manufactured. The gold thread of today is either Chinese or more frequently Japanese gold. These are made in the same way, with gold on paper wound round a silk core, but they vary in colour, the Chinese being a paler and cooler gold than the Japanese.

gold thread: small Chinese purse, 19th century.

Gothic Word with several meanings but which generally applies to the style of architecture common in western Europe from the 12th to the 16th centuries, characterised by the pointed arch. It can also mean medieval (in the romantic sense) and barbarous.

Gothic revival The style of church building and furnishing revived by Pugin and his school of thought in the early and middle 19th century. Gothic was held to be the only style suitable, and not only did it apply to the architecture but also to all the furnishing such as tiles, glass, and embroidery.

gothic revival: the hood of a cope designed by Pugin, c.1840.

Gould, John (1804–1881) One of the foremost British ornithologists of the 19th century and an excellent and most accurate painter. In 1827 he became curator to the Zoological Society's Museum. His eighteen published works on birds include *Birds of Europe, Birds of Australia, Birds of Great Britain,* and a *Monograph of the Ramplastidae of the Family of Toucans.* He is of great interest to embroiderers as so many of his drawings and paintings were made into patterns for Berlin woolwork.

gown 1. Loose outer garment, now used in a special sense as barrister's gown, academic gown, and mayor's gown. These all derive from the medieval and early Tudor gown which was everyday wear for men. 2. For women, gown is often synonymous with dress, but with slightly different meanings at different dates. In the 18th century the word was used for a garment with a tight-fitting bodice and a flowing skirt, but in the 19th and 20th centuries the word dress is used for everyday wear, while gown is kept for more specialised garments such as tea gown, dinner gown, nightgown, or hospital gown.

grafting The invisible joining of two pieces of material. The word is used chiefly in connection with knitting, where the join at the toe of a sock, for example, is made by simulating the knitting stitch with needle and thread, and also with splicing or joining canvas where two pieces must be joined so that when worked over no line is visible.

grain The line of the warp in textiles. To cut horizontally, that is along the weft, is called cutting across or against the grain. In addition, the word is used in connection with dyeing. See also ingrain.

graph canvas Single-thread canvas with a blue line every ten squares, both vertically and horizontally. This makes it very simple to count squares from a chart.

graph paper see point paper.

grass embroidery Caribbean embroidery using dried and dyed grass as the thread.

grecian Twisted gold or silver metal cord, used in ecclesiastical embroidery, modern collages, and panels.

Greece Few embroideries of ancient Greece survive, but fragments found in burial mounds in southern Russia indicate a variety of patterns and techniques covering a period from the 5th century BC to the time of Roman domination. A line drawing used as a pattern was found with one embroidery fragment that showed an Amazon dressed in a short green chiton and high shoes, riding a galloping horse. During the classical period, border bands predominated but human and animal figures were also portrayed, and geometric patterns were used in an allover pattern. Woollen thread on woollen fabrics was sewn in a type of chain and satin stitch. Greek embroideries were imported then copied by the Scythians through whom the Greek style survived for centuries, and there is a collection of these embroideries in the Hermitage, Leningrad. (Tolmachoff 1942) See also Greek islands, Janina embroidery.

Greek embroidery 1. Described by Caulfeild and Saward (1882) as a modern work consisting of appliqué in various fabrics on cloth or silk, sewn down and decorated with different stitches. The design was based on Mohammedan motifs such as arabesques. 2. See Greece.

Greek Islands While most islands off the Greek and Turkish mainland have their own special style of embroidery, there is a generic feeling for the whole area based on tradition and history. Until the late 12th century the islands were part of the Byzantine Empire, but after the sack of Constantinople (1204), Venice ruled the majority, and then from the middle of the 16th century they were under Turkish rule. These three influences show in the embroideries of the area, especially in the designs, which are in general stylised birds, animals, and flowers, together with geometric shapes and patterns. There is a great deal of cross stitch worked on hand spun linen, with pulled fabric stitches, drawn threadwork, and darning. Embroidery was much used on household articles, especially *bed tents, sheets, pillows and cushions, and also on dress. (Johnstone 1972) See also Greece.

Greek Islands: detail of a bed curtain from the Cyclades.

greek plait Five-strand plait, used in making fringes. It is made in the same way as the ordinary three-strand plait, except that the outer strands pass over two strands to the middle instead of one.

Greenaway, Kate (1846–1901) Daughter of a London wood engraver, she specialised in portraying artless children in pseudo early 19th century costume for book illustration. Her work had a great vogue from 1879 and the children were copied and embroidered in outline stitch on articles such as aprons, children's clothes, towel ends, splashers, quilts, etc.

grenadier caps Uniform caps worn by regiments of grenadiers in the 18th century. Originally they were designed to be more stable than the more normal tricorne. They had a wide headband and a soft crown and sat well down on the head, but the front could be up to 12 inches (30.5 centimetres) high and was shaped like a bishop's mitre. In the first half of the century in the standing army, and afterwards in the militia, these caps were heavily embroidered with regimental devices and mottoes.

grisaille beadwork Monochromatic *beadwork designs on a ground of Berlin woolwork. Black, grey, white (both clear and opaque), and steel beads are used. It was very popular in the mid 19th century and was made up into articles such as banner firescreens, mantel covers, and teacosies.

grisaille beadwork: 'Morning' by Thorwaldsen in beads on a banner firescreen, 19th century.

grommet Ring of metal whose outer perimeter is open so that it may be fastened round a leather or fabric hole to make an eyelet.

gros point Cross stitch. However, the term is often misapplied to canvas work done with a large tent stitch, and sometimes is even used for the whole piece of work, as 'my gros point'.

ground downs Sewing needles shorter than *sharps. so called because they were ground down from sharps instead of being cut the right length (Caulfeild and Saward 1882). They are now called *betweens.

guanaco Wild South American mammal resembling a deer and of the same family as the alpaca and llama. It has a soft, beige coat from which the *guanaco cloaks of Patagonia were made.

guanaco cloaks (of Patagonia) Fur robes of the southernmost Indian tribes of South America including the Canoe Indians of Tierra del Fuego and the nomadic Tehuelche of Chaco who spread the technique and patterns. These robes are made mostly of guanaco skins painted on the bare side with predominantly red designs and then stitched with whale or animal sinew, and are worn with the fur-side in. Two pieces of skin are joined by using a sharpened nail or birdbone 'needle' to punch closely-spaced holes, and the thread is inserted to make fine stitches and a neat seam. Some robes alternate as many as twelve skins head to foot in rows, so that the white bellies and coffee-coloured backs form a mosaic of handsome colour and pattern. Guanaco robes had great commercial value—more than 24,000 skins were shipped from Patagonia in 1924. (Lothrop 1929)

guarded Term meaning edged with lace, braid, or embroidery, frequently used in the 15th and 16th centuries and found in a number of inventories.

guard hairs The long lustrous hairs which protect the underfur of animals. They are used, especially those of the moose, as threads for embroidery by some North American Indians.

Guatemalan silk Artificial embroidery silk used in the San Bartolome de Los Llanos area of Mexico on the elaborately worked marriage skirts, which have geometric, floral, and animal figure embroidery decorating the seams and top and bottom borders.

Gubbay collection (Clandon Park, Surrey) Comprehensive collection made by Mrs David Gubbay of mainly 18th century furniture, ceramics, jade, glass, metalwork, and textiles. It was left by her to the National Trust in 1968 and is now housed at *Clandon Park. The textiles are of great interest and include some fine needlework rugs, most of them worked about the middle of the 18th century and still in very good condition.

Gubbay collection: an English 18th century firescreen.

Guernsey rug   see Caswell carpet.

Guild of the Needle and Bobbin Crafts   Educational guild in America, composed of the People's Institute and a branch of the *Needle and Bobbin Club, and formed in 1920 to encourage immigrants to retain their own embroidery techniques. The guild provided employment for many women in the same way as the *exchanges for women's work had done.

guilloche   Figure, used chiefly in architecture, in which two bands cross each other at regular intervals in a spiral. It has been used in embroidery, particularly as a border, with the areas enclosed by the bands filled in with various stitches.

guimped embroidery   Type of embroidery where 'the pattern must be drawn on the material, and the figures of the pattern also cut in parchment, vellum, or cloth, over which the gold or silver is sewn with a fine silk thread' (Miss Lambert 1843). Nowadays this method of slightly raising or padding gold work is considered one of the techniques used in metal thread embroidery rather than a type of embroidery on its own.

guipure d'art   see net laces, lacis.

guipure work   Indefinite term with a variety of meanings, including lace with a raised thread, darned net or filet, 'a form of embroidery in which almost all the ground material was cut away leaving the parts of the pattern joined together only by narrow bars or brides' (Levey 1971). The word comes from the French *guiper* meaning to cover a thread with silk. According to the OED, it was used in England no earlier than 1830, and can be taken to refer to 19th century adaptations of the 17th century Venetian laces, the 16th and 17th century cutwork, and the earlier lacis.

Gujarat   Province of northwest India famed for its embroideries. These were introduced to England by the *East India Company as early as 1614, and a few had even arrived in the 16th century, brought by the Portuguese. The embroideries most prized in London were bedcovers and hangings worked in multicoloured silks on a cotton or satin background, probably in chain stitch. The quilts (not necessarily quilted) from Gujarat were also known as Patania quilts in the 17th century. (Irwin & Schwartz 1966)

Gujarat: detail of a petticoat, late 19th century.

gunny   Coarse sacking. Originally it was a strong coarse calico used for sacking and as a covering for bales, and was woven in the Rajapur and Kanwar areas of India. Later it referred to jute or hemp sacking, and is known in America as *burlap.

gusset   Triangle or strip of material sewn in between two seams to strengthen the join or to give extra width. In needlework, they were usually let in at underarm and shoulder on smocks, shirts, shifts, and chemises, and nowadays they are also used in knitting, toymaking, and in making bags.

gusset: detail of an English chemise, late 16th century.

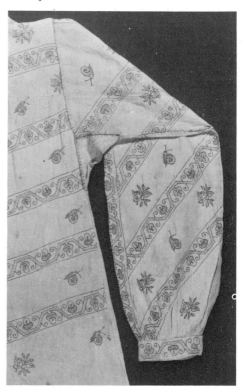

Hh

haberdashery (notions) Small practical items for personal or household use, including all kinds of sewing equipment, found on the haberdashery counter of a draper's shop or departmental store in Britain or in the notions department of a store in America.

hair In embroidery, human hair was used for fine drawing and for types of printwork of the late 18th and early 19th centuries, while animal hair, particularly from the reindeer and moose, was used for the embroideries worked by North American Indians, Laplanders, and those living near the Arctic Circle.

Hale, Sarah Josepha (1788–1899) American author, feminist, and editor of the *Ladies' Magazine* in Boston from 1828–1837. From 1837–1877 she was the influential editor of *Godey's Lady's Book*, dictating the tastes and interests of American women.

half back stitch see running stitch.

half cross stitch see tent stitch.

half-silk Equivalent to what is now called *union of silk and cotton. These were woven together and used as a ground fabric for embroidery in medieval Europe. Half-silks are found in Fatimid work. (Schuette and Müller-Christensen 1964)

halo Plain golden disc surrounding the heads of saints and martyrs in all art forms. In embroidery it is generally represented by circles of gold thread couched down in a brick or a wheeling pattern. See also nimbus, splendour, mandorla.

hammock Shape used in quilting, especially in borders.

hand coolers Egg-shaped lumps of certain minerals that do not conduct heat, such as marble, Derbyshire Blue John, or stone. These 'eggs' were kept in the workbasket and could be held in the hand at intervals to cool it. It is important when working white embroidery or using metal threads that no heat or stickiness is transferred to the thread which can quickly discolour.

hand finished Term referring to machine-made garments which have the finishing touches such as buttonholes, saddle stitching, or embroidery, done by hand. It applies particularly to the underwear trade, and knitwear.

handkerchief The word is difficult to define and is inextricably mixed with pocket handkerchief, kerchief, half-kerchief, neckerchief, and muckinder, but the general meaning is a square of fabric, plain or decorated, which can be used in one of several ways. A pocket handkerchief is used to blow the nose or wipe the face or eyes, and it may also be called a handkerchief or kerchief. A child's handkerchief used in this way and fastened to the girdle or waist belt was called a muckinder in the 16th and 17th centuries. In the middle ages a kerchief or coverchief was a square of light linen thrown over the head.

handkerchief: Turkish, given by the Sultan of Turkey to the French Ambassador's wife in 1866.

The Elizabethan handkerchief could be either for the hand or the neck, and those in the lists of New Year gifts to Elizabeth I (1588) are ambiguous: 'By Mrs Smithson, two handkerchers of Holland wrought with black silke' (Nichols 1823). In the 18th century, handkerchiefs, kerchiefs, and half-handkerchiefs were generally worn round the neck, the half-handkerchief being the square cut in half to form a triangle. There are many references to handkerchiefs in Nancy Woodforde's *Diary* (Woodforde 1932). 'Aug 3 1792 Mrs Custance shewed me a new Fashion Black Silk Handkerchief with a Colour'd work'd border.' 'Aug 7 . . . she brought a Cloak for me to make a Handk out of part of it like my new one, which I offered to do for her.' The main point is that all these squares, used for whatever purpose from the middle ages until today, have been decorated in any technique of the time, some of them quite exquisitely. (Colour illustration p.115)

handkerchief: English, 19th century.

Indian embroidery: detail of a hanging from Kathiawar, late 19th or early 20th century. This type of work was done by women for use in their own homes.

overleaf (p 126)
Indo-European embroidery: detail of a cotton hanging in polychrome silks in chain stitch, 17th century.

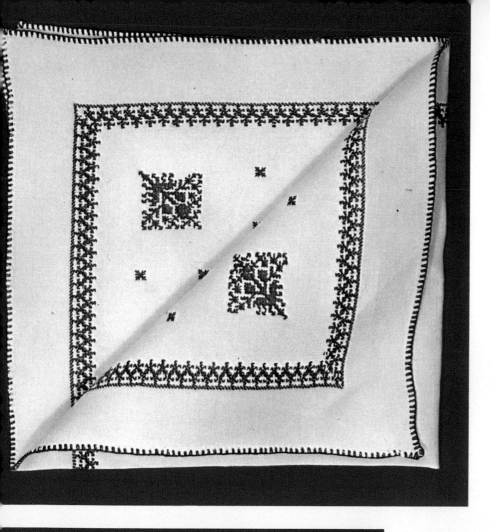

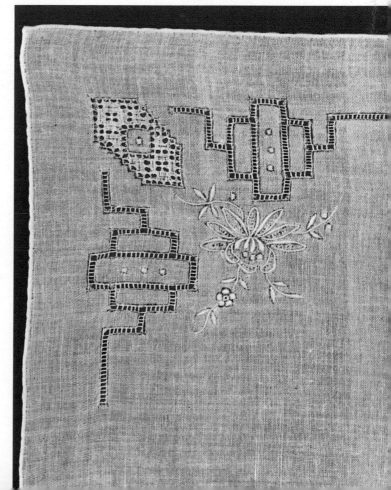

handkerchief case Receptacle for keeping handkerchiefs in. Certainly known in the 18th century and probably used much earlier, they have generally been embroidered in the fashion of the day, and being small have been excellent test-pieces for young needleworkers. When it was usual to have a plethora of cases to put things in, they were in great demand at sales of work and as Christmas presents.

hand-ruff In the Tudor period either a turned back cuff, a hanging ruffle, or a wrist ruff matching that worn round the neck. They were sometimes ornamented with blackwork or other embroidery or lace.

hand-ruff: from a painting of Elizabeth Brydges by Custodis, 1589.

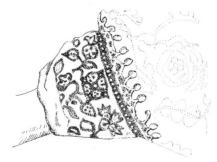

overleaf (p 127)
Italy: four modern examples of embroidery. Top left, a mat worked in cross stitch; top right, detail of a tablecloth in satin stitch and shadow work; bottom left, the corner of a napkin; bottom right, detail of a handkerchief with drawn threadwork.

Japanese embroidery: a 19th century picture worked in silk on a satin ground in raised brick stitch and satin stitch.

handscreens: English, mid–19th century.

handscreen Small screen on a handle held to protect the face from the heat of a fire. They were made in a variety of materials, for example, wood, papier mâché, and feathers, but a large number were embroidered in Berlin woolwork (with or without beads), chenille work, cut cloth work, or any other suitable technique. They were popular during the late 18th and 19th centuries.

hanging Large piece of fabric, plain, embroidered, or tapestry woven, originally for covering blank walls and keeping out draughts, but now used just for decoration. They give scope for large-scale pictorial embroidery which can seldom find a home elsewhere.

Han silk Product of a famous Chinese silk industry—that of the Han dynasty of China, 206 BC to AD 220. Han silk patterns follow the rhythmical movement of the painted cloud bands typical of Han lacquer work. The embroideries too use free pictorial decoration rather than symmetrical fields. Usually threads of one colour provide the dominating bright value in the embroideries on dark backgrounds; on light backgrounds dark embroidery is used sparsely and blended with intermediate colours. Some fragments of Han silk in good condition have been dated 2 BC by an inscribed lacquer cup found with them at *Noin Ula, and are now in the Hermitage, Leningrad. (Salmony 1942)

haqueton (haketon, acketon, acton, ackton etc) Either a leather jacket plated with mail, or a quilted leather jacket worn under armour to prevent chafing.

hard and soft silk Hard silk is that which has the natural gum from the cocoon left in it, while soft silk has had the gum removed by scouring. (Caulfeild and Saward 1882)

Hardanger embroidery Counted thread embroidery originating in the Hardanger district of Norway. It is characterised by the ground of open-weave double-thread canvas. The thread used is a fairly thick cotton or linen, and the designs are built up between blocks of geometrical satin stitch (called kloster blocks) and squares of cut threads. This type of embroidery is both hard wearing and decorative. It was revived in the US about 1900.

Hardanger embroidery: 20th century.

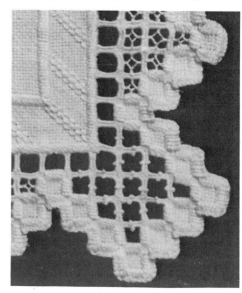

Hardwick Hall (Derbyshire, England) Late 16th century house built by Elizabeth, Countess of Shrewsbury (known as *Bess of Hardwick), and now belonging to the National Trust. To students and lovers of needlework one of the main features of the house is the number of Elizabethan embroideries there, and also the fact that in 1601 Bess ordered that an inventory of the contents be made. This inventory was published in 1971 by the Furniture History Society and gives an excellent idea of the embroidery used in a great house of that time.

Harrison, Edmund (1589–1666) Embroiderer to James I, Charles I, and Charles II, who lived in Cripplegate, London. In 1628, when he was warden of the *Broderers' Company, he presented the company with a cup and cover of silver gilt. After the Restoration he petitioned Charles II to be his embroiderer again: 'the Broderers Coy certify as to his skill, that he is the ablest worker living, and as to his loyalty, that he preserved the King's best cloth of State and his rich carpet, embroidered with pearl, from being cut in pieces or burnt, and that he restored these and many other goods to His Majesty.' The king agreed to pay Harrison £341 per annum, but in two months he relinquished his office. He is best known for his large pieces, *The Visitation, The Bethrothal*, and the *Adoration*, which are from a series made for William Howard, Lord Stafford. (Holford 1910)

Harrison: 'The Adoration of the Magi' embroidered in silk on canvas, c. 1637.

Haslemere Peasant Industries: 'The Spies' designed by Geoffrey Blount.

Haslemere Peasant Industries One of the offshoots of the *arts and crafts movement. It was founded in 1896 by Godfrey Blount, and was designed to bring back simplicity of stitch and decoration to help village embroiderers earn money. Blount made most of the designs which were usually carried out in a flat, pictorial applied work.

hassock see church kneelers.

hat Covering for the head, generally distinguished by having some form of brim, or a headband which fits the head without having to be tied on. It can be made of any fabric or material which can be plaited, blocked, or cut and sewn, and may be strictly utilitarian, frivolous, a status symbol, or the mark of degree in a profession. (Colour illustration p.116)

hat: made of straw, American, 20th century.

hatband The band which goes round a hat to hide the join between crown and brim. It could be expensively decorated and was sometimes moved from hat to hat. In the wardrobe account (1607) of that extravagant young man Henry Prince of Wales is an entry for 'Embroidering an hat band with several sorts of pearle, having set among the pearle rubies, emrods, and opals; having also three score great pearls, 26 l [pounds]' (Bray 1793).

hatchment Square or lozenge-shaped panel painted with the arms of a deceased person, and hung on the front of the house, generally over the door. After a certain length of time it was put in the church. In New England in the 18th century, and particularly between 1750 and 1770, there was a custom of embroidering hatchments which were carried in funeral processions and then hung in the church, and an advertisement in the *Boston Chronicle* for 1769 states that Amy and Elizabeth Cummings at their school for needlework 'instruct young ladies in embroidery, Coats of Arms . . .' See also heraldic embroidery.

hatchment: the arms of Isaiah Thomas of Boston embroidered in coloured silks on black satin, early 19th century.

Hatton Garden hangings One of the most interesting embroideries in the Victoria and Albert Museum (London). These hangings were found behind many layers of wallpaper in an old house in Hatton Garden, and they consist of six panels 7 feet 9 inches high by 4 feet wide (2.4 by 1.2 metres). They are worked in wool on linen canvas and date from about 1690. The designs, based on Corinthian pillars entwined by luxuriant foliage, with birds and animals, are alike in the main but differ in detail. The interesting point is the variety of canvas stitches used, including tent, cross, gobelin, rococo, hungarian, rice, eye stitches, and french knots.

Hatton Garden hangings: a detail showing the variety of canvas stitches used.

Hausa African tribe of Northern Nigeria and Ghana who are renowned for magnificent embroideries. Silk is produced locally and is used in its natural colour or dyed gold, green, red, purple, and brown. Breeches and *rigas are embroidered in traditional patterns of circles, triangles, and squares, and many beautiful examples can be seen in ethnographical museums including the Museum of Primitive Art (New York) and the Museum of Archaeology and Ethnography (Cambridge, England).

havenese embroidery Described by Caulfeild and Saward (1882) as 'a modern embroidery formed of buttonhole stitch, worked with coloured silks or crewels upon crash, cloth, or any thick material.'

Hawaiian quilts: in this example the symbolic design represents Queen Kapiolani's fans and 'Kahilis' (processional canopies).

Hawaiian quilts Patchwork quilts made in Hawaii. These differ from the more usual American quilt in that they are always made of new material, are in two colours only, and the design consists of one motif repeated four times which is cut out and applied to the ground fabric. (Ickis 1949)

hearse cloth see pall.

heart One of the shapes used in quilting.

Hedebo embroidery Danish embroidery originating in the flat heathland west of Copenhagen. It started in the middle of the 18th century as a peasant craft worked on a coarse homewoven linen. Hedebo embroidery has had three stages: from about 1760 to 1820 it consisted of a small amount of cut and drawn threadwork with a lot of surface embroidery; between about 1820 and 1850 various cutwork fillings based on Italian reticella work were added, and the designs became more formal; then after this, when Hedebo became popular as a

Hedebo embroidery: detail of a towel inscribed and dated 'K.F.D. 1840'.

form of embroidery in other countries, a number of elaborate lace stitches were added to the drawn threadwork and very little surface stitchery remained.

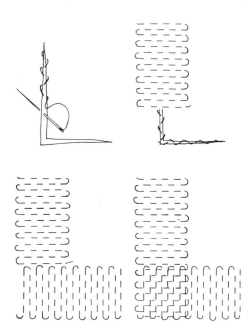

helmet Hard, protective head covering. It may appear an unlikely object to be connected with needlework, but at least two kinds were embroidered. For Queen Victoria's Golden Jubilee (1887) the units of the British Army in India had their white tropical helmets embroidered with the emblems of the British Isles. Also, some Indian helmets were partially quilted.

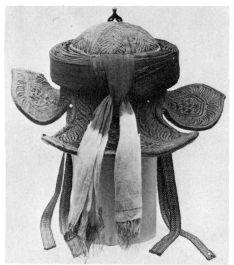

helmet: in quilting taken from Tipu Sultan's palace, Indian, 19th century.

hemming bird: cut steel, early 19th century.

hedge tear darn (angular tear darn) Used to repair right-angled tears in clothing. Each leg of the tear is darned separately so that at the weakest point there is a double darn.

heelball Compound of lampblack and hard wax, normally used by shoemakers to polish the sides of the soles of shoes, but it can also be used to transfer a design onto fabric. After the design has been pricked, a pad is dampened with petrol or benzene, rubbed onto a heelball, and then over the pricks. To make it, 2 lbs beeswax are mixed with 3 oz suet, and 4 oz ivory black and 2 oz powdered rock candy are stirred in. When partly cold it is poured into moulds. See also prick, pounce.

heer bharat Type of embroidery worked with floss silk (heer), the thread used by some of the embroiderers of India. Heer bharat is distinguished by the play of light on geometrical patterns, and is similar to *phulkari. (Dhamija 1964)

Heilmann, Josué (1796–1848) The inventor of the first machine which simulated hand embroidery on material. He belonged to a firm of cotton manufacturers who made India muslins at Mulhouse (France), and in a time of economic depression he had the idea of inventing a machine which could embroider. By 1828 he had evolved one in which the needles were pointed at both ends with an eye in the middle, and the fabric, held in a frame, was moved to meet them rather than vice versa. Though the machine has since been very much modified, the basic principles have not changed. See also machine embroidery.

hem The edge or border of a piece of clothing or a domestic article which is sewn in such a way that it will not fray. Generally it is considered to be the raw edge of the fabric turned under (to the wrong side) and sewn down. There are various types of hem: 1. the fold is turned under and secured by hemming; 2. the raw edge is bound and secured with slip stitch; 3. the raw edge is caught down with herringbone stitch; 4. the edge is narrowly turned and machine stitched, then the edge is cut close, turned again, and stitched. See also rolled hem.

hemmed fell seam see run and fell seam.

hemmer see attachments.

hemming (felling) The usual process by which a *hem is sewn down. Hemming, or the making of a hemming stitch, consists of taking a small stitch through both the single fabric and the fold in a slanting direction. The stitches should be small and regular and look the same on either side of the fabric.

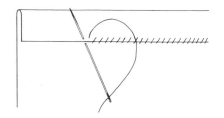

hemming bird (sewing bird) Metal object cast in the shape of a bird and used as an aid in sewing. Underneath the body is a clamp which can be fastened to a table, and by pressing or pinching the tail of the bird the beak is made to open and close. Fabric is held tight in the beak so that tension can be applied, thus making sewing quicker and easier.

hemp Annual plant, a native of western and central Asia, whose fibres, as well as being made into ropes, can be woven into a strong cloth. In Tudor times it was grown on practically every farm in England, as well as being imported from Northern Europe, to make ropes for the Navy and to be woven into canvas for sails, bedsheets, and rough clothing. Nowadays it is made into fabrics such as hessian, which can be used as a ground for embroidery.

hemstitched flat seam Join sometimes worked on lingerie or linen chemises, but which cannot be worked on a curve. About three threads are drawn $\frac{3}{4}$ inch (19 millimetres) from the raw edge on both pieces of fabric. One piece has a $\frac{1}{4}$ inch (6.4 millimetres) turning to the wrong side of the fabric and the other the same turned to the right side. The two pieces are then laid one over the other, the fold in each case exactly meeting the drawn thread, and two rows of *hemstitching are then worked, catching in the folds at every stitch.

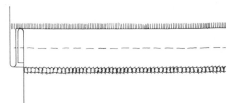

hemstitching Used to form a decorative hem. The hem is turned and threads are drawn where the inside fold meets the ground fabric. The number drawn depends on the variation of hem stitch being used, but in general the fewer the better as the drawing of threads weakens the fabric and strength must be put back. The working thread then ties the ground threads into little bundles, at the same time stitching in the hem. If more than one or two threads have been drawn, the other side must be worked as well and here many patterns can be evolved.

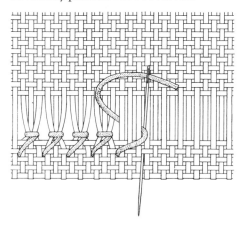

heraldic beasts Real and mythical animals which have been used in the science of heraldry, in England by the College of Arms and by its respective counterparts in other countries. While actual beasts, birds, and fish are common, so too are mythical creatures, including the wyvern, dragon, phoenix, winged horse, cockatrice, and unicorn. In embroidery they have usually been portrayed as supporters to coats of arms (for example, the lion and unicorn in the English royal coat of arms), or as crests of charges. They are generally found on state beds, firescreens, panels, herald's tabards, and regimental colours, and in former times on the surcoats of the heraldic knights and on their standards.

heraldic beasts: detail of a Swiss tablecloth depicting a griffin, 14th century.

heraldic embroidery The representation of coats of arms, crests, and insignia on textiles. It is used on the robes of the different Orders of Chivalry, standards and colours, herald's tabards, and also articles such as blazer pockets. Because a considerable knowledge of heraldry is necessary, as well as great skill in metal thread embroidery, it is very seldom attempted by amateurs. See also hatchment.

herald's tabard 'The official dress of a herald or poursuivant; a coat or jerkin having short sleeves, or none, and emblazoned with the arms of the sovereign' (OED). In the middle ages every sovereign had his heralds who, as his messengers, wore a representation of the sovereign's coat, which covered the armour and had the arms embroidered on the back, front, and short sleeves (if worn). The custom has been kept up to the present day in Britain, when the Heralds of the College of Arms wear the tabard on ceremonial occasions.

herald's tabard: sleeve of an English tabard, 18th century.

herringbone stitch (catch stitch, mossoul stitch, russian stitch, russian cross stitch, witch stitch) Used in plain sewing as well as in embroidery and has many variations. It is a simple interlacing stitch and is good for holding down raw edges, especially in fabric which does not fray. When worked with no space between the stitches it makes two rows of back stitch on the reverse side, and is then known as closed herringbone or double back stitch: this is used in shadow work.

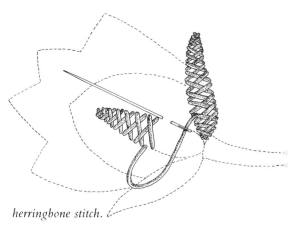

herringbone stitch.

Hertz and Wegener German publishers of Berlin woolwork patterns in the early 19th century.

hessian Strong coarse cloth, woven from hemp and jute in a rather open tabby weave. It is used for covering bales of goods but it can also be dyed attractive, subtle colours and used as a general ground fabric for coarse embroidery on articles such as gardening aprons. In addition it forms the base for many thrift rugs in England.

Hewson, John (1745–1822) English textile printer who went to America in 1773 and established a textile bleaching and printing factory near Philadelphia. During the Revolution, while he was a captain in the American army, most of his factory was destroyed by the British, but he re-established his business after the war, printing handkerchiefs, yard goods, bedspreads, and quilt centres. It has been said that Martha Washington dressed in calico printed by him. Numerous quilts with entire tops or centres in his fabrics have been discovered, and are in the collections of the Philadelphia Museum, St Louis Art Museum, and Cincinnati Museum of Art, among others.

Hewson: detail of a coverlet in printed and quilted cotton, American, 1807–19.

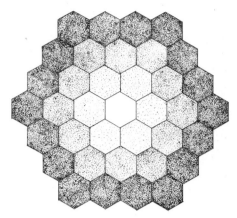

hexagon Six-sided shape commonly used in patchwork. One hexagon surrounded by six others makes a flower or rose. See also honeycomb quilt.

Hiberian embroidery Named variation of satin embroidery, worked in the late 19th century. Caulfeild and Saward (1882) describe it as 'An embroidery with Satin and Buttonhole stitches upon velvet, silk, or net foundations, with coloured silks or filoselles. It is used for banner screens, cushions, and dress trimmings, and is but little distinguishable from Satin Embroidery.'

hobby sampler Needlework *sampler form which evolved in America during the 1930s in which recreations such as fishing, hunting, sailing, and other sports and pastimes were depicted, sometimes with the addition of a verse.

holbein stitch (holbein work) see double running embroidery, double running stitch.

holland One of the basic domestic fabrics from the middle ages until now. Originally it was linen and was made in the Low Countries, but now it is generally cotton. It was used for many different domestic furnishings such as sheets and bed curtains, and also for smocks and shirts.

Holme, Randle (1627–99) English genealogist, heraldic painter, and collector of manuscripts. His father and his son (both named Randle) also followed the same trade. In 1688 he published *The Academy of Armory* 'or a Storehouse of Armory and Blazon containing the several variety of created beings and how borne in Coats of Arms, both Foreign and Domestic with the Instruments used in all Trades and Sciences, together with their terms of Art.' From the needle-worker's point of view it is the last part which is interesting, because he describes the 'terms of Art' of the school mistress who teaches sewing, and the tools of the

embroiderer, and he gives a list of stitches in current use. The manuscripts collected by the family were sold to Robert Harley in 1753 and now form part of the Harleian Manuscripts in the British Museum (London).

Holte, Mary (1684–1759) Daughter of Sir Charles Holte of Aston Hall near Birmingham (England), who is remembered by the canvas work hangings she embroidered there. They cover two of the walls in what is now known as Lady Holte's room and show Aston Hall and another house belonging to the family, Brereton Hall, framed in cartouches surrounded by flowers, figures, and foliage. On one there is the inscription: 'God be the Guide/And the work will abide/Mary Holte spinster aged 60 1744'.

Holte: detail of one of the canvas work hangings, c.1744.

Home Arts and Industries Association Association set up in 1883 which acted as an umbrella to small local groups of craft workers. Under the presidency of Lord Brownlow, it was concerned with all crafts and the teaching of them, and embroidery was included with wood-carving, metalwork, and leatherwork. The association was influenced by the teaching of John *Ruskin and his insistence on the importance of manual crafts, and the *Langdale and *Fisherton-de-la-Mere groups eventually became part of it. It is no longer in existence.

homespun Fabric made from yarn spun at home, either wool or linen, and so by inference rather coarse, plain, and uneven in texture.

honeycomb quilt Early American style of patchwork quilt where the patches are cut to a uniform* hexagon shape and sewn together in a random colour pattern.

hood Head covering which can be either attached to or separate from a garment. The medieval hood has survived in two forms. The academic hood is worn to denote the degree held by the wearer. The ecclesiastical hood is still part of the cope, though generally in a very attenuated form, and in the past some of the finest embroidery has been concentrated on it.

hood: of a modern caftan from Morocco.

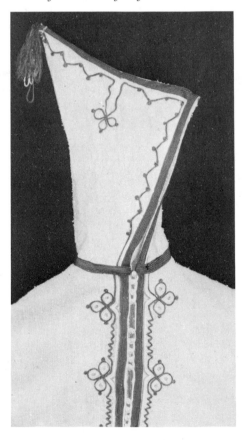

hooked rugs American folk art which gained popularity during the 1850s when burlap, used as the base for these rugs, became more available. The technique is simple, requiring only a hook similar to a crochet hook, burlap, and strips of fabric which are pulled through the backing to make the pile. Although designs were sometimes stencilled onto the rugs many were produced by the worker, incorporating mottoes, flowers, animals, ships, and geometric patterns. They are similar to the English looped rugs.

hoop see embroidery hoop.

hope chest In America a more modern name for a *dower chest; the chest and contents were more varied and less frequently handmade.

Hopi embroidery Fine embroidery done by the men of the Hopi tribe of North American Indians for their own use, for trade, and for other *Pueblos. Since all examples are done in wool it is assumed that embroidery replaced painted designs when the white man introduced sheep to the area. Designs are conventionalised, abstract, and geometric. The embroidery cloth is stretched on a frame of sharp pointed sticks, and the pattern is built up by counting the threads on material folded to make a centre line so that the border, worked in each direction, will come out even. Formerly done with bone awls, steel darning needles are now used for the simple back stitch (pueblo stitch) which leaves much of the yarn on the right side and picks up only a few threads on the underside. White meander lines are made by carrying the yarn under certain threads, leaving the natural white cotton base exposed to give an off-balance effect intended to exaggerate the movements of the dance. Formerly all Hopi men were skilled embroiderers and weavers, but today only one in ten practises the craft. (Roediger 1941, Dockstader 1964)

Hopi embroidery: an American Indian manta.

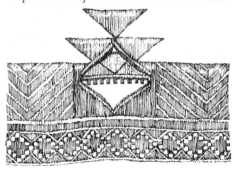

Hopi wedding robe Two large rectangles of white cotton woven for a bride of the Hopi tribe of *Pueblo Indians in North America at the time of her marriage, and worn as a dress and a mantle. Later both are embroidered top and bottom with wide coloured bands by her husband or a male relative for her to wear at tribal ceremonials. Similar style garments are worn by female and god impersonators and priests at Pueblo dance ceremonies. (Roediger 1941)

Horae Successivae see bookbindings.

horse furniture Trappings or furniture for horses, which are often superbly

horse furniture: housing and holster caps belonging to the first Duke of Marlborough, c. 1705.

embroidered for ceremonial occasions, and include saddle-bags, saddle-cloths, housings, holster caps, and neckcloths. The type of work varies from the heavy raised metal thread embroidery used in the British Army to the less formal but no less decorative beadwork on the horses of North American Indians, and the silk and spangled neckcovers of the horses in northern India.

horsetail silk see maltese silk.

hose Covering for the leg which, at different periods, was tied to the *doublet with points, reached to the knee, resembled a pair of tights, or else meant breeches. They have been, and are, worn by men and women, but those for women have generally ended just above the knee and been fastened with garters. Until the 16th century, hose were cut from cloth and seamed up the back, but with the wider use of hand knitting and the stocking frame, knitted hose which had elasticity (and therefore fitted well) became universally worn. See also stockings, clocks, chevening.

hosiery Branch of the draper's trade which includes all types of stockings and socks for men, women, and children.

hospital quilts (scripture quilts) Quilts used in the Poor Law Institutes of 19th century England. They were padded with brown paper and often the tops were of red and white patchwork squares with texts embroidered on them. (Colby 1972)

huckaback Coarse linen fabric with a loose weft thread which makes it very absorbent and good for making towels.

huckaback embroidery Kind of embroidery worked on huckaback linen or on any other similar fabric, in which the loose weft thread is picked up with coloured threads, and patterns of a darning type are made.

Hudson's Bay Company Joint stock company founded in 1670 in London, granted sole trading rights in all land drained by streams flowing into Hudson's Bay, Canada. Forts serving as protective and trading centres were built, slowly opening the country as far as the Pacific. The company traded extensively with the Indians, exchanging barter goods, blankets, beads and other items with which to do their embroideries, and also cloth for furs. In 1821 they joined rival trading companies and maintained a monopoly on the fur trade until 1859.

Hudson's Bay Company Museum

Hudson's Bay Company Museum
(Winnipeg, Canada) Collection of historical exhibits, hair embroidery, and artefacts of the Governor and Company of Adventurers of England Trading into Hudson's Bay.

huipil The blouse-like cotton upper garment worn by the women of Guatemala. They are almost always handwoven by the women themselves and some women still spin the cotton. Others spin a two-ply thread from fine commercial yarn. Ornament is usually woven stripes, fancy weaves, brocading, applied work, embroidery, or often a combination of two or three of these. Huipils worn by children in the Yucatan are embroidered with indigo blue yarn which is said to protect them against 'bad air'. (Mozzi 1968)

huipil: detail, from the Amusgo Indians of the Ometepec Region.

humeral veil Long oblong vestment of silk worn round the shoulders of Roman Catholic priests to envelop their hands when carrying the sacred vessels. It should be light enough to drape well and can be decorated with embroidery.

hungarian point see florentine embroidery.

hungarian stitch One of the grounding stitches used in work done by the counted thread, either in fine canvas work and needlepoint for stool tops, hassocks etc, or for rugs. It consists of a short upright stitch covering two threads followed by one covering four threads and one covering two threads and then a space of one thread. The second row fits into the spaces left by the first.

Hungary: detail of an apron from Mezőkövesd, 19th–20th century.

Hungary Eastern European country with a long tradition of embroidery, where originally, as in most places, the best and richest work was done for the church and the nobility. It is probable that the world famous florentine embroidery originated in Hungary through a number of Italian craftsmen who had settled there in the 15th century. Later embroideries fall into two categories: those worked by women for their dress or their homes on homespun linen, and those worked on frieze or leather by men to order and for sale. The home embroideries centred round decoration for the bed, including bands of work on the ends of sheets and on the many pillows which were piled on top of the bed in the daytime. These, as well as embroidery on costume, were either worked by the counted thread with stylised birds, animals, and flowers, or were worked freehand, using the same homely designs in a different way. One characteristic of Hungarian embroidery is the even spacing and near equal sizes of the design motifs. The stitches are those common to eastern Europe, but they are sometimes used in a special way, as for example the outlining of motifs worked in satin or basket stitch with chain stitch, and the use of open chain, or 'small writing' and closed square chain or 'big writing' worked in a thick twisted thread to give a braid effect. The work of the male furriers and embroiderers is quite different—theirs is an ancient trade which was controlled by the artisans' guilds and is entirely commercial. The spectacular cloaks (*suba) and jackets (*ködmön) are made from sheepskin, and the mantles (*szür) from frieze, and all are embroidered either in applied work using leather, or in freehand wool embroidery, or perhaps a combination of the two. (Fél 1961)

hungary stitch see florentine stitch.

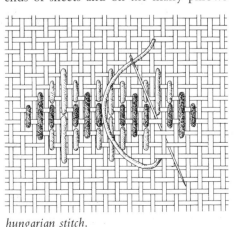

hungarian stitch.

jean: detail of an embroidered patch pocket on a pair of Levis jeans, worked by Anne Meshe.

hungertuch: made at the village of Telgte near Munster in Germany, 1930.

hungertuch (fastentuch) The hunger or fast cloth hung in some churches during Lent, especially in Germany, to separate the chancel from the nave. They were often embroidered in white on white. In the village of Telgte near Munster (Germany) is a hungertuch which was worked there in 1623. It has squares of plain linen alternating with squares of filet, darned with representations of the Passion, Adam and Eve, the Ark, etc. In 1930 another hungertuch was made using the same techniques but in a modern way, and every square was worked by a different villager. (Anon 1960). See also Lenten cloths.

Huron Large Indian nation which lived in southeast Ontario (Canada) until disrupted by the Iroquois in 1650. One remnant settled in Lorette, near Quebec, about 1721 and was greatly influenced by the convents. Poor farmland and fewer herds to hunt led them to copy French living conditions and turn to manufacturing, and a highly organised village industry was developed producing snowshoes, fancy goods, canoes, and especially

Leek Embroidery Society: detail of a piece of printed silk on which the printed design has been embroidered over; English, 19th century.

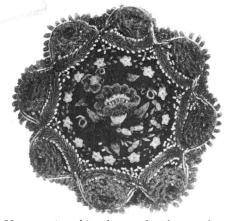

Huron: pincushion decorated with moose hair embroidery and beadwork.

hair-embroidered moccasins which were cut out at the hide plants, then decorated and assembled by the women at home. The railroads expanded the markets, and by 1898, using mass methods of production, the Hurons produced more than 140,000 pairs of moccasins in a year. (Turner 1955)

hussif (housewife) Folding bag for travelling which contains all the basic necessities for sewing and mending. They are used particularly by men, and were issued to all soldiers and sailors in Britain.

Hussifs got their name from the fact that they acted in place of a wife. Generally they are very utilitarian but some decorative ones have been made for women. In 1860 *Godey's Lady's Book* offered a roll case pattern called 'A Housewife for a Gentleman' which was considered a 'suitable gift from a lady' (Harbeson 1938).

Hutton, Miss Catherine (1756–1846) Spinster lady whose letters and memoirs were published in 1891 under the title *Reminiscences of a Gentlewoman of the last century,* which gives some idea of the needlework output of a lady of that time. She told a friend in 1845 that 'I have made shirts for my father and brothers, and all sorts of wearing apparel for myself, with the exception of shoes, stockings, and gloves. I have made furniture for beds, with window curtains, and chair and sofa covers; these included a complete drawing room set. I have quilted counterpanes and chest covers in fine white linen, in various patterns of my own invention. I have made patchwork beyond calculation, from seven years old to eighty-five ... Here ended the efforts of my needle; but before this I had worked embroidery on muslin, satin, and canvas, and netted upward of one hundred wallet purses, in combined colours and in patterns of my own invention.' (Beale 1891)

Ica shawls Shawl-like garments from the Ica Valley, one of three pre-Columbian valley communities (the others are the *Nazca and Acari) reported to have had a cultural and perhaps political unity c AD 900-1400. Ica embroideries are therefore sometimes referred to as Nazca. The shawls are almost completely covered by repeating figures embroidered in even stitches and varying colour combinations on loosely-woven, wool-gauze fabric. The decorative yarn is laced a full turn about pairs of the warp or weft and forms a ribbed surface on the back that changes directions with the altered direction of the embroidery on the surface. Some Ica shawls were worked in chain stitch. The designs are arranged as units in horizontal bands, diagonal rows, and within squares. (Bennett and Bird 1960)

Ica shawls: detail showing the embroidery technique.

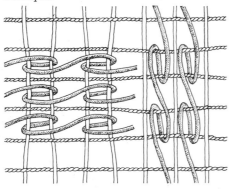

Iceland Although a small country, Iceland is rich in embroideries which are varied both in style and content. Medieval designs are closely related to contemporary manuscript illustrations and it appears that the artists of the day drew the embroidery patterns. A number of designs are enclosed in circular or polygonal frames. Embroideries are worked for the church, the home, and on costume (limited to the hem and bodice), and they include altar frontals, bed valances from the 17th and 18th centuries often darned in many coloured wools on white linen, coverlets, and cushion covers. The stitches most commonly seen include cross, long armed cross, darning, eye, stem, and split, with drawn threadwork and laid and couched work. (Gudjónssen 1970)

iconography The representation of a person or object by any form of design. This often refers to saints and prophets where they are shown with the objects which has become associated with them. such as the keys of St Peter or the gridiron of St Lawrence. In some medieval paintings and embroideries it is only these objects which identify the person.

Ida canvas Canvas introduced into America in 1889. It was loosely woven and looked as though it had been unpicked.

ikat Method of weaving in which either the warp threads alone or both the warp and weft are dyed off the loom before being woven, making a slightly fuzzy but beautiful pattern. In warp or single ikat the fuzzy pattern only appears down the length of the fabric, while in double ikat it shows in both directions. See Ship of the Dead embroideries.

imbrication Distinctive bead decoration resembling a shingled or tiled surface, generally used on coiled baskets made by the Paiute Indians of Nevada.

imbrication : a beaded basket from Nevada.

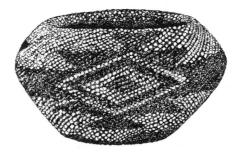

impresa 'Emblem or device, usually accompanied by an appropriate motto' (OED). The 16th century in particular was the great age of emblems, anagrams, devices, and hidden meanings, and most important people chose an impresa and used it as a badge or personal symbol. For example, *Mary Queen of Scots chose the marigold which turns its face to the sun, and for the accompanying motto, she chose *Sa Virtu m'Atire* (its strength draws me), which was an anagram on her name Marie Stuart.

inch Measure of length equal to one-twelfth of a foot. It is a very old measure, certainly pre-Norman, and is supposed to represent three barley corns laid end to end. The metric equivalent is 2.54 centimetres. See also nail.

incrust To ornament a surface with a layer or crust of another material, most commonly jewels, gold cord or braid, and lace, the latter being very common in the late 19th and early 20th centuries.

incrust: consecrated hat given to Ferdinand V in 1582 incrusted with pearls.

Index of American Design Collection of more than 17,000 carefully documented watercolours of American decorative arts from 1700 to 1900, including embroideries, furniture, glass, ceramics, and folk sculptures. It was made by American artists under the Works Progress Administration during the late 1930s. Now housed in the National Gallery of Art, Washington DC, it is often on special exhibition, and many of the watercolours have been published by Clarence Hornung in *Treasury of American Design* (1972).

Iceland: a wall hanging worked in coloured worsted on coarse canvas.

India cloths Fabrics originally manufactured only in India of which the chief are Dacca muslins, chintz, cashmere, and jaconet.

Indian embroidery The modern history of India started with the founding of the Mughal Empire in 1526. Though of central Asian origin, the Mughals had assimilated the culture of Persia, and Emperor Akbar (b 1542), keenly interested in the arts, brought Persian craftsmen to India where they worked with the natives in workshops or kharkhanas. The result was a blend of the two cultures which has remained the dominant characteristic of Indian embroidery. In general it is typified by the use of chain stitch worked with a hook called an *ari, metal threads, mirror glass or shisha, beetle wings, and exquisite work on very fine muslins. However in such an enormous subcontinent it is natural that there should be many local traditions: see bagh, chamba rumal embroidery, chikankari, kasuti embroidery, phulkari. (Irwin 1951, Dhamija 1964) (Colour illustration p.125)

indigo Substance obtained in the form of a blue powder from plants of the genus *Indigofera* and used as a dye. The indigo grows wild in the East Indies, Caribbean countries, and Australia, and varieties also producing the same colour are found in China, Japan, America, and Egypt. (Woad, the same colour as indigo and extensively used as a blue dye-stuff in early Britain, is produced from the plant *Isatis tinctoria*.) Although it has been associated with the dyeing of fabrics and threads all over the world, indigo is usually thought of in connection with the early settlers in America. The plant grew wild there and it became one of the first and only dyes available. Home vat dyeing was the custom, and a 'bluepot' was usually kept steeping on the hearth or in the shed to provide the colour-fast blue dye in varying shades—a distinctive characteristic of the wools and crewel embroidery of colonial America. See also Deerfield Society of Blue and White Needlework.

Indo-European embroidery Embroidery which came to England from India in the 17th century and was thought for many years to be truly Indian. However Irwin (1959), keeper of the Indian section at the Victoria and Albert Museum in London, has shown conclusively from the records of the *East India Company that this work was in fact embroidered from designs and suggestions sent to India from England, and worked by the Indian in his own idiom. See also Indo-Portuguese embroidery. (Colour illustration p.126)

Indo-Portuguese embroidery: detail of a bedspread, late 17th century.

Indo-Portuguese embroidery Adapted style of Portuguese European embroidery which developed in India after the Portuguese infiltration, beginning in 1501. The Portuguese Jesuit missionaries arriving about 1542 set up schools and brought with them illustrated books, religious vestments, and church furnishings. This may well have inspired new design motifs of Old Testament themes, European hunters, and classical Graeco-Roman legends, which combine with the traditional Hindu mythological heroes, animals, and decorative motifs. Examples of this work can be seen at the Museum of Fine Arts in Boston, and the Museo Nazionale in Florence. (Fanelli 1970) See also Indo-European embroidery.

infulae The two *lappets which hang down from the back of a bishop's mitre. Originally they were probably longer and tied under the chin, but for many hundreds of years they have been merely ornamental appendages which are either sewn or hooked onto the mitre.

ingrain Word describing yarn that is dyed before being woven (as opposed to dyeing the finished fabric). Both Turkey red cotton and red marking cotton are ingrain.

initials see lettering.

inkle Narrow linen tape used until the end of the 17th century for many purposes such as shoe and apron strings. It often had yellow or blue-and-red stripes and was occasionally embroidered. This material was used more by the poor than by the well-to-do.

inlay Type of patchwork still done today, suitable only for materials which are close textured or closely woven and which do not fray. It lends itself to counterchange designs and was much used in the 14th and 15th centuries by the Spaniards and Italians, but the work started in the East and is known in Iran as *Resht work. See also pieced patchwork.

INRI Initials standing for *Iesus Nazarenus, Rex Iudaeorum*, or Jesus of Nazareth, King of the Jews. This was written on the cross on which Jesus was crucified by Pontius Pilate, and these letters appear in most representations of the Crucifixion, whether in embroidery or other arts.

insertion Length of fabric, lace, ribbon, tape, or embroidery with both edges identical which can be let in (inserted) to make a decorative join. They are often found on babies' gowns and lingerie, where as well as being used in a seam, they are sometimes let into the fabric as decoration. Coarse linen insertion is also suitable for curtains and brise-bises, bed-spreads, and tablecloths. See also entre deux.

insertion: handworked for the English royal household, c.1920.

insertion stitches Stitches making an *openwork or decorative seam, some-times referred to as *faggoting. To make them the two edges must first be prepared by roll hemming, making a very narrow hem, or binding. In order to keep the stitches equidistant it is best to tack the two edges to a shiny surface such as *toile cirée, parchment, or even greaseproof paper. Faggoting and variations: bar, buttonhole, and pyramid stitches. Insertion stitch and variations: buttonhole, interlacing, italian buttonhole, knotted (open cretan, trellis), laced, plaited, twisted (faggoting).

Instruments of the Passion Christian symbols often embroidered in red cotton thread on drab-coloured linen for lenten altar and church furnishings, the Instruments may include the crown of thorns, the ladder, the dice, the seamless robe, the cock, the sword, the spear, pincers, hammer, pillar, scourge, reed and sponge, nails, and thirty pieces of silver, all of which played a part in the Passion and death of Christ.

interchange Similar to *counter-change, but refers to colour as well as design.

interchange: red velvet ground with green silk ornament changes to green ground with red velvet ornament.

interlining Extra layer of material placed between a fabric and its lining either for strength or for warmth.

inventory List of goods and chattels owned by a person at a given time. An inventory may be taken on death (the big majority), on sequestration by the Crown or country (Dame Agnes Hungerford and Charles I), for insurance purposes (most present-day inventories), on marriage (princess Elizabeth, daughter of James I), or for some particular reason now unknown (the Hardwick Hall Inventories); also, in the case of church goods, on the occasion of Archdeacons' visitations. Most old inventories have details added to the description of goods which are our main source of knowledge about such objects as bed hangings, clothes, coverings for furniture etc.

invisible hemming see blind hem-ming.

invisible mending see fine drawing.

Iranian embroidery see Persian em-broidery.

Ireland There is no embroidery of a specifically Irish style known before the 19th century when, because of the extreme poverty of the peasantry, various types were started either by nuns or landowners' wives. Generally they were based on European laces, and sold very well as lace was so popular and the Irish embroideries were considerably cheaper than the real article. See Carrickmacross, Limerick lace, Mountmellick work.

Irish guipure see Carrickmacross.

Irish linen Even, soft, and slightly glossy linen which is good for embroidery. The climate of Ireland is particularly suitable for the cultivation of flax so the weaving of linen has been one of the country's main industries for several centuries.

irish stitch see long and short stitch, florentine stitch.

ironing (pressing) The smoothing of fabric with an iron. Originally ironing and pressing were different but now the words are synonymous. At one time all flat articles were folded and put, slightly damp, into a linen press which was screwed down so that creases were smoothed out, but the sharp folding lines remained. Then, with the advent of irons, creases could be removed by heat. Embroidery should always be pressed from the back with a thick blanket under it so that it is not flattened.

Iroquois League of five Woodland Indian nations: the Mohawks, Senecas, Onondaga, Oneida, and Cayuga. They stayed in one place and were agricultural, peace-loving, skilled in quillwork, and, with the Algonquins who surrounded them, were the first Indian contact for most early settlers along the east coast of North America. The Iroquois were greatly influenced by the French, and quickly adopted European methods in agriculture, and they also used French patterns brought over by the *Ursuline nuns in their moosehair embroidery.

Irwin Untermeyer collection (Metropolitan Museum of Art, New York) Extensive collection of artefacts, porcelain, metalwork, furniture, textiles, and embroideries from the middle ages onward. It was made during the 20th century by Judge and Mrs Irwin Untermeyer of New York, and includes embroidered panels, pictures, caskets, vestments, and clothing accessories in all varieties of techniques, as well as what is probably the finest collection of English needlework extant. (Hackenbrock 1960)

italian cutwork see reticella.

italian hem Decorative hem used on lingerie or for edging tray cloths, tablecloths, runners etc. A separate piece of fabric, sometimes of a different colour, is seamed onto the back and brought over to the right side. A simple design such as a scallop is marked onto the hem which is then cut off $\frac{1}{8}$ inch (3.2 millimetres) outside the design, the edge is turned in, and the hem worked with an ornamental stitch such as point turc or pin stitch, or simply hemmed down.

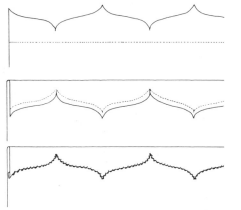

italian quilting One of the two types of *cord quilting. Two layers of fabric are used: a top one preferably of silk, though satin and some cottons can be used, and an underlayer of butter muslin. The design, which must always consist of a pair of parallel lines, is run or backstitched through both layers of fabric. Then from the back a soft cord is run between the layers and between the double lines, so bringing the design into relief.

Italy Modern Italy has been formed from a collection of states, each once self-governing and each with very different characteristics in art, so it is not possible to speak of Italian embroidery as a whole. In the 15th century the ecclesiastical embroideries of Florence (opus florentium) had a great reputation, and the designs were generally produced by the well-known artists of the day such as Antonio del Pollaiuolo and Mantegna's master Francesco Squarcione, who was an embroiderer until the age of 29. In *The Lives of the Painters*, Vasari mentions other artists who designed for embroidery and whose ambition was to produce embroideries which looked as much like paintings as possible. Italian *cutwork or *reticella was the inspiration which eventually produced all the needlepoint laces of Europe, and it is from Italy that the early pattern books came, such as *Les singuliers et nouveaux pourtraicts et ouvrages de Lingerie* by the Venetian Federic di *Vinciolo. See also Assisi embroidery, florentine embroidery. (Colour illustration p.127)

Italy: detail of a panel depicting the Labours of the Months, 17th century.

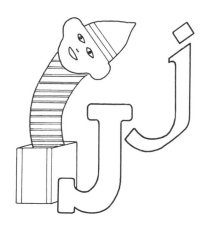

jack 1. Short jacket worn by men and women in the 14th century. 2. Sleeveless tunic or jacket of quilted leather, sometimes plated with iron, worn by foot soldiers between the 14th and 17th centuries.

Jacobean embroidery see crewel work.

Jamieson, Mrs Skilled needlewoman who was one of the agents for the flowered muslin industry of West Scotland at the turn of the 18th century. In 1814 she was shown a beautiful baby's robe, worked by a Frenchwoman, which was inset with lace stitches. She copied these stitches and taught them to the women she employed, who then added them to the flowered muslins to form the distinctive type of embroidery known as *Ayrshire. (Swain (1955)

Janina embroidery (Joannina embroidery) In the late 18th and 19th centuries Janina (Greece) was famous for its gold embroideries for costume, which it exported. Pesel (1921) shows a table cover from there in double running and fine darning whose design is based on that of Italian brocade with the colours reminiscent of tiles.

janina stitch see romanian stitch.

Japanese embroidery The art of embroidery in Japan has been complementary and often subordinate to the arts of weaving and dyeing in which the country has been pre-eminent, and it was often used just to highlight and enhance dyed or brocaded textiles. However it came into its own in periods when those crafts were for some reason or other in decline. In the 18th and 19th centuries the nature-loving Japanese embroidered their flowers in as naturalistic a way as possible, using few stitches—mainly satin, long and short, stem, and chain—but getting their effects by the perfect placing and direction of the stitch, often using an untwisted floss silk as thread. Much gold thread is used for highlighting coloured embroidery or dyeing, or by itself on coloured ground. Modern Japanese work still emphasises the importance of embroidery and dyeing together, rather than one overriding the other, and although as in other countries commercial considerations are now more important than the purely artistic, there is still much beautiful work being produced. (Johnstone 1957) (Colour illustration p128)

Japanese embroidery: an 18th century cover.

Japanese gold Thread made by winding strips of paper covered with gold leaf round an orange silk core. It was not introduced into England or America until about 1860.

japangi Large scarlet cape with brilliant embroideries worn in Scutari (Albania) by married Catholic women for outdoor wear. It has a rectangular piece of material which hangs down the back but can be pulled over the head and kept in place by the wearer holding two cords, one on either side. (Start 1939)

japangi: from Scutari, late 19th century. Above is a detail of the embroidery; below is the embroidery complete.

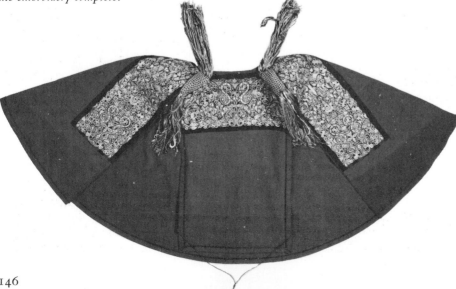

Jarvis collection see Nathan Sturges Jarvis collection.

Java canvas Originally known as Panama canvas, it is closely-woven with several threads to each warp and weft, available in several colours and thicknesses. It was popular in the late 19th century as the ground could, if required, be left plain, and it was used for bold, simple designs on mats, slippers, and cushions.

Java cotton see kapok.

jean Strong, twilled cotton cloth, a variety of fustian. It is a fabric with a very long history which has been much used in the corset trade, especially when it has a satin weave, and many of the lightweight women's boots of the first half of the 19th century were made of jean or satin jean. Nowadays it is used for pockets and linings. The trousers called jeans are

jean: appliqué denim jeans with scallops of denim and felt.

generally made of *denim, a very similar fabric, and there is a current fad for having them elaborately embroidered. (Colour illustration p.137)

jelek Little sleeveless jackets or zouaves worn by women in Albania. They are beautifully embroidered or else decorated with braid by Albanian tailors. (Start 1939)

jerkin Jacket with or (more frequently) without sleeves, worn by men in the 16th and 17th centuries, and with sleeves by men, women, and children today. It could be very plain and utilitarian, perhaps made of leather, or else very decorative. Planché (1847) says that 'in 1535 a jerkin of purple velvet, with purple satin sleeves, embroidered all over with Venice gold, was presented to the King [Henry VIII] by Sir Richard Cromwell', and in the wardrobe account of Henry Prince of Wales (1608) there is an entry for 'Embroidering a jerkin and a pair of panes of perfumed leather, wrought about with gold, silver and coloured silk, 45l' (Bray 1793).

jerkin: detail from a 16th century portrait.

Jesse cope One of the fine pieces of opus anglicanum in the Victoria and Albert Museum (London), worked between 1295 and 1315. The cope, which has been mutilated, is made of rose-coloured silk twill, embroidered with silver gilt, silver thread, and coloured silks, and it depicts a vine springing from the body of Jesse, sheltering prophets and ancestors of Christ within its convolutions. (King 1963)

jet 'Hard compact black form of "brown coal" or lignite, capable of receiving a brilliant polish' (OED). It has been used in needlework as a bead or jewel for many hundreds of years.

jewel embroidery thread see coton perlé.

jewels The various descriptions in inventories and wardrobe accounts, from the middle ages onwards, show that jewels were frequently used in embroidery in conjunction with metal threads, and that great personages literally tottered under the weight of them. Mrs Christie (1909) quotes the story that Marie de' Medici, at a royal baptism in 1606, wore a robe decorated with 3200 pearls and 3000 diamonds and that, perhaps not surprisingly, she never wore it again. Copes especially were often heavily bejewelled, as were the mitres, sandals, and buskins worn by bishops. However the surviving number of pieces of embroidery worked with jewels is small, largely because either the work was mutilated when the stones were removed and sold, or else because wear has caused the thread with which the stones were sewn down to fray so they have fallen off. In the East the use of precious stones in embroidery has always been even more lavish than in the West. See also pearl embroidery.

jewels: glove of Frederick the Great, Sicilian, early 13th century.

Jewish ritual embroidery As in all religions, the embroidery on objects used in the rituals of the Jewish faith is the best and most sumptuous that can be worked, allied to designs which are full of symbolism. Embroidery has always been a feature of the faith going back to the Old Testament with its description of the curtain in the Tabernacle, 'And thou shalt make a vail of blue, and purple and scarlet, and fine twined linen of cunning work; with cherubims shall it be made' (Exodus 26.31). This command is remembered on the embroidery of the parokheths hung in front of the Arks. Other decorated objects include the binders or wimpels which hold the scroll together, and the mantles which cover it. The prayer shawl or tallith, worn by men, may be quite plain with fringes at the four corners, or may be beautifully embroidered as one worn by a bridegroom at his wedding. (Cohen 1966)

John of Thanet panel *Panel of opus anglicanum in the Victoria and Albert Museum (London) worked between 1300 and 1320. It was probably part of a cope and shows Christ enthroned, blessing. Over the figure is an arch inscribed Johannes de Thaneto.

Jones, Mary Famous quilter and designer of quilts who trained apprentices. She lived in the village of Panteg in Cardiganshire (Wales), and died in 1900. (Colby 1972)

Judgment of Solomon One of the themes from the Old Testament which excited the imagination of the 17th century embroiderer, and was interpreted in countless tent stitch and raised work panels. The story (1 Kings 3) tells of two harlots living in the same house who each had a child. One child died, and its mother stole the child belonging to the other woman. She then accused the thief, who denied the charge. The case was taken to Solomon, and he ordered the executioner to cut the remaining child in two and give one half to each mother, whereupon the real mother, not being able to bear to see her child killed, offered to give it to her rival, and so Solomon knew which was the mother and gave her back her child.

Judgment of Solomon: embroidered panel after Rubens, English, 17th century.

jupon (gipon) 1. 'Close-fitting tunic or doublet, especially one worn by knights under the hauberk [coat of mail], sometimes of thick stuff and padded; later a sleeveless surcoat worn outside the armour, of rich materials and emblazoned with arms' (OED). 2. 'Short kirtle worn by women' (OED). 3. Woman's skirt or petticoat. The variety of these definitions makes it very necessary to establish the context when reading the word. The jupons or surcoats worn by knights in the middle ages were usually emblazoned with applied work.

jute Fibre of the jute plant grown mainly in Bengal but also in other parts of India and in Ceylon and China. It is woven into canvas, sacking, duck, and twine, and being silky it is also mixed with other fibres, sometimes with pure silk.

jute embroidery canvas Double-thread canvas with comparatively small holes used for making rugs, especially in surrey stitch.

kaftan see caftan.

kalangas Wall hangings used in the past in Burma to decorate temples and the houses of the wealthy. They were taken from place to place and, on journeys to feasts, they adorned the bullock carts. No exotic fabrics were used, though sequins and braids were added, and the whole hanging, with its figures, animals, and stylised designs, was worked in appliqué in a rough but exciting way with the minimum of stitchery. (Krishna 1962 and 1963)

kameleika Waterproof garment worn by the Aleuts, made from seal intestines. Collars and cuffs are embroidered with delicate hair embroidery and seal gullet borders are applied onto the bottom of the skirt. See Aleut embroidery.

kanthas Quilted coverlets and shawls made entirely from waste fabrics by the women of Bengal. The running stitches which form the quilting are worked in whirling patterns of flowers, animals, and scenes of domestic life. When this is finished, extra medallions are embroidered on top. (Irwin and Hall 1973)

kanthas: Indian, 19th century.

kapok (silk cotton, mockmain, Java cotton) Short-stapled, silky fibres which surround the seeds of a tree found in the East Indies *(Eriodendron anfractuosum)* and were first introduced into Britain in 1851. These fibres can be used as a cheap filling for cushions, pillows, and quilts but are not used for good-quality articles as they tend to become lumpy.

kapporeth Short valance which often hangs in front of the Torah ark curtain in synagogues.

Kasai velvet see embroidered pile cloth.

kashmir (fabric) see cashmere (fabric).

Kashmir shawls Since the 15th century shawls have been woven in Kashmir. One 19th century type, called an *amli, had designs embroidered rather than woven in. (Irwin 1973)

kasuti embroidery Embroidery worked in Deccan and parts of Mysore in India, which is composed of stitches worked by the counted thread, including double running, zigzag running, plain running, simulating weaving, and cross stitch. The word is a variation of kashida meaning embroidery. (Dhamija 1964)

katab Applied work of Kathiawar (India) which uses coloured cotton cloths, red and blue usually predominating on white or unbleached cotton. Geometric patterns are combined with animals, men, and plants. Much use is made of counterchange, but here, instead of the pieces exactly interlocking as in true counterchange, they are turned under and hemmed down leaving a narrow strip of the white cotton ground showing. (Irwin and Hall 1973)

Kay-Shuttleworth, Hon Rachel see Gawthorpe Hall.

Keith, Dora Wheeler (1856–1940) American textile and embroidery designer, daughter of Candace *Wheeler, and a member of *Associated Artists after 1883. She designed several series of needlework tapestries, one of which was

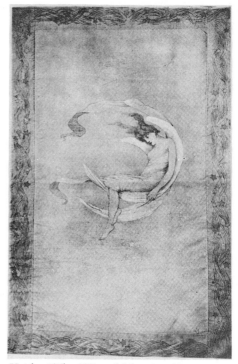

Keith: 'The Winged Moon', 1882.

for the Cornelius Vanderbilt II mansion Fifth Avenue, New York. This five-panel set, worked on salmon pink in greys and purples, includes the Water Spirit and the Winged Moon. (Faude 1975)

Kells embroidery Embroidery in which the designs are based mostly on the illustrations in the *Book of Kells* and ancient Celtic manuscripts, used on curtains and portières as well as smaller pieces. It was worked on handspun, vegetable-dyed linen, wool, or Galway flannel with polished flax thread. The famines in Donegal (Ireland) in the early 1880s prompted a Mrs Ernest Hart to set up an organisation known as the Donegal Industrial Fund which taught crafts to the starving women and girls and sold their work, and this was one type of embroidery they learnt. (Morris 1962)

kersey Cloth woven from long staple wool, which is coarse and generally ribbed. With references to it going back at least to the 14th century, it is one of the earliest known woollen cloths. It was woven in different parts of England and was known as Devon kersey, Hampshire kersey, Suffolk kersey, and so on, and it made a good foundation for embroidery, though the ravages of moths have meant that few early pieces remain.

kharkanas Court workshops set up by Emperor Akbar in India in the 16th century, where Persian and Indian workers collaborated and the specifically Mughal types of design first appeared. They were large halls in which artisans such as embroiderers, tailors, joiners, goldsmiths, and others worked, each trade being superintended by a master. (Irwin 1951) See also Mughals.

khirka Veil worn by the women of Ramallah in south Palestine. It is made of two pieces of white linen joined lengthways and embroidered all over with stylised designs. (Weir 1969)

khirka: from Ramallah, Palestine, c. 1870.

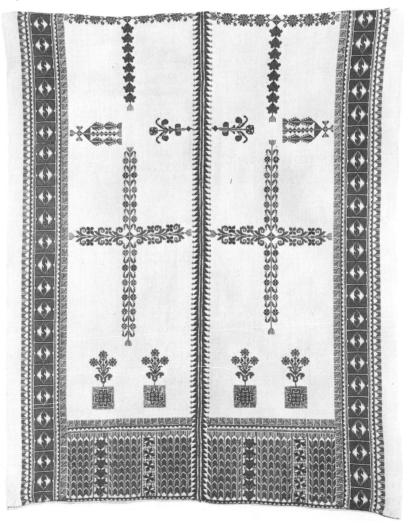

kilt 'Pleated wrap-round skirt reaching from the waist to the knees, originally of tartan plaid and worn by men and boys in Scotland; term now applies to anything that resembles a kilt in form, in any fabric and for either sex' (Webster). Certain American Indian tribes wear kilts for ceremonial dances, often of apron style, which are embroidered or decorated with shells and appliqué in designs of stylised animals or mythological creatures. A fringe sewn round the bottom is sometimes trimmed with puffin beaks and deer hooves that rattle as the dancer moves. (Roediger 1941, Dockstader 1964) See also dancing aprons, Pueblo Indians, Hopi embroidery.

kilt: from the Northwest Coast of America.

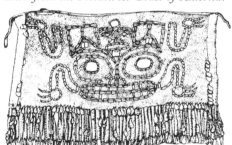

kimono Long robe with loose sleeves, fastened with a sash or obi, and worn in Japan. They are often lavishly and beautifully embroidered, especially those for ceremonial occasions. During the 20th century the Western world has adapted the kimono to its own use for dressing gowns, beachwear etc, and used the sleeve shape (kimono sleeve) in other types of garment.

kimono: for ceremonial use, Japanese, 19th century.

kirtle 1. Tunic or coat worn by men which reached to the knees or lower, but Fairholt (1846) mentions that it could also mean a monk's gown. The use of the word applying to male garments ceased at the end of the middle ages. 2. Gown for women in the middle ages, but later a skirt or a petticoat designed to show. In 1578 Elizabeth I was given 'a kyrtyll of purple satten, with roses of white lawne embrodered with golde unlyned' (Nichols 1823). In some dialects, notably in East Anglia, it was the word for a safeguard or dust cover worn when riding pillion. 3. Blouse of cotton or linen of the late 19th and early 20th centuries. It was sometimes smocked, was worn by schoolboys, and had a leather belt.

kits Method of selling supplies for embroidery and rugmaking which has gained great acceptance since the Second World War. Everything necessary for a piece of work, including the design, threads, needle, and detailed instructions, is packed together so the embroiderer has no decisions to make. In the 1930s it was possible to buy an etching embroidery which had the design ready traced on linen, packed together with a skein of black thread, but it went no further than that, and it was not until the 1950s and 60s that the selling of kits became common.

kloster blocks Blocks of geometrical satin stitch which edge the cut threads in Hardanger embroidery.

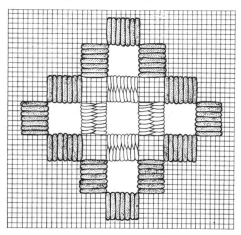

kloster stitch see couching stitch.

knife case Cover for the knives which were used for cutting up food and which were kept as personal possessions until the general use of table cutlery came in in the 17th century. The knives owned by wealthy people had rich and decorative handles and were kept in a case which was often embroidered.

knife case: a pair of knives and their embroidered case.

Knole: the Spangle Bedroom.

Knole (Kent, England) House belonging to the National Trust which is particularly rich in embroideries, some of which date from James I's reign. These include the bedhead, tester, and bedspread in the Venetian room, the embroideries in gold appliqué and silver spangles in the Spangle Room, and the furnishings of Lady Betty Germaine's room of a slightly later date. A workroom has now been set up in the house where those embroideries most in need of attention are being repaired.

knot The interlacing of one or more threads which can be used in many ways in such diverse crafts as rugmaking, macramé, weaving, upholstery, and knotting. In needlework a knot is most commonly used at the end of a needleful of thread to prevent it being pulled through the fabric, and in embroidery in stitches such as french or pekin knots. Silk, leather, or cord interlaced in the design called Turk's head can be used as a button.

knot garden Formal flower-beds outlined by low-cut hedges forming arabesques or complicated fret patterns, like those seen in pattern books and furnishings of the time. They were one of the inspirations of the Elizabethan embroiderers, and still offer a fruitful source of design today. (Digby 1963)

knotted stitch see french knot.

knotted stitches Stitches used to give a definite texture. They can be detached points, or knots close together, or knots made as an addition to another stitch. Stitches in this group are: armenian edging; braid edging (braid); bullion or bullion knot (caterpillar, coil, grub, knot, point de rose, porto rico rose, post, roll,

worm, wound); *chinese knot (pekin knot); coral (beaded, coral knot, german knot, knotted outline knotted, snail trail) and variations: double, spanish (teardrop), tied, zigzag; dot (simple knot); double knot (danish knot, old english knot, palestrina, smyrna, tied coral); fourlegged knot; *french knot (french dot, knotted, twisted knot, wound knot); knot (Antwerp edging, knotted blanket); knotted buttonhole; knotted cable; knotted chain, knotted feather (spanish knotted feather); knotted stem; *tailor's buttonhole.

knotting Craft akin to embroidery, which was practised in England in the 17th and 18th centuries. By means of a shuttle known as a knotting shuttle (larger than a tatting shuttle), knots were made at about quarter inch (6 millimetre) intervals in lengths of thread that might be string, linen, silk, or wool. The thread between the knots was then sewn to a suitable ground, either covering it completely or in a pattern. At *Cotehele House there is a set of chairs covered in knotting in a design of flowers of many colours and shades, and here the knots are sewn so closely together that the ground is invisible. In the 17th century, linen doublets were sometimes decorated with knotting, as were bedspreads and curtains, and lengths of knotted yarn were made into fringes in the 18th century. The craft was given a great fillip by Queen Mary (wife of William III) who could never bear to be idle and who, in the words of Sir Charles Sedley, 'when she rides in coach abroad is always knotting threads'. Two references in the Hardwick Hall inventories (1601) may refer to knotting, but could equally apply to embroidery worked in french knots: 'fyve Curtins of blewe cloth with black silk knottes' and 'an other long quition of silke nedlework wrought with knottes' (Boynton 1971). Finally, in 1750 the indefatigable Mrs Delany wrote to her sister 'I ... am sorry I have no knotting of the sort you want done, I cannot promise too much for you till I have finished a plain fringe I am knotting to trim a new blue and white linen bed I have just put up ... send me the sized knotting you want.' Knotting with a shuttle is no longer done today. (Llanover 1862)

Knowles, Mary (1733-1807) One of the British embroiderers of the last half of the 18th century who made a practice of copying prints and paintings in stitches

Knowles: embroidered self-portrait, 1779.

angled to represent the strokes of a brush. She was well known to George III and worked a portrait of him in crewels, dated 1771, taken from the portrait by Zoffany, and then in 1779 she embroidered a picture of herself working at the king's portrait. Both these now belong to HM the Queen.

ködmön Sleeved jacket of various lengths, made of sheepskin, and worn by Hungarian men and women. The front and sides consist of one skin, which is sewn to a narrow back part. As most of the decoration is on the seams it means that the embroidery, which is either of applied leather or satin stitch (sometimes combined), is concentrated on the back of the jacket. (Fél 1961)

kokanwuqtl see spider woman.

koleto (colletto) Fichu or tippet of fine linen or silk gauze worn round the shoulders by the women of Crete. They are decorated with insertions of Cretan bobbin lace and with metal thread and silk embroidery. (Johnstone 1972)

Kwakiutl Indians One of the seven major tribes of the northwest coast of western Canada. Their settlements on the northern coast of Vancouver Island and on the mainland opposite are permanent, with red cedar houses. The cedar is also used for masks and totem poles, and the bark fibres are woven into clothing, mats, and baskets. Ceremonial clothing includes *dance aprons, leggings, and *button blankets decorated with buttons, bells, and thimbles, and embroidered with traditional clan motifs. (Hawthorn 1967)

Kwakiutl Indians: button cloak from Aleut Bay.

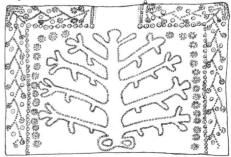

lace 1. Fine, openwork fabric of three main types: bobbin or bone lace made by twisting threads; needlepoint made by looping and knotting threads; and machine made. For needle-made simulated laces see net laces. 2. Cord used to draw together two edges, as stay lace, shoe-lace or tie for a mantle or cloak. See also point (number 2).

lace joins Method of joining two pieces of lace by laying the ends one over the other, in pattern if possible, and working close hemming or overcasting round the edge of a motif. The surplus fabric, both top and bottom, is then cut away close to the stitching.

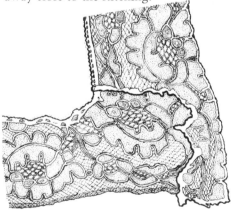

lacer In America, a blunt needle-like device sometimes used for lacing braid to braid with carpet thread when making braided rugs. (*McCall's Needlework* 1972)

lace scissors Specially designed scissors which make it easier to cut away the surplus of fine lace or muslin motifs applied to net, as in Honiton or Carrickmacross laces. They have a tiny rounded piece of metal at the back of one of the points which prevents the scissor point from cutting through the base fabric.

lace stitch see point turc.

lacet work Method of using lacet *braid, either by itself or in conjunction with tatting or crochet, to form patterns which can be made up into work for the church, or for mats or other articles. A ground fabric is prepared with a suitable design and the braid, which is narrow

with a looped edge, is sewn down following the pattern. The different parts of the braid are then joined by bars or brides.

lacis Handmade, square or lozenge-shaped meshed net with the pattern darned in using the same kind of linen thread as that used for the net. This was a very early technique known all through the middle ages, especially in Germany. The earliest English piece recorded is one belonging to St Paul's Cathedral (London) in 1295. Other names for this work include filet, opus araneum, opus filatorium, spiderwork, and guipure d'art. Modern lacis work, which may be machine made, often consists of insertions for articles such as tablecloths, tray cloths, and chair backs. It is also used to make table mats, dressing table sets etc. See also darned net, net laces.

lacis: detail of a pillow bere, English, 16th century.

ladder stitch see open chain stitch.

Ladies' Ecclesiastical Embroidery Society Association founded in 1854 'to supply altar cloths of strictly ecclesiastical design either by reproducing ancient examples or by working under the supervision of a competent architect.' The society was formed by the architect G. E. *Street, his sister, and Miss Agnes Blencowe. See Bodley, G.F.

ladies' fairs Fund-raising events in America at which ladies donated hand-worked items for sale. One of the most famous was the Bunker Hill Monument Fair, held in September 1840 to raise money to complete the Bunker Hill Monument begun 15 years previously (the Battle of Bunker Hill in Boston between the Americans and the British started the War of Independence in 1775). Ladies from Boston and vicinity, Norwich, Connecticut, and Brooklyn, were among those who provided a 'rich array of useful and choice articles . . . the proof of women's industry and ingenuity, and of the efficiency of the "polished shaft".' In the seven days of the fair about $27,000 was raised. See also Sanitary Fair.

Lady's Magazine, The or entertaining companion for the fair sex Magazine published in Britain between 1770 and 1832 which contained among the usual articles, gossip, and fashions excellent designs for embroidered accessories. So popular were these that it is rare to find copies with the designs intact—they have been torn out, pricked, and used for embroidery. Most of the designs were suitable for the popular whitework of the day and were used on articles such as handkerchiefs, watch bottoms, aprons, caps etc.

laidwork The laying down of a foundation of long threads which are then tied down in pattern by other threads crossing them. This type of embroidery has been popular at various times in most parts of the world, and different countries have interpreted the basic definition in different ways, with the result that there are three distinct varieties. 1. Solid, where the ground threads are placed touching one

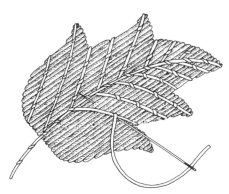

lambrequin: in crazy patchwork, late 19th century.

another. This type can be found in parts of the *Bayeux tapestry and in various pieces of opus anglicanum. 2. Open, where the threads are laid at intervals, with the crossing thread laid at the same interval to form open squares which are then tied down at the corners. This kind can often be seen in English crewel work hangings of the 17th century. 3. Oriental (which is really a form of *couching), where the same thread both lays and ties, as in the medieval white embroideries from Germany and Switzerland. (Forbes 1966) See also couching.

lama (lame) Very thin gilded or plated sheet of metal which can be cut into shapes or strips with scissors or a punch and which is much used in Indian embroidery for decorating net, muslin, and other suitable fabrics. If the pieces punched out from the metal sheet are very small they are termed paillons. The name is also given to a fabric woven from metallic thread. (Lambert 1843)

lama: Indian, late 19th century.

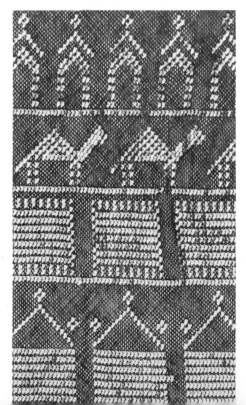

lambrequin 1. In the middle ages, a piece of fabric worn over the helmet to protect it from the heat and wet; also in heraldry, a scarf hanging from the helmet with a pointed or jagged end. 2. In 19th century USA, a cornice or the material hanging from a cornice, mantelpiece, or shelf, that could have had a vandyked or scalloped border, and is still used above windows.

landscape picture embroidery Favourite type of embroidery in England and also America. Many late-18th-century pictures were worked on silk taffeta, in which the faces, hands, and skies were painted, and the landscapes were embroidered in long stitches in filoselle. This kind of pictorial embroidery has also been done in canvas work (particularly petit point) and crewel work. See also embroidered pictures.

Landseer, Sir Edwin Henry (1802–1873) One of the foremost English animal painters of his period, whose pictures were generally based on some moral or sentimental idea which appealed to the Victorians. Many of his paintings were translated into patterns for Berlin woolwork, including *Monarch of the Glen, Dignity and Impudence, There's life in the old dog yet*, and various portraits of pets belonging to Queen Victoria.

Langdale Linen Industry A small weaving industry in Westmorland, England, set up by John *Ruskin and Albert Fleming in 1893 to help local workers. Working teachers first produced an evenweave linen, then added cutwork designs based on old reticella lace.

lappet 1. Loose flap or fold on a garment; also a lapel. 2. Appendage to a lady's cap. Generally they are the two pieces that hang down, either at the sides or back of the head, and are often embroidered en suite with the cap. 3. The *infulae or lappets hanging from a bishop's mitre.

lap robes In America, blanket which covers the knees, thighs, and lower part of the body. Necessary in carriages and the early days of cars, they were made of wool, fur, felt, or medium-weight fabric and were embroidered, appliquéd, or monogrammed with the name of the owner.

lap seam Method of joining materials which do not fray, used generally for outer wear. The two edges are laid one over the other facing in opposite directions, and two parallel rows of stitching are worked, one from the right side and one from the wrong.

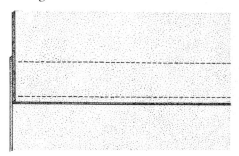

latch hook (latchet hook) Tool resembling a crochet hook but with the addition of a small hinged spoke or latch below the hook. Thus a loop of thread or yarn in the hook can be held there by the latch which is pushed upwards when the head of the tool is pulled through fabric. Latch hooks are used in various sizes in making hooked rugs, in turning bias rouleau, and to pull up dropped stitches in knitted fabric.

Latin cross see cross.

Laudian frontal (altar carpet, thow-over frontal) One of the two types of *altar frontal, so called after Archbishop Laud who reintroduced it into the Anglican church in the 17th century. It consists of a single piece of fabric, large enough to throw over the altar and hang to the ground on all four sides, thus making it suitable for a free-standing altar. Because of the shape and the folds at the corners, it is not so easy to decorate as intensively as the other type (the frontal or antependium), so the embroidery generally only consists of a large motif in the centre front.

lawn Originally a fine linen fabric, but now it is usually made of cotton. It has always been used for the finest lingerie, baby clothes, handkerchiefs, and for the lawn sleeves worn by a bishop.

layette Complete outfit for a newborn infant, including garments (many of which may be handsewn and embroidered) and, in America, bedding and furniture.

lazy squaw stitch Method of attaching beads by stringing several on a thread and stitching to the ground fabric only at the ends. It is practised by, among others, the eastern Plains and Woodland Indians of North America.

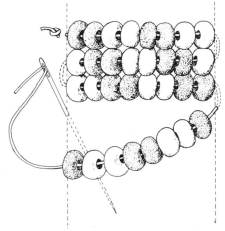

lazy squaw stitch: detail below of a Yakima Indian woman's beaded buckskin dress.

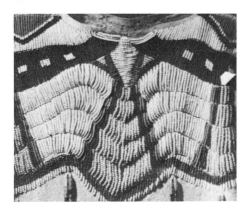

lea (lay) Measure of yarn. According to the *Encyclopedia Britannica* (1882) it equals the Scottish 'cut' of 300 yards (275 metres), while Bowman (1885) says that it is the seventh part of a hank, which in worsted is 80 yards (73 metres), and in cotton and silk is 120 yards (110 metres).

lead cushion Very heavy cushion which was (and sometimes still is) used when sewing long seams by hand. The *Ladies Treasury* (1887) says 'The lead should be oblong, about 7 inches long by 4 inches wide [18 by 10 centimetres] covered with a piece of canvas . . . A flannel bag to fit the top of this to be filled with Oakeys Wellington knife polish, or the usual emery powder. Sew this cushion to the canvas. Make up the whole cushion.' The work was then pinned to the cushion which was heavy enough to withstand the tension necessary for even sewing. In America these are called weight or weighted pillows, and they can be bought in a store and put into any type of needlework cover.

leaf stitch see long and short stitch.

leather The skin of animals, birds, or reptiles prepared for use by tanning or similar process which, because of its wind-resisting and hardwearing qualities, has been used for clothes since earliest times. Though it is often left plain, people in many countries decorate it with embroidery and beads: for example the deerskin robes of some north American Indians, the chamois gloves and leggings from Mongolia and Siberia, and the braid trimmed parkas (anoraks) of the Eskimos. In the 16th and 17th centuries in Europe, gauntlet gloves were often embroidered. Elizabeth I was given in 1599 'By the Lady Digbye, two square cushions . . . thother redde leather, embrothered with flowers of silke' (Nichols 1823). See also sheepskin.

leather appliqué The application of leather to a cloth or leather ground. This form of applied work is particularly suitable for counterchange and inlay as leather does not fray. In modern embroidery, especially ecclesiastical and collage, there is a vogue for applying gold and silver kid, often padded.

letter-case: the naturalistic floral sprays are embroidered in polychrome silks on a satin ground, each of the five pockets worked with a different flower; English, 18th century.

overleaf (p156)
lettering: detail of a modern children's alphabet panel designed and worked by Mrs Pat Russell. The panel itself is four feet long and two feet wide.

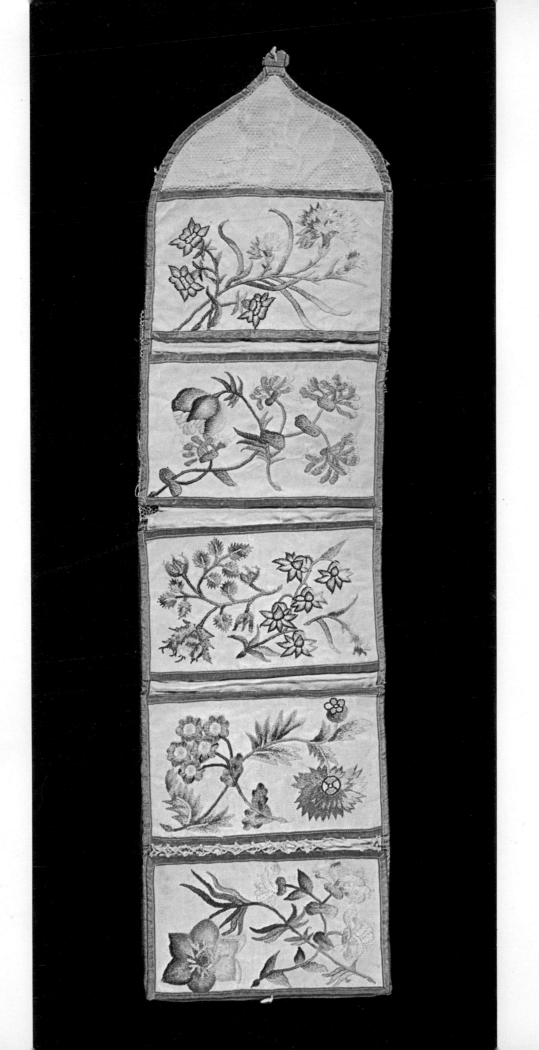

Leek Embroidery Society: photograph of Mrs Wardle.

Leek Embroidery Society Formed in 1879 by Mrs Wardle, wife of Thomas Wardle, President of the Silk Association of Great Britain and Ireland. It was natural that such a society should be in Leek (Staffordshire) as practically all the materials necessary for embroidery were made there. The production of spun silks, sewing silks, and embroidery silks was the staple industry, silks and brocades were woven, chenille and many kinds of trimming were produced, and in addition there were dye houses and fabric printing works. The style of work for which the town was famous was brocade embroidery, and two of the best known pieces of work are a green altar frontal at All Saints' Church, Leek, designed by Norman Shaw, and a memorial cloth in Cheddleton Parish Church designed by Gerald Horsley. (Parker 1893) (Colour illustration p 138)

leno　see gauze.

___

overleaf (p 157)
machine embroidery: a modern panel, 'Astral Light', by Joy Clucas. The background is made up of several pieces of coloured fabric joined together; the light is composed of many layers of coloured dress net; the centre is a shape of applied glossy rayon thread stitched on with transparent thread starting from the outside using zig zag. All the other shapes and joined pieces are held together with multiple zig zag.

Mary Queen of Scots: detail of the needlework bed hangings at Hardwick Hall, thought to have been worked by Mary.

lenten cloths Hangings used during Lent in both the Roman Catholic and Anglican churches are often of natural or ash-coloured linen embroidered in a very plain style in red or black. As well as the usual frontal, burse, veil, and pulpit fall, Lenten cloths sometimes include covers for all the rich metal, gilt, or painted objects in the church, such as processional or altar crosses, retable, and pictures, but excluding the *stations of the cross. In the middle ages Germany was especially noted for these cloths, which were generally worked in white on white, using a variety of stitches and patterns to give relief to the plain colour. See also hungertuch. (Shepherd 1960)

lenten cloths: an example from Germany, 13th century.

letter-case Cases used in the home were generally referred to as letter-cases, while those for carrying papers from one place to another were more usually called portfolios, or sabretaches in the British Army, where they used to be part of the uniform. In the 17th and 18th centuries, letter-cases were sometimes shaped like wallets or like bags with stiff sides, and were beautifully decorated. They were made of leather, satin, silk, or canvas, and were embroidered in some appropriate technique. (Seligman and Hughes n.d.) (Colour illustration p 155)

lettering The use of alphabets, initials, monograms, and numbers in embroidery has always been a most important branch of the art, and never more so than today. The letters and numbers so frequently seen on 18th and 19th century samplers were not intended to be decorative but were a training for the marking of household linen and underwear in exquisite, fine cross stitch, marking stitch, or brave bred stitch. Lettering as part of an overall design was used in the middle ages, especially in the whitework of Germany, and it is sometimes possible to identify early pieces of work from the inscriptions or signatures on them. In the 19th century great emphasis was put on monograms etc in embroidery, and many pattern books were published, often with Gothic or Old English alphabets. Towards the end of the century there was a reaction against flowery decoration, and Ann *Macbeth in particular designed using clear plain letters as an integral part of her work. Today lettering is used especially in church work and again there is a strong move to improve the quality of the script. The use of monograms and initials on household linen by hand or machine is still popular, especially in the US, and there is a vogue for lettering in canvas work (needlepoint). (Colour illustration p 156)

lettering: detail of a sampler worked at the Mountmellick Boarding School in 1811.

leviathan work Canvas work, similar to Berlin woolwork, which was popular during the last part of the 19th century. It was very quick to do because the canvas was large meshed, and was made into articles such as banner firescreens, needlemade rugs, and piano mats. The *Englishwoman's Domestic Magazine* sometimes carried supplements with designs for the work from Germany or France.

leviathan work: detail of a hearth-rug pattern, late 19th century.

Limerick lace: stole, mid-19th century.

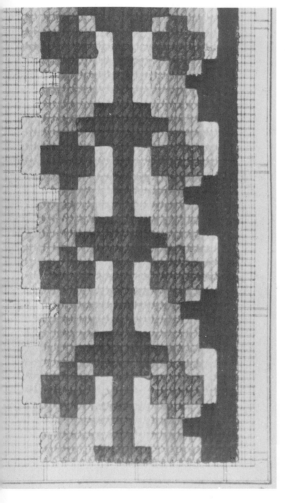

Liberty's (London) Shop started in Regent Street in 1875 by Arthur Lazenby Liberty, which has had a great influence on the taste of America, France, Holland, and Britain during the last 100 years. Originally specialising in fabrics and embroideries from Japan and the East, it made available to customers work which they might not otherwise have known, and helped to start the Japanese cult of the 1890s. In the dress department they were outstanding in their use of smocking for both adults and children, and while the fashion for women has changed, that of dresses smocked from yoke to waist or just below the yoke for children has lasted until today. (Adburgham 1975)

Limerick lace Not a lace in the true sense, but embroidered net, made in Limerick (Ireland) in the 19th century. The net was both tamboured and needle-run and in addition many filling stitches were used. The industry was started in 1829 by an Englishman, Charles Walker, who saw that his lace business would do better in Ireland where labour was cheaper than in England. It eventually declined with the increasing use of machine-made lace. (Wardle 1968) See also net laces.

linen Cloth woven from the fibres of flax. It has the longest known history of any fabric and probably originated with the Egyptians. It is cool to wear, absorbent, hardwearing, washes well, and has the advantage that it makes a perfect background for many types of embroidery. Nowadays the prefix linen or cotton is used when referring to fabrics that may be made from either, such as lawn, cambric, canvas, dowlas, or holland. The growing of flax and manufacture of linen is now mostly done in Ireland and Belgium.

linen embroidery Generic term for the types of embroidery worked on even-weave linen (including freehand embroidery) in a variety of stitches, for example counted thread embroidery, blackwork, drawn threadwork, and drawn fabric work. Embroidery on linen canvas is generally classed as canvas work or needlepoint. Caulfeild and Saward (1882) define linen embroidery as a specific type, not unlike Assisi work but with the ground formed by drawing some threads and overcasting the remainder. However, nowadays the term has a wider meaning.

linen thread Yarn used for embroidery and lacemaking. It is becoming more and more difficult to obtain and has a habit of fraying in the needle, but work in this thread has an unequalled lustre and beauty.

line stitch see double running stitch.

lin floche see flourishing thread.

lingère Maker by hand of dresses and underwear in light fabrics.

lingerie In the early 19th century, lingerie was informal dress worn at home, but in the 20th century it has come to mean underwear, made not only of linen but of any suitable fabric. Often these garments are finely and beautifully embroidered.

lingerie: American slip made by Lucille, 1919.

lingerie hem see shell edge.

Linwood, Mary (1756–1845) Accomplished English embroiderer, a native of Birmingham, who lived and worked in Leicester. Although not the first, she was the most noted exponent of the craft of making embroidery look like painting. She worked in specially-dyed crewel wools on a specially woven, coarse, linen tammy cloth, and her stitches were designed to look like brush strokes. An astute businesswoman, she had many exhibitions and valued her pictures very

Linwood: detail of her portrait of Napoleon completed in 1825.

highly—she was offered (and refused) 3000 guineas for what was considered her masterpiece, a copy of *Salvator Mundi* by Dolci, which she bequeathed to Queen Victoria, but after her death the value of her pictures dropped considerably. Among the best known were copies of the *Madonna della Sedia* (Raphael), *Head of King Lear* (Reynolds), and the *Emperor Napoleon I*, now in the Victoria and Albert Museum (London). (Whitcomb n.d., Trendall 1926)

list Border or selvage of cloth usually woven with a different and stronger thread than the main fabric. The word can also mean a strip or band, and in the Hardwick Hall inventories (1601) is 'a quition of lystes' (Boynton 1971).

list cloth Wool broadcloth of New England manufacture, distinguished by a striped selvage (list) about 1 inch (2.5 centimetres) wide. It was used by American Indians as the ground fabric for beaded decoration.

llama South American mammal resembling a camel without a hump, and of the same species as the alpaca and guanaco. It was domesticated in pre-Columbian Peru as a beast of burden and as a source of wool for their highly developed weavings and embroideries. The wool was sometimes used in its natural tan, black, and white, and sometimes dyed to brilliant colours. See also pre-Columbian embroidery.

locked-weave canvas American canvas with single warp thread and two fine weft threads which interlock in weaving and so prevent distortion while working. It is good for pre-printed designs and suitable for florentine work and needlepoint.

locker hook Tool resembling a large crochet hook with a needle eye at the end opposite the hook, used in the making of *locker rugs.

locker rugs Made with 6 ply rug wool, rug canvas, and a locker hook. The eye on the needle-end of the hook is threaded from the ball of wool and several yards are pulled through the canvas from back to front. The hook is put through a hole and picks up a loop of wool from the back; this continues until there are twelve or so loops on the hook, when the needle is pulled through the loops on the front, locking them firmly onto the canvas.

lock stitch The stitch made by the majority of domestic sewing machines since the 1860s. Two threads are used, one runs along the top of the work and the other underneath, and they twist round each other and lock together at every stitch. It has the advantage over machine chain stitch in that it is not possible to undo the whole row by pulling one end.

log cabin patchwork (Canadian log patchwork) Type of patchwork which simulates the construction of the log cabins of North America. Starting from the middle, a small square of fabric is tacked onto a foundation fabric, and then narrow pieces are sewn on with running stitch round each side of the square in turn so that the foundation is gradually covered with strips. The squares are then joined together in pattern. The advantage of this patchwork is that small cut-off lengths of fabric and ribbon can be used up.

long and short stitch (brick stitch, embroidery stitch, featherwork or opus plumarium, plumage stitch, irish stitch, shading stitch, tapestry shading stitch, leaf stitch) One of the most familiar and useful of stitches, often called feather stitch or opus plumarium in the middle ages, not to be confused with modern feather stitch. In long and short stitch only the first row of stitches is in fact alternately long and short; the others are all the same length and fit into the first row. It looks best when worked in floss silks or fine crewel wools, and takes variation in colour beautifully, being frequently used for shading the petals of flowers. See also opus plumarium.

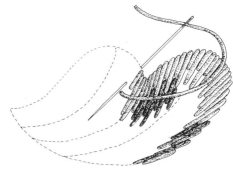

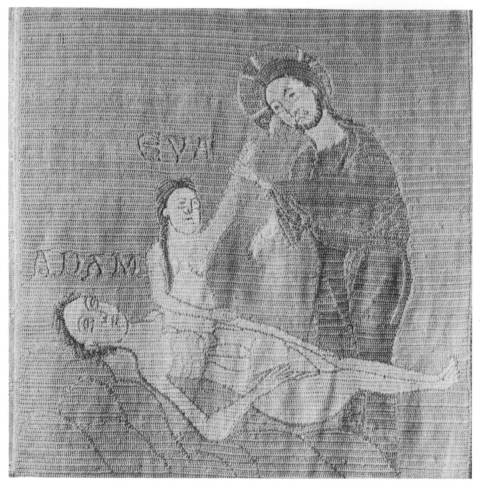

long armed cross stitch: detail of a wall hanging depicting Adam and Eve.

long armed cross stitch (long legged cross stitch, plaited slav stitch, portuguese stitch) Variation of cross stitch which is very popular for canvas work (needlepoint), especially for small articles such as church hassocks, as it is very strong. It is also used in needlemade rugs. The first diagonal stitch of the cross, upwards from left to right, is twice the length of the second arm of the cross and so a plaited effect is obtained. Unlike cross stitch, where it is possible to work the first half of each stitch all along a row and then return, each long armed cross must be finished before the next is started.

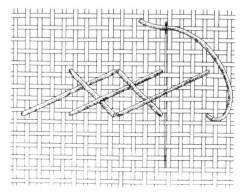

long shades Term describing Berlin wool in which the shades or colours, from lightest to darkest and back, change very gradually over a long length of the wool; in *short shades the complete change comes within a yard (metre).

looking glass (mirror) The earliest looking glasses were of burnished metal and it was not until the 16th century that the art of backing glass with quicksilver became known. Even at the end of the century these mirrors were rare and costly, but by the 17th century they were often framed with embroidery, especially raised work. Though some were for dressing tables, others were made to hang on walls. From the Hardwick Hall inventories (1601) is 'a looking glass with a border of imbroderie' (Boynton 1971). Small discs of mirror glass are sometimes used in Indian embroidery: see abhla bharat, shisha.

looped stitches The group of stitches in which the thread is taken around the needle in a loop. These are generally line stitches, although a few can be used in isolation, but as in all the groups they can be adapted to fill special needs. The stitches are *blanket (open buttonhole);

*buttonhole and variations: angular, closed, crossed, double, hedebo, slanting, up and down; ceylon; cretan (fish, long armed feather) and variation: open cretan; *feather (briar, single coral) and variations: chained feather, closed feather (double chain), double feather (double coral), long armed feather (cretan, stacked feather), single feather (slanted buttonhole), stacked feather (long armed feather); fly (open loop, Y); ladder; loop; looped braid; pearl; rope; scroll; sword edging; vandyke; wave.

Louis-Quinze lace One of the types of embroidery worked in the late 19th century which simulated the heavy Venetian lace of the 17th century.

lozenge (diamond) Geometric shape with two acute and two obtuse angles. In needlework it occurs most commonly in patchwork where, as one-third of a hexagon, it is often used in the building up of patterns. It is also used in heraldic embroidery—since the 16th century the arms of spinsters or widows have been emblazoned in a lozenge.

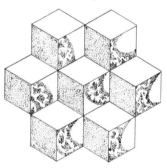

lunch cloth 19th century American term referring to a small linen damask table or stand cover, which had fringed ends and openwork borders.

Lunéville work The art of applying beads to fabric by means of a tambour hook, so called because it appears to have started in Lunéville (France) in 1878. (Edwards 1966) See also tambour beading.

lurex Metallic thread which will not tarnish. It was developed in America and is based on aluminium. When woven it is mixed with other yarns.

lustrine work Kind of embroidery described in the first volume of *The Needle* (1903) which was designed to exploit the thread lustrine. This was mercerised and was made in many varieties such as cable, Bulgarian, twisted, and flossette. The designs were mostly flowers worked in a semi-naturalistic style.

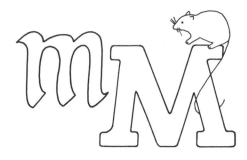

Macbeth, Ann (1875-1948) Scotswoman who trained at the Glasgow School of Art. In 1901 she became assistant to Mrs J. R. *Newbery in the needlework, embroidery, and appliqué class, and on Mrs Newbery's retirement in 1910, became head of the department, a post she held until 1928. She was a prolific worker, designing for linen and thread-manufacturing firms, undertaking private commissions, and publishing books and articles, and her influence on the embroidery of the first half of the 20th century was very great. (Swain 1974)

Macbeth: table centre, early 20th century.

machine embroidery (free embroidery, freehand embroidery, art embroidery, free motion embroidery, flat embroidery) Work done either on a domestic sewing machine or on a trade machine designed especially for embroidery. The earliest embroidery machine was invented by Josué *Heilmann of Mulhouse (France) in 1828 and the patent rights were bought by Henry Houldsworth of Manchester (England) in 1829. At the Great Exhibition of 1851, Houldsworth & Company displayed 'specimens of patent machine embroideries' which were polychrome on various fabrics. Switzerland was well known for fine cotton embroidery on muslin and there the new machines were used to develop this kind of work. Soon the quality was high enough to compete successfully with hand embroidery, and by the 1850s and 1860s the industry had become very prosperous. In the 1870s women's dresses were loaded with trimming of every kind, for which the machine embroideries were admirable. By the turn of the century the Cornely machine had been adapted for beadwork and the Irish machine which made a zigzag stitch was in use. It was not until the late 1920s and early 1930s that the idea of creative embroidery by machine was born. Until then its only use had been for repetitive designs for household and dress articles, but Miss Thomson, head of the Women's Department of Bromley School of Art, felt that it should be possible to use the machine in a bolder and freer way. From that point on, the possibilities of machine embroidery have been exploited in every way and colleges of art have trained embroiderers whose work on the machine, though completely different, challenges even the best hand embroidery. Since the availability of the swing-needle domestic machine, this kind of embroidery has become a popular homecraft. (Risley 1961) (Colour illustration p 157) See also Cornely machine, Schiffli machine, Heilmann.

machine twist Thread of silk or mercerised cotton for use in sewing machines.

Madeira work Development from *broderie anglaise which was so popular in the mid 19th century for trimming dresses and underwear. The technique was taken by nuns to Madeira, an island off the north-west coast of Africa, where it was taught to the peasant women and subsequently has become one of the major exports and tourist 'buys' of the island. In addition to the plain overcast holes and buttonholed edges of broderie anglaise, Madeira work has a small amount of surface embroidery, and is usually meticulously worked.

Madras work Embroidery covering the design and borders of silk or cotton handkerchiefs from Madras. Except for the fact that it is always worked on these handkerchiefs, Madras work is very little different from *Anglo-Indian embroidery.

Malterer hanging Wall hanging worked with wool on linen, whose theme is the evil consequences of earthly love. It was probably embroidered between 1310 and 1320 and is unusual in that in spite of its religious overtones it is basically a piece of secular work, and there are very few in existence of that date. It was given by the Malterer family to the Convent of St Catherine at Freiburg-im-Breisgau (Germany) where Anna Malterer was a nun, and this explains its good condition. It can now be seen in the Augustiner Museum in Freiburg.

Malterer hanging: detail, South German, .1310-20.

Maltese embroidery Popular late 19th century embroidery which originated in the island of Malta in the Mediterranean. It consisted of the making of lots of little tassels with a many-plied cotton thread to form a pattern on a ground of some strong fabric. The stitch used to make the tassels is very similar to *smyrna stitch, which is used in knotted rugs.

maltese silk (horsetail silk) Fine strong silk thread used to couch metal threads. As it is used for little else it is only obtainable in two shades of gold and a silvery grey.

mandarin square Embroidered or woven panel applied to robes worn by Ming and Ching dynasty Chinese officials and their wives to denote civil and military ranks.

mandorla Almond-shaped decorative space which in religious art sometimes surrounds the figure of Christ or the Virgin Mary. Often it is rayed as in a *splendour or glory.

mandorla: Czechoslovakia, c.1420.

maniple (fanon) Strip of fabric embroidered en suite with the stole, which is worn over the left forearm of a priest, deacon, or sub-deacon at the celebration of the Eucharist in the Western church. It symbolises the towel used by Christ when washing the feet of the disciples. The maniple of St Cuthbert (worked between 909 and 916) is one of the oldest pieces of opus anglicanum, and can be seen in Durham Cathedral, England.

maniple: which belonged to St Cuthbert.

manta Wrap or cloak worn in Spain and Mexico.

mantle: detail of an altar frontal depicting the Countees of Westmorland, 16th century.

mantle 1. Outer garment like a cloak which has been worn at different periods by men, women, and children, with slight variations in shape. Nowadays the word is more likely to refer to either the outer garment worn by the sovereign and peers at a coronation, or the garment worn by women in the last quarter of the 19th century which was like a cloak but was slightly shaped to the body and sometimes had wide elbow-length sleeves. 2. The beautifully and richly decorated covering for the Scroll or Sepher Torah, the most sacred object of the Jewish faith. The mantles are generally professional work of the highest standard, using rich fabrics and metal threads, cords, and purls. See also Jewish ritual embroidery.

mantua makers' seam Join which is useful either where a close fit is not necessary or where there is a selvage and·

a raw edge to be stitched together. A plain seam is made, the raw edge is trimmed down, and the selvage edge is then turned over it and stitched through. This is very similar to a *fell seam. (Hind 1934)

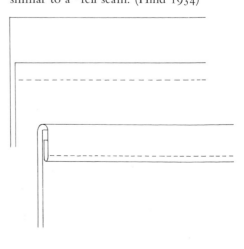

map sampler: of Boston Harbour worked by Lydia Withington at Miss Rowson's school in 1799.

marguerite Daisy-like flower made from two rows of gathered ric-rac braid stitched to a silk-covered button mould. Alternatively the centre of the flower could be of clipped wool pile. They decorated many kinds of household articles in the late 19th century.

Marie de' Medici (1573-1642) Wife of Henry IV of France. A notable needleworker, she set the fashion for embroidering with floral designs (soon followed by the ladies of the French court), and an anthology of flowers, or florilegium, by Pierre Vallet was dedicated to her.

marking When household articles and underwear were made in dozens it was necessary to mark them, not only with the name or initial of the owner, but also with the date and the number in the dozen. This was usually done in fine cross stitch using a red or blue ingrain marking cotton. Nowadays most marking is done with printed or embroidered name tapes.

map sampler Late 18th and early 19th century *samplers which generally depicted the world or else the county, state, or country in which the embroiderer lived. Their popularity coincided with the interest in travel and geography and the use of the globe, which was considered an essential part of a young lady's schooling at that time. They were worked on a fine silk canvas in tent or cross stitch, or sometimes in cross stitch on satin or taffeta in which case they might have swags of flowers embroidered in the corners. There was usually an elaborate cartouche for the title and they were signed and dated—the earliest found so far is 1777. See also globe sampler.

map shawl *'Amli shawl from Kashmir, produced in the second half of the 19th century and embroidered in the form of a pictorial map of the capital, Srinagar. (Irwin 1973)

map shawl: detail.

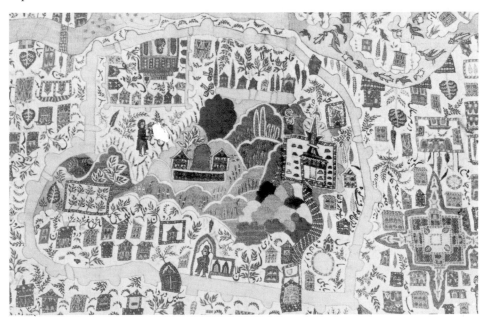

marking cotton Cotton, *ingrain sewing thread specially spun for marking, most commonly Turkey red and less frequently blue.

marking stitch see brave bred stitch.

Mary Queen of Scots (Marie Stuart, 1542–1587) One of the best known embroiderers of all time, about whose work we know more legends than truth. There are far more pieces of embroidery said to be hers than is either possible or credible, but she certainly loved the work and found great solace in it. The main pieces which can definitely be ascribed to her, and which usually bear either her crowned initials or her cipher, are the Oxburgh hangings at *Oxburgh Hall, a cushion cover at *Hardwick Hall (Derbyshire), and a pair of child's reins now at Arundel Castle (Sussex). (Swain 1973) (Colour illustration p 158)

Mary Queen of Scots: monogram 'Marie Stuart' crowned, with thistles, her cipher and motto.

mat Domestic and household article for protecting and decorating floors and furniture. Most mats are used to keep heat or scratches from polished surfaces, and in the late 19th and early 20th centuries, in conjunction with doilies, they proliferated until there was not an article of furniture which was not covered with several of them. For the embroiderer they have the advantage of being quite small and flat and so lend themselves to different techniques and many experiments. See also needlemade rugs.

mattress needle Double-pointed needle with an eye at one end. It is usually about 6 to 8 inches (15 to 20 centimetres) long, and is used for making the tufts that hold the stuffing of a mattress in place.

matzoh cover Embroidered cover for the sabbath breads used during the Kiddush (sanctification) of the Jewish sabbath.

McCormick collection see Elizabeth Day McCormick collection.

meander (vermicular) Pattern much in vogue for the ground in quilting in the early and mid 18th century. It was usually worked in back stitch and is named from the wandering worm-like design that covers most of the background and ensures even distribution of wadding.

meander: detail of a quilted bonnet, English, late 17th century.

medieval Term referring to the middle ages in Europe, roughly from AD 1000 to 1500.

medieval: detail of an Icelandic wall hanging, 14th century.

mellore Tool with one pointed end and one rounded, spatula-shaped end, formerly used when working with metal threads. The point was for making holes and the rounded end for flattening the threads. The use of a mellore ensured that damp and sticky hands did not touch the thread more than was absolutely necessary.

melon seed embroidery Embroidery using the seeds of the small musk melon, which are first washed and dried. In the *Ladies Treasury* of 1887, a design of barley is shown to be embroidered on black lace, with the grains of melon seeds and the leaves worked in silk. This embroidery was intended 'for blouse frontals and insertions in the upper parts of sleeves'.

melon seeds Tiny frogs made in China from scraps of cloth. See frogging.

mending cottons Threads dyed in shades of beige as well as pastel colours and sold in small balls, plaits, or braids of mixed colours for mending stockings, underwear etc.

mercerised cotton thread In 1844 John Mercer (1791–1866), a dye chemist of Accrington, England, discovered how to treat cotton thread with a solution of caustic soda which both strengthened it and gave it a silky lustre. Although he patented his invention in 1850 it was not used commercially until 1895. Since then many cotton weaves as well as threads have been mercerised, of which the best known for embroidery is stranded cotton.

(opposite)
mittens: one of a pair of babies' mittens, English, 18th century.

(overleaf, p 168)
Morris: detail of a watercolour design for embroidery by William Morris, English, 19th century.

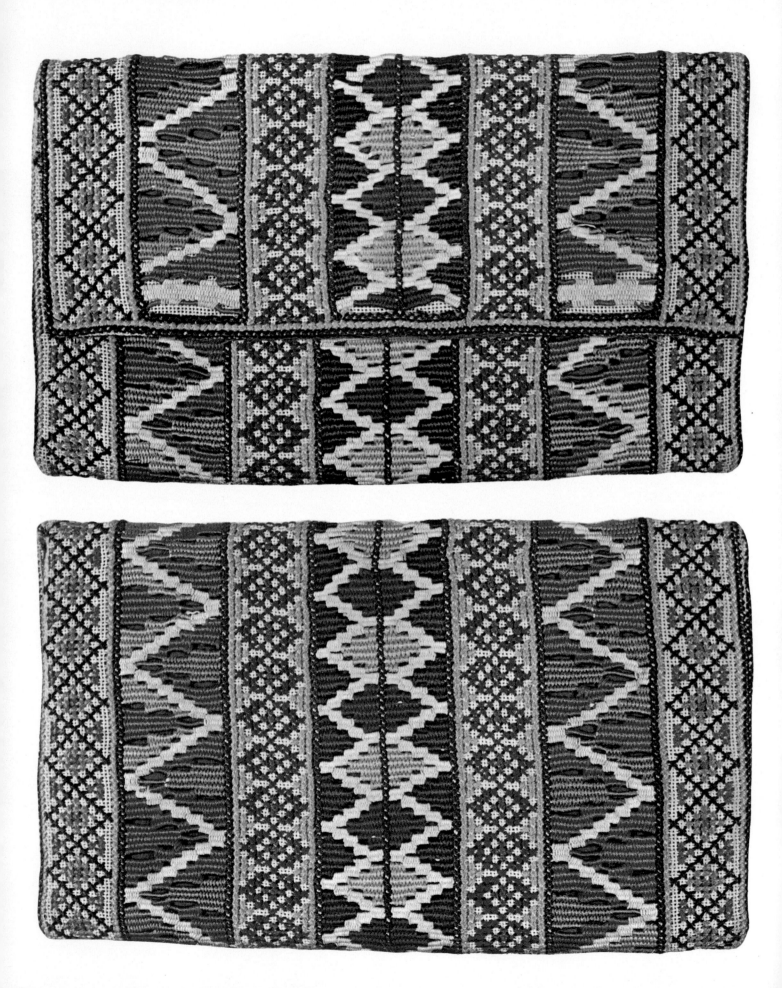

Merian, Maria Sibylle (1647–1717) Botanical and entomological artist, born in Germany. Her Swiss father died when she was a baby and her Dutch mother then married the Dutch flower painter Jacob Marnell, and Maria was later to marry one of his pupils, Johann Graff. She had always had a bent for drawing and took with enthusiasm to the production of volumes of engravings, hand-coloured, of European and South American insects. In 1680 she brought out *Neues Blumen Buch* in which the plates, adapted from those in *Diverses Fleurs* by Nicholas Robert, were intended to provide designs for embroidery. She was also an excellent needlewoman. (Blunt 1950)

mesh 1. Space or intersection of the threads in canvas or net. 2. Tool for regulating the length of the stitches in French raised work of the mid 19th century. It was of boxwood or steel, and had a sharp edge or a groove for scissors or a knife when cutting the stitches.

metal thread embroidery Embroidery worked with threads of gold, gilt, silver, aluminium, or copper, and metal spangles or sequins, and sometimes called gold embroidery as gold thread is most often used. At one time it was almost synonymous with *ecclesiastical embroidery because although metal threads were used in *heraldic work and for badges, these were always worked by professionals. Nowadays metal threads both genuine and synthetic are much used in all types of panels and collages. See also guimped embroidery.

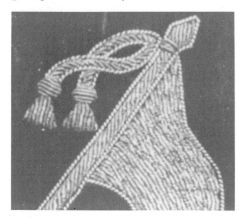

(*overleaf, p 169*)
Nazca: detail of a feather mantle from Peru.

(*opposite*)
needleweaving: front and back of a bag, American, 20th century.

metre Metric measure of length equal to 100 centimetres, or to 3 feet 3.37 inches.

Metropolitan Museum of Art (New York) One of the great collections of religious embroideries from Western Europe, America, and other parts of the world. Flat textiles, costumes, and accessories, as well as furnishings, are housed in various departments of the colonaded Fifth Avenue building. A textile study room contains examples of various embroideries (including the *Irwin Untermeyer collection) and can be used by appointment, and the *Caswell carpet and a bed rug of 1796 are also to be seen. Most of the medieval collection is housed at the Cloisters in Fort Tryon Park.

Metropolitan Museum of Art: back of a chasuble, opus Anglicanum, 1330–50.

Mexican drawnwork Traditionally done on native Mexican cotton cloth. The main centres for these drawn threadwork centrepieces, samplers, doilies, and handkerchiefs are Aguascalientes, Celaya, and Guanajuato. See drawn threadwork.

Mexican drawnwork: detail of a sampler with designs in reds and greens, 19th century.

Mexican/Spanish samplers: this example is signed, and dated 1738.

Mexican/Spanish samplers Spanish *samplers were decorative, usually larger than those of other countries, and used more flat stitches, which were worked in many brilliant shades of silk or in the popular combination of plain black and white. Since they were often made in convent schools in *Spain, when these religious orders established schools in the new world, the same patterns and techniques followed to those areas, especially Mexico. (Horner 1971)

Mexico: needlework panel, c.1750.

Mexico *Huipils, *quexquemitls, and samplers are all part of the Spanish and convent-influenced form of Mexican embroidery. Examples predating the conquest of the Aztecs by the Spaniard Cortez, in 1519, were mostly destroyed, but one remaining piece of featherwork is a crown given to Cortez by Montezuma. Mexican patterns are characterised by floral or geometric designs worked in cross or satin stitch with bright silk threads. Reds, greens, and blues with the addition of metallic threads are used on skirt borders, blouse yokes, and as decorative seam joinings, and samplers on cotton backgrounds are worked mostly as pattern records incorporating various embroidery stitches and drawnwork. See also featherwork, feather embroidery, Spanish-Mexican samplers.

mica Mineral characterised by its shiny look. While not as clear as glass, it is transparent and it has been used in embroidery, especially Indian work, to give glitter.

Middleton collection Well-known English collection of early 17th century embroidered garments belonging to Lord Middleton, which are on permanent loan to Nottingham Museums. It is unusual to find a quantity of clothes of this date anywhere, and it is even more unusual to find so many in such excellent condition and of such good quality. There are nightcaps, coifs, forehead cloths, stockings, bodices, and jackets, as well as minor items.

mide bag Medicine bag used by members of the Midewin or Grand Medicine Society, a secret society which cured the sick of the *Woodland tribes of North American Indians. The bags were family or tribal property and were passed down from generation to generation. They were made from skin decorated with quill-work. (Feder 1971)

military Pertaining to soldiers in the armies of the world. In the field of embroidery it refers to the uniforms and accoutrements of the soldier (and in the case of cavalry of his horse) and the colours of the regiment or unit to which he belongs.

military skirt (waffenrock) Heavy skirt worn by soldiers in the 16th century and probably earlier. It was about 21 inches (53 centimetres) long, closely pleated with two rows of braid holding the pleats in place, and quilted.

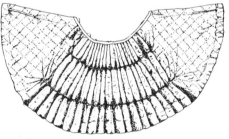

Middleton collection: man's cap, English, 18th century.

milliner's needle see straws.

millinery Nowadays, all head coverings worn by women and girls. However in the 18th century it had a wider meaning, nearer to the modern haberdashery, and included all those small articles of dress originally made in Milan, such as bonnets, gloves, ribbons etc.

miniatures Small embroidered portraits of the 17th century which are not copies of painted miniatures but are originals. Though there are a few of other people, most are of Charles I of England (beheaded in 1649) and they resemble, with many small variations, his portrait by Van Dyck. These are now considered to have been worked in the latter part of the century. The majority are in fine silk in long and short stitch but there are one or two worked in hair.

minikin Literally a small person or thing, but in embroidery a fine gold wire known as pearl-*purl.

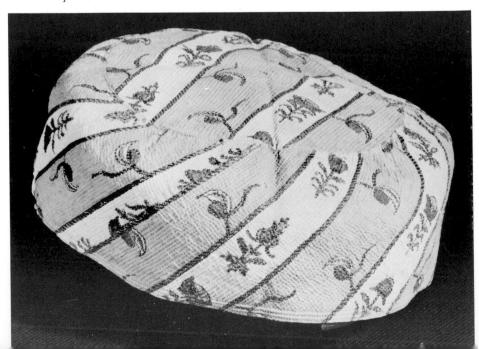

miracle warp base canvas Double-weave fabric which permits stitching into its strong surface threads yet leaves a solid canvas back, used in the mid 20th century for latch hook rugs and needlework rugs worked with a Giordes knot.

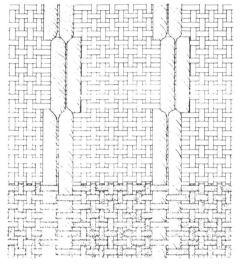

Miroir or Glasse of the Synneful Soul see bookbindings.

mirror see looking glass. For embroidery with mirror glass see abhla bharat and shisha.

mitered bargello see four-way bargello.

mitorse silk Lightly-twisted silk embroidery thread used in the 19th century. Miss Lambert (1843) considered it to be superior to floss silk as it was less likely to fluff up, but it needed care in working to make it lie evenly. It is similar to the thread used by the Chinese in their double embroidery.

mitra The Eastern equivalent of the *mitre worn by Western bishops. Until the early years of the 15th century they were only worn by the Patriarch of Alexandria in the Greek Orthodox church, but later some if not all Greek bishops wore them, and after 1589 the Russian bishops too. The earliest style was a round, flat-topped cap embroidered with a scene on top and scenes or figures in arcaded sections round the side. Later the top of the mitra became higher and more rounded, eventually assuming the beehive shape of the 19th century. (Johnstone 1967)

mitre Originally a pointed head-dress; the term was also applied, because of the shape, to a right-angle with a bisecting line. Hence it is both the shaping of a right-angled corner or hem to make a neat finish by turning the corner or hem and cutting away the material to make a seam at an angle of 45° to the edge of the article, and a bishop's head-dress. The

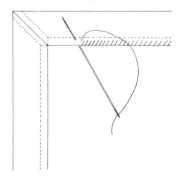

earliest mitres were bands or fillets of linen, but by AD 1000 they had become circlets which were often embroidered or jewelled. Gradually the sides became raised with the centre depressed to form a crescent shape. By the time of St Thomas à Becket the hollowed-out centre had risen with the point forming an obtuse angle, but over the succeeding centuries the point has risen until it now forms an acute angle, and the sides are generally curved. Depending from either side are two embroidered lappets called *infulae, which probably originally tied under the chin. For festal occasions, the mitre has always been very richly embroidered and jewelled and some very early ones have been preserved. Among those which can still be seen is the mitre of Jean de Marigny (mid 14th century) in the Evreux Museum, France; the mitre from Sainte Chapelle (1380-90) in the Musée de Cluny, Paris; and that of opus anglicanum showing the stoning of St Stephen and the Martyrdom of St Thomas à Becket (late 12th century) in the Bayerisches Nationalmuseum, Munich. In modern times some beautiful mitres have been made and embroidered, notably that for Guildford Cathedral, Surrey. See also mitra.

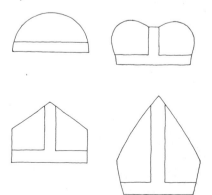

mitten Covering for the hand which differs from a glove in that it has no separate fingers. It was also a 19th century fashion for lace or finely knitted hand coverings which reached only to the base of the fingers. Mittens are sometimes worn for warmth, to prevent injury to the hand, or in certain occupations, but from time to time they have been a fashion article and elaborately embroidered. One of the New Year (1578-9) gifts to Elizabeth I was 'By Sir William Drury, a paire of myttons of blake vellet embraudered with damaske golde and lyned with unshorne vellat carnation' (Nichols 1823). Today children's mittens are sometimes embroidered with their names, and Norwegian ones have folk or flower designs in wool. (Colour illustration p 167)

mitten: detail in quillwork, made by the Cree Indians.

moccasin Soft shoe of leather, especially that worn by North American Indians, which is often decorated with beads, moosehair, or porcupine quills. The amount of bead decoration varies from tribe to tribe—the uppers of the moccasins used by Cheyenne, Arapaho, and Sioux Indians were completely covered with beadwork, while Blackfoot decoration was simple and limited almost entirely to the toe and instep.

mock hemstitch see pin stitch.

modano lace General term in Italy for *lacis or filet work with a square-mesh ground.

Modern Priscilla, The (1887-1930) Popular American needlework and crafts magazine. It introduced many new styles such as Bulgarian embroidery, Turkish work, Mountmellick embroidery, and Battenberg lace, and offered special booklets and samples of thread, fabrics, patterns, and pre-painted canvases for needleworked cushions.

Moguls see Mughals.

mola Word meaning both the blouse and the two panels forming the blouse, worn by the Cuna women of the San Blas Islands in Central America. The panels (one for the front and one for the back) are worked in reverse appliqué and may have as many as five layers of different coloured cotton in them. Occasionally a small amount of surface stitchery is added. Each design is an expression of feeling on the part of the worker and may represent tribal or Christian beliefs, the world around them, or native flora or fauna. They can either be drawn on the top layer of cloth with pencil or worked direct with no guide. It seems that the tradition is not more than 150 years old and as the humidity of the tropics is not kind to textiles, few pre-1920 examples remain. At the present time there is much interest in these panels and they are being made in great quantities as a tourist attraction, unfortunately with consequent loss of technique and good design. There are molas in the Brooklyn Museum, and the Museum of the American Indian, and there is a collection of 177 molas in the British Museum Department of Ethnology. See also Cuna Indian embroidery, Sappi Karta tree.

mola: detail, 20th century.

Moldavian Wallachian embroidery Tradition of Romanian embroidery which evolved during the 13th and 14th centuries as a result of the Greek Orthodox church forbidding all free artistic representation of the human figure. Geometric and floral patterns were embroidered in wool on fur jackets, blouses, and hats, using stem, cross, double running, and chain stitches.

mollusc A shellfish, the source of a purple dye in ancient South and Central America and still used in Guatemala in the mid 20th century. Thread is dyed in the saliva produced by rubbing the molluscs together. This has a seaweed smell and salty taste, and Indians first chew a thread to make sure they are buying the genuine product. A related shellfish produced the famous Tyrian purple of classical Mediterranean days. (Kelsey and Osborne 1952)

monk's cloth Heavy. coarse, cotton fabric, loosely woven in a 2 × 2 to 8 × 8 thread basket weave, and often used as a ground for embroidery. Although usually oatmeal coloured, it may also be obtained in stripes or solid colours. In America it is also known by other names such as abbot's cloth, belfry cloth, and druid's cloth, but is unknown in England.

mono canvas Unstarched single-mesh canvas used for needlepoint (canvas work) and florentine embroidery. It has a surface very suitable for pre-painted designs. In the UK it is called congress canvas.

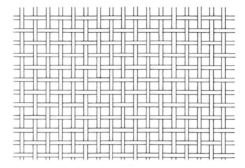

monochrome Embroidery worked in a single colour or in shades of one colour. See also polychrome.

monogram see lettering.

Montacute House (Somerset, England) Elizabethan house owned by the National Trust. Among its many treasures, including a number of pieces of needlework, are the hangings originally in Stoke Edith, Herefordshire. Two of the panels are very large and show typical country house gardens of about 1720—very formal with grass, statues, fountains, trees in pots, and members of the family and their servants disporting themselves. The third panel is classical and shows Aeneas and Achates near Carthage, meeting Venus in disguise. They are all worked in tent stitch.

monthly magazines Ladies magazines were a phenomenon of the 19th and early 20th centuries in America. Usually sold by subscription or through a club, they contained articles and stories, music, fashion, household recipes, and instructions for the latest ideas in needlework. *Godey's Lady's Book* began the trend, and others followed such as *Arthur's Home Magazine, Graham's American Monthly Magazine, Petersen Magazine, Demorest's Family Magazine, The Delineator,* and The *Modern Priscilla,* to name but a few. They were influential in setting tastes in America. The same pattern was followed in England and most European countries. See also Englishwomen's Domestic Magazine.

moose Large mammal of the deer family found in coniferous forests from Scandinavia to the Atlantic coast of Canada and across the northern US. A small pouch of hairy skin called the bell or dewlap hangs from the neck and it is from this bell that the best hairs for embroidery are found, along with hairs from the mane, cheek, and rump. Most of the hairs are pure white except for dark tips, which is surprising since the animal always appears to be a dusky brown. (Turner 1955) See also Huron, Ursuline nuns, moosehair embroidery.

moosehair embroidery Indigenous craft of the North American Indians, changed by the influence of the *Ursuline nuns in Canada in the 17th century. Dyed moosehair couched onto birch bark or leather was a form of decoration which had been practised by the Indians for many years. When the nuns settled in Canada they brought their embroidery

skills with them but because silks were difficult to obtain, they had to use moosehair instead. The result was that the French designs became grafted onto the North American materials, and delicate flowers were worked by Indian girls trained in the convents, using moosehair for thread and birch bark or broadcloth backed by birch bark for the ground. See also quillwork. (Turner 1955)

Moravian embroidery 1. The embroidery peculiar to Moravia, a province now in Czechoslovakia, but formerly part of the Austro-Hungarian Empire. It is a slav type of peasant work, making great use of geometric satin stitch as well as chain and stem stitch, and is found on dress and household articles. 2. Lacemaking and tambour work produced in Ireland by the Moravians, members of a Protestant sect who fled from Moravia in the 18th century and settled abroad, some 400 of them in County Antrim, Ireland. 3. The work done by the Moravian sisters who settled in Bethlehem (Pennsylvania) in the 1740s. They established a school and taught to a high standard 'floral embroideries in silks, ribbon, and crêpe work, mourning and embroidered pictures.' They not only taught but accepted commissions for work among which was the *Pulaski banner. They also did *Dresden work.

morocco leather Shiny, predominantly rusty-red coloured leather, made in and exported from Morocco, and used for shoes, fans, horse furnishings and other objects. Decoration on the leather includes embroidery (often chain stitch) and appliqué. Ornamental shoes from Morocco were a popular accessory during the mid 19th century.

Morris, May (1862–1938) The youngest daughter of William *Morris. She designed textiles and wallpaper for Morris & Co, and in 1885 took over the embroidery section of the firm. Her influence on embroidery was very considerable and she lectured on the subject in England and America. She was far more interested in design than in stitchery, and her work is characterised by large, rather untidy stem stitching following the lines of the form.

Morris, William (1834–96) English designer, artist, poet, and printer who probably had more influence on the crafts of his time than any one person has had before or since. He believed in the dignity of the craftsman, deplored mass production, and fought against the evil results of the industrial revolution. In 1853 he went to Exeter College, Oxford,

Morris: detail of the Battye Tapestry.

with the intention of becoming a clergyman, but on inheriting £900 in 1855 he decided to be an architect instead and entered the firm of G. E. *Street. He had already met the pre Raphaelite artist Burne-Jones at Oxford and in 1856 he abandoned architecture and took up painting. In 1861 he became one of the founder members of Morris, Marshall, Faulkener & Co, a firm set up to produce wallpapers, embroideries, furniture, etc. which later (in 1875) became Morris & Co under his sole direction. Not only did he design a large proportion of their output but he also taught himself all the techniques such as tapestry-weaving and bookbinding, as well as furniture-making and embroidery. His influence is incalculable and has lasted until the present revival of interest in his work and designs. A lifelong socialist, he founded the Socialist League in 1885.

morse The clasp which fastens a cope. As it suffers much handling, it is generally jewelled or enamelled, but is sometimes embroidered (especially on modern copes), in which case any fine flat stitching is usually protected by raised metal threads or braids.

mosaic Any surface decoration composed of many carefully-fitted, small pieces of material. Originally the term applied only to glass or stone, but now it also includes fur, feathers, and cloth worked in a similar manner. See also guanaco robe, feather cape, Eskimo pieced fur work.

mosaic art embroidery Type of braiding popular in the late 19th century. Coloured braids were stitched onto cloth in a pattern and the spaces filled in with flowers and leaves in satin and other stitches. (Caulfeild and Saward 1882)

mosaic beadwork Method of making beads strung on thread into a solid material. A number of large beads were strung and the end of the thread was fastened. In the next row the thread between the beads was looped round the thread of the row above, and this process was continued with subsequent rows until a flat surface was built up which might be used as a border to embroidery or as a mat or other article. It was popular in the mid 19th century. The same effect in a slightly different technique was achieved by the Peyote Indians of North America. (Levey 1971)

mosaic canvas The finest size of canvas in any fibre, used for embroidery.

mosaic patchwork see pieced patchwork.

Moskowa canvas Late 19th century canvas, woven in pattern with coloured threads of gold, silver, black, and blue. When used for embroidery the ground could be left plain if required. (Caulfeild and Saward 1882)

mossoul embroidery Late 19th century English embroidery which used oriental designs. It was the colouring, which had to be 'artistic', and the filling-in stitches which gave it its character, rather than the design. According to Caulfeild and Saward (1882) 'it is a pleasing variety to Crewel Work as it possesses all the artistic attributes of that work'.

mossoul stitch see herringbone stitch.

moss work Type of 16th and 17th century embroidery which has not been identified, though from its name it would appear to consist of french knots close together, or perhaps the dyed purl thread that is so often found in embroidery of that time. In the list of Elizabeth I's wardrobe (1600) is: 'Item, one cloake of heare-coloure raized mosseworke embrodered like stubbes of dead trees', and 'Item, one rounde gowne of heare-coloured raized mosse-worke, embrodered all over with leaves, pomegranets and men' (Nichols 1823).

mother-of-pearl work see nacre work.

motif Part of a design that can be isolated as a unit; it may appear only once, be repeated, or be varied. The word also refers to small embroidered or beaded pieces that can be bought ready-made and applied.

mould (mold) 'Frame or body on or round which a manufactured article is made' (OED). In needlework this definition has several applications. 1. Wooden shape, often covered with silk or other thread or beads, which is used as the basis for tassels. 2. *Button mould. 3. Moule turc, a wooden mould like a very large thimble which was covered with rows of buttonholing and was used to make small purses or bags in the 19th century. 4. The moulds of wood, cotton wool, or ravellings which formed the basis of the hands, faces, and (sometimes) architectural features in 17th century raised work.

mould: moule turc, first half 19th century.

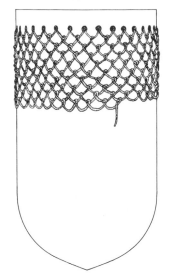

Mountain Artisans, The Non-profit-making Appalachian craft co-operative comprising of West Virginia women who do extensive piecing and quilting for the home and fahion fabric market. In the 1960s Mrs J. F. Kennedy chose some Mountain Artisan fabrics when she re-decorated the White House. Various attempts have been made since the 1930s to organise a cottage industry and training centre in Virginia, but The Mountain Artisans is the first successful venture.

Mountmellick work Type of embroidery developed (supposedly by a member of the Society of Friends) at Mountmellick near Waterford (Ireland) in the 1840s. At this time there was great hardship in Ireland and various crafts were taught to the peasants all over the country to try to alleviate distress. The embroidery is in a thick white cotton thread on white satin jean, and was made mainly into bedspreads but also into smaller articles. Though in white on white, the work is strongly textured, much difference being made between the flat and raised stitches. The designs are usually of . wild flowers and fruits, especially the blackberry.

mourning picture: American, embroidered on painted satin ground, 19th century.

mourning pictures Framed and glazed embroidered pictures in vogue in the early 19th century. At this period 'sensibility' and what would now be considered an exaggerated insistence on the outward appurtenances of death were in fashion. These pictures were very similar to printwork and usually showed a widow drooping over a tomb or an urn with a weeping willow tree somewhere in the composition. They were generally finely and beautifully worked.

Moyses Hall (Bury St Edmunds, England) Small Suffolk museum mostly devoted to local archaeology which has among its collections several superb pieces of needlework.

muff Covering usually of fur or rich padded material and generally cylindrical, into which the hands are put in cold weather, and which has been used at different periods by both men and women. The early muffs often had the fur inside, with the outside of satin or velvet, generally embroidered. In the wardrobe account of Henry Prince of Wales (1608) is 'Embroidering two muffs, viz. one of cloth of silver embroidered with purles, plates and Venice twists of silver and gold, the other of black satten embroidered with black silk and bugles.' (Bray 1793)

Mughals (Moguls, Moghals) Race of central Asian origin who conquered India in 1526 and ruled there until after the Indian Mutiny in 1858. Their emperors, especially Akbar (1542–1605), encouraged the arts including embroidery.

Mughals: detail of a satin coat embroidered in coloured silks.

mules Backless slippers for men and women. Known since the 17th century, they have generally been for informal or bedroom wear and so have been made of soft materials such as velvet, satin, and light leathers. They are often quilted or decorated with embroidery, and needle-point kits can be bought.

mull (mull muslin) Very soft muslin, sometimes used as a backing for *Italian quilting and *trapunto. It was also used for tamboured dresses in the late 18th and early 19th centuries.

mummy bundle Barrel-shaped pre-Columbian mummy encased in a woven outer sack (some with geometric design), and topped by a flat, stylised head with a primitive painted face and stone nose. The body was placed in the foetal position in a basket, and wrapped first in a fine, plain white cotton shroud sometimes 13 by 18 feet (4 by 5.5 metres), and then in additional layers of smaller coloured cloths of alpaca and a large, elaborately embroidered burial mantle. Food, clothing, weapons, pottery, and gold ornaments for the dead were tucked into the folds of the wrappings which formed a fat, round bundle often 5 feet (1.5 metres) wide. No embalming was used as the desert dryness of the Peruvian Peninsula where the deep tombs were located preserved the bodies and also the many layers of cloth. The most noted burial ground, 2000 years old, was that at Paracas Necropolis where 429 mummies, many of chieftains and priests, were found wrapped in beautifully woven cloth and superbly embroidered mantles. Another site at Paracas Cavernas contained outstanding gauzes, but most of the textiles were inferior to those of the Necropolis. (Mason 1957 and 1973, Leonard 1967) See also Paracas embroideries.

mummy canvas In America, a natural canvas woven with a close, irregular mesh. Chair backs, cushions, and sofa pillows were worked on it in crewels and silks.

mummy cloth (Egyptian cloth) Fabric, used as ground for embroidery, which is an imitation of the cloths used to wrap round mummies in ancient Egypt. (Caulfeild & Saward 1882)

Munster web canvas see pattern weave canvas.

Musée Historique des Tissus (Lyon, France) Museum devoted entirely to the display and study of textiles, working in conjunction with the famous silk manufacturing industry of Lyon. There

Musée Historique des Tissus: orphrey, opus anglicanum, *c.1330.*

are many fine embroideries there including a piece of opus anglicanum—the orphrey of a chasuble dating from about 1330 depicting the *Tree of Jesse—and one of the St Martin embroideries.

Museum of Fine Arts (Boston) Contains one of the oldest and, with the Metropolitan in New York, one of the largest and most representative collections of early Peruvian textiles and embroideries in the US. In addition, a stump work casket, quilts, crewel bed hangings and matching chair seats, and European American, and Greek embroideries are

all to be found there. The collection of *Elizabeth Day McCormick, the oldest known New England embroidery pattern, and one of the *fishing lady embroideries are also in the museum.

Museum of International Folk Art (Santa Fé, New Mexico) Contains major collections of costumes from Palestine, Mexico, and Scandinavia, and textiles from Mexico, Guatemala, and southwest United States, and it also houses the *Whiting collection. Inscribed above the entrance of this unit of the Museum of New Mexico is 'The Art of the Craftsman is a Bond Among the Peoples of the World'.

Museum of the American Indian (Heye Foundation, New York) One of the most extensive collections of artefacts from Indian cultures of North South, and Central America. Wide-ranging exhibits include numerous examples of tribal styles of beadwork, quill decoration, pieced work, feather and skin appliqué, and embroidery.   skinap

Museum of the Plains Indians (Browning, Montana) In the centre of the Blackfoot reservations near Glacier National Park, it contains a large collection of Plains Indians artefacts, clothing, and bead and quillwork. It is the headquarters of the *Northern Plains Indian Crafts Association.

mushroom see darning egg.

muslin Fine fabric woven from cotton thread. Originally it came from India and Persia where it was made in many grades and was manufactured in Europe from the late 18th century. It was first woven in Scotland in 1780 by James Monteith of Blantyre, and from then on formed a large part of the Scottish weaving trade. In America it was first woven in 1790 in a mill in Rhode Island by Samuel Slater. Muslin has many uses in fine embroidery, especially for accessories, but it was probably most used for the tamboured dresses of the late 18th and early 19th centuries, and for the collars, cuffs, and pelerines of the mid 19th century.

muslin appliqué The application of muslin to other fabrics, especially net. It was in vogue in the late 19th century and was most popular when worked in Ireland under the name Carrickmacross.

Mylar Trade-name for a strong, flexible, metalised, polyester film used in sheets or strips both as a decorative fabric and an embroidery thread, and as an alternative to gold kid.

nacre work (mother-of-pearl work) Embroidery using small pieces of mother-of-pearl cut into paillettes. These are sewn onto velvet or satin indesigns of birds or flowers, with details worked in gold thread. Miss Lambert (1843) says 'it is not, however, commonly to be met with, and is seldom practised in this country'.

nacre work: purse, 19th century.

nail Measure of length equal to $2\frac{1}{4}$ inches (5.7 centimetres), and in use until about the middle of the 19th century when it was completely superseded by inches. It is then opened out and pressed flat.

nail guard Small U-shaped piece of metal which fits onto the forefinger of the right hand, and is used by Indian embroiderers when working chain stitch embroidery with an *āri.

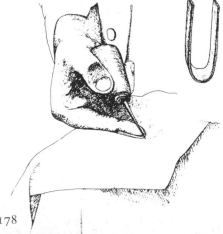

nakshe Persian word meaning embroidered, and applied to the women's trouserings of rich pattern so much in vogue up to the end of the 19th century. The Victorians called them gilets persans (Persian waistcoats), because waistcoats or vests were a more acceptable item of dress than trousers. The designs are always of diagonal parallel bands filled in with close floral ornamentation, either woven or embroidered.

nap (pile) Raised surface of cloth or carpets, made by one of three methods: 1. Teasing up the smooth surface with an instrument such as the head of a teasel plant, or with machinery; 2. Weaving in raised loops which are subsequently cut and smoothed as in velvet; and 3. Making loops by hand on canvas as in plush stitch or surrey stitch, which are then cut and sheared to the requisite depth.

napery hem (damask hem) Type of hem that appears the same on both sides and so was used when hems were hand-worked on damask tablecloths and napkins. The raw edge is turned and turned again as for a normal hem, and then turned back and creased, and stitched with fine overcasting through hem and crease.

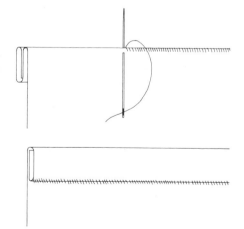

Nasca see Nazca.

Nathan Sturges Jarvis Collection The most important single collection of early Plains Indian artefacts dating from 1833–1836 which were collected and catalogued by Dr Nathan Jarvis (1801–1862) while stationed at Fort Snelling, Minnesota. While there he met George *Catlin who offered to buy Jarvis' entire collection. Today it is at the Brooklyn Museum, and includes pieces added by Dr Jarvis' son. (Feder 1964)

Nathan Sturges Jarvis collection: tobacco pouch in quillwork and hide, Sioux or Chippewa Indian, c.1830.

nati Hooded cap for a child made by professional embroiderers in Kutch, India. They are made like a skull cap with a deep curtain of the same material hanging from the sides and back, and are embroidered with silk on silk and sometimes discs of mirror glass. (Irwin and Hall 1973)

(opposite)
Newark Museum: detail of the ceremonial canopy for a Tibetan lama's throne worked in silk and peacock feathers thread.

(overleaf, p 180)
or nué: detail of the Mass Vestments of the Golden Fleece, Burgundian, mid-15th century.

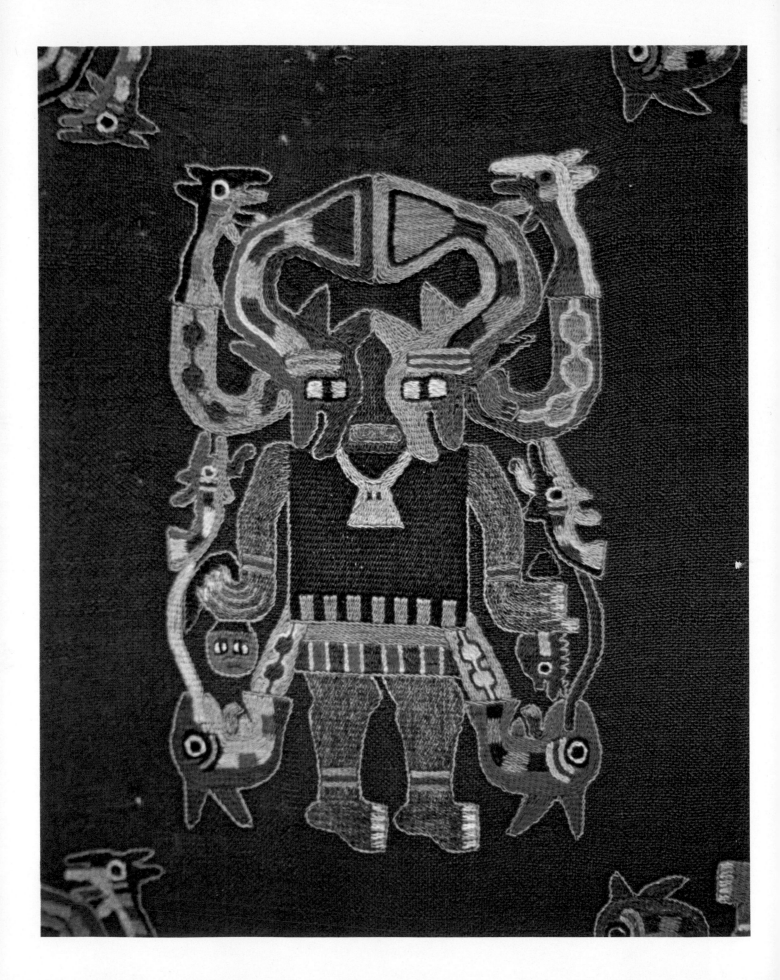

National Army Museum (Chelsea, London) Collection devoted to the history of the British Army before 1914. It may seem an unlikely place for a needle-worker to visit but there is a wealth of excellent embroidery, especially metal thread work on uniforms, and the colours, standards, and guidons of the regiments.

National Army Museum: detail of an officer's coat 1737-40.

National Trust British organisation founded in 1894 in England and later in Scotland, with the aim of preserving for the nation lands and buildings of historic and architectural interest. Some of the finest houses in Britain belong to the Trust and many of them contain excellent examples of needlework—some large, some small, but all interesting. See Anglesey Abbey, Clandon Park, Cotehele House, Gawthorpe Hall, Hardwick Hall, Knole, Montacute House, Oxburgh Hall, Polesdon Lacey, and Wallington Hall.

National Trust for Historic Preservation National preservation organisation in America, founded in 1949 and chartered by the United States Congress. It works with historical preservation societies not only by providing information on techniques and procedural matters, but by maintaining various properties as examples of what can be done. Regional offices are information centres for area projects and problems.

(overleaf, p 181)
Paracas embroidery: detail of a mantle of the pre-Columbian period discovered at the burial site of Paracas in Southern Peru.

(opposite)
panel: depicting a rolling landscape. The main areas of this modern example are appliquéd in materials including flannel, tweed and shunting; trees and bushes are over-embroidered.

Nazca (Nasca) Pre-Columbian culture which emerged about AD 200 from the Paracas culture in the same area of southern Peru. The Nazca weavers continued the Paracas textile tradition, adding many intricate weaving techniques, but never equalled their fine embroidery. They are known for three-dimensional needle-knitted borders and for gauze embroidery with delicate designs in wool stitched on fine, loosely-woven backing in a technique very like the Italian *burato. Their textiles never showed realistic human forms—in some early examples (AD 200-600) decorative mythological figures are somewhat conventionalised, embroidered in crewel stitch and outlined in black crewel, but later (AD 900-1400) gauze embroidery used more geometric forms worked solidly in wool in darning stitch. (Means 1932, Leonard 1967) See also Paracas embroidery, pre-Columbian embroidery. (Colour illustration p 169)

needle Steel implement, pointed at one end and with an eye at the other, for taking a thread through material. Originally they were probably made from fishbones or thorns, and later from bronze, but steel needles were used in China several centuries BC, and the art of making them had spread to the Near East and, via the Moors, to Spain by the 16th century. During the reign of Elizabeth I they were known in London as Spanish needles. In England, needles have been made in the area round what is now known as Redditch in Worcestershire since Roman times and possibly earlier, and the industry was actively encouraged by the Cistercian monks at the abbey of Bordesley nearby. After the dissolution of the abbey in 1538 the needlemakers scattered into the surrounding villages and carried on their work, and eventually in the mid 19th century the trade was concentrated at Redditch. Other manufacturing centres in England were Long Crendon (Buckinghamshire), Chichester (Sussex), and London. (Rollins 1969)

In 1688 Randle *Holme in his *Academy of Armory* gives a list of types available: 'Sorts of Needle. Pearl needle, is the least size of needles. The *first, second* and *third* sort of Needles, according to their sizes; so numbered till you come to ten. *Ordinary needles. Buth Lane* needles. *Glovers needles* have square points. *Book Binders* needles are long and round points. *Sow-gelders* needles are flat pointed. *Chyrurgions* needles are the same, flat pointed. *Pack needles*, crooked at the point, and some flat; others three square; others with a Back and Edge (like a Knife) at point.'

When the settlers in Virginia were

ordering their manufactured goods from England they specified Whitechapel needles (1771): 'One pound of coloured Taylors thread—three hundred best white Chapel needles' (Mason 1968). By the 19th century there was a specific type of needle for every purpose: see between, blunt, calyx-eyed, candlewick, chenille, crewel, curved, darning, glover's, sewing machine, pack, sharp, straw tapestry. Needlemaking did not become an important manufacture in America until the last decade of the 19th century.

Needle and Bobbin Club Organisation founded in 1916 in the USA by Gertrude Whiting to encourage, maintain, and promote interest in all kinds of fabrics and textiles. The name originally applied to lace needles and bobbins, but soon the objects of the club were widened to include everything to do with weaving and embroidery as well. Their excellent bulletin is published once a year.

Needle and Thread (1914) British magazine devoted to the study of all fine needlework. Edited by Mrs *Christie and published by James Pearsall & Co., (thread manufacturers), it was a casualty of World War I, surviving only for one year.

Needle Arts Publication issued quarterly by the *Embroiderers' Guild of America Inc.

needlecase Any container for needles. In the early days a needle was a rare and precious household necessity and had to be cherished and kept safely. Anglo Saxon needlecases were attached by a chain to a lady's girdle, and medieval ones were often tubeshaped, the needle being stuck into a piece of fabric which was then drawn up into the tube. In the 18th century the cases were, like so many other accessories, made of exquisitely-worked materials, such as ivory, piqué, or vernis Martin (a kind of lacquer), and some of the most charming are those made in imitation of the shaped knife boxes of the time in silver and tortoiseshell, which held little packets of fine needles. The 19th century cases were often made more as toys and knick-knacks, perhaps shaped like umbrellas, bellows, or butterflies, and in every conceivable material, while the 20th century has become strictly utilitarian, and needlecases are, for the

needlecase: ivory with flanges representing polar bears, Eskimo.

needlecase: a collection of 19th century needle-cases.

moment, out of fashion. The Eskimos used small engraved or carved containers made from a single hollow piece of bone or ivory to hold their copper or bone needles. They have been found at excavation sites from Alaska to Labrador, some as much as 1000 years old. The older needle cases were engraved with geometric designs; later ones added carved wings and knobs to represent animal and human forms. A toggle, attached to a sealskin thong for drawing out the needles, often fitted on top of the case to suggest the head of a human figure—always female since though men did the carving the women did the sewing. (Groves 1966, *Britannica* 1932) See also needle skins.

needle etching see etching embroidery.

needle knitting (needle coiling) Dainty ancient Peruvian sewing which looks like knitting but is actually an embroidery technique, probably done with a needle. Buttonhole stitch is worked on tape, completely covering it in 2 ply yarn, 20 loops to the inch (8 to the centimetre) in five or six bright colours, to produce tiny, realistic three-dimensional figures mostly of birds or flowers. These were made as a border or fringe and sewn to the edge of Nazca fabrics, and are found in all periods of southern and central pre-Columbian Peru. (Crawford 1916, Mason 1973)

needlemade rugs (embroidered rugs) Rugs or carpets made by hand using some type of sewing needle, wool, or thrift materials, and canvas, hessian, burlap, or other sacking. The homemade rug can be a beautifully planned and executed article, worthy to rank with the finest carpets, or else equally well planned but homely and cheap to make. They can be flat, worked with stitches suitable for canvas work or needlepoint, or have a pile. The stitches which produce the most attractive results are cross, tent, gobelin, hungarian, knitting, soumak (kelim), and knotting. It used to be the custom to make short-pile rugs either by needle tufting or by the short-pile method, but the invention of surrey stitch has superseded the others. See also acadian rugs, button rugs, Caswell carpet, chenille rugs, locker rugs, needlepile rugs, stitched rugs, yarn sewn rugs.

needlemade rugs: detail of a rug in petit point, English, 18th century.

Needle Makers, Worshipful Company of Incorporated by Oliver Cromwell in 1656, the needlemakers were later than most other companies in being united into a whole, probably because the centre of the trade was not in London but in Worcestershire. The three needles on the arms of the company gave the name to the street in London where most of the needlemakers' shops were situated, Threeneedle Street, later corrupted to Threadneedle Street.

needle painting (pictorial or coloured embroidery) Technique of reproducing a painted picture in needlework, even to the extent of imitating the brush strokes. This, to many people, seems a wrong and unnecessary use of needlework skills, but it must be admitted that some exponents of the craft have achieved pleasing and accurate results. In America these works are called pictorial or colored embroideries. See also Linwood, Mary and Knowles, Mary.

needlepile rugs Kinds of rugs made using a rug needle, rug or jute embroidery canvas, and either 6 ply rug wool or thrums. In each case a series of knots is made in the canvas and each stitch is joined to the next by a loop. It is the size of the loops when cut which determines the length of the pile. 1. Short-pile rugs: double-thread canvas is used with a gauge to regulate the length of the pile. The gauge is laid across the canvas just below a row of holes and, with the needle threaded, the end of the wool is laid under the gauge with the needle above it. The needle is inserted between the double thread of the canvas, the left-hand one is picked up, the wool is pulled through, both threads towards the right are passed over, and the right-hand thread is picked up so the needle comes out through the space between the two threads of canvas. The needle is then passed downwards over the gauge and up behind it. At the end of the row the loops are cut through. 2. Needletuft rugs: single-thread canvas is used. A thread of canvas is picked up with the needle from right to left. The wool is drawn through till about $\frac{3}{4}$ inch (2 centimetres) is left, and this end is held

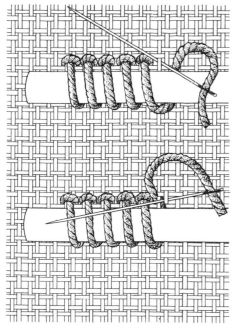

needlepile rugs 1.

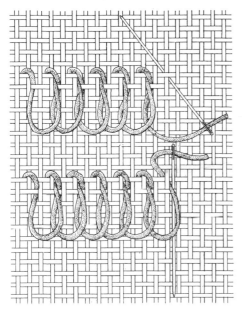

needlepile rugs 2.

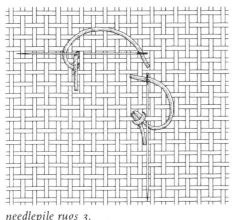

needlepile rugs 3.

with the left hand. The horizontal thread next to but a row below the last stitch is picked up and the wool is pulled tight. In each row this stitch goes into the spaces left in the row before. At the end of the row the loops are cut. 3. Surrey stitched rugs sewn on single or double canvas. Two horizontal threads (from top to bottom) are picked up and pulled through leaving about $\frac{3}{4}$ inch (2 centimetres) which is held towards the worker with the left hand *over* the working thread. The working thread is swung round from left to right and two vertical threads from right to left are picked up, diagonally above the first threads picked up and with the needle kept in front of the working thread, which is pulled tight. This is probably the most economical, satisfactory, and attractive of the short-pile methods. (Roseaman 1949, N.F.W.I. 1951)

needlepoint 1. Lace made with a needle as opposed to bobbin lace. 2. In America, all types of *canvas work, especially in tent stitch.

needlepoint: detail of a chair seat worked by Sarah Tyler of Boston, 18th century.

needlepoint stitch see tent stitch.

Needle's Excellency, The Small volume of patterns for embroidery published in London by James Boler in 1631 and 'sold at the sign of *The Marigold* in Paules Churchyard'. It ran through many editions, the twelfth coming out in 1640. The patterns were copies from various books by Sibmacher. The book is chiefly known from the introductory poem *The *Prayse of the Needle* by John *Taylor. (Nevinson 1938)

needle skin Small triangle of embroidered skin used by the Angmagssalik Eskimos to store their valued bone or walrus ivory needles. Their skin sewing bags were similarly decorated with sewn-on bands of ornamentation and embroidery. (Birket-Smith 1935)

needle threader Small implement which enables the needleworker to thread a needle easily. Many types have been tried out over the years but the one that is most used consists of a loop of fine wire which is pushed through the eye of the needle; the thread is put through the loop, and the wire is then pulled back bringing the thread with it.

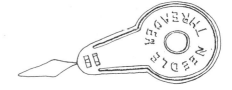

needletuft rugs see needlepile rugs.

needleweaving (Swedish weaving, Swedish darning) Embroidery based on drawn threads, in which coloured threads are woven or darned in pattern to take their place. It is generally used for the borders of household articles such as curtains and cloths, but is also used to decorate costume in many of the Slav countries. Another variation is darned on a warp stitches onto the background.

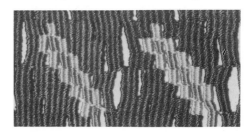

needlework: Dutch panel, 1659.

needlework Any form of embroidery, plain sewing, or machine sewing that is done with a sewing or machine needle.

Needlework Development Scheme In 1934 the firm of J. P. Coats of Glasgow set up this scheme with the aim of improving embroidery technique and design, using lectures, loan collections of historic work, and cheap publications for schools and the general public. The scheme closed in 1962.

Needlework School of the Museum of Fine Arts (Boston) One of the first schools to attempt to improve the quality of embroidery, it was founded in 1879 under the influence and inspiration of William *Morris, and was part of the beginning of the art needlework movement in America.

needlewoven tapestry see American tapestry.

neo-classic Movement that started in Italy in the mid 18th century inspired by the discoveries of Herculaneum and Pompeii. It was a reaction against the exuberance of the baroque and rococo and was expressed by simple lines, patterns such as the Greek key taken from the art of Greece and Rome, and in needlework by great use of white with very restrained decoration. In England the movement was at its strongest between about 1790 and 1810. See also Federal period.

net Openwork fabric made either by hand or machine, which consists of twisting or knotting threads to make meshes of various sizes. Those used in needlework are generally fine and light, as for bridal veils and dress trimmings, but they may be thicker as in lacis. Net may be darned, as in Limerick lace or Nottingham darned laces, or it can have small motifs of lace or embroidery applied onto it, such as in Carrickmacross embroidery.

net canvas 1. Very open mesh canvas, simulating hand netting, on which embroidery called *lacis was worked (the canvas itself was also known as lacis). In the 19th century this canvas was made in white, ecru, and other light colours. 2. See also railroad canvas.

net embroidery The decoration of net with embroidery stitches or appliqué. Satin stitch, looped and eyelet stitches, and others were used on this popular late 19th century work, which was made up into caps, scarves, and trimmings. See also Carrickmacross and net laces.

net embroidery: babies' bonnet, English, early 19th century.

the possible addition of a little embroidery, and is known as needlerun net or darned net. This was the beginning of the enormous Nottingham lace industry when hundreds of lace-runners were employed to work in the pattern on the machine-made net. Later, machines were developed which could pattern the net themselves and Nottingham lace became entirely machine made. A rather more elaborate net lace is called net embroidery; it is the same as needlerun net but has far more embroidery stitches added, the best known of this type being Limerick lace. Bordados lace from Spain is a darned net resembling blonde lace, where the darning has been done with a thick, loosely-spun silk on a fine silk net. Fine net or tulle can also be embroidered with a tambour hook and this too is done in Limerick. The last type of net lace is another Irish one, Carrickmacross, which is a combination of appliqué and embroidery stitches.

In the late 19th century there was a revival of the early filet or lacis. Sometimes called guipure d'art, it was generally worked in squares which were put together with plain linen or cutwork to make tablecloths or similar articles. When made with a very fine thread, the motifs were let into underwear as decoration in the period from 1910–30.

netting frame Frame about 9 inches square with rounded corners made of tubular steel wound round with tape. To this frame are fastened interlaced and knotted threads which form the basis of darned net or lacis.

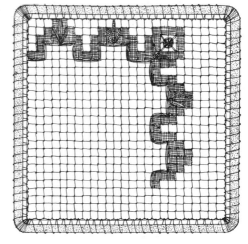

netting silk see purse silk.

Newark Museum (New Jersey) Crewel embroideries, Berlin woolwork, quilts mostly from New Jersey, cardwork, Assisi embroidery, and a fine collection of embroidered *t'angkas are all included in the textile and oriental departments.

net laces Here taken to mean net, either machine or handmade, worked with darning or other flat stitches to simulate lace. The dividing line between lace and embroidery is narrow, especially as lacemaking developed in the 16th century from two kinds of embroidery—cutwork and lacis (a kind of darned net). The net could be used plain for curtains, bed furniture etc, in which case it was called reseau, but when darned it went under the names lacis, opus araneum, spiderwork, opus filatorium, darned netting, or filet. A pattern book by Frederic di Vinciolo first published in 1587, has designs for cutwork, lacis, and burato work, all hovering on the border between embroidery and lace.

Net lace was still popular in the 17th century as can be seen by the amount which is on the whitework samplers of that period, but like all school work, samplers tended to be behind the fashion rather than level with it. The 18th century simulated lace was drawn fabric work on muslin, generally known as Dresden work, and it was not until the very beginning of the 19th century that the big revival in the production of net lace started. This was brought about largely through the invention in 1801 of a machine net which did away with the necessity for making the ground of the work and also produced a very much finer lace. The simplest was one where the design was worked by darning, with

Newbery, Mrs J. R. (1864–1948) Pioneer embroiderer in the modern approach to needlework. Jessie Rowart, better known as Mrs Newbery, took a general training at the Glasgow School of Art, and in 1889 married the principal. A friend of Charles Rennie Macintosh and a follower of the ideas of William *Morris, she taught needlework at the Glasgow School, both to the students and any interested outsiders, and insisted on clear design with equal emphasis on pattern and space and good lettering. She did not follow the fashion of her day for tight corsetting, but designed clothes for herself that were comfortable and becoming. In 1910 she retired from teaching and was succeeded by Ann *Macbeth who carried on her ideas. (Swain 1973)

New England needlework pattern The earliest known surviving needlework pattern from New England is on parchment and was used in 1720 to record a deed of sale of land by Stephen Dudley of Exeter to 'John Proctor of Boston in the County of Suffolk in New England, Scrivener'. Although part of the design was erased to make room for the deed of sale, much of the inked scroll and floral pattern remains. Perhaps intended for embroidery, or perhaps for lace, the original designer is unknown. It may have been John Proctor, a scrivener and schoolmaster, or one of the master scriveners in Boston to whom he would have been apprenticed. It is now in the collection of the Museum of Fine Arts. (Terrace 1964)

New Zealand There is little indigenous embroidery among the Maoris of New Zealand who are primarily carvers, but they excel in *featherwork, making brilliant polychrome capes from birds with exotic plumage, worn by high-ranking Maori women. The feathers are stitched to a fibre mat backing and the edges are embroidered in coloured cottons.

nightcap 1. Cap worn in bed by a man or woman to keep the head warm or to cover the hair arranged for the night. 2. Cap worn by men in the house from the 16th to the 18th century. They were usually made of four sections meeting at the top with a broad cuff turned up all round, and were often superbly embroidered with trailing scrolls enclosing birds, flowers, and insects, worked in silks and metal threads.

nightcap: for a man, embroidered in wine and sage-green silks, English, 18th century.

nightdress (nightgown) Woman's or child's garment for wearing in bed during and since the 19th century. Early on, they were handmade in white cotton or linen, and decorated with tucks and embroidery stitches, often feather stitching. However, with the gradual change in taste towards coloured and thinner underwear, nightdresses have been made from the end of the century in fabrics such as lightweight cottons, crêpe de chine, and later rayons, seersucker, and manmade fibres. In the 1930s especially, many were exquisitely embroidered, often in France.

nightdress case Bag for holding a nightdress which sits on the bed in the daytime. It can be worked to match the bedspread or decor of the room, but is more often of any technique which takes the fancy of the embroiderer.

nightdress case: English, early 20th century.

nimbus Elaborate type of halo which in art surrounds the head of Christ, God, the Virgin Mary, and sometimes the evangelists and apostles. It usually takes the form of a *halo divided by a cruciform cross.

Ninhue embroideries Contemporary embroideries inspired by the surroundings of the Chilean village of Ninhue and

Ninhue embroideries: 'Backyard Scene' by Ema Vergara, from Ninhue, Chile.

worked by the local women. Described as 'drawing in wool', the work is done with 2 ply wool yarns on linen or cotton, in traditional English and American crewel stitches taught to the villagers by Carmen Benavente de Orrego-Salas who lived in the area, moved to the US, and returned in 1971 to teach the villagers the almost lost craft.

noil The waste fibres of wool left on the teeth of the comb after drawing out the long staples, used in the manufacture of cloth. The word is often used, apparently incorrectly, for silk made from waste, which makes an excellent ground for embroidery.

Noin Ula Burial site in northern Mongolia for the chieftains of the Hiung-nu people, called the Huns in Europe. It is significant for the excavation of quantities of *Han silk and woollen stuffs that provided a key to the evolution of both Western and Chinese textile art. Most of the silks found in the tombs were made by the Chinese for their own use and sent as tribute to appease the warlike marauding Huns. A letter written by the Emperor in 174 BC lists an embroidered garment, unwadded, lined with silk, and woven with flowers, and a long tunic, embroidered and unwadded. The barbarians used these delicate, splendidly decorated fabrics indiscriminately: their jackets, trousers, caps, and shoes were often formed of a patchwork of Chinese materials; embroidered silks were found nailed haphazardly to the tomb walls; and a Chinese wool embroidered with a

tiger skin design, was used as a tomb roof. Native felt, however, was the material of honour at Noin Ula—a large carpet of felt with appliqué work and fringes protected by delicate silk casings was spread under the coffin. Woollen stuffs were of secondary importance, and were attributed at first to Western or Greek origins, but one large carpet, done in the same chain stitch used on Chinese silk embroideries, with the design of a hanging tiger skin typical of Han art, seems to refute the theory that the Chinese did not use wool for any fabric. The Noin Ula textiles are now preserved in the Hermitage in Leningrad. (Salmony 1942)

Normandy canvas Type of canvas woven in Normandy and used for household linens in the early 16th century.

Northern Plains Indian Crafts Association Co-operative organisation of Indian craftsmen first set up in 1936 by the education division of the US Indian Service to revive the Blackfoot tradition of expert craftsmanship and to make craftwork a source of income through greater production and better marketing.

northwest coast Indians The numerous tribes of Indians inhabiting the coastal areas from Yakutat Bay in Alaska to Vancouver in British Columbia, including among others the Haida, Tsimshian, and *Kwakiutl. Because of the temperate climate and a wealth of natural resources—salmon and other fish, game, and forests—they lived in stable

communities and had extensively decorated household goods and wearing apparel. See also button blankets, dance aprons.

Norwegian embroidery Norway is in an isolated position in northern Europe but it has always been a seafaring nation, and the early embroideries from the age of the Vikings (8th to 10th centuries) show Assyrian and Egyptian influence. Then, after the 10th century, the country was virtually cut off from foreign influence, so her arts and especially her embroidery developed in their own way. Flax is grown in Scandinavia so linen is always obtainable for a ground fabric, as in the famous Hardanger linen embroidery from the west coast. Homespun wool was also used in the peasant rosesöm or rose embroidery in which swirling rows of satin stitch form gay roses. By the 18th century, pattern books from Italy and Germany were obtainable and the designs from these influenced the local work. Drawn fabric work was popular and it was the custom for a bride to embroider shirts for her husband-to-be and herself in these stitches, taking great pains to create beautiful garments, many of which have become treasured heirlooms. Nowadays beautiful table-linen comes from Norway. (Donaldson 1941, Engelstad 1960)

Norwegian embroidery: detail of an embroidered stocking.

nun's cloth (toile de nonne) Woollen, tabby-woven fabric used as a dress material in the mid 19th century and, because of its even weave and many colours, as a ground for embroidery. In America this is known as *bunting.

nun's cotton The 19th century term for fine, white embroidery cotton, so called from its use in embroidery worked on linen by nuns. The label was often marked with a cross, hence the occasional name 'cross cotton'.

nuns' work At some period or other the following crafts have been known as nuns' work: crochet, knitting, netting, cutwork, drawn thread and drawn fabric work, pillow and needlepoint laces, satin embroidery, and ecclesiastical embroidery. See also convent influence.

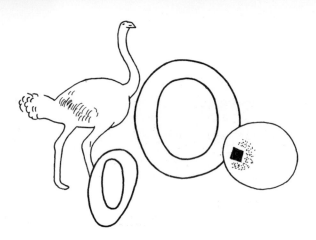

oes (owes) Small metal circles with a hole in the middle, like eyelets, used for trimming articles of dress in the late 16th and early 17th centuries.

ogee 'Continuous double curve, convex above and concave below' (OED). Though the word is usually applied to architectural mouldings, the shape is used in various crafts including embroidery.

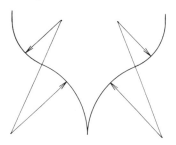

Ojibwa coats Coats of unsmoked buckskin in the *Prince Albert style which were very popular with the Ojibwa Indians of the northern plains. These Indians had early contact with traders from whom they copied the style and then made the coats for them, often exquisitely decorated with quillwork. Long leather fringes on the sleeves, shoulders, and round the hems were not only decorative but useful in shedding rain.

ombré Term meaning shaded, and applied to thread which is shaded along its length from light to dark to light again, always in the same colour; and also to *shadow work, when a softened colour is obtained by working embroidery stitches in a bright silk thread, or applying a piece of bright silk or satin under a transparent fabric.

onlay see applied work.

ONT Initials standing for Our New Thread, a cabled thread consisting of three 2 ply yarns twisted together, manufactured by George A. Clark in Newark (New Jersey) about 1866. This six cord cotton thread became a standard sewing machine thread in America.

opanke (opangi, opintsi) Outer pair of socks worn by men and women in Yugoslavia, Albania, and Romania. They are of thick knitted wool and are elaborately decorated with applied work and embroidery. Worn under a leather sandal and over another pair of socks, they act as slippers when the sandal is taken off on entering a house. Modern versions worn in many countries often have leather soles sewn to knitted socks with thick brightly-coloured wool. (Start 1939)

OP beads Large cylindrical beads of opaque glass exported from Germany about the middle of the 19th century. It is not known what the initials stand for, but they are proably a trader's (as distinct from a trade) term.

open buttonhole stitch see blanket stitch.

open chain stitch (square chain stitch, small writing, ladder stitch) Variation of chain stitch popular in Hungary, where complete designs on household linens are carried out in it. The name 'small writing' comes from the traced or 'written' line over which the stitch is worked. It is very like ordinary chain stitch but a little wider, as the needle does not go in at the same place as it came out, but just to the right.

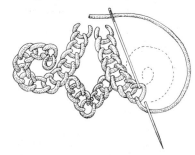

open groundwork see punch stitch.

openwork Generic term referring to embroideries in which the threads are either removed or drawn apart, as for instance in drawn thread or drawn fabric work. It includes such embroideries as broderie anglaise (eyelet), Hardanger, Ayrshire etc.

openwork seam The joining of two pieces of fabric by means of decorative stitches. Each piece must have its raw edge finished off, either by whipping or rolling the edge on fine fabric, or by turning and stitching a tiny hem on calico or linen. They are then joined by any of the many insertion stitches. See also veining.

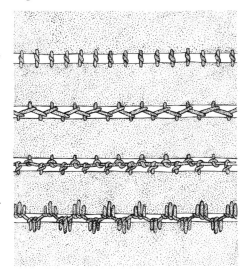

openwork stitch see punch stitch.

opus anglicanum Literally meaning English work, and applied to the English embroidery, chiefly ecclesiastical, worked from approximately AD 900 to 1500. Embroidery in England has never reached a higher peak of excellence than it did at this time, so much so that it was thought unnecessary to specify a type of work; English work meant embroidery. Fortunately there still remains a considerable quantity of opus anglicanum in different parts of Europe and America, but there was probably also a large amount of secular embroidery of the same type which has practically all disappeared.

opus anglicanum: the mitre of St Thomas à Becket, late 12th century.

Opus anglicanum was worked on heavy linen with silk and metal threads, enriched with pearls and jewels, and the skill is not so much in the workmanship, good though that is, as in the drawing and designing, especially of the figures. A fine split stitch was used for the details, and in the faces the stitches were worked spirally to give an effect of being slightly raised. Much of the background was worked with gold thread in underside couching, and since this method of working is very secure, there being no couching stitches on top to break away, many pieces are still intact. Though a number of museums, churches, and cathedrals have examples of opus anglicanum, it can best be studied at the Victoria and Albert Museum (London), the Metropolitan Museum of Art (New York), and the Museum of Art (Philadelphia).

opus araneum   see lacis.

opus conservetum   Applied work used in conjunction with quilting for hangings in Italy from the 16th century. It is still used for the heavy quilted leather curtains which substitute for doors in some Italian churches. (Webster 1915)

opus consutum   see applied work.

opus filatorium   see lacis.

opus plumarium   Work embroidered to look like feathers, not the modern feather stitch with which it is often confused. The term appears in 13th and 14th century inventories and no one knows exactly what it means, but it is generally thought to be either long and short or satin stitch.

opus teutonicum   Name used in the middle ages for German whitework. Schuette and Müller-Christensen (1964)

opus teutonicum: 'The Chase of the Unicorn', 14th century.

say that this typical embroidery might have been the result of the extreme poverty of north German convents, but even if this were true and the work was originally just a cheap alternative to the elaborate jewelled and silk ecclesiastical vestments of other countries, it developed a very high level of craftsmanship in its own right. White linen thread was used with a variety of stitches, including many composite ones, and some openwork effects.

organzine   The best quality silk thread, thrown and hand-twisted, used for the warp of good silk fabrics.

oriental carpet   The *American Ladies' Memorial* of 1849 discusses 'oriental' carpets worked on canvas, and says: '. . . for Pic-nic carpet seats, the parts are usually worked separately, and then sewed together. Smoking carpets are of various sizes and shapes, and are useful to place upon a lawn in fine weather. They are wadded and quilted at the back. Any pattern may be adopted, but flowers are the most appropriate.'

oriental couching   see romanian stitch.

oriental embroidery   Loose late 19th century term which included various techniques associated with the East but interpreted by western women. These included Indian, Japanese, and Chinese work, a form of crazy patchwork, and the embroidering of Persian and Indian printed cloths. (Levey 1971)

oriental embroidery: detail of an apron, late 19th century.

ornaments rubric   The part of the prayer book of the Church of England that states what vestments and hangings may be used in churches. These rubrics were established in 1549 during the reign of Edward VI.

or nué Technique in gold embroidery in which gold thread is couched down with coloured silks, close or far apart, making a shaded pattern on the gold. This method of couching, which was used in the middle ages and up until the 17th century, is found particularly on draperies, and it gives the richest effect of all gold techniques. The finest work in or nué was done in Burgundy in the 14th and 15th centuries. (Colour illustration p 80) See also Burgundian embroidery.

orphrey Word derived from the Latin auriphrygium, meaning gold embroidery. It now refers to bands of embroidery, often of gold or silk thread, on the front edges of copes, the backs of chasubles, and on some altar frontals. Fairholt (1846) says that the apparels of the amice and alb and any fringes or laces added to vestments were also called orphreys.

orphrey: depicting the crucifixion on a German chasuble, 15th century.

oshvitza Small worked borders that form the collars and outline the front openings of the shirts worn by Yugoslavian and Albanian women. The borders are worked separately and are then attached to the shirt with plain or fancy stitches. (Start 1939)

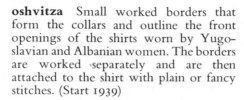

otolith embroidery Late 19th century embroidery in which the wings of the rose-beetle and the small bones from the heads of haddock, whiting, gurnard, and cod were sewn onto a dark cloth or velvet. The fishbones were cleaned, boiled, and dried to make them transparent and shiny. (Howe 1973)

Oudry, Pierre Professional embroiderer to *Mary Queen of Scots. He was one of the ten or so embroiderers who worked for her in France, and he apparently followed her to Scotland. It also seems that he was with Mary while she was in captivity as his name is on her portrait painted at Sheffield Castle and now at Hardwick Hall (Derbyshire).

ouragan Algonquin Indian name for birch bark boxes, leather cases, and bags decorated with porcupine quills and moosehair.

outing flannel see domett.

outline embroidery Popular late 19th century embroidery which consisted of designs worked mainly in outline stitch. A few other stitches could be used, but not so as to fill in any part of the design. It was used particularly on household articles so it had to be worked in such a way that it could be frequently washed and ironed. Some of the most popular designs were of Kate *Greenaway girls in bonnets with watering cans, umbrellas, pet lambs, and other animals.

outline stitch see stem stitch.

overcasting 1. In plain sewing, rather widely-spaced oversewing worked over raw edges to prevent them from ravelling. 2. In embroidery, a series of tight small stitches worked over a thread or a line of running. It can be used for fine outlines and stems or to form letters in monograms.

overhanded seam (french fell seam) Handsewn seam which is very like *run and fell except that instead of the second line of stitching being worked as hemming, the main fabric is folded back and a line of overhanding or oversewing is worked.

overhanding see top sewing.

overlaying Method of working cross or tent stitch on a material in which threads cannot be counted. Canvas is tacked over the ground, the pattern worked through both materials, and then the canvas threads are pulled out.

overlay stitch see spot stitch.

Oxburgh Hall (Norfolk, England) National Trust property containing (on loan from the Victoria and Albert Museum, London) those pieces of needlework worked by *Mary Queen of Scots during her captivity, called the Oxburgh Hangings. From 1482 the Hall has been the seat of the Catholic family of Bedingfeld and the hangings seem to have been brought to Oxburgh in 1761 through the marriage of Sir Richard Bedingfeld to the Hon Mary Browne of Cowdray. Swain (1973) thinks it is likely that the hangings originally belonged to the Duke of Norfolk and that they went from Arundel to Cowdray. Be that as it may, the needlework on the hangings is of the greatest importance as the motifs that make it up are among the very few pieces which can confidently be ascribed to Mary. The work is carried out entirely in tent stitch on canvas and consists of isolated units either square, octagonal, or cruciform mounted on green velvet. One section, made up of 34 units, is known as the 'Marian hanging' because each unit contains Mary's name, initial, or cipher. The designs, which in most cases contain a play on words or the *emblems so loved and well-understood in the 16th century, are taken chiefly from the bestiaries of the time.

Overlord Epic piece of embroidery commissioned by Lord Dulverton to commemorate the Second World War, culminating in the invasion of Normandy in 1944, the code name for which was Overlord. It is 272 feet (83 metres) long, which is 42 feet (13 metres) longer than the Bayeux tapestry. It has 34 panels each 8 feet by 3 feet (2.4 by 0.9 metres), was worked by 23 girls at the *Royal School of Needlework taking five years to complete, and was designed by Sandra Lawrence. It has been shown in America and England but as yet no permanent home has been found for it.

oversewing   see top sewing.

Overton, John   English publisher of pattern books in the mid 17th century. He was the successor to Peter *Stent at the White Horse, Little Old Bailey, without Newgate, London, and he published *The Second part of Fower-fotted creatures, A New and perfect Book of Beasts, Flowers, Fruits, butterflies & other vermine Exactly drawne after ye life and naturall by W. Hollar,* and *A New Boock of Flowers and Fishes,* all of which were of great value to the embroiderer.

owes   see oes.

Oxburgh Hall: motif from the hangings worked by Mary Queen of Scots.

oversewn seam (top sewn seam)   Join in which the raw edges of two pieces of fabric are each turned in, the pieces held together (raw edges inside), and a straight overcast or overhand stitch worked along the top from right to left. It is also used when joining two selvages and it may be made decorative by sewing with a thick, coloured embroidery thread. In English pieced patchwork the same seam is used for joining the pieces except that it is worked from the wrong side.

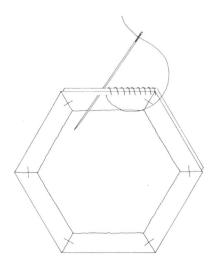

pack needle Large strong needle for sewing up packs. In the days when the majority of goods were moved about the country by pack horse, and articles being exported or imported went in small damp ships, the correct and careful sewing up of the packs in canvas was of great importance.

padding 1. Material sometimes called wadding used as the interlining for quilting or the filling for flat cushions etc. It may be cotton wool, kapok, sheep's wool, plastic foam, or any other suitable material. 2. Material, generally string, felt, or card, used to build up all types of padded embroidery, especially gold work. 3. Compressed cotton wool used to pad the faces and bodies in raised embroidery. See also moulds (number 4).

padding stitches Sometimes it is desirable to raise stitches, especially satin stitch, in order to give a little modelling, in which case another stitch has to be worked first, underneath the main one. The two stitches generally used as padding are satin and chain. When satin is used over satin, the two layers are worked at right angles to each other, and this is the method employed in the fine French white-on-white embroidery of the 19th and 20th centuries. Padding in other techniques sometimes makes use of string, card, parchment, wool etc.

paillette see spangle

paintings Needleworkers can use paintings in two ways. 1. As a source for the study of embroidery. Italian paintings from the 12th century onwards frequently show dresses with embroidered motifs or borders, and some of the paintings of early Fathers of the Church, saints, and bishops clearly illustrate the worked stoles, apparel, and insignia. Later, in the portraits of Tudor and Stuart times, great care is taken in the delineation of collars, cuffs, ruffs, and costume embroidery, all of which help to give an understanding of the needlework of the

paintings: 'The Descent from the Cross' after Rubens, 19th century.

period. 2. As a source for design. Much inspiration can be drawn from the study of period details, which can prove a very fruitful source of design. It is however questionable whether paintings should be copied in another medium, ie needlework, but this has frequently been done, especially in the 17th, 18th, and 19th centuries, not always with the happiest results. See also Linwood, Mary and Knowles, Mary.

paisley pattern Modern term wrongly applied to designs incorporating the pine cone or buta. While fabrics and shawls with this motif were made in abundance in Paisley (Scotland) in the 19th century, the motif did not in fact originate there but in India, and it was equally used in France and Austria as well as in other towns in Britain.

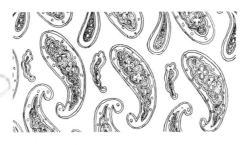

pall Word of many meanings including a rich fabric, an altar frontal, and a canopy, but now generally used in the

pall: detail, from the Upper Rhine, second half of the 15th century.

following senses. 1. Cloth which covers a hearse, tomb, or coffin. There are still some 15th and 16th century palls in existence which show superb embroidery, among which are the Bakers' pall and the Fishmongers' pall (both belonging to livery companies of the City of London), and the Sudbury and Fayrey palls. 2. Small, white, stiffened linen cloth which is used to cover the chalice at Holy Communion. It generally has a simple cross embroidered in white on it.

pallium Distinctive garment of scholars and teachers in ancient Greece and as such used by the early Christian church to represent dignity.

Panama canvas see Java canvas.

pane Word with several meanings, and care must be taken when reading old inventories to distinguish between them. 1. Pane can be a width of cloth, a counterpane, or a strip of cloth to be joined to another. 2. Panes (always plural), sometimes known as fendu, are the cuts or slashes made in material so as to show other material underneath. This was a favourite form of decoration on 16th century dress, and was especially popular in Switzerland. The underneath material could be pulled through the slits in puffs. 3. Paned can also mean striped.

panel: Greek, 18th century.

panel 1. Loose width of fabric, often embroidered, hanging from the shoulder or waist of dresses of some periods, notably the 1920s. 2. Piece of embroidery, generally unglazed, which is purely decorative and is meant to hang on a wall. It is difficult to differentiate between an embroidered picture and a panel, but generally the latter is non-representational and often experimental. (Colour illustration p 181)

pansa Crape-like, hand-woven cotton or linen fabric on which most Romanian embroideries are worked.

pantofles (pantobles) Indoor slippers, often embroidered, of any period but chiefly 1550–1650. The word also applied to galoshes or overshoes, as well as to the very high chopines worn on the continent.

papoose see baby carrier.

Paracas embroidery Skilful, intricate embroidery of the pre-Columbian period of 100 BC to AD 200, first discovered in the burial sites of Paracas Cavernas and Paracas Necropolis in southern Peru. The embroideries, on a loosely-woven background of wool or cotton, are minutely worked with small figures of animals or mythological creatures sometimes intermingled with geometric designs. Forms are repeated many times in complex horizontal, vertical, or chequerboard pat-

terns, and in many colour combinations. The stitching closely follows the weave, with each minute stitch enveloping a single thread of the cloth, almost completely veneering it with embroidery. Because of their size, often 4½ by 8 feet (1.4 by 2.4 metres), Paracas embroideries are thought to have been made purely for mortuary purposes, and because of their remarkable preservation in the dry burial sites, a large number have survived and can be found in many collections—notably the Metropolitan Museum, New York; the Brooklyn Museum, New York; the Peabody Museum, Harvard University; University Museum Philadelphia; and the National Museum of Anthropology and Archaeology, Lima, Peru. The Paracas tradition for fine embroidery was continued but was never equalled by the later *Nazca culture (AD 200). (Mason 1957, Leonard 1967) See also mummy bundle. (Colour illustration p 182)

Paracas embroidery: a mantle from the south coast of Peru.

Paravicini, George Known only through his very interesting trade card, now in the Pepysian Library in Magdalene College, Cambridge (England). It was one of a collection made by Samuel Pepys, and as he died in 1703, it probably dates from the last quarter of the 17th century. It reads: 'George Paravicini. At the Blackamore's head in Bedford St

(sometimes called Half-Moon St) Pinker Cutter And Raiser of Sattin. He also Draweth all sorts of Point Patterns, & Patternes for Beds Petticoats, Wastcoats Quilts and all sorts of Indian Patternes for Japan or Quilting.' (Heal 1933)

parchment The dressed skin of sheep, goat, or other animals prepared for use as a writing material before the introduction of paper. Being fairly stiff, embroiderers used it for padding gold work, and also to back *cutwork while it was being done, after which the parchment would be removed. Vellum is better quality parchment.

Parham Park (Sussex) Privately-owned Elizabethan manor house (open to the public at stated times) with arguably the finest collection of needlework in any house in England. The range is varied both in time and style, but outstanding are the chair and sofa coverings, the collection of 17th century canvas work panels, and the Florentine work bed hangings. Every room has its complement of superb embroidery, making a visit there a 'must' for every lover of fine needlework.

Parham Park: detail of the 17th century florentine hangings, English.

paris embroidery Late 19th century form of embroidery, described by Caulfeild and Saward (1882) as a 'simple variety of Satin Stitch worked upon Piqué with fine white cord for washing articles, and upon coloured rep silk, or fine cloth with filoselles for other materials.'

paris point see pin stitch.

parokheth see Torah ark curtain.

partlet Panel which filled in the decolletage of a bodice in the 16th century. It was generally embroidered en suite with the sleeves in contrast to the bodice or doublet. Though generally considered to be feminine wear they were sometimes worn by men. In the inventory of Dame Agnes Hungerford (1523) is 'Item, viij partlettes of sypers, iij of them garnysed with gold and the rest with Spanyshe worke.' (Nichols 1859)

passement (passemayne, passementerie) Term which includes gold and silver lace, braids, gimp, beaded edgings, and trimmings ornamented with metal threads, tinsel, gold, silver, and jet. In the 16th and 17th centuries it also included bobbin and needlepoint laces (the lacemakers were known as the passementerie). In the late 19th century when a lot of dresses were trimmed with jet in passement.

passing thread Very smooth metal thread which can be used in the needle like ordinary thread, but the needle should have a large eye so that the passing does not fray. As well as gold and silver, it can now be obtained in aluminium and copper and in various synthetic substitutes.

passion cross see cross.

Patania quilts see Gujarat.

patch 1. Piece of fabric used to cover a worn place or hole in clothes or household articles. They are sewn on as invisibly as possible and different fabrics have different methods of attachment. See calico patch, flannel patch, and print patch. 2. In patchwork, a piece of fabric which is either a specific shape (eg a hexagon) as in pieced patchwork, or an indefinite shape as in applied patchwork. 3. Term used in North America for

patch: on romper suit, English, 20th century.

machine-embroidery appliqués of flowers, animals, and slogans (eg 'danger, curves', and 'make love not war') which are then stitched to jackets, shirts, jeans, and other clothes.

patchwork The putting together, by one method or another, of pieces of material of different colours, types, and sizes to make a pleasing whole. What was, up to a few years ago, thought to be the oldest piece of needlework in the world is patchwork—the canopy of dyed gazelle hide cut into many patterns, dating from about 980 BC, which is in the Boulak Museum in Cairo (Egypt). It is both a form of thrift and a decorative technique, and a feature of the craft is that it is world-wide: there are few races or countries which have not used it in one form or another at some date. The bigger the surface to be covered the more elaborate and decorative the pattern, which means that it has been used extensively for bed furniture and large wall hangings. In the minds of many people the words patchwork and quilt go together like bread and butter, but like them they can and do stand alone. Patchwork is not all quilted, and quilts are not all patchwork, and the two words should always be clearly differentiated.

There are four basic types of patchwork. 1. *Applied work or appliqué or onlay, which is the sewing of pieces of material cut to certain shapes onto a

patchwork: pincushion with added beads, English, 19th century.

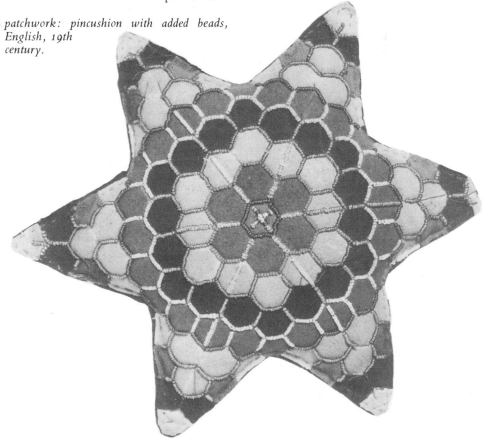

ground material. 2. *Pieced or mosaic patchwork or inlay, including Resht work and counterchange, which is the joining together of regular shapes to make a whole. 3. *Log cabin patchwork which is the joining of long narrow strips of ribbon or fabric in extending squares, which are then sewn together to make the whole. 4. *Crazy patchwork which is the sewing down of irregularly shaped patches onto one another with no set pattern and no foundation fabric showing. This type has decorative stitchery covering the joins. (Colour illustration p 199)

patchwork pillowcases pieced and/ or applied Pennsylvania German pillowcases, some signed and dated (from the late 1830s to the late 1860s), which matched quilts. So far they have only been found in Pennsylvania, mostly in Lancaster, York, and Dauphin counties. (Carlisle 1969)

patent canvas see french canvas.

paternayan wool Trade-name for long-fibred wool with a sheen, available in a wide range of colours, and now used in America for needlepoint (canvas work). The Paternayan brothers went to the United States in 1923 and began by selling Persian wools specially dyed for the repair of Aubusson and Persian carpets, later turning to needlepoint wools.

pattern books Books containing patterns and designs drawn for embroiderers to copy have been produced at all times from the 16th century until today. The earliest known, dated 1523, is in German, and was quickly followed by one in 1527 from Italy, French and English ones coming a little later. At that time there was no copyright law and publishers copied shamelessly from one another so that very few of the early books are entirely original. Also, sadly, few are still complete as many pages were torn out and used as patterns. However they ran through many editions, and one book, The *Needle's Excellency by James Boler, is only known by its 10th edition of 1634 and 12th of 1640, making it clear that many copies must have been used up and thrown away. The best known early pattern books published in England are by Thomas *Geminus, William *Barley, Richard Shorleyker (A *Scholehouse for the Needle), Peter *Stent, John *Overton, Robert *Furber, and Thomas *Trevelyon. The 18th century saw the start of women's magazines which, among other items, had designs for needlework, and again it is noticeable that many of the copies of, for example, The *Lady's Magazine have had the patterns torn out. These were sometimes pasted into a book for reference by the individual embroiderer, and there are many sketch books of designs in pen and wash in existence, obviously collected from different sources to be used as needed. In the 19th century the manufacturer of embroidery materials produced and sold, not always under his own name, innumerable pattern books of different techniques, and this tendency has become even stronger in the 20th century, so that today pattern books on every imaginable technique are available.

pattern books: an early 19th century American example.

pattern drawer Man or woman who draws designs for someone else to work; also, especially in the 19th century, a man who travelled round drawing designs on quilts. Most embroiderers have little skill in designing and so rely on people who can put a good design directly onto the fabric for them. It is likely that many well-known professional embroiderers have also drawn patterns for other people, for example Pierre *Oudry who was embroiderer to *Mary Queen of Scots probably drew out some of the designs she used. However, generally these men and women were not well known, and travelled from place to place in much the same way as the itinerant artists who painted inn signs in exchange for a meal or a lodging. One man who is recorded is the quilt drawer George *Gardiner and his apprentice Elizabeth *Sanderson. By the 18th century it had become a recognised trade and Campbell (1747) says in The London Tradesman that they are employed to draw patterns on paper or 'Shapes and Figures upon Men's Waistcoats to be embroidered, upon Women's Petticoats, and other Wearing Apparel', and he goes on to say that the trade requires a 'fruitful Fancy' and 'a wild kind of Imagination' and that it is better if he has a 'natural Turn for Designing' when 'his Works must have more of Nature and cannot fail to please better than the wild Scrawls of a mechanical Drawer'. Colby (1971) quotes an advertisement from a Boston (USA) newspaper of 1747: 'Sarah Hunt, dwelling in the house of James Nicol in School Street, also stamped Counterpins, curtains, linens and cottons for quilting with Fidelity and Despatch.'

patterns Designs printed on paper or cloth and used as a guide by the embroiderer. In the 16th and 17th centuries many pattern books were published and 18th century magazines such as The *Lady's Magazine had embroidery patterns in among their stories, fashions, and hints. The 19th century brought the great influx of printed designs, largely charts on graph paper for Berlin woolwork. These originated in Germany in the early years of the century and for several decades sold in enormous quantities. With the revival of interest in all types of embroidery at the end of the century, several magazines devoted entirely to the craft appeared (mostly sponsored and published by firms selling threads, materials, and fabrics) and they printed designs for all techniques. In recent times people have tended to draw their own designs from natural objects or to use geometrical motifs, but although there are a growing number of embroiderers who are able to do this there will always be those who cannot. Nowadays they are helped not only by magazines and books, but by the production of numbers of *kits providing everything necessary for a piece of work, including the design.

pattern shirring Method of gathering fullness in pattern which was still practised at the beginning of this century in the district around Monti Aurunci near Cassino, Italy. It was used for holding the fullness at the neck and sleeve in women's blouses. The method of working is not unlike that used in English *smocking, but in pattern shirring the pattern is formed by the gathers and there is no surface stitching. (Scanno 1914)

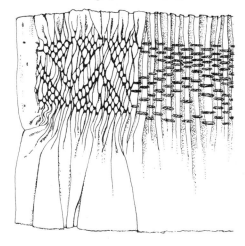

patchwork: an American quilt worked in the popular 'double wedding ring' design made from remnants of the maker's daughter's dresses, 1930.

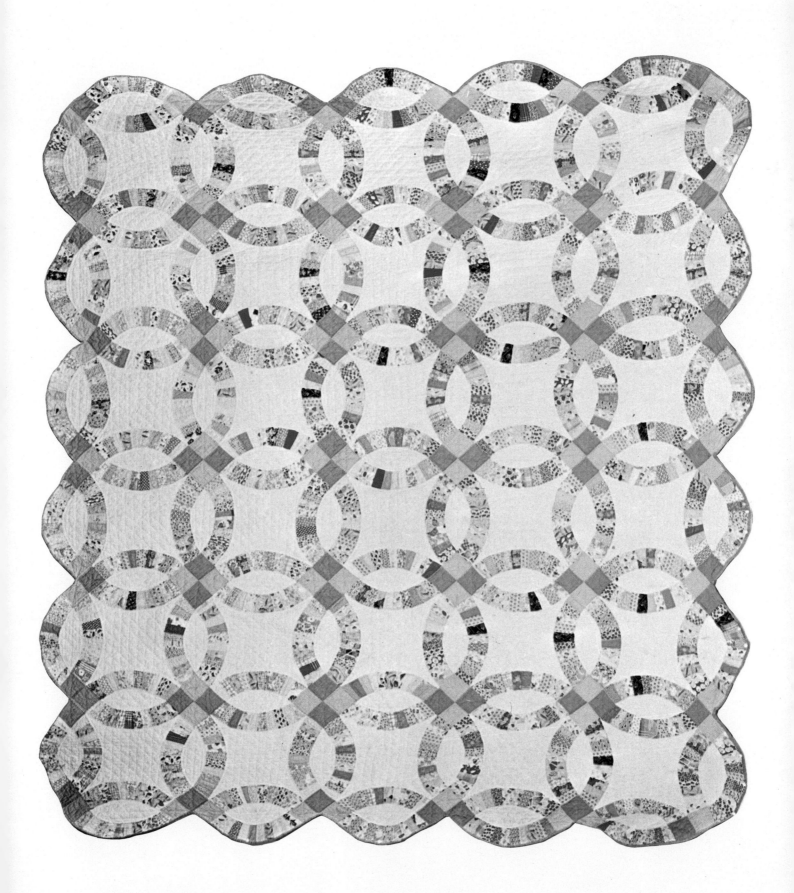

pattern sources: detail of a 16th century panel depicting beasts from Revelations and scenes from Greek and Persian history.

pattern sources The complete gamut of books, drawings, pictures, and the world of nature from which designs and patterns used in embroidery are derived. At different periods different sources have been popular, and at the present time great emphasis is placed on working from nature, either directly or from a stylised drawing, on which subject many books and articles have been written. In the 16th and 17th centuries a number of pattern books were published, and bestiaries, emblem books, prints, and book illustrations were also used. With the advent of magazines in the 18th century, designs appeared in each number, while in the 19th century large quantities of embroideries were worked from charts and designs already prepared. One interesting exercise practised today is discovering the exact source of many of the 17th century tent stitch pictorial embroideries, a number of which for instance are derived from illustrations to Virgil's works, Ovid's *Metamorphoses*, and other books.

quillwork: this form of embroidery was practised by the Canadian, eastern and central American Indian tribes. This vest embroidered with porcupine quills was made for a member of the Santee Sioux tribe.

pattern weave canvas Prepatterned cotton canvas of multiple threads, prepared for canvas work (needlepoint) embroidery. In Britain it is known as Munster web canvas.

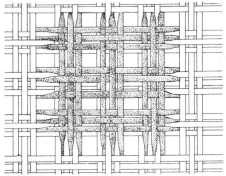

pearl Bead used in embroidery, which is either obtained from a freshwater mollusc that is distributed throughout rivers, lakes, and streams of most continents, or is an imitation of this. Real pearls were often used on the rich ecclesiastical embroideries of the middle ages as well as on the costume of royalty and nobility. In his will (1399), John of Gaunt leaves to the minster at Bury St Edmunds, Suffolk, 'un petit frontier pur l'autier de velvet vert enbroude de perill' (a little altar frontal of green velvet embroidered with pearl) as well as a set of vestments 'en chescune un masche de la frette un angnell de perill, en chescune autre masche un escochon de perill, faite des armes de Saint George' (embroidered with pearl angels and pearl escutcheons of the arms of St George) (Nichols 1780). Small freshwater pearls were used in the raised work embroideries of the 17th and 18th centuries for added richness and decoration, but sadly many of them have been removed or have fallen off, leaving only the marks where they were sewn on. Pearls, made from fishscales, glass, and other substances, have also been used in embroidery.

pearl: detail of the Mass Vestments of the Golden Fleece, 15th century.

pearl embroidery Embroidery using pearls from freshwater molluscs, especially as practised in tsarist Russia. Here there were two methods of attaching the pearls—by threading and by placing: in threading, a mesh of pearls was created and applied to fabric; in placing, the pearls were first threaded onto a length of white silk or linen thread which was then couched onto fabric or else a knot was made between each one. They were one of the most frequent decorations applied to embroidered clothing, ecclesiastical embroidery, head-dresses, and shoes, especially pre-17th century. (Edwards 1966)

pearly Colloquial term for a costermonger or barrowboy in the East End of London. On special occasions some of these families wear outfits covered with pearl buttons, sewn on in many patterns and leaving little of the cloth to be seen. This applies to both sexes and the outfits include hats, caps, dresses, coats, suits and shoes.

pearly: 'pearlies' from London's East End.

pede cloth The carpet or rug between the altar and the altar rails. In the 19th century they were usually in cross stitch on canvas and were considered suitable objects for societies or guilds to work, so they were often designed in squares with one person working each, which were then joined to form the carpet. Much thought was given as to which symbols or designs would be most suitable for treading underfoot. (Miss Lambert 1844)

pegs Metal or wood pegs used for holding the stretchers and runners of a rectangular embroidery frame in position.

pekinese stitch (chinese stitch) Composite stitch with back stitch as its basis. This is worked first, rather large, and then a second thread is laced through the stitches, going forward two and back one. A firm thread is needed for the lacing to keep its shape.

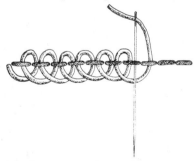

pekin knot see chinese knot.

pelerine Waist-length cape or tippet, often made of embroidered muslin, lace, or net, which was worn in the middle of the 19th century.

pelisse Full-length coat, often made of silks or lightweight fabrics and decorated with rouleaux or embroidery, which were worn by women in the late 18th and early 19th centuries.

penelope canvas (duo canvas) The first canvas to be woven with double instead of single threads. It was invented in the 1830s and called Penelope after the wife of Ulysses, who spent her nights

unpicking the work she had done during the day—the two-thread canvas looked to needleworkers (who had only been used to single thread) as though the work had been unpicked. It rapidly became, and still is, a very popular medium for fairly heavy-weight work, especially as it is possible to separate the threads and do both coarse and fine work on the same canvas.

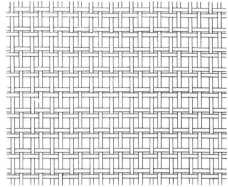

Penobscot Indians One of the tribes of the Algonquin federation, living along the Penobscot River in Maine and in New Brunswick, Canada. They were basket-makers, but were also extremely skilled in fine ribbonwork embroideries outlined with tiny seed beads, which decorated their clothing, and these reflect the influence of the French-Canadian *Ursuline nuns.

pentagon Five-sided shape used in patchwork, whose sides may or may not be of equal length. Twelve pentagons fitted together make a ball.

pentalpha Five-pointed star often used as a symbol in ecclesiastical embroidery.

perfume bag (perfume sachet) Ingenious little bags in all possible shapes used for carrying perfumes in the 17th and 18th centuries. The use of perfume was widespread and necessary both to enhance charms and to be used as an antiseptic and antidote to bad smells. These bags were made in any technique which could be adapted for the purpose, but generally silks and metal threads were used. (Seligman and Hughes n.d.)

perle cotton see coton perlé.

Persian embroidery Persia (now called Iran), being in the direct line of the silk road from East to West, has always been famous for textiles and even more

Persian embroidery: a 19th century prayer carpet, details.

for design. As a predominantly Moslem country the representation of living creatures is rare, formal pattern and stylised figures taking its place, and the influence of Persian design on other countries, both East and West, has been very great. When the Mughals conquered north India, the emperor Akbar brought Persian embroiderers in to work with the Indians and much Indian design shows this combination of talent. Neighbouring countries such as Afghanistan, Turkestan, Turkey, and Syria also show Persian influence in their designs, and with the imports of goods from the Near and Far East, England too succumbed to the fashion. Over the centuries three main motifs emerged which appear to us as typical: the *Tree of Life which gradually evolved into a stylised bunch of flowers; the cypress tree with its narrow upright shape; and the carnation, stylised or naturalistic, all used over and over again. The embroidery designs are based on those of woven textiles and carpets, and the stitches generally used are double darning, chain, stem, and long and short. See also Resht work.

perspex (plexiglas) Unbreakable, transparent, man-made substance resembling glass. It is often used for making templates, especially those used in patchwork, and can be a substitute for mica or mirror glass in collage and other embroideries.

Pesel, Louisa Frances (1870-1947) English embroideress and author who was brought up in Bradford, Yorkshire. She studied design and drawing with Lewis Day and on his recommendation went to Greece in 1903, where she became head of the Royal Hellenic Schools of Needlework and Laces in Athens. She returned to England in 1907, and in 1908 was elected a member of the *Embroiderers' Guild, of which she was president from 1920-1922. She will be remembered particularly for two things. First, she was commissioned by the Victoria and Albert Museum (London) to work a set of samplers of the stitches used in English embroidery. These are still in the textile study room at the museum for everyone to see, and they form the basis for many drawings of stitches in this book. They were photographed and published in 1913 as *Stitches from Old English Embroideries* with two other portfolios, *Stitches from Eastern Embroideries* and *Stitches from Western Embroideries*. Second, she was the inspiration and leader of the Winchester Broderers who, from 1931 to 1936, worked cushions and kneelers for Winchester Cathedral, the first of many such projects all over the world.

pessante see double darning.

petit point see tent stitch.

petticoat Literally a little coat, and originally applied to a short coat for men worn under armour. Over the centuries there have been several other meanings: 1. In the 17th and 18th centuries, the skirt of a woman's riding habit; 2. In the 16th and 18th centuries, the skirt worn under an open robe, decorated to match or contrast with the robe; 3. At all times from the 16th century, the undergarment generally hanging from the waist but sometimes from the shoulder, worn under a dress or skirt for warmth, modesty, or to produce a certain shape in the top skirt; and 4. from the 16th to the end of the 19th century, the dresses worn by small boys before they were breeched.

The petticoats worn by women have been embroidered in many ways. In 1599 Elizabeth I was given 'By the earle of Cumberland one pettycote of white sarcenett, embrothered all over with Venyce silver plate, and some carnacion silke like columbines' (Nichols 1823), while the 18th century petticoats were often of silk and satin, padded and quilted, or of the same fabric as the gown and embroidered to match. The undergarment of the 19th and 20th centuries has varied greatly in shape, fabric, and decoration, from the voluminous petticoats of cambric worked with flounces of broderie anglaise (eyelet embroidery) to the attenuated garments of crêpe de chine so popular in the 1920s, which were often decorated with very fine hemstitching, shadow work, and other fine sewing. See also slip.

Philadelphia Museum of Art (Pennsylvania) Contains a fine collection of quilts (among them a *Hewson quilt), embroideries, and samplers, including the recently acquired *Whitman samplers.

Philippine Islands The embroidery of these islands is an example of how nuns and missionaries have grafted the craft of their native lands onto local fabrics. The islands grow pineapples in abundance, and from the leaves a fibre is extracted which is woven into piña or pineapple cloth. This is normally as fine as lawn and of a delicate straw colour, and is embroidered with drawn fabric stitches or surface stitches in a matching thread.

Philippine Islands: detail of embroidered piña cloth, 20th century.

Philipson, Herr According to the Countess of Wilton writing in 1840, 'About the year 1804-5, a print-seller in Berlin, named Philipson, published the first coloured design, on checked paper, for needlework'. And so to this almost forgotten German printseller belongs the credit for producing the means by which the enormous industry of canvas work (needlepoint), including Berlin woolwork and all other types evolved since, has been built up.

Phrygia In ancient times Phrygia was part of Asia Minor and it was noted for the beauty of its needlework, especially gold work, for which both the Greeks and the Romans had the greatest esteem. Roman generals wore the *toga picta* decorated with Phrygian embroidery at their triumphs, as did the consuls when they celebrated their games. For this reason the Romans called embroidery Phrygian, and gold work auriphrygium. (Townsend 1899)

phulkari Literally flowered work, it is embroidery worked by the women of the *Punjab for head veils and other garment pieces. Floss silk is used on a coarse cotton known as kaddar cloth, and darning stitch is worked from the back of the cloth leaving the long threads on the right side to form the pattern. The design is worked both vertically and horizontally and it is the play of light on the smooth silk which gives phulkari embroidery its unique character. See also Indian embroidery.

piano furniture Embroideries for decorating and protecting pianos in the 19th and early 20th centuries. They could consist of a front which was placed along the front of an upright piano; a key cover which was placed on the keys to keep the dust off (rather than shutting the lid); and with grand pianos, a shawl or piece of embroidery which draped over the body of the instrument.

piano furniture: detail of a front panel, 19th century.

picot Small loop of twisted thread, generally but not always forming an edging to lace or embroidery. It can also mean a raised loop or bead representing things such as a grain of corn or the vein of a leaf. Picot-edging was a term widely used in the 1930s when many bias-cut dresses had their hems finished with machine hemstitching which was then cut through the centre leaving tiny tufts of thread.

pictorial or coloured embroidery see needle painting.

pieced patchwork (mosaic patchwork) The sewing together of patches of different patterns and colours cut to a regular shape to make a complete design. These designs are always geometric in style, although with skilful use of fabric a softer look can be achieved. The great tradition of pieced bedspreads on both sides of the Atlantic has chiefly used hexagons, lozenges or diamonds, squares, and triangles as the basis for the work, and on this simple foundation patterns of great complexity and beauty have been built up. Many have been given names such as the Star of Bethlehem or the Wild Goose Chase, but these names can vary from place to place, especially in America. There is now a vogue in Britain for a softer, more floral look achieved by using fabrics with a less clearly defined design than have been used in the past. Of all types of patchwork this is considered the easiest to make

pieced patchwork: detail of a 19th century American quilt worked in diamond shapes.

(most workers graduate from pieced to applied work). The pieces are small, light in weight, cheerful to look at, the basic technique is simple, and the small objects which can be made give much pleasure. One modern use for the craft is in occupational therapy as it has been found very suitable for the handicapped or the bedridden. See also Resht work, counterchange, inlay.

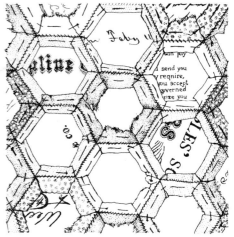

piecing Mending of partially worn articles such as sheets. For instance it could imply the turning of sheets sides to middles, or the introduction of extra pieces of fabric as patches. The term is also used in patchwork.

Piegan One of the tribes of the *Blackfoot nation of North American Indians, now located on a reservation in Alberta, Canada. Early embroideries were created with few beads in simple designs but by the 1880s wider polychrome strips were being applied to shirts and leggings. Great care went into making and decorating ceremonial suits—the fastest beadworking to complete a man's shirt and leggings with real beads took three weeks, and with seed beads a month.

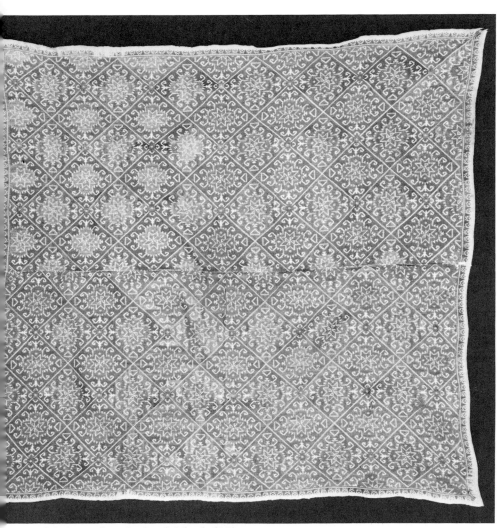

pillow bere: from the Greek Island of Naxos, 19th century.

pillow bere (pillow case) Word used until the end of the last century for what is now a pillow case for the bed. In 19th and early 20th century America pillow cases which are closed on three sides and open on the fourth were favourite items to decorate with hemstitching, monograms, embroidery, tatting, and crochet for sale at fairs and church bazaars.

pin Thin piece of wire with a sharp tapered point at one end and a small knob at the other, and certainly one of the most universal of all articles from earliest times until today. In the middle ages pins were used, often with guards over their points, to keep various garments and parts of garments together, and even today some orders of nuns use them on their dress rather than any other form of fastening. Originally they were expensive and considered a very acceptable present, and then as now the spending money given to a woman by either her husband or her father was known as pin money. During their long history there have been many

different sorts, but never more than in the last hundred years, when it has been possible to buy the ordinary household pin of brass or steel, toilet pins of blued steel with black glass heads, fine steel pins with coloured glass heads, pins which are very short, entomological pins which are very fine and ideal for using on fabric which marks easily, dressmaker's pins of well-shaped steel, and florist's pins which are long and thick. There have also been all types of pins used on costume, such as hat pins, lace pins, corset pins, and shawl pins. Although now usually sold in boxes, from at least the 18th century they were sold stuck into paper, and the phrase 'paper of pins' has passed into folk song.

piña cloth   see Philippine Islands.

pinafore   Washable covering to protect a child's or woman's dress. They were commonly worn in the late 19th century, especially by children, and could be very ornamental. They differ from an apron in being fastened above the waist at the back and in having armholes.

pincushion (pinpillow) Stuffed cushions of many shapes and sizes used for keeping pins in. As long as there have been pins there have been receptacles, either utilitarian or decorative, for holding them, and these have needed some form of stuffing (eg sawdust, kapok, foam rubber) to protect the points. The cushions have usually been embroidered in whatever technique was in fashion at the time: for example, tent stitch in the 17th century, flat stitches on silk in the 18th, and cross stitch and patchwork in the 19th. One type of which there are many in collections is the christening or layette cushion, popular as gifts in the 18th and early 19th centuries. These were often made of white satin and were stuck with pins of different sizes making a pattern and expressing an unexceptionable sentiment such as 'Welcome, sweet babe' or giving the name and birth date of the child. Generally these pins were not used and the pincushion has remained intact. In the 19th century there was a fashion for making pincushions resembling extremely unlikely objects such as wheelbarrows, bellows, books, jockey caps, or teacups, which were made from ivory, bone, wood, or patchwork with stuffing added somewhere into which the pins were stuck. A further type was the pincushion made as part of another sewing accessory such as a netting or sewing clamp or a hemming bird, and they were also made weighted with lead with an embroidered top for use instead of a clamp. In the 20th century they tend to be less decorative, or else worked in some derivative historical form. See also pin poppets, and pinballs.

pincushion: with chenille bird, American c.1850.

pincushion cover Described in the *Ladies' Work Table Book* (1858) in the following way: 'A large pincushion, having two covers to it, should belong to each toilet table. The covers are merely a bag into which the cushion is slipped. This may be either worked or plain and should have small tassels at each corner, and a frill or fringe all round.'

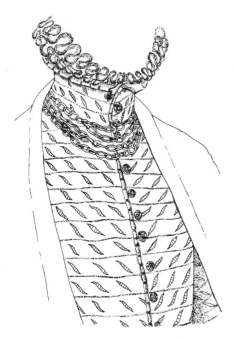

pinking: detail from a portrait by Hans Eworth, 1560.

pinking The ornamentation of material by cutting or punching different shapes in it; also the decoration of a raw edge by punching out a pattern on it which also has the effect of preventing fraying. It was a very usual form of decoration in the 16th century when various shaped eyelets and slashes were cut into the surface fabric of doublets and gowns to show a contrasting colour and texture underneath, but in the succeeding centuries it had a more practical use as a seam finish to prevent fraying. Until about the 1920s the same method was used for both these forms—that of using a mallet to hit a punch or knife (which were made in many different shapes to give the required effect) through the material onto a lead block. In the late 19th century, in an effort to speed up the seam finishing of dresses, a small machine was invented where the fabric was fed into a drum, and when the handle was turned a cutting blade made a continuous saw-tooth edge.

pinking knives.

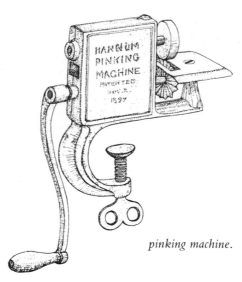

pinking machine.

In the 20th century the simplest method of all came into use with the invention of pinking shears, which are scissors with a serrated edge to each blade. Nowadays these are in the workboxes of most home dressmakers and embroiderers.

pinking scissors.

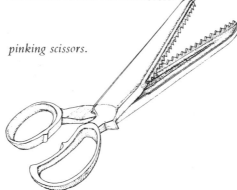

pinpillow   see pincushion.

pin poppet Small decorative case of ivory, wood, or metal which held a pincushion. They were used in the 17th and 18th centuries to carry the pins needed for running repairs to a gown.

pin stitch (point de paris, paris point, mock hemstitch) Drawn fabric stitch used to make a decorative join or to apply lace, often in lingerie, which is worked with a thick needle and a fine thread on firm silk or cotton, and relies on the holes so formed to make the decoration. It is not so strong a stitch as point turc and the raw edge must be neatened.

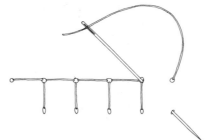

pinwork Small crescents or spines made on needlepoint lace or used as edgings in fine lingerie. A loose stitch is taken from one point to another about $\frac{1}{4}$ inch (6 millimetres) away, and taken back to the starting point. The loop so formed is then covered with buttonhole stitch, thus forming the crescent. The spine (or thorn) is made the same way but with a longer loop finishing closer to the starting point, and the point of the loop is held with a pin until the buttonhole stitch has been worked. This type of edging is often seen on the babies' caps of the 18th century.

pipe (pype) Small, hollow, shaped glass tube used as decoration on dresses and doublets in the 16th century. They were imported from Venice and are mentioned in the 1582 *Book of Rates* (Willan 1962).

pipe bag Long, narrow, skin bag elaborately decorated with beads and/or quillwork which is used to store the long-stemmed pipes central to all Plains Indians ceremonies—hunting, war, or council—between two people. Every man had his own pipe stored in his own pipe bag.

pipe bag: in beaded deerskin, Crow Indians of Montana.

piped seam Join which is finished with *piping. These seams were used on many dresses in the 19th century, on the edges of decorative rouleaux, and they often form a finish to articles such as cushions and chair covers. The piping may be of contrasting or matching fabric.

piping (welting) Strip of fabric, usually bias-cut, which may or may not enclose a thin cord. It is inserted into a plain seam to form a decorative trimming.

piping cord String or cord of various thicknesses covered by a strip of fabric and used in a piped seam. In America this is known as cable cord or dressmaker's cord, and may be used in corded shirring or as an edge finish.

piqué embroidery Embroidery which has a cord outlining the main part of the design, with filling stitches imitating a figured fabric. This type of work was popular in the 19th century and was used extensively on children's clothes and certain household articles.

plain seam The joining of two pieces of material by means of stitching, either by hand or by machine. The join is then pressed open and the raw edges neatened. This is the seam most often used in dressmaking as well as in other forms of needlework. See also seam finishes.

plain sewing Term meaning needlework which is useful rather than decorative, though it may have some decoration as a finish. Before the domestic sewing machine became generally available in about 1860, all dresses, underwear, men's shirts, and children's clothes came into this category. Nowadays it is generally confined to the making of underwear and baby's clothes by hand, and includes techniques such as mending, patching, making buttonholes etc, as well as those seams appropriate to handwork.

plain sewing: Norwegian marriage shirt, 19th century.

plain sewing stitches Stitches used for making up articles and garments by hand, rather than decorating them. Beautiful, fine, even stitchery which we call plain sewing was at its most perfect in the late 18th and early 19th centuries. After the general introduction of the sewing machine in the 1860s the craft deteriorated, but there are still many people who either have no machine or prefer to make things by hand. In this group are *back stitch (stitching), *basting, *blind hemming, *brave bred stitch (marking, true marking, two-sided cross), catch stitch (see herringbone stitch), *fly running, *french stemming, half back stitch (*running), *slip stitch, *stab stitch, *streatley stitch, *tacking, *whip.

Plains Indians Nomadic tribes of the great plains of North America, ranging from the Rocky Mountains to the Mississippi River, and from Texas to southern Canada. Buffalo, which they hunted on horseback, were a source of food, shelter, clothing, and trade, and items made from the buffalo skin were usually elaborately embroidered with porcupine or birdquill embroidery, or later with trade beads. Depending on the region and period, the patterns varied from geometric to floral, from solidly beaded areas to delicately outlined patterns, and from four to five different colours to as many as twenty on a single item. *Sioux, *Blackfoot, *Crow, Arapaho, Shoshoni, Commanche, Chippewa, and Cheyenne are among the best known of the Plains tribes.

Plains Indians: leather bag with beaded decoration, Sioux.

plain weave see tabby weave.

plait 1. In England, it now means the interweaving of fabric, straw, or hair to form a rope, but originally, up to the end of the 19th century, the word plait was interchangeable with *pleat. 2. In America plaiting is the English pleating, and the interweaving of fabric etc is braiding, not plaiting.

plaited slav stitch see long armed cross stitch.

plate Strip of metal, generally gilt, which is flat, bright, and shining and is used in ecclesiastical and metal thread embroidery. It is usually couched down with a matching or contrasting thread, either in a straight line or folded so that the couching thread does not show. Crimped plate is made by pressing ordinary plate along the ridges of a screw. Lately, synthetic threads have been made, both smooth and textured, which go under the name of plate.

pleached alley Formal walk bordered with trees all cut to the same height whose branches meet overhead making a tunnel. They were included in most large gardens of the 16th century and were a source of inspiration for the needleworkers of that time.

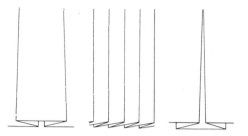

pleat: box, knife, and inverted.

pleat (plait) Fold of cloth or flattened gather used as a means of controlling fullness. It can be made in many different ways, and the main types are accordion, box, bulgare, cartridge, fan, goupil, inverted, knife, and watteau.

plexiglas see perspex.

plumage stitch see long and short stitch.

plush Fabric with a *nap longer than that of velvet, in cotton, silk or wool, and used for upholstery, liveries, and dresses. The look of plush was simulated in embroidery with plush stitch and in French raised work.

plush stitch (velvet stitch, rug stitch, tassel stitch, raised stitch, astrakhan stitch) Counted thread stitch making a series of loops which may be cut or left uncut according to the design. Each loop is held in place by a tent or cross stitch. It was very popular in the mid 19th century when sculptured effects in Berlin woolwork were common, and in the 17th century panels it was used to depict fur on costume and the coats of some animals in raised or stump work. Plush stitch can also be used for rugs.

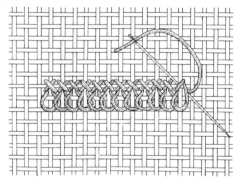

ply (filé) Threads or yarns twisted together for strength. They are usually bought in 1, 2, 3, or 4 ply thicknesses.

pocket In the 18th and mid 19th centuries a pair of pockets was worn attached to a tape which tied round the waist, underneath the skirt and petticoat. They carried feminine necessities such as keys, handkerchiefs, purse etc. In the

pocket: English, 18th century.

19th century they were very utilitarian, plain, and dull, but in the 18th century they were generally embroidered, many being obviously cut from another worn out embroidered article such as a bedspread. Very few of the surviving pockets appear to have been specially embroidered. On modern garments the patch pocket sometimes carries an embroidered badge or motif.

point 1. The three fine *tucks on the back of a glove. 2. Tie or lace, especially that tying the doublet to the hose in the 16th and 17th centuries. 3. The French word for a stitch, hence point turc, paris point etc. 4. Abbreviation of needlepoint in the phrase 'point lace'.

point couché rentré ou retiré see underside couching.

point de paris see pin stitch.

point de saxe see Dresden work.

point d'hongrie see florentine embroidery.

point paper (graph paper, quadrille paper) Paper printed with a grid of equidistant vertical and horizontal parallel lines, often with every tenth one thicker. It is used for the charts of all designs worked by the counted thread, each small square representing one stitch, and was first used for this purpose in the early 19th century. Weaver's paper is very similar.

point turc (three-sided stitch, bermuda faggoting, lace stitch, turkish stitch) Useful stitch for making a decorative join in firmly woven fabric, as all surplus can be cut away close to the stitch. It is worked with a thick needle in fine silk and consists of a row of joined triangles, the holes forming the decoration.

pole screen Framed piece of embroidery mounted on a decorative pole with feet. The frame can be adjusted to any height on the pole and is placed so as to keep the heat of the fire from anyone sitting too near it. These screens can be large or small and are generally very elegant with exquisite needlework of the period. See also banner firescreen, firescreen, and handscreen.

pole screen: American, 18th century.

(opposite)
raised work: detail of a panel of an English casket, c.1660.
(overleaf, p 210)
rococo: detail of an English 18th century pillou bere with the characteristically opulent decoration of this style.

Polesden Lacey: detail of an English embroidered chair back, 18th century.

Polesden Lacey (near Leatherhead, Surrey) National Trust property among whose many treasures are a considerable number of 18th century chairs upholstered in needlework of the time, some with marked *chinoiserie features.

polychrome Term describing the use of several colours in a piece of work.

polyester fiberfill see terylene filling.

poncho In Latin America, a blanket with a slit in the middle for inserting the head, and worn as a cloak. If it is sewn up the sides with decorative stitching it is known as a poncho-shirt. They have been worn since pre-Columbian times, the earlier ones often being short and elaborately woven, or embroidered, in vicuna wool, or else decorated with bands, fringes, and borders around the V-necks. Long poncho-shirts like those introduced in the Tiahuanaco period (AD 700–1100) can still be seen in the Andean Highlands today.

(overleaf, p 211)
Romania: an embroidered waistcoat showing the Slav love of colour and repeated motifs.

(opposite)
Roosevelt: firescreen depicting a leapard, worked by Mrs Theodore Roosevelt Jr.

ponto grado canvas Large scale penelope or double-thread canvas used for making rugs, and called rug canvas in the UK.

pony beads (big beads) Irregular, opaque china beads about ⅛ inch (3 millimetres) in diameter, manufactured in Venice. They were imported into North America and taken to the Plains tribes by pony pack trains from about 1800–1840. They were mainly blue, white, yellow, and black, and were used as trade goods.

porcupine quill Quill of the New World porcupine with the necessary qualities for embroidery: they are long enough to be easily handled, thick enough to be readily visible, light in colour so that they can be dyed easily, and capable of being folded, flattened, or creased sufficiently to obscure the thread used in stitching. North American Indians use them extensively for embroidery. See also quillwork. (Turner 1955)

poncho: from the Paracas culture of the south coast of Peru.

portière Curtain hung over a door, doorway, or arch to give privacy, to exclude draughts, or for decoration. As they are big and flat they lend themselves to large scale embroidery, often applied. They were used in medieval houses and were popular in the interior decoration of the late 19th and early 20th centuries.

portière: designed by Queen Victoria's daughter, Princess Louise.

portrait: English, 17th century.

portraits Although embroidery has never been a good medium for portraiture, it is possible to show strong emotions in a stylistic way, as was so frequently and beautifully done in opus anglicanum and other medieval embroidery. In the 17th century the attempts made at representing faces mostly produced rather wooden results. However at various times portraits have been attempted though not often at first hand, generally being copies of paintings, like those of Mary *Linwood. Realistic portraits in a stylised way can be seen in *Overlord, where the faces of George VI, Winston Churchill, and service chiefs are completely life-like.

Portugal While Portuguese embroideries frequently resemble those of her near neighbour, Spain, they have in some cases evolved a distinct style of their own. In the 15th and early 16th centuries, Portugal was the greatest maritime nation in Europe, and in 1510 conquered Goa

Portugal: corner of a linen coverlet, second half of the 16th century.

and in 1511 Malacca, while commercial treaties were made with China in 1517 and Japan in 1542. The result was that for a time Lisbon became the clearing house for oriental goods and so the first

of the influences from the East spread to the rest of Europe via Portugal. This combined with trends from the Moors who had occupied the country until the 12th century, and from South America brought in by Spain, to produce an embroidery of many styles in the 16th and 17th centuries. However one particular type stands out which was worked in monochrome (often a reddish brown) with a very hard linen thread in a mixture of knotted and raised stitches, giving depth and interest to what could otherwise be a dull piece of work. It was used for bedcovers and hangings as well as altar cloths and often church work, and is perpetuated today in the Caldas da Rainha (or Queen Leonora) embroideries. The Castelo Branco district is known for work using a long satin stitch couched in straight lines, while around Viana in the north of the country much chain stitch is used, and the stylised flowers and leaves tend to have solid centres with light lacy surrounds. Guimarães, also in the north, is a centre for the sale of local embroideries including drawn threadwork.

portuguese hem Decorative hem used as a finish to underwear and some household articles when there is a straight line at the edge and no curve. The finished effect shows a series of triangles or vandykes sewn down to the body of the garment either with hemming or a more decorative stitch. (Armes 1939)

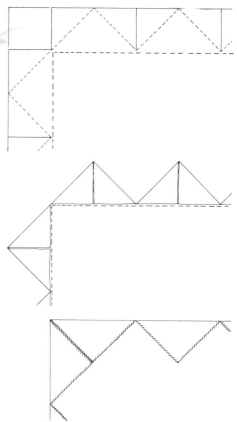

portuguese stitch see long armed cross stitch.

pouch Receptacle for carrying small objects or money; also, sometimes a pocket. Whether made of leather, birch bark, or cloth, some have been beautifully embroidered, and they have been used by many different people, from soldiers who used pouches for ammunition and other necessities, to fashionable women who at different times have used a pouch handbag or poche. See also alms purse.

pouch: English 16th century.

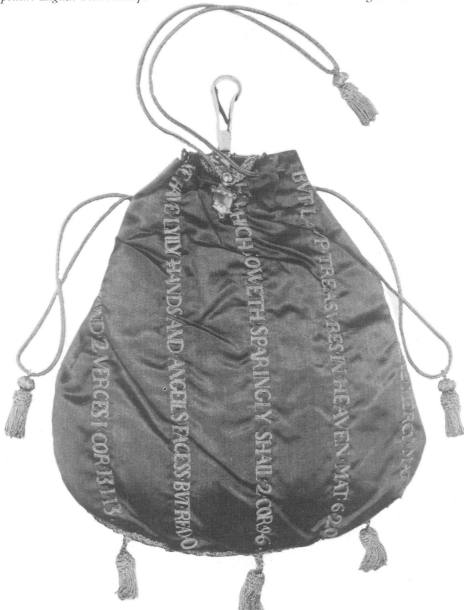

pounce Fine powder, such as powdered charcoal or powdered cuttlefish, used to rub through the perforations of a design on paper to transfer it to the fabric underneath. The design is fixed by painting over the pounce which is then blown away. See also prick.

pound beads Beads imported from Italy and Germany in the 19th century and sold by weight. They were of transparent glass dyed in a wide range of colours. See also beadwork.

pourpoint Something quilted, either the padded and quilted doublet worn under armour in the middle ages, or a quilted bedspread. The word itself refers to the stitching which was sometimes called pourpointing.

powder In embroidery to scatter jewels or small motifs over a ground.

powder sprinkler Container with a perforated top, generally made of bone, ivory, or wood and kept in the workbox. They were filled with powder which could be sprinkled on the hands to prevent them becoming damp and marking the embroidery.

Practical Embroiderer Embroidery aid produced in England in the 1930s by H. Kay and, according to the manufacturer, 'acclaimed as the most ingenious method of embroidery ever discovered' and also surprisingly, 'sanctioned by Education Authorities for use in schools'. It consisted of metal templates in basic

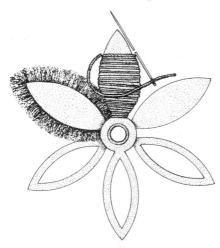

shapes which could be combined to form a number of designs by passing layers of coloured wool over them and through the ground fabric. When sufficient layers had been arranged the wool was cut and fluffed up, and other embroidery stitches were added.

prayer desk see faldstool.

prayer mats (prayer rugs) Used in the household of every Moslem, with smaller versions to go with him on his travels. They are made in all the Eastern carpet techniques, and can also be worked with a needle, quilted, or be of printed fabric. The design is of a single or triple prayer niche at one end, supported on columns, and generally a hanging lamp in the centre. (Mathews 1960)

prayer mats: detail of a Persian example quilted in back stitch with a chain stitch design, late 18th century.

Prayse of the Needle, The Poem written by John *Taylor in 1640 and included in *The *Needle's Excellency* by James Boler. It is quoted in part in many needlework books and is reproduced in full from the *Handbook of Needlework* (Miss Lambert 1843) on the endpapers.

pre-Columbian embroidery Highly skilled needlework that accompanied a sophisticated textile development in the cultures along the western coast of South America from 2000 BC to the time of Columbus (1451–1506). It reached its peak between the 3rd century BC and the 3rd century AD with the *Paracas embroideries. They were mostly worked in wool, with buttonhole, darning, double darning, knit stem stitch, and variations of plain stem among the stitches used to achieve a variety of spectacular effects with ease of execution. See also mummy bundles, needle knitting, Ica shawls, Nazca.

Pre-Raphaelite Brotherhood Group of artists in England who in 1849 decided to model their work on that of the Italian painters before Raphael. The original members were Hunt, Millais, D. G. Rossetti and his brother William, Collinson, Stephens, and Woolner. Their work was attacked by many people including Dickens, but *Ruskin came to their defence. In the 1850s this group dissolved and Rossetti formed a second Brotherhood at Oxford with *Morris and Burne-Jones. The work of both these groups influenced many other artists, a number of whom designed embroideries.

presentation quilt see album quilt.

presser foot see foot.

prick In embroidery to outline a design on paper by pricking it with a needle so that the paper becomes perforated. The holes so formed are then rubbed through with *pounce to transfer the design onto fabric.

pricker Needle or fine sharp steel wire inserted into a handle and used for pricking. They could be very decorative and often the sharp point was screwed inside a bone or ivory case so that it could neither do damage nor get broken. An adequate substitute for a pricker is a needle with the eye stuck into a cork. See prick.

prie-dieu (vesper chair) Chair used in the home, particularly in the 19th century. It consisted of a low seat with a high back and a ledge on top. Although its main purpose was for family prayers (the seat was knelt on and the prayer or

hymn book placed on the ledge), it also made a good sewing chair. Many were upholstered in Berlin woolwork.

prince albert Long, double-breasted frock coat for men, named after Prince Albert Edward, later Edward VII of England who set the fashion for wearing it. The term and the fashion were very popular in America in the 1890s, and Buffalo Bill Cody wore a prince albert made of buckskin together with wide-cuffed gauntlets, both elaborately decorated with beadwork, in his Wild West Show which started in 1883.

prince albert: Buffalo Bill Cody wearing a buckskin coat beaded by the Sioux.

print patch Repair for a cotton print. A new square of fabric is chosen and the edges turned in so that the pattern matches the pattern of the main fabric. It is then top sewn from the right side. On the back the hole is cut to correspond to the turned edges and they are blanket stitched together.

printwork The copying of prints in needlework. Usually a cream silk or taffeta ground was chosen and the reproduction was worked in fine silk in black, sometimes including greys. Printwork was popular in the early 19th century and was revived at the end of the century as *etching embroidery.

printwork: English, early 19th century.

pucker Term used for areas of embroidery which will not lie flat because they are too tightly worked. Puckering also occurs in applied work which has not been properly smoothed on, and when one type of fabric does not stretch equally with another.

pueblo embroidery stitch Variety of back stitch invented by the *Pueblo Indians in about the 16th century and used ever since. A two-ply, lightly-twisted wool yarn is usually used on a wool or cotton background.

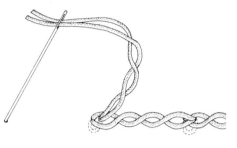

Pueblo Indians American Indians living in permanent communities in New Mexico, Arizona, Colorado, and southern Utah. The white settlers introduced wool which the Indians used for fine embroideries, an art form not previously developed. Although both quality and quantity have declined they still produce a great variety of art and craftwork, and serious efforts are being made to revitalise the old skills. See also Hopi embroidery, kilts.

Pueblo Indians: dance kilt.

Pulaski banner Banner embroidered on red silk made by the Moravian nuns at Bethlehem (Pennsylvania) and carried by the dragoon legion of Count Pulaski (1748-1779). He was the Polish patriot brigadier-general who fought in the revolutionary battle of Monmouth (New Jersey) in 1778 and was killed in 1779 in a cavalry charge against the British at Savannah (Georgia). See also Moravian embroidery.

Pulham work Type of work mentioned in 16th century inventories which is now unidentifiable. It apparently originated at Pulham in south Norfolk (England) where there was a celebrated manufactory of coverlets, so presumably it was embroidery on bedspreads. In the inventory of Jeffery Cobb (1591) there is 'A covering of Pulham worke', in the inventory of Stephen Atkins (1588), 'one coverlet of pullham worke', and in the inventory of Sir Roger Wodehouse (1588), 'A hanging of Pulham work'.

pulled fabric work see drawn fabric work.

punch Metal tool for cutting shaped holes such as eyelets in material.

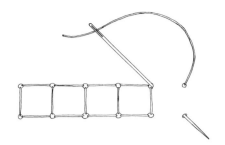

punch stitch (four-sided stitch, open groundwork, openwork stitch, single faggot stitch) Drawn fabric stitch which may either be used in a single line to form a decorative join or to apply lace, or (worked in a different way) as a filling stitch. It consists of a series of joined squares, and can be worked on a firm fabric with a thick needle and fine thread, or on loosely-woven scrim or linen when used as a filling. Punch stitch makes a very strong joining stitch and surplus fabric can be cut away. It is used in Rhodes work or *punch work.

punch work (Rhodes work) Variety of drawn fabric work which employs punch stitch. Generally in drawn fabric work many ground stitches are employed but in punch work only one is used. The design is outlined in stem stitch and then the whole of the ground is covered with punch stitch.

punch work: detail of a Turkish cloth, 19th century.

Punjab Region of the Indian subcontinent, now partly in India and partly in Pakistan. It was largely composed of hill states with a fighting tradition, and many of the embroideries depict warriors and battle scenes; they also reflect a strong Mughal influence. The main varieties of work are the *chamba rumals and the domestic *phulkari or flowered embroidery.

punto The Italian word for stitch and used in the same way as the French word *point. It in fact means a stitch made in needlepoint lace, but in various forms of cutwork which were the antecedents of lace, punto is used with another word to describe early techniques; for example, punto tagliato (cutwork), punto tirato (drawn threadwork), and punto in aria (needlepoint lace).

purfle To ornament or decorate with a border of embroidery, lace, or trimming.

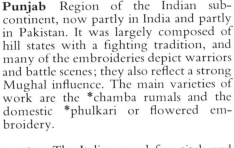

purificator Small square of linen used to wipe the chalice at Holy Communion. They are about 9 inches (23 centimetres) square, hemmed, and have a small cross embroidered in the centre of one edge.

purl 1. Type of 17th century metal embroidery known as purl embroidery. 2. The tiny loop or twist at the edge of a piece of lace or braid. 3. The gold wire with which purl embroidery was worked. There are several kinds in use today, their common basis being that the coiled wire is hollow so that the metal can be cut and a length used like a bead. Pearl-purl (wire purl, Jaceron, badge purl, or bead purl) is heavy and can be sewn like a bead, but it can also be slightly drawn out before use so that the sewing thread clips between the coils. Smooth purl (shine purl) is pliable, bright, shining and smooth; rough purl (matte purl) is duller; while check purl (frizé purl) has an angular look and is very bright and sparkling. The purl of the 16th and 17th centuries was often dyed in colours that give the embroidery a rather stiff but naturalistic effect. 4. Stitch in knitting.

purlette Cord sewn down with widely-spaced buttonhole stitch and used as an edging for applied work in America. The thread for the stitching can be silk, cotton, chenille, etc.

purse Bag for carrying money and other necessities, which at various times has been embroidered, notably in the 16th, 19th, and 20th centuries. In the 16th century they were used for presenting gifts of money and there are many references in the *New Year Gifts to Queen Elizabeth*, such as (in 1561) 'By the Earle of Darbye in a purse of crymsen satten, embraudered with golde, in dimy soveraignes . . . 20.0.0' (Nichols 1823). While women wore pockets under their dresses, purses were not essential, but by the 19th century they had become necessary and were made in every conceivable technique such as netting, knitting, crochet etc, as well as embroidery. Early in the century purses were known as reticules, were often of satin, and were embroidered with wreaths of flowers in fine cross or tent stitch. Late 19th and 20th century purses became larger in size and were known as handbags, but some of these

purse: English, 17th century.

purse: North American Indian beadwork.

continued to be embroidered, especially those used in the evening, and they still are today, while small change purses are also used.

purse silk (netting silk) Hard-twist, round, even silk thread of the 19th century, used especially for the netting or crocheting of purses but also for embroidery. It took dye very well and when worked closely made a good matt surface which did not fluff up. Miss Lambert (1843) says that in certain kinds of work it can be mistaken for gold thread, and so was very suitable for ecclesiastical embroidery. It was similar to the French cordonnet.

putting in In quilting, the art of fastening the edges of the bottom piece of fabric to the frame, spreading the wadding over it, and putting on the top piece of fabric ready for sewing all three together.

puzzle patchwork see crazy patchwork.

pype see pipe.

quadrille paper see point paper.

quatrefoil Literally having four leaves, the term generally refers in embroidery to a four-petalled flower or to the architectural detail sometimes found in opus anglicanum where an arch or opening is so shaped as to give the appearance of a four-petalled flower.

Queen Anne quilting see false quilting.

Quentell, Peter German author from Cologne of one of the earliest *pattern books *Eyn new kunstlich boich* (1527). It contained medieval and arabesque borders and alphabets to be worked in embroidery and lacis. (Palliser 1869)

quetzel Dove-sized South American bird with a scarlet breast and iridescent green to midnight blue feathers. These feathers, which are easily removed from the bird, were used on ceremonial capes worn by the Aztec and Mayan chiefs. They were also used with humming-bird and rhea (American ostrich) feathers to embellish head-dresses, shields, garments, and standards. A beautiful quetzel feather tiara which was given to Cortez by Montezuma is now in the Volkerkunde Museum in Vienna. See also featherwork.

quexquemitl Upper garment shaped like a cape or poncho worn by the women of Guatemala. While they often have the patterns woven into the fabric some are embroidered in cross and double running stitch in formal patterns of flower sprays in vases, birds, animals etc. (Start 1963)

quille see quilling.

quill embroidery see quillwork.

quill holder Long cigar-shaped bladder container used to store quills of the same size and colour before they are used in *quillwork.

quilling (quille) Pleated, braided, or gathered trimming for dresses, bonnets etc, which often resembled rows of quills. It was usually made from lightweight fabrics such as chiffon, aerophane, and taffeta, and was sometimes used as a border on samplers in Pennsylvania in the early 19th century.

quill patchwork Variety of patchwork practised in the 1880s. It consisted of folding small scraps of fabric into pointed 'quills' and then sewing them in straight overlapping rows onto a stout foundation such as ticking. (Morris 1962) See also button rugs.

quillwork (quill embroidery) Universal form of embroidery among the Canadian and eastern and central US Indian tribes, using dyed porcupine or bird quills on birch bark or hides. Sinew was used for thread and an awl or sharp thorn instead of a needle to pierce the hide or bark. First the quills were softened by soaking, and then flattened by pulling between the fingernails or teeth. They were not themselves sewn but they were formed into shapes held in place with stitches which were always hidden, except in the link-chain technique where the holding stitch is part of the pattern. Originally quillwork was regarded as a

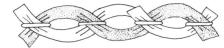

link-chain quillwork

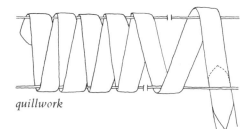

quillwork

sacred craft. Young women were ceremonially initiated into the art of handling the sharp and pointed quills, then taught by the older women the various methods of sewing, plaiting, weaving, and wrapping. (Ewers 1945) (Colour illustration p 200)

quilt Word often used to mean all bedspreads, but here confined to those which are actually quilted. Quilting has probably been a thrifty as well as an ornamental practice since fabric was woven and warm bedcovers needed—they are certainly mentioned in very early inventories. Quilts originally came from the East, and as early as 1516 a Portuguese traveller in India, Duarte Barbosa, was sending back reports saying that 'They also make here very beautiful quilts and testers of beds finely worked and painted and quilted articles of dress.'

In England they were part of the very important beds with all their furniture which were used by the wealthy and carefully left to their descendants: in 1381, Philippa Countess of March left to her son Esmond her bed of blue taffeta with a matching embroidered quilt, and another quilt stitched in white. Throughout the centuries, quilts have never lost their popularity though there have been many different styles. In the 18th century rather less value was placed on warmth and rather more on decoration, and many were embroidered, often in chain stitch,

quilt: patchwork and quilting are combined in this American example, c.1824.

as well as quilted, mostly in Queen Anne or *false quilting. The 19th century saw the zenith both in England and America of *wadded or Durham quilts and patchwork covers quilted to plain backs. Fortunately there are still people today who admire these beautiful and useful articles, and spend hours making them. Splendid quilts were and are associated with American needleworkers, both in the Colonial period and since. See also bedcovers, patchwork, quilting, kanthas, sujanis.

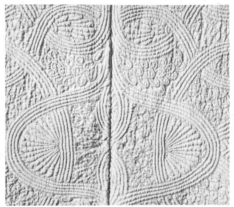

quilting: detail of an early 18th century English quilted bodice.

quilting The stitching together of two or three thicknesses of fabric to make something which can be warm, protective, or purely decorative. One of the oldest of needlework techniques, it certainly originated in the East, and it is such an obvious method of providing warmth with the maximum re-use of old fabrics that it must have been used very early in all cold countries. Quilting has been used for many different types of objects. It was discovered early on that the interlining made an excellent defence against the weapons of war, so quilted jerkins and *haquetons were worn both

quilting: detail of a modern picture quilt.

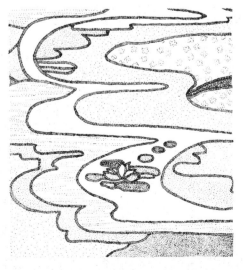

by knights under their armour to prevent chafing and by foot soldiers to turn the point of a sword or lance. The definition given by Randle *Holme in *The Academy of Armory* (1688) shows that by that date the beauty of the article was of paramount importance: 'Quilting is to put cotton wool of an equal thickness between two Silks, or a Callicoe or other Cloth undermost, and a Silk above, which is wrought in scrolls, flowers, etc, to keep the cotton from shifting its place.' Also, in the *New Years Gifts of Queen Elizabeth* (1599-1600) is 'By Sir Henry Burker, one pettycote of taffeta scarcenet quylted all over with a border, imbrothered with golde and carnacion silke with poyntes' (Nichols 1823). See also trapunto, italian quilting, cord quilting, false quilting, wadded quilting.

quilting bar or guide   see attachments.

quilting bee Favourite form of social gathering in the pioneer days in America when neighbours were not too close and did not meet very frequently. The hostess, who would have patched a quilt, would put it with the interlining and backing onto a frame, mark out the design, and then invite friends and neighbours for the day to help her do the *quilting. She would have prepared food for everybody, and her guests would sit

quilting bee: an anonymous painting, c.1854.

both sides of the frame, in relays if need be, and run in the design for her amid much chat and general enjoyment. In the north of England these gatherings were known as quilting feasts or quilting parties.

quilting hoop Double-ring embroidery frame resembling a tambour frame which is sometimes used for quilting small articles or, with extra careful preparation, even a full-sized quilt. See also embroidery frame.

quilting needle In America a short, sharp, pointed needle designed for making fine stitches and available in sizes 7 and 8.

Quintain French lawn made in Quintain, Brittany, in the 16th and 17th centuries. According to Palliser (1869) it was used in the making of early cutwork.

quirk 1. The part of a loose cover for a chair or sofa in front of the arms. 2. The small gussets between the bottom of the fingers and the palms in some makes of glove. 3. The earliest known appearance of the word is in Salesbury's *Welsh Dictionary* (1547), where kwyrk-hosan is given as the equivalent of the English *clock on a stocking.

quition   see cushion.

quiver Case for carrying weapons such as arrows or harpoons. Embroidered sealskin quivers are used by some Eskimo peoples for carrying their harpoons.

quoif   see coif.

saddle-bag: detail of a Piegan Indian saddle-bag in scarlet cloth applied with navy blue and beaded.

raffia (rafia, raphia) Soft fibres from the leaves of the raphia palm from Madagascar, used for embroidery in many African countries, the Caribbean islands, as well as Britain and America. It has the disadvantage of being uneven in width, and now a plastic substitute of absolutely even quality is made. See also raffia embroidery.

raffia embroidery (Madagascar straw embroidery) Kind of embroidery using raffia as the thread, which is suitable for rather coarse work on raffia cloth, canvas, crash, or hessian. Kuba and Kasai tribes in Africa use such techniques as over-sewing, openwork, eyelet, or buttonhole stitching and *embroidered pile cloth. Raffia can be dyed bright colours and so lends itself to decoration on garden hats and aprons, workbags etc. As it is comparatively cheap and covers the ground quickly, raffia has always been one of the threads used in teaching embroidery to small children.

rafugar Embroiderer in Kashmir. In the early 19th century there were only a few of them, and their job was to sew together the pieces from various looms to make the finished shawl. However the advent of the *'amli or embroidered shawl created the need for more needlemen, and by 1825 there were probably about 5000. With the decline of the shawl industry in the late 19th century the rafugars had to adapt themselves to embroidering bedcovers, tablecloths etc for the tourist market. (Irwin 1973)

rafugari work Embroidery of Kashmir worked by the *rafugars.

railroad canvas (net canvas) Stiff linen and cotton fabric in black or white, woven with a large, open mesh. Double worsted thread is needed to fill in the meshes and it is considered equally suitable for cross stitch and star stitch.

---

sampler: in cross stitch and satin stitch, English, signed and dated Jane Dobson Battle, 1838. This type, probably worked at school, combined religious training with needlework teaching. Later, alphabets and numbers were more usual.

raised Term applied to fabric partly woven with a pile, so that some of it appears to have been cut away leaving the other part raised. Also it applies to all embroidery which is not flat but is worked in relief by means of card, parchment, string, cotton wool, or just by the use of thick thread. It is extremely difficult to sort out all the different types of embroidery which have the word 'raised' in their title and confusion is bound to arise, but in all cases it is the result of a wish to introduce modelling into a flat design. A raised technique usually becomes fashionable after a long period of flat techniques: for example, modelling in gold work came towards the end of the long period of opus anglicanum; the 16th and even more the 17th century raised or stump work came after the blackwork and flat polychrome embroideries of the 16th century; French raised work was an antidote to the flat Berlin woolwork; and today collage with its very three-dimensional effects comes after a long period of linen embroidery, pulled and drawn work, and flat pictorial effects.

raised: detail of a pair of Chilean dancer's trousers from Santiago.

raised appliqué Embroidery with applied pieces of material padded and so raised from the ground fabric. Embroiderers have always exploited the possibilities of slightly three-dimensional work and never more so than at the present time, when gold or silver kid is often used for raised medallions, giving a great deal of depth of light and shade. See stumpwork.

raised Berlin work see french raised work.

raised cut work see French raised work.

raised embroidery Type of 19th century embroidery consisting of flowers and buds worked in satin stitch over a pad of cotton wool which was carefully cut to shape and fastened to the ground fabric with a large cross stitch. Next satin stitch in embroidery cotton was worked over the pad, and finally satin stitch in the appropriate thread and colours.

raised stitch see plush stitch.

raised work (embossed work, stump work, cut canvas work, embroidery on the stamp) Embroidery with a three-dimensional effect made by using small wooden moulds or pads of cotton wool and by adding loosely attached details in lace stitches. It was a favourite form of work with the young ladies of the 17th century when it was called raised or embossed work, but later it became known as embroidery on the stamp, and later still (during the 19th century), stump work, though why is unclear. Raised work appears to have been the culmination of a girl's training in stitchery—she would progress from a polychrome sampler to a cutwork sampler, and from there to panels of raised work, made up into a casket, cabinet, cushion, mirror frame, or panel. The work is distinguished by its naive charm, complete impracticability, and meticulous detail, but it can never have been boring to do. The themes were generally taken from Old Testament stories with the characters in modern dress, or were representations of the current king and queen, with any spaces left being filled

raised work: panel depicting 'The Judgement of Paris', English, 17th century.

with unrelated birds, animals, and insects. Sometimes the whole design would be worked in long and short stitch and then the padded features and loosely hanging pieces would be added later. This type of raised work was done during a fairly short span of about 40 years in the middle of the 17th century.

Rasmussen collection One of the extensive collections of northwest coast Indian art, including textiles, which was acquired in 1948 by the Portland Museum of Art. The objects were collected by Alex Rasmussen throughout Alaska between about 1926 and 1945.

rational (pectoral) Ornament of metal or embroidered cloth formerly worn over the chasuble and pallium by bishops when saying mass. It was suspended by a gold chain or fastened with pins, and derived from the breastplate of the Jewish High Priest. It was not used after the 14th century.

ravel To remove the weft threads of a piece of cloth so that the warp threads are left as a fringe. This is a normal finish to a number of articles such as scarves or table mats. Randle *Holme in *The Academy of Armory* (1688) describes it as 'Ravell, or Rovell, vulgarly Rove, when threads come out of the edges of the cloth.'

ravelling (roving) The threads pulled out from a piece of cloth. When rolled together they can be used as the filling for handmade buttons or other purposes. See also drizzling.

raw edge The unfinished edge of cut fabric.

raw silk Silk reeled off from the cocoon but not yet spun and woven. There are three kinds, *floss, *organzine, and *tram, and it is in this state that silk is bought by the manufacturer.

rational: south German, c.1320–40.

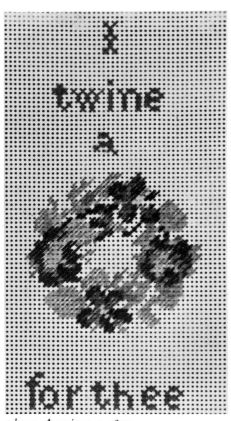

rebus: American, c.1850.

rebus Mild form of puzzle in which the syllables of a name or word are pictured together to suggest the whole, or a simple story is told with pictures in place of some words. They are found in the embroidery of the 16th century when all forms of emblems and hidden meanings were enjoyed, and again in the 19th century when rather simpler games and puzzles, such as anagrams, were popular.

reducing see enlarging.

reed Long, cylindrical, hard-stemmed grass, quill, or stick used to regulate the size of loop and the pile of stitches. It was probably used in America when making *bed rugs, hearth rugs, and other looped pile fabrics. See also gauge and mesh.

reel holder see spool knave.

Reformation The great religious revolution of the first half of the 16th century in which most of the churches of the northern part of Europe ceased to belong to the church of Rome. The main effect of this from the point of view of embroidery was that there was no further need for all the embroidered

vestments and hangings which had adorned and beautified the churches, and so this particular branch of needlework virtually ceased to exist in Germany, Scandinavia, and Britain, while it continued in France, Spain, Italy, and the Greek and Russian Orthodox churches.

Regency Strictly speaking, the period in British history from 1811–1820 when George, Prince of Wales, acted as Regent for his father, George III, but in all the arts generally accepted as a longer period, from about 1800–1830. It was the time of neo-classicism when all things Greek and Roman were particularly admired, and embroidery followed the same lines with the use of classical motifs, much embroidery on white fabrics, and embroidered pictures portraying the simple life.

reindeer hair Used as embroidery thread wherever there are herds of reindeer, ie the arctic and subarctic regions of Europe, Asia, and America (in North America the hair of the caribou, a type of reindeer, is also used). The embroidery is similar to that worked in *moosehair.

Reformation: an English panel depicting Henry VIII humbling the Pope, 16th century.

Renaissance Period in European history of classical revival, marking the end of the middle ages and the birth of modern Europe. It started in Italy in the 14th century, spread to other countries during the 14th and 16th centuries, and was characterised by a great love of beauty in all its forms, coupled with a new feeling of freedom and sensuality. In the realms of embroidery this meant exuberant and rioting forms with spirals, tendrils, and coils, together with all the flowers, beasts, and foliage then known.

Renaissance embroidery General term meaning lace and embroidery worked from old designs, but specifically a form of whitework in which the patterns are entirely in buttonhole stitch. The ground fabric is cut away and the parts of the design are strengthened by connecting buttonhole bars. The outside edge of the design may be edged with picots. This type of work is used on household articles and was sometimes put onto petticoat flounces. See also Richelieu embroidery.

Renaissance embroidery: an English 19th century parasol.

Repository of Arts, literature, commerce, manufactures, fashions, and politics Well-known magazine published in London by Rudolph Ackermann from 1809-1828. It promoted interest in fabrics, fashions, and needlework, contained numerous lithographed illustrations, and had actual samples of fabrics stuck in.

réseau In the 16th century a network of square meshes, either used plain for bedcurtains, valances etc, or with a pattern darned on it, when it became *lacis. Later réseau came to mean the ground of bobbin lace.

Resht work: detail of a prayer mat.

Resht work Type of applied work made in the 18th but especially the 19th century in and around the town of Resht (Iran) on the Caspian Sea. It consists of cut out pieces of cloth applied to a different coloured background, each piece being outlined by cord or by chain stitch, with details occasionally added in embroidery. Sometimes the work approaches inlay patchwork with some of the pieces being let into the ground fabric. The designs are typically Persian and the work is used for prayer mats, saddle cloths, and covers.

Restoration Period of English history marked by the restoration of Charles II to the throne (1660) after the austere Commonwealth, and implying a return to gaiety, life, and colour for the people. The embroideries usually described by this name are large crewel work hangings, tent stitch pictures, and raised or stump work, though all these types were worked for a considerable time before and after 1660.

reticella (Italian cutwork) Italian needlepoint technique which is on the border between embroidery and lace. It is one of the cutwork variations of the 15th, 16th, and 17th centuries, coming chiefly from Venice. The earliest work was made with a basis of fabric from which most of the threads were drawn or cut, forming squares. These were buttonholed round and then crossed with threads in pattern which were also buttonholed. Another and rather later method was to work the lace directly on a parchment pattern in buttonhole stitch.

reticella: border.

reverse appliqué Form of *applied work, sometimes called découpé, in which the design is cut out of the top layer of fabric to show the ground material underneath. It is also possible to cut down through several layers showing some part of each layer on each 'step', and this is practised by the Cuna Indians of the San Blas Islands in making their *molas.

ribbon quilts English version of the *log cabin patchwork quilts of North America. During the last quarter of the 19th century they were made from the ribbons used for trimming hats.

ribbonwork 1. Form of applied work used extensively by the eastern Plains and Woodland Indians of North America as decoration on skirts, leggings, moccasins, and robes. It became a decorative form after the introduction of needles, thread, and scissors as trade items in the 18th century and was greatly increased by the availability of vast quantities of French silk ribbons about 1800. Geometric patterns were cut into one ribbon which was then applied onto another of a contrasting colour, and several strips were used to make a panel and applied to the ground fabric. As much as 16 yards (15 metres) of red, white, yellow, and light and dark blue ribbons might be needed to decorate a skirt. Later, for economic reasons, yard goods were used instead. This work is also known as ribbon appliqué and silk appliqué. 2. Nowadays in North America and Britain, ribbons are used to make various forms of craftwork.

rice embroidery (rice grain embroidery) Late 19th century embroidery, either all white or coloured, in which the principal stitch used was rice stitch (not to be confused with the more usual rice stitch of canvas work). The effect was of grains of rice scattered carelessly over the surface of the design, which was outlined in stem stitch.

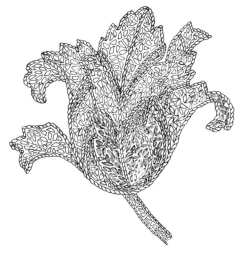

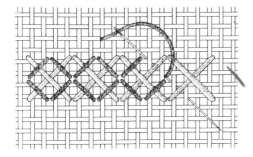

rice stitch (crossed corners cross stitch) Variation of cross stitch much used in modern canvas work and needlepoint, which is important for its texture and because it covers the ground completely. First, a series of large cross stitches covering four threads of canvas is made and then each arm of each cross is crossed, sometimes with a different thickness or colour of thread.

Richelieu embroidery Type of whitework where, as in Renaissance embroidery, the design is outlined in buttonhole stitch, the fabric cut away, and the spaces joined with bars or brides. The difference between the two types is that here the joining bars are decorated with picots.

rick-rack braid see braid.

riga Voluminous robe, often as much as 100 inches (2.5 metres) wide, worn by various African tribesmen, especially Nigerians. Often they are elaborately embroidered, the quantity of work indicating the wealth of the wearer.

ring work Simple late 19th and early 20th century work in which curtain rings are covered with buttonhole stitch in wool or thickish silk, and are then joined to make mats or baskets. Larger rings covered with raffia are made into shopping baskets nowadays.

robings Trimming or edging on women's gowns in the 18th century. They were narrow (about 2 inches or 5 centimetres wide) and went down the edge of the bodice and often continued down the front of the open skirt.

rocailles Trade-name for transparent glass beads used in embroidery. They are sub-divided as 1. round rocailles or seed beads which are round with round holes; 2. toscas or square rocailles which have square holes but are round outside; and 3. charlottes which are faceted on the outside. (Edwards 1966)

rococo Style of furniture and architecture originating in France at the time of Louis XIV and XV, from about 1700 to 1770. It was based on the shell motif and was characterised by a curvilinear style with scrolls and much rather florid, ornate, and meaningless decoration. The effect of embroidery in the rococo style is opulent, with much shining silk and glittering gold.

rococo stitch Counted thread stitch very popular in the 17th century and revived in the late 19th century. It consists of small bundles of stitches drawn together with holes between each bundle. A straight stitch is made over two threads of ground fabric and tied down from right to left taking in the right-hand vertical thread of fabric, and then three similar stitches are made over the same threads, the tying stitch for the left-hand one taking in the left-hand vertical thread. These groups are continued alternately up and down working from right to left.

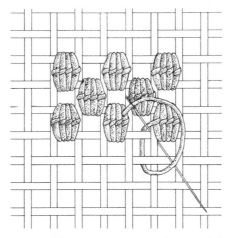

rococo stitch: châtelaine pin cushion made by Walter Cornell, Providence, Rhode Island, 1780.

rococo work Late 1880s work of which there were two types. 1. Revival of the *china ribbon embroidery of the early 19th century, worked in the same way adding coloured silks and chenille, but using designs with a French flavour, such as small bunches of flowers tied with ribbon bows. 2. Form of *cutwork in which a design was outlined with rows of buttonholing, and the ground fabric in between was cut away.

roll hem Type of hem for edging fine or transparent fabric, and used for headscarves, handkerchiefs, and the edges of the georgette and chiffon dresses of the 1930s. The raw edge is rolled towards the worker and either the sewing thread is taken right over the edge enclosing it in the stitch, or a slip stitch is made in the hem.

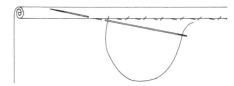

Roman cutwork (Roman work, Ragusa guipure, Strasbourg work, Venetian cutwork) Popular late 19th century form of cutwork, done on strong washable fabrics. The outline of the design is worked in close buttonholing, with the edge of the stitch on the outside of the design. The fabric between the buttonhole lines is then cut away and the spaces filled with bars and wheels. It resembles Richelieu and Renaissance embroidery.

Romanesque Architectural style of Romanised Europe between the classical and Gothic periods, and especially evident in some French cathedrals. The term is used in embroidery when describing designs based on this form of architecture.

Romania In common with most Slav countries, the embroidery of Romania shows a love of brilliant colour and repeated motifs. The majority of the work is on costume and household articles such as towels, rugs, curtains etc. The fabric used as a ground is a homespun called pansa which ranges from coarse to fine in a union of cotton and wool, and on it embroidery is worked by the counted thread, using cross, back, double running, hem, buttonhole, and eyelet stitches. Early Romanian embroidery (pre-18th century) should not be forgotten, for many beautiful church embroideries with a strong Byzantine influence were worked in the monasteries, especially in the parts then known as Moldavia and Serbia. See also Moldavian Wallachian embroidery. (Colour illustration p 211)

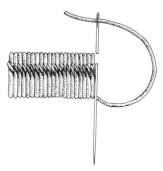

romanian stitch (janina stitch, figure stitch, oriental couching, antique couching) Couched stitch consisting of a thread taken across the design and then crossed by a small stitch in the centre. It is the angle of this crossing stitch and the number of times the laid thread is crossed which makes for the variety of names. For example, romanian stitch has one cross at a slight angle, romanian couching has several crosses at the same angle, while oriental couching and figure stitch have such oblique crosses that there is no effect of a marked line. The New Mexican version is colcha stitch.

Roosevelt, Mrs Theodore, Jr Daughter-in-law of Theodore Roosevelt, 26th President of the US, and an embroideress known for her *conversation pieces, some of which depicted in careful detail various animals which her husband captured during hunting expeditions throughout the world. She also worked one to commemorate US recognition of the USSR in 1933. (Colour illustration p.212)

rose blanket (rose wheel blanket, Cherokee rose blanket) White woollen blanket embroidered with a circular medallion in each corner. In England these medallions are of very simple design in red; in America they are generally sewn in herringbone stitch (or a variation) in rose, olive green, brown, and gold handspun yarns, with a red closed buttonhole or herringbone stitch border. The blankets were used both in England and America in the early 19th century but the reason for their decoration is unknown.

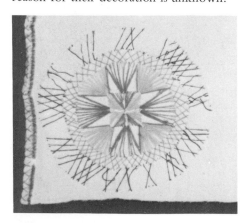

rosette: Sioux, 1825–75.

rosette One of the oldest folk art designs found in almost every culture and at most periods. In needlework it generally means 'like a rose' and has been used as a decorative motif on clothes and household articles in most parts of the world. Probably originating as a circle with a point in the centre, it became increasingly elaborate, varying from a first century Palestinian hexagon within a circle to intricate encircled swirls of the 17th to the 19th centuries.

rosette: Crow Indian beaded horse ornament, late 19th century.

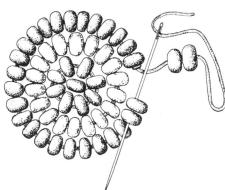

Ross, Betsy (1752–1836) Possibly the maker of the first American flag. According to legend, George Washington, Robert Morris, and George Ross (brother of her husband) came to her upholstery shop in Arch Street, Philadelphia, asking her to make the flag. At her suggestion, to make it easier, the five instead of six-pointed star was chosen, and on 14 June 1777 the Continental Congress voted to adopt the flag as the national emblem.

rouleau Any trimming or part of an article which is rounded or rolled. It may be in the form of piping or may mean a turned hollow tube as in the 'shoelace' shoulder straps of the 1930s and 1940s. Rouleaux first became used as a decoration in the early 19th century when many dresses and pelisses were trimmed with fabric made into bows and other shapes edged with very fine piping.

roundel Circular piece of embroidery sewn onto a garment; also, any round part of an embroidery design.

roving 1. Thick, loosely-twisted, single-strand cotton, often used in America instead of candlewicking for candlewick beadspreads. 2. See ravelling.

Rowson, Susanna (1762–1824) English actress-author who went to America in 1766 and again in 1793 on an acting tour, and in 1797 opened a school in Boston teaching young ladies arithmetic, reading, writing, and needlework. Later she taught 'Plain and Muslin work . . . Landscape and Figures with Embroidery, Print Work . . .' Embroidered pictures, mourning or historical, were a speciality of the school until it closed in 1882, and many fine examples exist at the Bostonian Society in Boston, New Hampshire Historical Society, and Old Sturbridge Village. (Giffen 1970)

Rowson: 'Cymbeline' embroidered in silk by Ann Trask at Susanna Rowson's school.

Royal College of Art As part of a plan to encourage good design in industry, one of many Government Schools of Design was inaugurated in 1837 at Somerset House, London. By 1857 it had become the National Art Training School and had moved to South Kensington, London. It became the Royal College of Art in 1897 and in a scheme for its reorganisation it was stated that the 'the school should return to its original purpose of the direct study of design' including 'special technical courses in the various branches of design where an intimate knowledge of the conditions of handicrafts and manufactures could be acquired', a function the college is still carrying out.

Royal Ontario Museum (Toronto, Canada) Contains an extensive collection of textiles and embroideries including more than one hundred 18th and 19th century oriental robes, a Ching dynasty embroidered velvet robe never made up, vestments, and western European, African, and ethnic embroideries, among them *szur coats and a tunic from Yoruba.

Royal Ontario Museum: American Indian dance shirt with shark motif.

Royal School of Needlework Founded in London in 1872 under the presidency of HRH the Princess Christian of Schleswig-Holstein (daughter of Queen Victoria) 'for the two fold purpose of supplying suitable employment for Gentlewomen and restoring Ornamental Needlework to the high place it once held among the decorative arts' (from the prospectus). It was originally called the School of Art Needlework and was in Sloane Street, but in 1875 it moved

Royal School of Needlework: sampler worked by Dorothea Nield when a student at the school.

to Prince's Gate, London (where it still is), and was granted the prefix 'Royal'. Later the word 'Art' was dropped from the title so it is now known as the Royal School of needlework.

Ruffini, Luigi Embroiderer who came from Italy and, in 1782, set up a workroom in Edinburgh (Scotland) to train apprentices in fine embroidery, Dresden work, and tambouring. Three years later he had 70 young girls learning the trade, first working on linen and then on muslin as this new cotton fabric began to be manufactured in Scotland. His training of his workers produced the expertise which in the next generation led to the Ayrshire embroidery industry. (Swain 1955)

ruffle Frill of lace, muslin, or cambric worn at the wrist or elbow at various times by both men and women. They were always of the finest workmanship and in the middle of the 18th century were often of Dresden work. Lady Mary Coke in 1767 mentions that she 'received some ruffles from Hanover that I had sent to be worked there', and she also says 'I shew'd her Ld Strafford's ruffles. She

admired them very much and was amazed at the cheapness. The two pair cost no more than four guineas and half a crown.' The frill down the front of a man's shirt is often referred to (inaccurately) as a ruffle.

rug canvas Single or double-thread canvas, sometimes with blue threads at regular intervals, of any sized mesh suitable for working knotted or canvas stitch rugs. Single-thread or mono canvas used for rugs is often called raffia canvas in the UK. In both the UK and the US the term rug canvas can imply any canvas of whatever description on which rugs can be worked.

rug stitch see plush stitch.

rumal In India, a small cloth cover which may be decorated with painting, printing, or embroidery. It is placed over an offering or a gift. (Irwin and Hall 1973)

rumal: embroidered in coloured silks, 18th century.

runner Length of fabric, embroidered in any style enjoyed by the worker, and used on tables, cupboards, and chests of drawers to protect the polished surface and as decoration. See also scarf.

running stitch The simplest and most basic of all stitches, which consists of passing the needle in and out of the fabric at regular intervals. When extra strength is required a back stitch is worked every two or three stitches, and this is known as half back stitch.

Ruskin, John (1819–1900) Painter, poet, and writer on art, socialism and economics. His influence, particularly his championship of the Pre-Raphaelite group, and his desire for social justice, encouraged many movements concerned with cottage industry such as Home Arts and Industries Associations, and the *Langdale Linen Industry.

Russia see USSR.

russia braid see braid.

russia crash Coarse, very hard-wearing linen or hempen cloth. It is always woven in its unbleached state (it is a donkey-brown colour) and it makes an excellent ground fabric for bold, thick embroidery.

russian cross stitch, russian stitch see herringbone stitch.

Russian embroidery (broderie russe) Late 19th century embroidery sponsored by the Broderie Russe Co of London and other continental capitals. The company sold genuine Russian embroideries, including peasant costume, and also fabrics printed with designs for customers to work themselves. Generally the stitches were double running or cross and the embroidery was used to trim children's dresses and for mantel covers, cushions etc. (Morris 1962)

rya Pile longer than one inch (2½ centimetres). The term is applied to long-pile rugs, including handmade ones. Strictly speaking, a rya rug is made with a space left between each line of knots, so that the wool lies flat, instead of being close together, with a plushy pile, as most deep-pile rugs are.

run and fell seam (sew and fell seam, hemmed fell seam) Type of seam worked on fairly light fabrics, commonly used for children's garments and undergarments, but now often superseded by other varieties. To work it, a plain seam is run with the right sides of the fabric together, one turning is cut down to half the width of the other, the turnings are pressed to one side, and the raw edge turned under and hemmed.

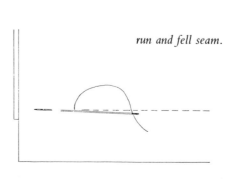

run and fell seam.

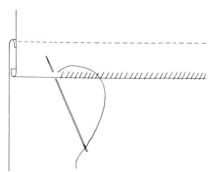

sabinilla Plain-weave woollen home-spun 20 to 24 inches (50 to 60 centimetres) wide, used as the ground for the New Mexican *colcha embroideries.

sabretache Cavalry officer's leather satchel hung on long straps from the left side of the sword belt. They were used to carry despatches, letters etc, and they ceased to be issued in the British Army in 1901. Those worn with dress uniform were heavily embroidered.

sabretache: embroidered in silver thread, English, 19th century.

Sabrina work Form of *applied work in which petals, leaves, or conventionalised flower patterns cut out of velvet, serge, cloth, satin, silk, or washable fabrics were sewn onto a ground with widely spaced buttonhole stitch. According to Caulfeild and Saward (1882) 'good effects can be obtained without much labour'. It was popular in the 1870s and 1880s.

sacking see burlap.

sacred monogram The letters IHS or IHC combined in a suitable, decorative fashion. They stand for the first three letters of the name Jesus in Greek, IHSUS or IHCUC, the letters S or C being variant forms, or for *Iesus Hominum Salvator* (Jesus Saviour of Men). It is frequently found in ecclesiastical embroidery.

saddle-bag One of a pair of bags joined together by a strap and laid across a horse; also a bag fixed to the saddle. They are used for carrying necessities and are very important pieces of equipment for peoples to whom riding is part of life, such as some North American Indian tribes who have gaily embroidered and beaded bags. Saddle-bags used by royalty and the nobility on ceremonial occasions are also splendidly embroidered. (Colour illustration p 221)

saddle-cloth Cloth put over the back of a horse or other riding animal underneath the saddle. While this may be quite plain, for special occasions it can be heavily embroidered, often with metal threads.

saddle cloth: Indian, 18th century.

saddle stitching Long running stitch in a thick thread used as a decorative finish to the edges of some garments such as coats, capes, and tailored dresses.

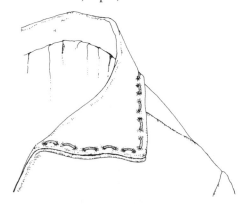

sailor's palm (thummel) Thimble traditionally used by sailmakers and anyone hand-sewing heavy-weight or hard fabric. An indented metal circle is fastened into a leather strap which is worn on the right hand with the metal resting on the palm by the base of the thumb. The needle is pushed through with the weight of the hand rather than a finger.

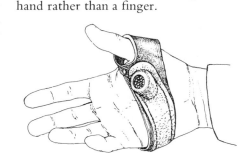

Saint Martin embroideries, the Set of 32 embroidered *roundels, 4 panels, and one oval depicting events in the life of St Martin. The series seems to be incomplete as various well-known episodes of his life are missing, and it is also not known whether they were part of an altar frontal or a cope, or who the donor was, but they were probably worked in Burgundy about 1440. Items in this superb series of embroidery can be seen in the Cooper Hewitt Museum and in the cloisters of the Metropolitan Museum (both New York), the Walter's Art Gallery (Baltimore), the Church of St Michael (Ghent, Belgium), and the Musée Historique des Tissus (Lyons, France). (Freeman 1968)

samite Rich fabric of the middle ages, constantly referred to in wills and inventories as well as poems and romances. Unfortunately its exact weave is now unknown, but it is generally considered to have been a heavy silk and was often embroidered.

sample books Specimens made up into books by manufacturers of fabrics to show prospective buyers their various ranges. Old sample books still in existence are of the greatest value in telling later generations what was in fashion at a particular date. In addition to books of plain and figured fabrics held in museums there are also books of machine embroideries still to be seen, which show the variety available in the 19th century.

sample books: machine embroidered samples, c.1880.

sampler (sam cloth, exampler) Collection of patterns, stitches, and techniques put together in a convenient form for reference. It seems as though the earliest samplers were worked towards the end of the 15th century, possibly in Italy or Germany, at a time when there were still no pattern books to use as guides, for there are references to them in wills, inventories, and literature from the beginning of the 16th century onwards. The earliest known dated example in England is that by Jane *Bostocke in 1598. At this time samplers were worked on linen 9 inches (23 centimetres) wide, then the normal width for linen, and they were around 2 feet (60 centimetres) in length. They were often all white showing patterns in cutwork, lacis, geometrical satin stitch, and double running stitch, but

sampler: Portuguese, 17th century.

there were others which were polychrome, with rows of stiff flowers and the little figures known as *boxers. These types continued during the 17th century, when the sewing of samplers ceased to be, as King (1960) puts it, 'embroidered memoranda of any interesting designs' but became part of the school curriculum for girls. In 1688 Randle *Holme, describing the 'School Mistris Terms, and things to work with', includes 'A samcloth, a cloth to sow on, a Canvice cloth' and then under her Terms of Art mentions 'a Samcloth, vulgarly a Sampler'. At the same time linen became wider and finer in texture and instead of being long and narrow, the sampler was more nearly square.

In the 18th century, with the change in emphasis towards sewing lessons, samplers became more stereotyped. They often had borders and designs from pattern books, a verse, possibly a house or animals, the worker's name and age and, with increasing frequency, an alphabet and numbers which were training for the marking of household linen. Then, towards the end of the century, the *map and *darning types appeared. The 19th century saw a proliferation of samplers, varying from charming to poor and boring, but they were practically all worked in schools and were quite obviously not enjoyed by the scholars. There was one kind, however, which escaped from the general mediocrity and reverted to the original use of being a collection of patterns: these were long and narrow, worked on a single canvas, and consisted of patterns for Berlin woolwork, placed higgledy-piggledy on the canvas with no design plan. Their edges were bound with ribbon, and they were then rolled up, sometimes round a wooden bar, and tied. After the indifferent school works of the 19th century, the working of samplers declined until the 1930s when, with the revival of interest in old techniques, collections of

patterns again began to be made, and charming examples in blackwork, drawn fabric, metal thread embroidery, and canvas work appeared. This trend seems likely to continue as most needleworkers find the making of a sampler an excellent introduction to a technique. Since the First World War many samplers have been worked commemorating special events and campaigns, such as coronations and the drive of the Women's Organisation of National Prohibition Reform. Good collections are at the Cooper-Hewitt Museum (Mrs Henry E. Coe collection); the Metropolitan Museum, New York (Mrs Lathrop C. Harper collection); the Museum of Art, Philadelphia (Whitman collection); the Fitzwilliam Museum, Cambridge, England. (Colour illustration p 222) See also hobby sampler.

sampler stitch   see cross stitch.

San Blas embroidery   see Cuna Indian embroidery, mola, Sappi Karta tree.

Sanderson, Elizabeth (d 1934) Yorkshire *pattern drawer who designed and marked quilt tops for the neighbouring quilters. She was trained by the better-known George *Gardiner, and she herself had several apprentices, two of whom in 1966 were still marking quilts sent to them from as far afield as Canada. Although she sometimes sewed a quilt herself, she made most of her living from stamping the design for others to sew for which she charged between 1/- and 2/6 per top, according to the intricacy of the pattern. (Ward 1966)

Sanitary Fair Fund-raising event sponsored by the US Sanitary Commission, which was founded in 1861 to look after sick and wounded soldiers and their dependents. An important one was the Chicago Sanitary Fair of 1864. Among the items auctioned at these fairs were

Sanitary Fair: doll and complete wardrobe, 1863.

sarcenet (sarsnet) Very fine, soft silk, woven plain or twill, now used chiefly for linings or as ribbon. The name comes from its having first been made by the Saracens, and it is one of the oldest recorded silks, always soft, supple, and expensive—in the 15th century it cost between 3 and 4 shillings (about 18p or 40 cents) a yard, while in the 17th it cost 7/6 the ell.

sari (saree) Length of fabric worn as the main garment by Hindu women. They are draped round the body with one end thrown over the head or shoulder. Saris may be of printed cotton, printed or beautifully embroidered silk, or, nowadays, of man-made fibres, and they have a narrow border at the sides and a deep border at one end.

sash 1. Length of fine fabric worn twisted round the head as a turban by orientals. 2. Length of woven, netted, or plaited fabric, often fringed at the end, worn either round the waist or diagonally across the chest from shoulder to waist as part of some military uniforms. See drum-major's sash. 3. Length of ribbon or fabric, plain or embroidered, worn round the waist or sometimes over the shoulder by women and children, generally tied in a bow or knot or with hanging ends, and often fringed.

sash: worn by a Menominee Indian photographed 1910–13.

dolls dressed in beautifully-made, fashionable attire, with complete wardrobes and trunks, an example of which is in the collection of the Brooklyn Museum (New York).

Sappi Karta tree 'Magic' tree growing in the high mainland mountains near the Panama-Colombia border, which is the home of the Spirits of the Arts of the Cuna Indians. According to legend, women who wish to made especially beautiful *molas ask the Spirit, through the Medicine Man, for help. Concentric dark lines which appear on the leaves of the tree during the dry season are believed to be the creative impulses of the god. A special salve is made from the leaves and applied to the eyes of the supplicant, thereby transferring the inspiration to the artist so she may make beautiful molas with magic patterns. See also Cuna Indian embroidery, mola.

Sarawak The tribes of Sarawak (north Borneo), especially in the Kenyan highlands, do beautiful work using nassa shells and beads sewn onto ceremonial dress as well as onto articles in more general use such as carrying baskets.

Sarawak: detail of a woman's ceremonial jacket of nassa shells.

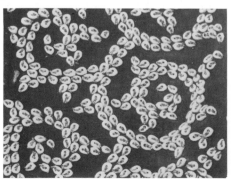

satin Correctly, a weave rather than a fabric. Satin is twilled but over an irregular number of warp threads so that the surface weft threads entirely hide the warp, producing a smooth surface which is afterwards *calendered and made glossy. It originally came from China and is generally made from silk, but it may also be made of wool, cotton, a mixture of wool and cotton, or synthetics.

satin embroidery see Hibernian embroidery.

satin stitch (geometrical satin stitch, surface satin stitch, sham satin stitch) Very simple stitch consisting of taking the thread over and over from one edge to the other of a design, keeping it perfectly smooth and even so that it resembles satin. There are many variations and it is often used in blocks or other groupings worked by the counted thread, when it is known as geometrical satin stitch. In satin stitch there is as much thread at the back of the work as at the front, and where economy is required, surface or sham satin stitch are worked. Here practically all the thread is on the surface, as, after taking the thread across the design, the needle picks up a small piece of the fabric and the next thread goes back across the design in the opposite direction to the first.

scalloped (scolloped) Term derived from the shape of the shellfish of that name, meaning edged with small semi-circular lobes. Scallops are used as a decorative finish and are often worked in buttonhole stitch or by facing or binding the edge.

scalp Among certain Plains Indian tribes, scalps were trophies of war and were stretched over a hoop, carefully dried and ornamented, and prized as a decoration to hang from garments, war clubs, bridles, or wigwams. Scalping did not necessarily kill the victim; the crown of the head was taken by slicing through the skin round it and tearing off a piece the size of the palm of the hand. When possible, the warrior took the rest of the hair for his wife to make into scalp locks to fringe the seams of his shirts, leggings etc. Horsehair wrapped with quills was similarly used as fringes.

scarf Length of fabric worn round the neck or over the shoulders for warmth or decoration. It is also one of the vestments worn by clergymen at church services other than Holy Communion. These are made of black silk pleated at the back of the neck and they hang loose to the knees. Originally the word scarf was synonymous with sash and was worn as part of military uniform. but it has been a very feminine accessory as well, often beautifully embroidered. Modern scarves, including head scarves, can be of a great variety of shapes and fabrics, from thickest wool to finest gauze, but they are not usually embroidered.

Schiffli machine Embroidery machine invented by Isaac Groebli in 1865, which combines the principle of the machine invented earlier by Josué *Heilmann with a continuous thread, as in the domestic sewing machine. The word Schiffli comes from the German word *Schiff* meaning shuttle, and it is the use of these shuttles which gives the machine its peculiar value. It can embroider up to 30 yards (27 metres) of fabric at one time and is capable of producing a very large number of entirely different effects, from guipure lace and broderie anglaise (eyelet embroidery) to free running stitch embroidery. (Elsey 1972) See also machine embroidery.

Scholehouse for the Needle, A English pattern book compiled in 1624 by Richard Shorleyker in Shoe Lane, London, at the Sign of the Falcon, with another edition in 1632. Shorleyker considers that the embroideress should be capable of adapting her own designs from those printed, and suggests that his book is for 'Teaching by sundry sortes of patterns and examples of different kinds, how to compose many faire workes; which being set in order and forme according to the skill and understanding of the workwoman, will, no doubt, yield profit unto such as live by the Needle and give good content to adorn the worthy.' The book is divided into two, and the title page of the second part says 'Here followeth certaine patternes of cutworkes, and but once printed before, also sundry sorts of spots as flowers, birds, fishes etc, and will fitly serve to be wrought, some with gould, some with silke and some with crewell or otherwise at your pleasure.'

schools Needlework has been part of the curriculum of girls' schools since they have been in existence. It used to be considered the most essential part of a girl's education, certainly more necessary than reading and writing, but nowadays it is a vocational option. The charity schools of the 18th and 19th centuries produced the most exact and meticulous work, and some of the sample books which have been preserved indicate the high standards the pupils were expected to attain. However when the domestic sewing machine came into general use in the 1860s, the need for this type of sewing declined. Needlework has seldom been taught in boys' schools, but in one at least, the Blue Coat school at Lincoln, beadwork was considered a suitable subject for boys of 14 in the 19th century. In the late 18th and early 19th century in America, Female Schools taught 'ornamental needlework . . . also every girl was taught to embroider the letters in marking stitch . . . Pocket books and cushions worked in crewel had given place to wrought muslin and pictures worked in satin. Mourning pictures were in vogue, though some preferred scriptual or classical subjects.' (Emery 1974)

schools: beadwork sampler worked by a Blue-coat schoolboy.

scissor cutting gauge (cutting gauge) Metal attachment slipped onto the blade of a pair of scissors which makes it easy to cut bias or other narrow strips exactly parallel.

scissors Instrument consisting of two sharp blades which, when put each side of material and brought together, cut through it. There are two designs: in one the blades have handles and pivot on a pin, while in the other the blades are connected by a spring, and these are generally called spring scissors or shears. Very large scissors such as those used by tailors are also known as shears. Both types were in use in early Rome, but in Britain the pivot kind did not come into use until the middle ages. Although the basic principle is the same all over the world, many different shapes are found. Chinese scissors have very short blades and curved handles large enough to take the whole hand; Persian scissors (though often made in Sheffield) have long dagger-like points; some French ones have fine engraving and decoration in the form of the cross of Lorraine; and there are the well-known stork scissors, with the beak forming the two blades and the pivot the eye of the bird. Various shapes of blade have been designed for specific purposes in needlework: drapers' scissors have rounded ends; embroidery scissors are small but have long, thin blades; and cutting-out scissors have one rounded and one straight blade. See also buttonhole scissors, pinking, lace scissors.

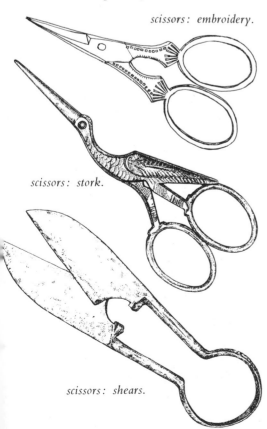

scissors: embroidery.

scissors: stork.

scissors: shears.

Scotland In general, embroidery in Scotland has followed the same lines as embroidery in England, but in some ways the country has made its own impact on the embroidery world. After several false starts, the weaving of fine muslin became a major Scottish industry in the late 18th century, and the 'sewing' (or embroidering) of muslins provided work for many of the women and girls in the country. An Italian, Luigi *Ruffini, started a school in Edinburgh for embroidering muslin with pulled stitches (Dresden work) and at the same time the girls in the west of the country were working little dots and small sprigs on muslin in the fashion of the dresses of the day. Eventually these two types merged through the agency of a Mrs *Jamieson of Ayr to produce the world famous Ayrshire embroidery of the 19th century.

In a different context, the Glasgow School of Art, especially in the late 19th and early 20th centuries, encouraged a clear-cut style through the personalities of Mrs *Newberry and Ann *Macbeth, insisting as they did on good lettering, good design, and fitness for purpose. Later still from the 1930s to 1960s Scotland put the embroidery world in its debt by the introduction of the *Needlework Development Scheme which did so much to inspire and help all needleworkers, especially the young. See also Fetternear banner.

screen Piece of furniture generally of two, three, or four hinged panels, which can be put up for privacy, to ward off a draught, or for ornament. These flat surfaces lend themselves to large pieces of embroidery, and though some were worked earlier, most screens were made in the 19th and 20th centuries. Some were designed with figures and foliage by the firm of Morris and Co; some were embroidered in the Japanese style prevalent at the end of the 19th century; while in the last 20 years there have been extremely successful pictorial screens showing landscapes in various forms. See also handscreens, firescreens, and pole screens.

scrim Fine, openweave canvas of a pleasant brown shade, originally made of low-grade linen, but now of cotton or a mixture. The best kind generally used for needlework was imported from Russia. Because of its open weave, scrim is very suitable for work done by the counted thread, and it is attractive enough in itself for the background to be left plain if necessary. In America it is used as a ground fabric for dresser scarves, samplers, chair tidies, and curtains, and the word also refers to a heavily starched and bleached cheesecloth.

scripture quilts see hospital quilts.

sculpturing The scissor-trimming of pile to emphasise design. This is done where a three-dimensional effect is required, and it is seen on some Chinese rugs and also in 19th century work where plush stitch has been used, often in conjunction with Berlin woolwork.

Seal Bag Bag which contains the Great Seal of England. The Keeper of the Great Seal (later known as the Lord Chancellor) keeps both seal and bag when any reign ends and a new one is made for the next reign. The bags which hold such important objects might be made from old vestments or other valuable fabrics, but more often were specially made and embroidered with coats-of-arms and other symbolic designs.

Seal Bag: belonging to Francis North, Baron Guildford, Chancellor of England, 1682–1685.

seal of Solomon Two equilateral triangles superimposed to form a six-pointed star, representing perfect God and perfect man. See Star of David.

seam Stitching, especially the join or
line of join made when two pieces of
material are sewn together. The join so
made can be worked by hand or machine
and may be plain or decorative. While it
is possible to join two pieces of cloth by
many methods there are traditionally
recognised ways for different weights and
types of cloth, as well as different purposes. Some seams have become less useful in modern times, but they are mentioned here as they are found when
examining old pieces of stitching. See
antique, double pinstitched, flannel,
french and overcast, french, hemstitched
flat, lap, mantua-makers', openwork,
overhanded (french fell), oversewn (top
sewn), piped, plain, prick, run and fell
(sew and fell, hemmed fell, fell), flat fell,
and shell seams.

seam allowance see turning.

seam finishes Methods of neatening
the raw edges left after sewing a seam.
The type of finish used varies with the
fabric, and includes: 1. overcasting by
hand; 2. overlocking or zigzagging on
the swing-needle sewing machine; 3.
binding with a bias strip; 4. blanket
stitching; 5. edge stitching or turning
under the raw edge and stitching it by
hand or machine; 6. pinking.

seaming 1. The joining together of
two selvages by overcasting. 2. Any
sewing, but especially the joining together of two pieces of material.

seam knife (seam ripper) Tool used for
unpicking seams quickly. Originally it
had a spade-shaped steel blade on a wood,
bone, or ivory handle. In America the
blade was often put on at right angles to
the handle so that the seam was ripped
rather than cut. The modern equivalent
tool has a U-shaped end with a very
sharp section at the base of the U, and one
prong is sharply pointed while the other
has a small blob on it to protect the fabric.

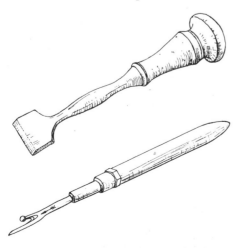

seam smoother Instrument for flattening seams. It can be in the shape of an
axe or in the shape of a clenched fist with
deep indentations for the fingers, and is
usually made of bone or ivory. Most
needleworkers now use their thumbnail.

seamster (seamstress, sempster, semp-
stress) Man or woman whose occupation is plain sewing, rather than dressmaking or embroidery.

seda floja Untwisted silk first imported by the Spaniards into Central
America, and still imported by Indians
for their finest textiles, but it is gradually
being replaced by synthetics and cheap
silk.

Sedding, John D. (1838–1891) English
architect who first worked under G. E.
*Street. After his architect's training he
spent most of his life designing embroideries, wallpapers, and goldsmiths' work.
He came under the influence of John
*Ruskin and so believed in working with
his craftsmen, and he thought that
natural forms should be used in church
embroidery. (Colour illustration p 239)

seed embroidery Embroidery using
the seeds of various plants such as the
melon, cucumber, or Indian corn. They
are dried, dyed if necessary, and sewn to
the ground fabric in the form of flowers,
while chenille and other embroidery
threads form the leaves and stems. It was
popular in England and Europe in the
late 19th century.

self-threading needle see calyx-eyed
needle.

selvage (selvedge) The edge of a
piece of woven cloth. Often the warp
threads at the edge are thicker or of a
different yarn to give extra strength.

semainier Long case of seven pockets
which could be folded or hung on the
wall. The pockets originally held prayers
and notes for each day of the week, and
as the cases were treasured possessions
they were often beautifully embroidered,
especially in the 17th century. Sometimes
a comb case with several pockets was
known as a semainier. (Seligman and
Hughes 1928) See also wall pockets.

semé Literally the sowing of seed, but
in embroidery and heraldry it means
powdered. Small dots embroidered on

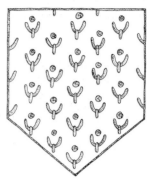

the muslins of the early 19th century are
semé and the term is also used of any
small, isolated pattern either woven or
embroidered on fabric.

Seminole Indians American Indian
tribe from the Everglade area of Florida,
known for the elaborate applied and
pieced garments worn by both men and
women. This style evolved during the
late 19th century, probably influenced
by the patchwork of the white settlers
and helped by the use of the sewing
machine.

*Seminole Indians: a woman working at her
embroidery.*

Sens Cathedral (S.E. of Paris) French
cathedral which has in its treasury some
superb embroideries, including the vestments of St Edmund Rich, the stole and
maniple of St Thomas à Becket, and a
mid 14th century aumonière.

sequin   see spangle.

sericulture   'The production of raw silk and the rearing of silkworms for this purpose' (OED). See also raw silk.

set   In *pieced patchwork the method by which the units or blocks are joined. They may simply be sewn together, but more often they are combined with strips, squares, or both, in white or one or two colours.

sew   To pass a thread in and out through holes made by a sharp instrument such as a needle or an awl. This is the basic method from which comes all needlework, dressmaking, and embroidery.

sew and fell seam   see run and fell seam.

sewing clamp   Embroidery tool, often decorative, which fastens pincushions, hooks for netting, hemming birds or, when used in pairs, revolving reels for winding thread, to a table. According to their period and use, they are made of metal, wood, ivory, or bone.

sewing cotton   Cotton thread, originally sold in balls as well as reels, but now, when obtainable, sold only in reels. In America they are known as spools. Before man-made fibres and mercerised cotton became so widely used, sewing cotton was in general use for all types of plain sewing and especially for making up household linens. It was available in a wide variety of thicknesses, from 200 which was very fine to 24 which was very thick. See also thread.

sewing machine   Machine which simulates hand sewing with speed, and is now widely used for plain sewing, dressmaking, and embroidery. The history of the domestic sewing machine is not a long one—the first to be used was invented in 1825 by a French tailor, Barthélémy Thimonnier. By 1831 he had 80 machines making army uniforms, but the opposition to their use was so widespread among tailors that they were wrecked. The first really practical machine was invented by Elias Howe of Boston (Massachusetts) in 1845. This was improved upon by Isaac Singer, also an American, who in 1864 formed the Singer Corporation to manufacture sewing machines in large quantities. From the point of view of the dressmaker this meant that by the early 1860s she could, and often did, own a machine capable of lock or chain stitch which would help her to make clothes and household linens in much less time, and which made possible the heavily trimmed dresses of the 1870s and 1880s. From then on many more machines were invented, in Europe as well as America, and it is remarkable that a number of these are still in use today, proving the excellence of the 19th century design and workmanship. It was not until the middle of the 20th century that the swing-needle machine became a household article, a machine able to overlock raw edges and do intricate embroidery. These are superb precision instruments and are all worked by electricity, but even so many housewives cling to their hand or treadle machines. (Bond 1963) See also attachments.

sewing machine: an early example, c.1850.

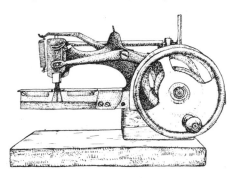

sewing machine needle   Needle specially made for use with the domestic sewing machine. They vary slightly from make to make but they generally have one grooved side, with the eye just above the point, and the top shaped to be held in the machine.

sewing silk   Thread made of silk for hand and machine sewing. In England the raw silk is imported from China or Italy, but America has attempted sericulture at various times. In the 1730s, silkworms were successfully raised in Georgia, and a little later in Pennsylvania, Delaware, and New England, and it was a moderately profitable home industry, lasting until the 1780s. After the Revolution it was revived but, because of speculation, collapsed in 1842, except for a few mills in New England from which was developed the first silk machine twist in about 1852.

shade   American term for a glass dome covering a fragile bouquet of feather, fabric, wool, or shell flowers. Eventually it came to mean not only the dome but also the arrangement. (Colour illustration p 240)

shaded embroidery   Embroidery which consisted of the drawing of naturalistic flowers and foliage on a suitable ground, determining where the light would fall, and working the flowers in long and short stitch to make them appear as real as possible.

shading stitch   see long and short stitch.

shadow quilting   In *italian quilting a shadow effect can be obtained by using a thin silk or cotton fabric for the top of the work and threading a brightly coloured thread through the back so that only a paler, shadowy colour can be seen from the front.

shadow work   Embroidery giving a muted and sometimes iridescent effect of colour. It is always worked on a sheer fabric such as fine lawn or a thin nylon, and consists of working closed herringbone stitch in a strongly coloured thread across the design from the back of the fabric. This shows from the front as a row of back stitches outlining the design, with the closed herringbone showing through the fabric much softened in colour. The technique is used particularly on children's dresses and lingerie. There is also another type where either a piece of white fabric or white stitching is worked underneath fine white linen as in Italian table-linen. Here no colour shows through and the effect is between semi-transparent and opaque.

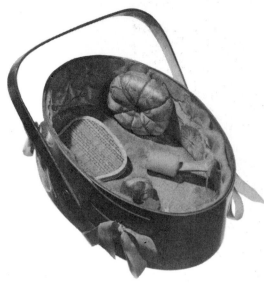

Shaker oval box: from the Sabbathday Lake community in Maine, 1900-10.

Shaker oval box   Oval workbox or sewing basket made by the *Shakers throughout the 19th century at the Mount Lebanon and Sabbathday Lake communities. They were made of pine with maple 'fingered' strips or lappers fastened with copper rivets, and were lined with silk.

Shakers   Originally part of the English Quaker church, the Shakers (Society of Believers) founded their first self-sufficient religious community, based on principles of equality and mass production, in 1787 near Albany, New York. They adhered to strict laws which forbade, among other things, the use of bone or horn spools and silver thimbles (which could, however, be lined with silver). Their work was of excellent quality and the simple, unadorned items produced in excess of community needs were sold to the outside world, and were in great demand: work baskets, 'emra' (emery) bags, beeswax, needlebooks, work and spool stands, 'tomato' pincushions, popple (poplar) oval fancy baskets, and candlewicking. See also Shaker oval box.

shako cover   Quilted linen cover made to fit over the shakos or caps worn by the British Army in the 19th century when on foreign service in very hot countries. They kept the rays of the sun from the metal and also provided a flap to shield the back of the neck.

sham   Decorative cover of fine fabric or lace for bed pillows when they are not in use. In some houses sheet shams are also used, and both may be embellished with embroidery or cutwork. See also show towel.

sham satin stitch   see satin stitch.

shank   Wire loop attached to the back of a metal button by which it is sewn to the fabric. Some handmade buttons may also have a shank consisting of loops of thread buttonholed over.

sharp   The most commonly used type of sewing needle. It is of medium length with a very sharp point and a small eye, and can be bought in sizes from thick (size 5) to very fine (size 12).

shawl   Fabric which can be plain, damasked, brocaded, figured, embroidered, lace, knitted, or crocheted, and is worn round the shoulders for warmth or decoration.

sheepskin   The skin of a sheep with the fleece still attached, which can be made into coats, jackets, hats, gloves, and boots, and is worn with the fleece inside for warmth in cold climates. Some countries, notably those of eastern Europe, have always had a tradition of decorating these garments, especially the coats and jackets, with embroidery worked in gay and very colourful wools and silks. See also Kodmön, szür.

sheer   Fabric which is so thin as to be transparent.

sheet and sheet end   Sheet for a bed, either embroidered all over or only on the turned-back end. They can very seldom have been worked all over as this would be unnecessary and wasteful, but one was certainly given to Elizabeth I in 1588: 'By Mrs Carre, one sheete of fyne camberick, wrought all over with sundry fowles, beastes, and wormes, of silke of sundry cullers' (Nichols 1823). More usual are the sheets of homespun with decorated ends which are found in some countries, notably Russia.

sheet end: detail of a Russian example, 18th century.

Shelburne Museum (Vermont) Folk museum founded by Mrs J. Watson Webb in 1947, and housed in 35 restored early American houses. Her late 18th and 19th century quilts from New England, New York, and Pennsylvania form the nucleus of an extensive collection which now includes examples from other parts of the US including Hawaii. This is one of the few museums to have a large collection of quilts on permanent exhibition.

Shelburne Museum: embroidered coverlet.

shell   Very popular motif in the embroidery of all periods. The shell or scallop is the device of St James the Great, the patron saint of pilgrims, and so it is frequently seen in ecclesiastical art and embroidery. It is also one of the most popular shapes of the *rococo period and was worked, often in metal threads, on the rather lush bedcovers, pillows, and curtains of the mid 18th century. In quilting and patchwork the shell is very common, in the latter often being called the clamshell.

Sedding: detail of an altar frontal designed by John D. Sedding for Holy Trinity church, Sloane Street, London, late 19th century.

shell edge (lingerie hem) Finish suitable for lingerie made in fine fabrics. A narrow hem is turned, and to commence, the thread overcasts the hem twice at the same place, the needle is run a little way through the fold of the hem, then it is brought out and two tight overcast stitches are again made. The effect of this is to leave the hem standing up between two depressions in the shape of a shell. If the fabric is very springy, two or three hemming stitches may be taken between each overcast.

shell embroidery In parts of the world where shells are abundant they have been used as decoration on costume and furnishings. For example, the cowrie shell, found in warm seas round the world and used as money, decorates costume in much the same way that many Eastern embroiderers use coins, especially in the US, Africa and the south Pacific; the American Indians use dentalium or tusk shells and discs cut from flat shells such as mussels; New Guinea tribes make much use of nassa shells on baskets, headbands, and costume; in the highlands of Mexico there is a tradition of using shells cut into bird, animal, and fish shapes and applied to garments; and there has been some use of mother-of-pearl in embroidery in the West. See also nacre work.

shell seam Join suitable for lingerie in fine fabrics. A *shell edge is worked on the two pieces to be joined, and the tops of the shells are sewn together with a double overcast stitch, the needle being run along the back to the next stitch.

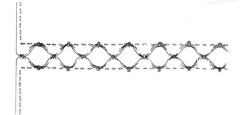

Ship of the Dead embroideries Embroideries of highly stylised ships on *ikat backgrounds, decorating ceremonial and ritual robe borders in south Sumatra (Indonesia). Big ship cloths were long and narrow and were used at weddings, funerals, and other ceremonies; smaller ones were used to cover bowls at funeral wakes. Some of these were worked on palm leaf fabric with shell and bead embroidered ships incorporating the *Tree of Life and animal, bird, fish, or

human motifs, and occasionally mica, tin foil, or paillettes were worked into the design. Although painted representations of these ships began in pre-Egyptian times, known examples of woven and embroidered Sumatran ship cloths only date from about the mid 19th century.

ship pictures Embroideries worked by sailors and fishermen in the 19th century. They appear to have been made both at sea to while away the long periods of inactivity when the sailing ships were in the doldrums, and on retiring from the sea. Generally they are naive but technically accurate representations of the ship in which the worker sailed, always in profile with no attempt at perspective or foreshortening, and always sailing straight into the wind, with streaming bunting. Ship pictures are worked entirely in straight stitches in wool, and are a form of needle painting.

ship pictures: an English example, c.1875.

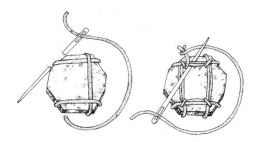

shisha Mirror glass or mica applied to cloth with embroidery stitches. It is a technique practised in areas of India and Pakistan, and now popular with workers of collage in America and the west. Because the mirror glass or mica has no holes with which to sew it down, it must be held by a criss-cross of threads, either by using an interlacing stitch as is done in India, or by using modern imaginative methods possibly involving gold kid, transparent fabric, metal eyelets, or other means. See also abhla bharat.

shirring Form of *gauging in which rows of stitches are drawn up in parallel lines, but with the stitches not exactly under one another. The result is a ruffled look rather than rows of parallel gathers. Gathering or gauging with elastic is also called shirring.

shirring thread see elastic thread.

shirt Basic garment or undergarment worn either by men or women but more generally considered to be for a man.

shoe-bag In America, white cotton bag the size of a pair of shoes with a drawstring top, or an envelope with several shoe-sized pockets usually monogrammed and embroidered to match *suitcase covers. Formerly considered a travel essential, shoe-bags are still used occasionally to keep shoes from soiling clothes in a suitcase (though disposable plastic is often considered more practical). In Britain they are still used by a large number of schoolgirls and boys for their shoes for games and gym.

---

shade: originally this term referred to the glass dome covering the arrangement but it has come to mean both dome and arrangement. This American shade was made c.1850.

shoes Covering for the feet. Embroidered and decorated shoes have been worn by the well-to-do at all times and the earliest known reference to them in England is the description of the 10th century shoes of silk embroidered with jewels found in the tomb of Queen Emma. During the middle ages, shoes, especially those worn by men, became very exotic with toes so long that their length, fixed by sumptuary laws, varied between 15 inches (38 centimetres) for the common people and 30 inches (76 centimetres) for the nobility, though as with all sumptuary laws it is very unlikely that this was taken seriously. The toes were often tipped with gold or gilt metal, and embroidery and the use of jewels was common. Backless slippers or mules were worn in the 17th century as an indoor shoe and the toes of these were decorated with metal threads, silks, and metal braids.

The 18th century was the period when embroidered shoes were at their most attractive and decorative—they ranged from brocaded with sharply pointed toes and high heavy heels at the beginning of the century, again decorated with metal threads, to the later flat slippers in fine kid or ticking with little or no heel. These were often embroidered on the toe with a design worked in chain stitch while those made in ticking were embroidered all over in a variety of stitches using the stripes of the ticking as a guide. Towards the end of the 19th century beaded shoes had become popular, with bronze-coloured beads worked on bronze kid, while the 20th century has seen many different kinds of embroidery on shoes, often but not always machine-worked. (Colour illustration p 249)

shoes: hand embroidered in the 1920s.

Shorleyker, Richard see Schole House for the Needle, A.

short-pile rugs see needlepile rugs.

short shades Term used in the shading of Berlin wool in which the entire gamut of shades or colours from light to dark and back to light occurs in a short length of wool of about one yard (metre). See also long shades.

shoulder pouch: in black buckskin with beaded decoration from Oklahoma.

shoulder pouch (bandoleer bag, friendship bag) Skin or fabric pouch with a shoulder strap used primarily by the Woodland tribes of North American Indians. The sides of the bag were elaborately embroidered with quills, moosehair, or bead embroidery. The Chippewa Indians were particularly famous for the beautifully beaded friendship bags given as gifts at inter-tribal meetings. In America the Pennsylvania Germans brought the custom from Germany in the 19th century, using cross stitch or drawn thread work, such as was also found in Alsace, the Tyrol and Transylvania.

show towel Beautifully made and decorated towel for putting over more utilitarian towels. It therefore resembles a sham. In the Near East, show towels are commonly used, and even today in some Western homes they are used when visitors are expected.

shuttle Thread holder—either the tool on which thread is wound, as in a tatting or knotting shuttle, or a boat-shaped container which holds thread already wound on a bobbin, as in weaving or in a sewing machine.

Sicily One of the places where, in the middle ages, East and West met, and a great tradition of embroidery combining the two cultures was founded, based on the workshops of the wealthy capital Palermo. Sicily had been in the hands of the Saracens from 827 but was conquered by the Normans in 1072, and in 1130 Roger II became king. Three years later the superb mantle, later to become part of the coronation insignia of the Holy Roman Empire, was made for him in Palermo. It is a vivid portrayal of a lion attacking a camel, and shows a combination of Islamic and Western traditions. The island also has a tradition of cutwork and other linen embroideries.

signature quilt Type of American *album quilt, often worked to raise money for good causes. The quilt was designed to accommodate as many names as possible, each person who signed paying a fee for the privilege. One example, worked in 1893 in Terre Haute, Indiana, has over a thousand names embroidered on it.

signatures The signing of embroideries has occasionally been done in the past and is more general nowadays, but it is regrettable that the practice has never been universal. So much interest is added to a piece which has a name and date on it; not only is it interesting historically and helpful for studying the development of techniques, but it adds a human quality to what is, after all, one of the most domestic and friendly of the arts.

silk The fibre produced by the larvae of certain bombycine moths which feed on mulberry leaves. It was the Chinese in about 700 BC who first managed to rear silkworms and draw off their silk, and so jealously did they guard the secret that it was not until the 6th century AD that two monks were able to bring some eggs to Europe. From them sericulture spread to Sicily, Italy, France, and Spain, and nowadays the principal silk centres are southern Europe, where the best silk is reeled, Japan, northern China, and India.

silk: Chinese panel embroidered in silk on silk.

Tussah or wild-grown silk comes from the two latter places. The beauty of silk thread lies in its lustre and suppleness, and it is better that it should have as little twist as possible so that the light reflecting from it can be given full value. The best quality silk used for producing first-class threads and fabrics is known as net silk, and the waste from this manufacture becomes second quality and is called spun silk. The thread takes dye perfectly and it can be woven into many different fabrics such as brocade, velvet, satin, and crêpe de chine, but owing to the expense it is now more difficult to buy fabrics of pure silk and the range of silk embroidery threads is becoming very curtailed. See also seda floja.

silkman Tradesman of the 17th and 18th centuries who 'buys raw Silk from the Importer and sometimes imports it himself and sells it to the Manufacturer' (Campbell 1747).

silk ribbon embroidery Type of embroidery popular in the 1870s, in which narrow silk ribbon was gathered up and formed into petals, the edges of leaves, and the insides of buds etc, and sewn onto cloth, with embroidery stitches completing the design. The ribbon had a silky, crinkly look very applicable to flowers such as poppies.

silk ribbon embroidery: detail of designs from 'The Queen' 1876.

silk twist (etching silk, buttonhole twist) Hard-spun silk thread. In America it is sold in skeins and used for outline embroidery, feather and buttonhole stitching, and is also called etching silk. In England it is sold in reels and spools, is generally used for working buttonholes, and is known as buttonhole twist.

sindon Fine linen fabric or a fabric resembling cambric or muslin. It was used in the middle ages for articles such as bed hangings and curtains (sometimes embroidered in silk), and was also used for shrouds and corporals.

sinew Strands of white fibrous tendon from the back of a horse, deer, or buffalo, which was used by the American Indians instead of thread. It is prepared by soaking in water to remove the natural glue, hammering to separate the individual strands, and rolling between the hands until it is pliable and elastic. A sharp point is obtained by wetting with saliva and rolling it into a point—when it is dry it is ready for use. Sinew was then used for attaching moosehair, quills, or beads, but is now used mainly for the sewing together of mocassins etc.

single coral stitch   see feather stitch.

single faggot stitch   see punch stitch.

singlesided foot   see attachments.

Sioux (Dahcotas) Migrating Plains Indian tribe (from the upper Mississippi to the Rockies), known for their *quillwork and *beadwork. They were great hunters of wild horses and buffalo and supplied the American Trading Company at Fort Pierre with quantities of buffalo and fur robes which were then sold in the east at great profit. As fighters, the Sioux created particular terror among the early settlers since *scalps were their honourable trophy of war. See also pipe bag.

sipers gold   see Cyprus gold.

size Gum-like fluid used for stiffening cloth and to strengthen warp threads in a loom before weaving. See also embroidery paste and dressing.

skanny (twisted gold) Spun silk and gold thread produced in Russia during the 15th and 16th centuries.

skein Yarn or thread wound off a reel and made into a hank. Some skeins, especially those of embroidery cotton or silk, are wound in such a way that one end can be pulled out from the encircling paper, while others have to be rewound into a ball.

skein holder

skein holder Yarn and embroidery threads, whether homespun or bought, were generally in skeins which had to be wound into balls before being used, and to save someone having to hold the skein while another wound, various devices were employed. 1. An upright bar, either standing on the floor or clamped to a table, with four folding lattice arms which could be pulled out to fit the size of the skein. 2. An upright bar standing on the floor with a box-shaped top, adjustable in size, which revolves as the thread is pulled; this type was used particularly in tambour work when a continuous thread was needed. 3. An upright bar standing on the floor with two adjustable knobs; the skein was placed over these for winding off. 4. Two small clamps with revolving heads for use on a table; these were fixed at a distance apart equal to the length of the skein, and the thread was wound off. See also thread winder.

skirt The part of a garment which hangs below the waist, or a separate garment hanging from the waist.

skunk bead Rare, blue trade bead used by the North American Indians with a raised pattern of meandering lines and flower buds in white and red. A necklace of them was worth a horse or robe. (Ewers 1945)

slate frame see embroidery frame.

slave silk see floss silk.

Slavonic embroidery Embroidery of the peoples of East Europe with a similar culture background, from the countries now called Romania, Hungary, Bulgaria,

Slavonic embroidery: detail of a skirt, Romanian, 20th century.

Yugoslavia, Poland, Czechoslovakia, and west Russia, generally known as the Slav races. In the 18th century and earlier, their embroidery was worked in a single colour on homespun linen or hemp, but in the 19th century cotton and muslin were added to the fabrics, and more colours as well as silk to the threads. Colours had a particular significance: yellow was considered to be health-giving, while red indicated innocence, joy, and contentment. The designs are either based on the structure of the fabric using counted thread stitches such as cross and double running, or are freehand using stem, satin, and a variety of filling stitches. Most of the embroidery on costume, often in the form of bands, is found on either side of the neck opening and on collars, cuffs, and hems. The motifs most often seen include crosses, *fylfots, birds (especially eagles with one or two heads), lions, riders on horseback, as well as many plant forms. (Bazielichowna 1953) See also Hungary, Romania.

sleave silk see floss silk.

sleeves The part of clothing worn between the shoulder and wrist, sometimes made in one piece with the garment, sometimes as a separate article which can be tacked, pinned, or tied onto the dress. In the 18th century it was the custom for the sleeves of a child's best dress to be detachable and as the child grew so the armhole was enlarged by means of an adjustable strap over the shoulder, and the sleeve reattached. These were frequently quilted. The separate undersleeves worn with women's dresses in the middle of the 19th century, called *engageantes, were generally of white cotton or net, often embroidered.

slip 1. Embroidery motif consisting of a flower with its foliage and stem with a small heel or piece of root attached. Sometimes they show fruit and flower together on the same stalk. They can be seen on a great deal of 16th and 17th century embroidery, especially on the raised and tent stitch work of the 17th century, and can also be found on panels with isolated motifs and slips which were worked ready to be cut out and applied. The Hardwick Hall inventories (1601) give 'fyve peeces of hangings . . . set with trees and slips and Griphons', and 'a footestool of oring tawnie velvet set with nedleworke slips and oring tawnie frenge' (Boynton 1971). 2. Twentieth century word for a petticoat, a one-piece undergarment full length or skirt only (half slip). 3. *Pillowcase.

slip: panel of slips with raised work and tent stitch, English, c.1600.

slipcase Cardboard or fabric-covered box open on one long side, sometimes elaborately embroidered, and used in America to protect fine books. See also book covers.

slip stitch Used to hold down a hem where it is important that the stitches show as little as possible on the right side. A single thread is picked up with the needle on the main fabric and then the needle slides along and takes up a small piece of the fold. This is not a strong stitch but is a most useful one in dressmaking and plain sewing.

small writing see open chain stitch.

Smithsonian Institution (Washington DC) Corporation comprising ten member museums, including the *Cooper-Hewitt Museum of Decorative Arts and Design, the National Museum of History and Technology, and the National Museum of Natural History. As well as American Indian artefacts and decorative art items, it contains an extensive collection of needlework, including a bed rug, sewing accessories, sewing birds, and thimbles.

smock 1. Undergarment worn by women and artists. 2. Outer covering garment worn by labouring men in the 18th, 19th and early 20th centuries. The 18th century smock resembled a shirt and was put on over ordinary clothes for protection. By the early 19th century smocks were worn as a garment in their own right. In the 1820s–30s the 'traditional' smock appeared, in two or three variations,

smock: detail of the back of a 19th century example.

with the front and back panel, the tops of sleeves, and the cuffs gathered, and the gathers held in position by ornamental stitching now known as *smocking. 3. In the 20th century the smock became fashionable for women, especially when pregnant, and children. Although the modern basic shape is the same, the ornament has largely disappeared. Practical versions are worn by men and women in the studio, house and garden.

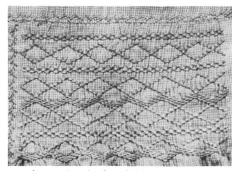

smocking: detail of a child's dress, English, 1930.

smocking The control of fullness by means of gathers fastened with ornamental stitching. Examples of this technique in a very simple style can be found on some 18th century caps and bonnets, but here there is no release of fullness—the main characteristic of the countryman's smock of the 19th century and of children's dresses of the 20th century. Evenly spaced gathers (tubings) are drawn up in the required number of rows, and are held in place with variations of two stitches, stem and feather. The stem stitch can be worked as outline, rope, cable, or wave stitch, while honeycomb stitch is a further variation. The gathering threads are then removed and the fullness released below the last row of stitching. In America the method is slightly different: dots are marked along the width of the fabric and the ornamental stitches worked without first drawing up gathers, the needle picking up a small piece of fabric at each dot.

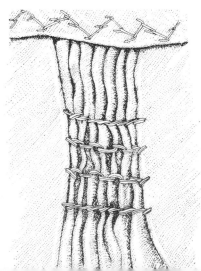

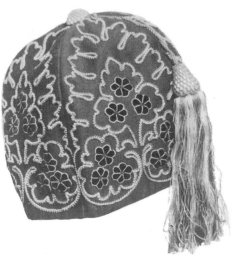

smoking cap: English, second half of the 19th century.

smoking cap Round cap with a long tassel commonly worn in the 19th century by men when smoking in order to keep the smoke out of their pomaded hair. They were simple to make and were often decorated with braidwork, but might be of any technique suitable for cloth or felt. Generally they were worked by the smoker's family.

smyrna stitch (double cross stitch, **star** stitch) Thick stitch which can be worked in two different threads and colours. A diagonal cross stitch covering two threads vertically and horizontally is worked and then this is covered by an upright cross stitch to give a star effect. Smyrna stitch is also another name for double knot stitch.

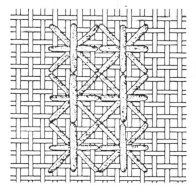

Society of Decorative Art American society founded by Candace *Wheeler and a group of ladies in 1877 in New York, after seeing the work from the *Royal School of Needlework on exhibition at the Centennial Exhibition in Philadelphia. She realised the need for a society to educate in design and to provide work for 'economically deprived gentlewomen'. Eventually there were more than thirty societies throughout the USA including branches in Hartford, Philadelphia, and Boston. (Faude 1975) See also exchanges for woman's work.

socks Short stockings. In the Anglo-Saxon period they were worn inside the shoe over the stockings, and like them were made of fustian or other fabric cut and seamed. However for wealthy people they could be far more decorative as is shown by an entry in the wardrobe account of Henry VIII (1533): 'It'm for making of foure [pairs of] sockis for our use, whereof one of taffeta, and three of Geneva clothe, everye of them embroidered with silke and lyned with skarlette.' (Caley 1789)

socks: in the Grecian style, early 19th century.

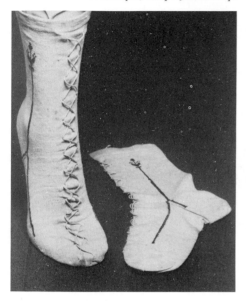

soft embroidery cotton Soft, slightly hairy thread made up of four two-ply threads twisted together. As it will not divide up and is rather thick it is generally used for couching. In the US it is known as coton à broder.

solid fillings Filling stitches which completely cover the ground, as distinct from lace and other light filling stitches. They were used particularly in 17th century crewel work, and often in ecclesiastical embroidery where there is a strong outline to the motif.

sol pattern Sun or wheel pattern found in fine Spanish drawnwork as early as the 17th century.

soumak stitch (kelim stitch) Used for making light, hardwearing rugs, simulating those from the Caucasus worked on a loom and known as Soumak rugs. The stitch is worked with the selvage facing the worker, and the beginning and end of each complete stitch splits the two threads of a weft double bar while the middle part of each stitch goes into the large holes of a double thread canvas, though a jute canvas may also be used.

Southwest Indians Indian tribes inhabiting Arizona, New Mexico, southern Colorado, and southeast Utah, including among others the Navajo, *Hopi, Apache, and *Pueblo. They were primarily stable, agricultural tribes who raised maize, cotton, and sheep. The Navajo were famous weavers, and the Indians of Acoma Pueblo produced beautiful embroidered mantas and shirts in pueblo stitch.

spacer see gauge.

soumak stitch.

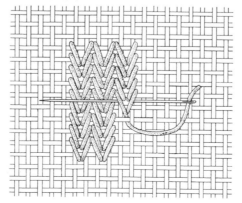

Spain: detail of an altar frontal.

Spain For the 800 years before 1492, Spain was dominated by the Moors, and after their expulsion she conquered parts of South America and Mexico. The result is that many of the designs in Spanish work are clearly derived from Arabic and, through the Arabs, Persian sources, to which are grafted on elements from Aztec and Inca art. Spain has always been a very religious country and so there are many Christian symbols in the folk embroidery, as well as superb ecclesiastical work such as altar frontals, copes, and chasubles. Following the Moorish tradition, one favourite colour combination was black and white, and this worked in stylised geometrical and flower designs on homespun linen is the 'Spanish work' or *blackwork which formed part of the trousseau brought to England by Katharine of Aragon in 1501 and which had a great influence on the English blackwork already known. Spanish embroidery includes many samplers, mostly signed and dated. Originally long and narrow, and later square, these are packed full of patterns and stitches, including pulled thread, using cross, geometrical satin, buttonhole, and double running stitches, among others. The folk embroidery varies from district to district, especially in colour, and is found on shirts and underclothes embroidered by girls for their future husbands and on the various household articles which form part of a bride's trousseau.

spangle (paillette, sequin) Small flat ornament used to add brilliance and glitter to fabrics or embroidery. They are usually of shiny metal (gold, silver, brass, or copper), and have a small hole for sewing them down. Though generally circular, the shape can vary as can the placing of the hole—sequins have the hole at one side, while paillettes are of various shapes, sometimes long and thin with a hole top and bottom for easier sewing. They were and are much used by couturières and dressmakers of the 19th and 20th centuries in jet and plastic iridescent material. Spangles have a long history, being known in Europe from the 15th century and probably much earlier in the orient.

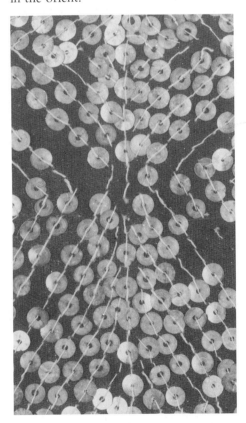

Spanish work   see blackwork.

sparver   Canopy for a bed, found in England in the middle ages and mentioned in wills and inventories as being of the same fabric and with the same decoration as the hangings. The word also applies to bed tents in the Dodecanese Islands of Greece (close to the mainland of Turkey), which are generally beautifully embroidered.

spider's web   Term for the stitches which look like a spider's web or a wheel, often seen in the corners of pulled thread work. It is formed by making spokes across the area to be filled and interlacing them in a spiral.

Spider Woman (kokyanwuqtl, Great Spider) In Navajo Indian mythology the Spider Woman was the greatest weaver of all times, but in Hopi Indian legend 'many designs were symbolic and were attributed to dreams sent by the Great Spider, who was the supreme master of the art of embroidery' (Terrell 1947).

spiderwork   see lacis.

spindle   1. Slender wooden rod, tapering at either end, onto which thread is spun. This meaning can be enlarged to include any rod made of any material which acts as an axis on which something revolves, such as the spindle of a sewing machine on which the shuttle revolves. 2. Measure of thread, the measure depending on the amount of any particular thread which can be wound on the spindle. 3. In some, but not all, senses the word spindle is synonymous with bobbin or spool.

spiral   Continuously increasing curve revolving round a fixed point. This shape is used in quilting and many other embroideries, including those of the Plains Indians of North America.

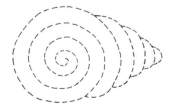

splasher   Piece of linen, lace, or other fabric, usually embroidered, which is fastened to the wall of a bedroom behind the washstand. In the late 19th and early 20th centuries these ornaments were often too decorative to be really useful.

splendour (glory)   In art forms, the surrounding of the sun, or representations of God, Christ, and the Virgin with rays. In embroidery the rays are generally worked in gold threads.

splicing   1. The joining of two ends of rope, cord, or yarn by unravelling the ends and weaving the strands together. 2. Method of joining strips used in rug braiding. 3. Method of joining two pieces of canvas, also known as *grafting. 4. Technique used in hair and quill embroidery for elongating a pattern line by overlapping or mingling the bundles of hair or quills.

split stitch   Because it looks like chain stitch, split stitch is put into that group but it is unique as it depends on being worked with a soft untwisted silk thread which can be split with the needle. It can be used for very fine line work or as a fine filling stitch, and was used extensively for depicting hands and faces in the opus anglicanum of the middle ages.

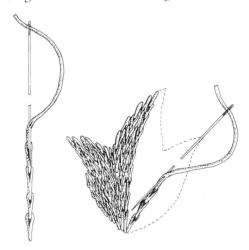

spool   1. 'Small cylindrical piece of wood or other material on which thread is wound as it is spun; a bobbin' (OED). 2. 'Small, shaped cylinder of wood on which sewing thread is wound; a reel' (OED).

spool knave (reel holder) Article worn suspended from the belt or apron which holds a reel or ball of thread or yarn, leaving the worker with both hands free to knit, crochet, or tambour. It hangs on a chain and has a semicircular frame with a pin across the bottom. This pin or bar screws into the frame and holds the ball in position.

spot stitch (overlay stitch) Variations of couching stitch for beads used by the northern Plains American Indians, such as the *Blackfoot, Sarsi, Plains Cree, *Crow, and Shoshone. If it is worked on skins with an awl and sinew no stitches appear on the back, but if on a fabric ground the stitches can be seen.

spot stitch: side view.

spot stitch: plan view.

spray Graceful sprig of some flowering plant or tree. The use of flowers, whether single or as sprays or *slips, is considered to be one of the characteristics of English embroidery design.

spring scissors (shears) see scissors.

spun yarns Although the phrase means any thread prepared by spinning, in modern usage it usually refers to second quality yarn—that which has been spun from short fibres put together, these being the waste from the long-fibred best quality.

squab Loose cushion with a flat top and bottom, fitting exactly into the seat of a coach, chair, or sofa.

square chain stitch see open chain stitch.

square stitch see double running stitch.

stab stitch Short running stitch used on thick materials including leather, and made by stabbing the needle straight down through the material and straight up a little further along.

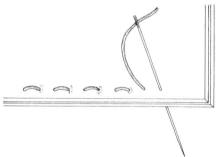

stalk stitch see stem stitch.

stamped linen Generic term for *art linen pre-stamped with designs specifically for items such as d'oyleys, splashers, tray cloths, and cushion (pillow) covers. Not only linen is used, but also canvas, duck, mummy cloth, muslin etc.

stamped velvet work Embroidery which merely consisted of outlining the pattern on embossed or stamped velvet with embroidery silks to give it greater prominence. This was done in the late 19th century when velvet was a fabric much used in upholstery.

staple Originally the purpose for which a wool or other fibre was suited and therefore the grade in which it was to be taxed and sold, but now a term generally accepted as denoting the average length of a sample of wool, cotton, or other textile fibre (Murphy n.d.). In wool the long staples make worsteds and the short staples make cloths, and in general it can be said that long staples make finer and better quality fabrics while short staples (often the waste from long) make second quality goods. Staple yarn is made from short, man-made fibres and is used to produce the dull-finish fabrics resembling cotton, linen, or wool.

star of Bethlehem Well-known quilt pattern consisting of an eight-pointed star. It may also be made up as one great star surrounded by smaller ones.

star of Bethlehem: American quilt made up of diamond patches in printed calicoes.

star-spangled banner This famous documented American flag was flown over Fort McHenry in Baltimore, Maryland, in 1812 and inspired Francis Scott Key to write the American national anthem. Made of English bunting, it is 42 feet by 30 feet (13 by 9 metres) with 15 inset stars, and was sewn by Mary Pickersgill, a flag-maker under contract to the US government for $405.90. (Cooper 1971)

star stitch Counted thread stitch consisting of eight spokes radiating from a central hole to form a square. If they are to be massed together it is necessary to use a thick enough thread to cover the canvas completely. See also smyrna stitch.

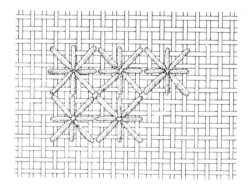

(opposite)
shoes: a pair of hand-embroidered shoes, 1930s.

(overleaf, p 250)
tent stitch: a detail of one of the 18th century Stoke Edith hangings now on display at Montacute House in Somerset.

stations of the cross The stages of Jesus Christ's journey to Calvary. They are often depicted on Lenten cloths and frontals and consist of: 1. Jesus being condemned to death, 2. Jesus receiving his cross, 3. Jesus falling the first time, 4. Jesus meeting his mother, 5. Simon of Cyrene helping to carry the cross, 6. Veronica wiping Jesus's face, 7. Jesus falling the second time, 8. Jesus speaking to the women of Jerusalem, 9. Jesus falling the third time, 10. Jesus being stripped of his garment, 11. Jesus nailed to the cross, 12. Jesus's death, 13. the descent from the cross, and 14. Jesus being laid in the sepulchre.

stem stitch (crewel stitch, outline stitch, stalk stitch, south kensington stitch) One of the most frequently used outline stitches. A long back stitch is taken with the needle coming out halfway along and just beside the stitch, and this is repeated. It is important that the thread should always be kept to the same side of the needle: generally if the thread is kept to the left it is called stem stitch, and if the thread is to the right (which makes a finer line), outline stitch. Stem stitch is also called crewel stitch because it was the stitch most commonly employed in the 17th century crewel embroideries, and

stem stitch.

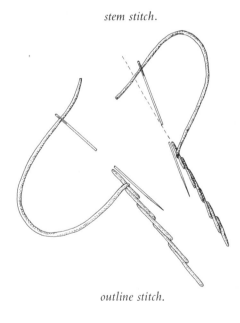

outline stitch.

(overleaf, p 251)
Thurstone, Mary and Sarah: the central motif of Mary Thurstone's coverlet, dated 1694.

(opposite)
toran: detail of this richly embroidered frieze which was hung over the door on festive occasions, from Kathiawar India, late 19th century or early 20th century.

south kensington because it was taught at what is now the *Royal School of Needlework in that area of London. Though mainly used for line work, it makes a very satisfactory filling stitch when worked in rows close together.

Stent, Peter English publisher of *pattern books for embroidery and other crafts in the mid 17th century.

stiletto (piercer, stylus) Very sharp, pointed instrument set into a handle and used for making eyelet holes in fabric in dressmaking (belts), staymaking (lace holes), and embroidery (broderie anglaise, or eyelet embroidery), and other techniques. Though it is generally made of steel, which is by far the most satisfactory material, it may also be made of bone, ivory, mother-of-pearl, or silver. See also awl.

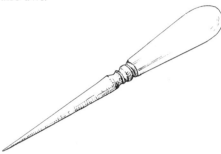

stitched rugs Thrift rugs made in the UK. Hessian or sacking is used as a foundation, and narrow strips of waste fabric such as cut up tights or stockings or lightweight dress pieces are threaded through a needle with a large eye. The design is marked out on the ground and is worked either with darning stitches or an overcast or satin stitch.

stitchery Term for any handwork done with a needle and thread—this includes dressmaking, plain sewing, and embroidery. The word was apparently coined by Shakespeare.

stitches The means by which, with thread and ground fabric, a given effect is created. It is true to say that all over the world for many thousands of years the same basic stitches have been used, and it is equally true that for a particular process, thread, or material a particular stitch has been invented. The result is that today there is a large group of well tried and indispensable stitches and round them are innumerable variations, each evolved for a certain purpose. It is nearly impossible now to create a new one; someone somewhere at sometime is bound to have tried it and, possibly because it did not do what was needed, discarded it. The thickness, pliability, twist, and strength of the thread has a great deal to do with the choice of stitch, as has the thickness, looseness, and evenness of weave, and the surface texture of the ground, so it is perhaps no wonder that there are so many.

One of the problems of stitches is in their nomenclature—since they are used in practically every country there are often many names for the same one, which can lead to confusion. Although there are many excellent books on the subject, there is as yet no absolute classification. The best that can be done is to use the most generally accepted name and list as many synonyms as can be found. The method followed here is to group similar stitches together (though some belong to several groups) and as many known variations as possible are listed, but this will inevitably fall far short of the actual number. A description and illustration of every asterisked stitch in the lists can be found under its own name, and also of every stitch mentioned throughout the text of the book. For the different groups, see chained stitches, composite stitches, couched and laid stitches, counted thread stitches, drawn fabric stitches, drawn thread stitches, eye and eyelet stitches, filling stitches, flat stitches, insertion stitches, knotted stitches, looped stitches, padding stitches, plain sewing stitches.

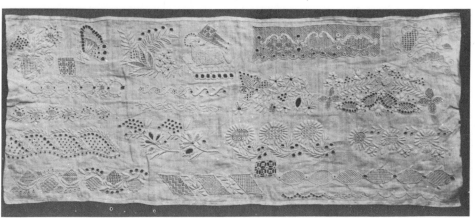

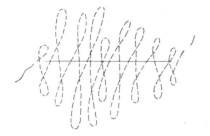

stoating Darning across a slit in thick cloth, using running stitch in an uneven figure-of-eight pattern. The darning is done on the wrong side of the fabric and the stitches should not show through to the right side. (Hird 1949)

stockings Covering for feet and legs. Knitted stockings have been known since the 4th century at least, but during the middle ages most people wore them cut from cloth and seamed. With the invention of Lee's knitting frame in the 16th century, the wearing of stockings knitted from wool, silk, or cotton, and more recently rayon and other man-made fibres, became general. Men's stockings were often embroidered in the 16th century, as can be seen in the full-length portraits of that period, but later this decoration became little more than a fairly discreet *clock. On the other hand, women's stockings became highly decorative in the 19th century, being embroidered sometimes with china ribbon, sometimes with silk, and often having a lacy pattern woven in. See also hose,

stockings: knitted in yellow silk embroidered in coloured silks, English, 1600-1625.

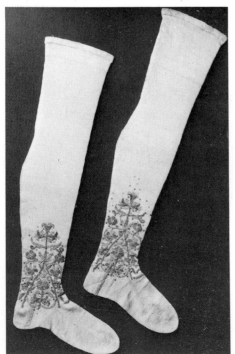

Stoke Edith panels see Montacute House.

stole 1. Narrow piece of fabric, frequently embroidered, worn round the shoulders and falling nearly to the feet of a priest officiating at the service of the Eucharist. A deacon wears the stole over his left shoulder. The garment derives from a linen handkerchief or napkin which had to be carried on the shoulder, as in ancient Greece and Rome there were no pockets. Ecclesiastical stoles were originally embroidered along their entire length, but in the 19th and 20th centuries it is considered sufficient to work a small panel above the fringed ends and a cross centre-back over the seam, and some excellent modern stoles have been made for various churches and cathedrals. The stole of St Cuthbert (909-916) can still be seen in Durham Cathedral, and that of St Thomas à Becket in Sens Cathedral (France). 2. Article worn by women round the shoulders for warmth, usually oblong in shape and made from fur, feathers, or fabric.

stomacher Triangular piece of fabric, generally richly decorated, worn with a robe open down the front, between the bust and the stomach, from the 15th to the 18th centuries. They were also worn by men in various ways from the 14th to the 18th centuries, but these were more like a waistcoat. Stomachers for women were sometimes boned or had other forms of stiffening.

stomacher: design from 'Nuouissimo Esemplace de Ricami', 1694.

stool Backless seat without arms for one person, also called a tabouret. In the 16th century when chairs were still fairly uncommon, most people sat on stools or

benches, and in royal circles in Europe the right to sit on a tabouret in the presence of the king or queen was a jealously-guarded honour. To palliate their excessive hardness, stools often had cushions or were upholstered, and often the coverings were embroidered.

strand Single filament or fibre which is one of many making a thread; also, one thread of a number forming stranded silk or cotton.

stranded cotton (art thread) One of the most versatile embroidery threads, consisting of six strands of mercerised cotton twisted loosely together. There are innumerable shades of colour obtainable, and any number of strands can be used in the needle.

Strangers Hall Museum (Norwich, England) Museum of domestic life from about 1500 onwards with a large number of textiles including costume and household furnishings. While it has many excellent and rare pieces of work, it specialises in the homely objects of the past which tell so much and are so rarely collected.

Strangers Hall: panel of applied work and stitchery in Art Nouveau style, c.1903.

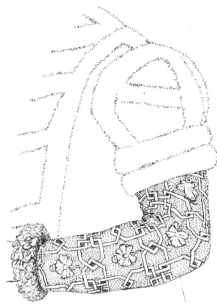

strap-work: detail of a painting by Hans Eworth, 1557.

strap work Style of ornament in vogue in the 15th and 16th centuries, consisting of interlacing bands. It was used in woodwork (on staircases, chairs, beds etc), plasterwork, and metalwork, as well as embroidery, and can often be seen in the patterning on costume of both men and women in 16th century portraits. It was carried out by the sewing down of braids or by stitches and possibly jewels outlining the strap shapes.

straw When woven into a fabric, straw can be a ground for embroidery, but this should not be confused with *straw cloth. Straw which is plaited and sewn into hats is often embroidered, and another use appeared in the 16th century when, in 1578, Mr Benedicke Spenolle gave Elizabeth I 'two fannes of strawe, wrought with silke of sondry collours' (Nichols 1823). These fans probably came from Italy where they were in general use.

straw (milliner's needle, beading needle) Very fine, long needle used in millinery and some kinds of bead embroidery.

straw cloth Mid 20th century fabric woven of cotton or man-made fibres, with a surface resembling straw. It makes a suitable ground for some types of embroidery, among them Dorset feather stitchery.

straw embroidery Embroidery using straw as the thread, sometimes in conjunction with other threads. In the 18th century ornamentation with straw became the rage and Beck (1882) says that in 1783 the *European Magazine* stated that to give an account of the straw ornaments

then fashionable 'would be tedious even to the votaries of fashion'. Coats called paillasses or straw coats were worn which were trimmed and ornamented with straw, and everything was decorated with it from the 'cap to the shoe-buckle'. It is not an easy material to handle and from its nature few garments worked with it have survived. In the early 19th century it could be found on such flimsy articles as bonnet veils, and later, though it still decorated jackets and sometimes skirts, it was used less for ornamenting costume than as a form of embroidery. Miss Lambert (1843) says that 'a flat plaited straw has been introduced into worsted work' and 'embroidery with split straw has also been done on velvet and silk and has a curious and beautiful effect'. In America as in England, work was done in the 1860s in which canvas had strips of straw laid on it which were partly covered and held down with wools in pattern.

straw embroidery: an unfinished piece, English, late 19th century.

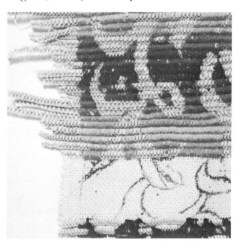

streatley stitch Used in glove-making. The two edges are held together and oversewn, but every stitch is worked twice, the result being one straight and one slanting stitch along the top of the seam.

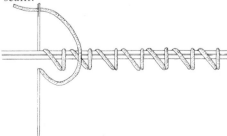

stretcher Wooden frame, usually of flat moulding, onto which a piece of embroidery can be fastened before framing. Nowadays a sheet of thick card is more often used.

stretching (blocking) Process of squaring and smoothing a finished rug or piece of needlework by dampening it with water and pinning it in shape to a surface until it is dry, after which it can be mounted or framed.

stroke stitch see double running stitch.

stroking gathers Technique in which a needle is used to straighten each of a row of gathers by running it along the vertical grooves from the top edge towards the bottom. This process makes the gathers lie parallel ready for the yoke or band to be sewn on the top edge, with one hemming stitch for each. To stroke gathers properly it is necessary to use cotton or linen because synthetics or crease-resisting fabrics do not make the firm, small grooves. See also gathering.

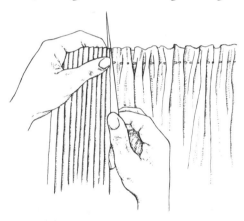

strouding Medium-weight woollen blanketing used especially by the *Iroquois Indian women for clothing, when it was decorated with seed bead embroidery. It was manufactured in Stroud (Gloucestershire) during the 18th and 19th centuries and was a barter item in trade with the American Indians.

Stuart In English history the period between 1603, when James VI of Scotland (James Stuart) became James I of England, and 1714 when Queen Anne died, thus generally taken to mean the 17th century. The period was interrupted by the Commonwealth (1649–1660) when such frivolities as embroidery were frowned upon, and the very strong Puritan element in the country forbade the representation of the Life of Christ or any New Testament subjects as idolatry. For this reason many 17th century tent stitch and raised work panels show scenes from the Old Testament but never from the New Testament. The other type of work so well known from this time is crewel work, which was usually made into large hangings.

stuffed quilting see trapunto.

stuffs Woollen fabrics distinguished from other cloths by having no *nap and being woven from long *staple wool. They are also lighter in weight than broadcloths and were part of the manufactures—the New Draperies—brought to England in the 16th century by the Flemish weavers. The word is sometimes used in a more general sense as applying to any textile fabric.

stump work see raised work.

style troubadour Particular style of design for Berlin woolwork, fashionable in the 1840s and 1850s. Based on the interest in medieval history so prevalent at that date, and fostered by the novels of Sit Walter Scott and by the Gothic revival, it consisted of romantic paintings by well-known artists made into patterns.

stylus see stiletto.

suba Embroidered sheepskin cloak traditionally worn by men and women in Hungary, now only surviving as museum pieces. They ase sleeveless and vary in size from the very practical which are no wider than necessary, to the very fine which when laid out were completely circular and took fifteen whole skins to make. These were prized possessions and might be handed down from father to son. The embroidery was worked in wool, mostly in satin stitch, round the shoulders and hem. Subas for women were only hip length. (Fél 1961)

Sudanese embroidery In the northern part of the Sudan, the embroidery is mostly done on the counted thread and is similar in style to Turkish and Persian work, using particularly double running, point turc, and geometrical satin stitches. Crowfoot (1950) thinks that this style of embroidery originally came to the country via Egypt. It is worked mostly on cloths for use in the household as towels, to cover food, to cover the table, or to wrap articles in to keep them clean. Until recently, with the advent of machine embroidery, there was little or none on women's clothes. In addition, the horsemen in the Sudan wear long padded and quilted coats but the quilting is done in straight lines with no attempt at pattern.

suede Word first used in the 19th century to denote undressed kidskin as used for gloves. Now the meaning is widened to include the undressed skins of other animals used for shoes, coats, etc. It has also recently been extensively used for appliqué work and piecing for everything from waistcoats, coats, and jackets to skirts, hats, and handbags, sometimes worked by hand, sometimes by machine. See also leather.

Suffolk puffs Form of patchwork in which circles of fabric of the same weight and type have a single hem turned onto the wrong side, which is then gathered with small, even running stitches. The gathering thread is pulled tight and fastened off, and the small circles are then joined together in pattern. They can be used as they are or mounted. This type of patchwork is of 20th century origin, and in the early part of the century was made into articles such as nightdress cases or table centres, while at the present time the idea is being extended to dress decoration and toys. Quilts made in America using this form of patchwork are known as yo-yo quilts. (Ickis 1949, Pickup and Field 1974)

Suffolk puffs: English nightdress case, 20th century.

sugi Leggings made of chamois skin worn by men and women in the Upper Iman River area of Manchuria. They are often decorated with decoupé or reverse appliqué.

suitcase covers (trunk covers, suitcase cloths) Large white cotton cloths usually hemmed with bright-coloured feather stitch and initialed in cross stitch in the corner. Often a part of a young woman's trousseau, they were used to cover the contents of a packed trunk or suitcase before it was closed to protect it from the dust and soot of travel. They were used in Edwardian England, Europe, and the US, and usually there were *shoe-bags to match.

suit of lights (traje de luces) Traditional bullfighter's suit consisting of an elaborately hand-embroidered padded jacket and a white linen shirt with lace or cutwork, worn with short tight trousers, pink stockings, ballet-type shoes, and a montera or pointed black hat. They are used in both Spain and Mexico, but most of the Mexican ones have been imported from Spain and are of softer pastel colours. These satin suits, often weighing as much as 25 pounds, gleam with

suba: spread out; each segment is a separate skin.

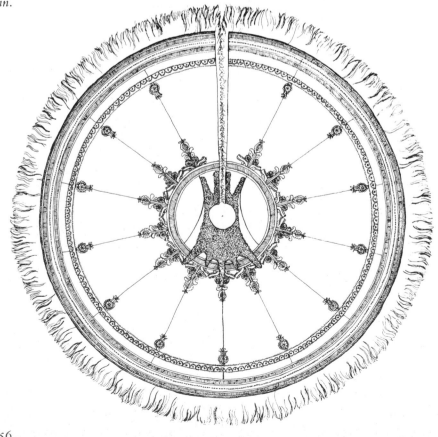

embroidery of gold or silver threads, which give them their name. The elaborate parade cape worn only when the matador enters the ring is worked with bright flowers surrounding an embroidered image of a patron saint.

sujanis Embroidered quilts from the district of Mithila, in Bihar (India). They are made from old fabrics pieced in layers and quilted with blocks of running stitches worked in straight lines. The outlines of the motif are worked in herringbone stitch in a dark colour. (Irwin and Hall 1973) See also kantha.

super frontal Narrow length of fabric hanging over the front edge of the altar, often embroidered to match the frontal. In the 19th and early 20th centuries they were sometimes made of an unrelated fabric such as crocheted lace, but now they generally match, or there may be none at all. See also altar frontal.

surcoat Outer coat or garment, often of rich fabric, worn by people of rank of both sexes in the middle ages.

surface satin stitch see satin stitch.

surrey stitched rugs see needlepile rugs.

suspenders see braces.

swastika see gammadion.

Swedish embroidery Sweden has a long tradition of embroidery, which in the middle ages was fostered by the church. As in other countries the convents played a large part in producing good work, especially that of St Brigitta in Vadstena, but with the Reformation the emphasis changed to embroidery for the king and court, and foreign influences, especially French, appeared, while England and the Netherlands provided the inspiration for the work done for wealthy merchants. One of the finest embroideries in Sweden is the suit of white satin worn by Gustavus Adolphus in 1620, which is worked in silver and mole grey with the motif of the Three Crowns and with arabesques and powderings. The embroideries of the peasants differed widely from district to district though very little remains from a date earlier than the 18th century. Linen was spun and woven at home, and threads were dyed with the berries and lichens found in the various districts, and also with specially grown woad. From Scania in the south come brilliantly coloured embroideries sometimes worked on black cloth, as well as work done on white by the counted thread. Hälsingland is well known for red embroidery on white, and Blekinge for pastel coloured linens, and these were worked for wall hangings, hand towels, pillow cases, and parts of costume such as hanging pockets, aprons, hoods, and dresses. Sweden suffered as much as other countries from the general decline in taste and quality of materials in the 19th century, and in 1874, inspired by William *Morris, an association was formed called the Friends of Needlework (*Foreningen Handarbetets Vanner*). This society started to produce designs based on traditional work, and as in other other Scandinavian countries it has grown into a large concern, selling designs, fabrics, and also finished work done under its auspices. (Kockum-Overengen 1951, Mattin 1962, Sturge 1934)

Swedish embroidery: back of Fredrik II's throne canopy.

Swedish weaving see needle weaving.

sweet bags Small embroidered bags of the 16th and 17th centuries frequently mentioned in inventories and lists of gifts. They held sweet-smelling herbs and were put among linen and clothes to help counteract the unpleasant smells so prevalent in Tudor and Stuart England. Elizabeth I was given many such bags between 1577 and 1600, which are recorded in the *New Years Gifts to Queen Elizabeth* (Nichols 1823), and there are thirty or more in the inventory taken at Kenilworth Castle in 1583, while that of the Earl of Northampton taken in 1614 mentions ten, including 'one small sweet bagge of Tent work the ground silver with pottes and flowers lined with greene sattin' and 'a smaller sweet bagge embroidered with highe embosted mosse-worke havinge two sea nymphes upon dolphins and other figures of fowles, edged about with lace of silver and gold, lined with carnation' (Shirley 1869).

swiss darning Method of repairing holes in knitting in which the stitches are reproduced exactly by means of needle and thread. The hole is first filled with single vertical threads to form a warp and then, working across, the needle fills in with stitches simulating knitted stocking stitch.

Switzerland As it is a small country in the centre of Europe, surrounded by Italy, Germany, Austria, and France, it is not surprising that the art and embroideries of Switzerland should owe so much to outside influences, especially German. The northeastern side of the country (St Gallen and Appenzell) is mainly famous for its whitework, which has been done in the area from the middle ages. It is characterised by a light design embroidered in many surface and pulled stitches in white on white, with possibly an outline stitch in coloured silk,

Switzerland: detail of a cover depicting 'The Senses'.

and it often strongly resembles the south German work of a comparable date. This tradition of fine whitework is still alive today.

During the last century and a half it is in the field of machine embroidery that the country has been pre-eminent. From 1828, when Josué *Heilmann of Mulhouse sold some of his newly-invented embroidery machines to François Mange of St Gallen, the Swiss have exploited the possibilities of the techniques to the full, especially on the white muslins for which the district was already famous. The main use to which the machines were put in the mid 19th century was the embroidering of borders and insertion for trimming dresses and underwear. The trade was further extended in 1855 when America became the chief market for these goods. By 1862 the Swiss machines could imitate hand-scalloping and by 1868 they could do eyelet work, and so an excellent reproduction of the popular broderie anglaise (eyelet embroidery) was possible. Until 1880 they virtually had the field to themselves, and even when other countries introduced machine embroidery, the Swiss kept the lead with their excellent work, so much so that the terms Swiss dotted, Swiss muslins, or Swiss braid have remained as a description of particular types of machine-embroidered fabrics.

symbol Material object, mark, or design which represents something immaterial, abstract, or sacred. In embroidery they are mostly found in ecclesiastical, heraldic, and allegorical work. Symbolism was very prevalent in the middle ages where examples such as a unicorn representing chastity or a white rose for purity would be understood by everyone. The science of heraldry is concerned with presenting the genealogy of a person in symbols.

symmetry The harmony and balance of parts with each other and the whole; also, in a more exact sense, the positioning of identical parts equally on either side of a dividing line or round a point.

Syon cope The most famous piece of opus anglicanum in existence. It was worked between 1300 and 1320, and can be seen in the Victoria and Albert Museum (London). The cope belonged to a group of nuns from the Brigettine convent of Syon in Middlesex, though its history before the foundation of this convent in 1414 is unknown. Originally a chasuble, it was remodelled as a cope when one row of scenes was cut away, and now there are three complete rows consisting of fifteen scenes, some from the life of Christ and some of the apostles. The embroidery consists of silver-gilt and silver thread and coloured silks in underside couching with split stitch and laid and couched work on linen. (King 1963)

Syon cope: detail showing Christ appearing to Mary Magdalen.

szür Mantle of *frieze worn by the peasants of Hungary in the 19th century. Although made like a coat with sleeves, it was worn like a cape, often with the lower part of the sleeves tied to act as pockets. The szür was very highly decorated with appliqué and wool embroidery, so much so that the government attempted (unsuccessfully) to enforce sumptuary laws regulating the amount allowed. (Fél 1961)

tabby weave The most common of all *weaves, sometimes called plain weave, consisting of warp threads interlaced with weft threads in a regular over and under sequence, with the return row being under and over.

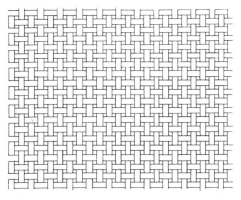

tabernacle veil Covering for the tabernacle. In a Roman Catholic church this houses the pyx which contains the consecrated Host. The veils are made of a soft, supple fabric, generally silk, and are embroidered with any suitable symbol.

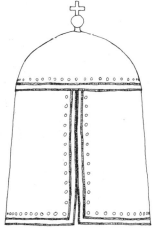

table-carpet 16th and 17th century carpet which was used in Europe to cover tables before the general introduction of floor carpets. They could be knotted pile carpets either of Turkish origin or English copies, or they might be embroidered in tent or cross stitch, or made of velvet or cloth decorated with applied work or embroidery in metal threads. Some of the most beautiful of those in the Victoria and Albert Museum (London)

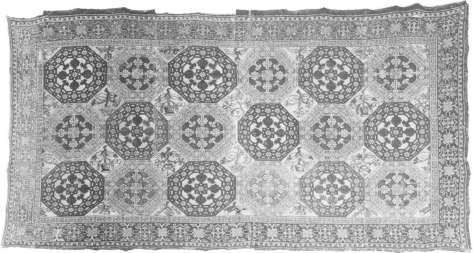

table-carpet: English, 1600.

are the St John of Bletso carpet in tent stitch with the arms of Gifford, the Bradford table-carpet, also in tent stitch with a deep border with scenes of rural life, and one in red velvet with pansies, columbines, and honeysuckle worked in silver-gilt and silver thread. In 1561 Elizabeth I was given 'By the Lady Knowlles, a fyne carpett of needleworke, theverende fricnged and buttoned with gold and silk' (Nichols 1823).

tablecloth Cloth used to cover a table, either for decoration only, when it may be of any suitable fabric worked in a chosen technique, or for use when eating when it must be of washable fabric and in a technique suitable for frequent laundering.

table-linen (napery) The fabric accessories for a table used for formal eating. These may include a tablecloth or place mats, table-napkins, doilies, fingerbowl mats, and glass mats. In the middle ages and later the cloth was usually of fine linen or damask, and a great number of napkins were used. It was not until the mid 19th century that the fashion of embroidered cloths came in, and it was the 20th century before the habit of using place-mats on a polished table became prevalent.

table-runner see runner.

table scarf (in America, long *runner) Table scarves are the exact width of a table but much longer. The ends hang down and may be embroidered in the current fashion. Table scarfs started their great popularity in the 1880s.

tacking The temporary joining of two or more pieces of fabric with a long loose thread. Nowadays the term is used synonymously with *basting.

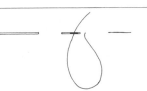

taffeta Fine, thin, tabby-woven silk fabric used in England since the 14th century. Originally it had no gloss, and according to some of the many references to it in inventories and accounts it could be expensive or cheap, wide or narrow, with a pile (tuft-taffety) or without. Alamode and lustring were other kinds of taffeta. In the 17th century a French manufacturer discovered that applied with a thin, wet, slightly glutinous substance and then put through heated rollers it became glossy, with an attractive watery look. Nowadays taffeta can be of silk, wool, or man-made fibres.

tag locks Yellowed ends of a sheep's fleece. When dyed with indigo a colour-fast green wool resulted which was used in *American crewel embroideries.

tailor's buttonhole Stitch which can be used for embroidery or as an edging stitch, but is most usually associated with the making of buttonholes. When edges are buttonholed in any form of cutwork, or slits are made for running ribbons through, ordinary buttonhole stitch is generally used for strengthening the edges, but for the buttonholes on garments which will receive hard wear, tailor's buttonhole with its double instead of single beaded edge is preferred. With the edge to be worked facing away, the needle is brought up from underneath and the thread drawn through until only a small loop is left. The needle is then put through the loop from behind and the thread drawn tight.

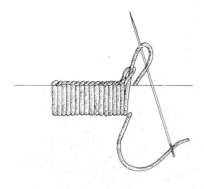

tambour 1. Frame shaped like a drum on which the embroidery known as tambouring was done. The original frames consisted of two hoops of wood, one fitting into the other, between which the fabric to be worked was stretched. The hoops were mounted on a curved wooden base which rested on the lap. Later this base was discarded and the hoops were mounted on a stand, which might have a reel underneath where the continuous thread was wound, or else they were fixed to a clamp which fastened to a table.

tambour: long muslin scarf, early 19th century.

2. Type of embroidery worked with a tambour hook or needle. This work, which has a marked resemblance to the chain stitch embroidery done in India with an *āri, is a quick method of working chain stitch on muslin and other fine fabrics. All designs for tambour are formed with a continuous line. The fabric is stretched across the tambour frame, the hook is held in the right hand above the frame, while the left hand under the frame controls the continuous thread. The hook is pushed through the fabric, picks up the thread, and brings it to the top in a loop; again the hook goes down through the loop and is brought up again with the thread, and the result is

a series of chain stitches. The hook or needle used is like a very fine metal crochet hook, and the tool, generally beautifully made in ivory or bone, has in its hollow handle spare hooks of varying sizes. The heyday of this work was between 1780 and 1850 when many dresses in white muslin as well as accessories like collars, cuffs, caps, and pelerines were tamboured. In 1849 the *American Ladies' Memorial* stated of tambouring that '. . . if it be intended to work in crewels, a colored pattern will also be of service as a guide to the selection of the worsteds, which are usually worked into very beautiful groups or wreaths of flowers, in their natural colors, principally for the bottom of dresses.'

3. Thread, a little finer than *passing, in silver gilt, silver wire, or one of the new synthetics which can be used threaded in a needle, unlike the thicker Japanese gold thread which must be couched. This is known as filé thread in the US.

tambour beading Method of attaching beads to fabric by means of tambouring. The same technique is employed as in tambour, but the beads are first threaded onto the continuous thread and the work is done with the wrong side of the fabric uppermost. Every time the hook goes down through the fabric and takes up the thread it leaves behind a bead which outlines the pattern. See also tambour (number 2), Lunéville work.

tambour thimble Thimble resembling a *finger shield but with a notch cut in the top. The thimble is worn on the left hand, and the notch receives and guides the metal hook when it appears underneath the frame in tambouring.

tammy cloth (tamis) Woollen cloth with a fine, even texture, originally used for sieving sauces. In the 18th and 19th centuries it was sometimes slightly glazed and often formed the ground fabric of samplers. It was also dyed in bright colours and exported to the West Indies.

Victorian: screen panel embroidered in silk and gold thread on satin, worked by Miss E. D. Bradby, and dated 1899.

Berlin bei L. W. Wittich Französische Str. No. 1845.

t'angka (tanka) Tibetan scroll painting or temple hanging. They are one of the glories of Tibetan art and usually show a cosmic diagram of a Buddhist deity surrounded by teachers, scholars, and scenes from his early life etc. Although generally painted on cotton, they were occasionally embroidered using the age-old appliqué method, and some of these, of the late 18th century, can be found in the Metropolitan Museum of Art (New York), the Newark Museum, and the Victoria and Albert Museum (London). (Lowry 1973)

t'angka: of applied and embroidered silk depicting a white Tara, 18th century.

tape measure (measuring tape) Length of linen tape, sometimes highly glazed or painted, marked with digits representing inches or centimetres, and used for measuring fabric. Today the utilitarian tape measure is plain white with black markings and two brass ends, but in the 18th and 19th centuries especially, they were very decorative additions to the workbox. They were often made of narrow ribbon wound on a pin which revolved in some kind of container, the measure being pulled through a slit. These containers could be made of ivory, bone, mother-of-pearl, Tunbridge ware, or any other material in any shape ingenuity could devise. Early measures (pre 1850) were often marked in nails (2¼ inches or 5.6 centimetres) and many had no digits, using instead the letters N, HQ, Q, H, and Y, standing for Nail (2¼

Wittich: example of a Berlin woolwork chart, produced by Wittich in the early 19th century.

tape measures: a collection dating from the 19th and early 20th centuries.

inches), Half Quarter (4½ inches), Quarter (9 inches), Half Yard (18 inches), and Yard (36 inches).

tapestry (opus saracenicum) Fabric with a pictorial design woven on a loom by a method different from that used in weaving cloth. In tapestry weaving there are numerous shuttles each containing a different colour, and instead of a single shuttle travelling across the entire width of the warp as in cloth weaving, each shuttle only goes as far as is needed for that particular colour and then turns back. The large tapestries which in the middle ages covered the walls of houses were gay and colourful and kept out draughts, and the majority told some story, often mythological, but these were only for the rich and well-to-do, and humbler people had to content themselves with stained or painted cloths. However in the 16th century the Elizabethans started to copy, if not tapestries themselves, the idea of tapestries in needlework, by using tent stitch in wool with some silk on canvas, and creating large pictorial pieces which could be hung on the walls as well as many smaller pieces. This practice continued into the 18th century, and because they simulated tapestries these pieces became known by the same name, giving

rise to a great deal of confusion. Nowadays in Britain, any piece of canvas work, large or small, is called tapestry work, which is a misnomer, while America, although not falling into that particular trap, calls canvas work needlepoint, which is also confusing as that word should apply to lace made with a needle.

tapestry needle (wool needle) Short needle with a large eye and a blunt tip used for wool work on canvas.

tapestry shading stitch see long and short stitch.

tapestry wool Strong, lightly-twisted wool in a large range of colours suitable for the coarser parts of canvas work (needlepoint). See also crewel wool, Paternayan wool.

tape work Type of embroidery which exploited the possibilities of ordinary linen tape. In the early part of the 19th century numerous lengths of narrow tape were joined with insertion stitches and treated as a fabric to be made into the high-waisted bodices then fashionable, both for women and children. Later, in the 1880s, a wider tape was used which was run in *chevron and drawn up.

tape work: bodice, early 19th century.

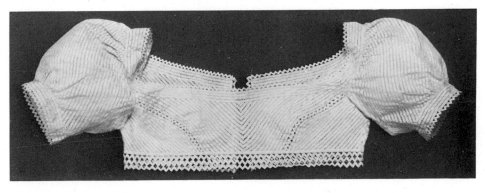

tapisserie d'Auxerre Popular in the middle and late 19th century, it consists of darning Berlin wools into a stiff, fairly large-meshed net. It could have beads added and was used for antimacassars or firescreens.

tassel Ornament consisting of a thick fringe of threads hanging from a metal or wooden mould or from a knob made of the threads. It may be purely decorative, used to give weight to a flimsy object such as a blind cord, or used to give a hold, as when on the end of a zip or zipper.

tassel stitch   see plush stitch.

Taylor, John (1580–1653) Thames waterman who was also called the Water Poet. He is chiefly known for his poem *The *Prayse of the Needle* which was printed in *The *Needle's Excellency* in 1640. This poem lists the stitches, domestic articles, and dress accessories in fashion at the time. In the book there were also six sonnets by Taylor praising famous needlewomen, and an ode to 'All degrees of both sexes, that love or live by the laudable imployment of the Needle'.

tele tirata Italian form of *drawn thread work of medieval times and later. There are two types: in the first, blocks of threads of both warp and weft are drawn out and the pattern is darned in

tele tirata: detail of Italian super frontal dating from the 17th century.

where necessary, the remaining threads being overcast to form an openwork background; in the second, the design is left as plain fabric and warp and weft threads are drawn from the background and overcast.

template Master shape cut in metal, wood, paper, ivory, or plastic. In patchwork it enables identical shapes to be cut from fabric, and in sewing it can be cut in a scallop or vandyke to use as a guide when working these patterns. It is also used in quilting.

tenchîfa (towel-scarf) Accessory used by women in Algeria at the public baths. It is a broad scarf, fringed at the ends and embroidered with patterns spread over the whole ground. These scarves are wound round the head, possibly several in succession, to dry the hair. (*Catalogue of Algerian embroideries* 1915) See also beniqa.

tension Term denoting how tightly a stitch is made. On a sewing machine a device regulates the tension or balance between upper and lower threads. Evenness of work implies perfect tension and is one of the criteria of good sewing.

tent (tenter)   see embroidery frame.

tent stitch (canvas stitch, continental stitch, cushion stitch, half cross stitch, needlepoint stitch, petit point)   One of the most generally used counted thread stitches, certainly dating from the 16th

tent stitch: worked horizontally.

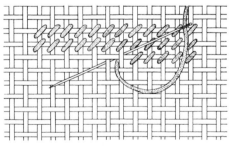

tent stitch: worked diagonally.

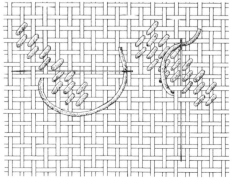

century and probably much earlier. It was frequently worked in Tudor households and professional workshops for the pictorial table carpets and hangings which often replaced the earlier tapestries, and later was worked on the finest possible scrim to make panels and pictures, as well as larger coarser work on upholstered chairs and sofas. In fact it has never gone out of fashion. Tent stitch can be worked either in horizontal rows, each stitch being taken diagonally over one thread, or in diagonal rows (basketweave stitch in America), which has the merit of not distorting the ground fabric and also of making a strongly woven back.

terry 'Loop raised in pile-weaving left uncut' (OED). The term can apply to any cloth which has uncut loops including a shaggy kind of cotton towelling, a velvet with uncut pile, or a poplin with silk warp and wool weft in which alternate warp threads are looped up to form a fine pile on the surface.

terylene filling (dacron filling, polyester fiberfill)   Modern filling for eiderdowns and quilts often considered preferable to the old sheep's wool or kapok on account of its lightness and washability.

tester Originally, the part of a four-poster bed behind the head which reached up to the top of the posts; now it means the canopy, which is either hung from the ceiling by chains or is held between the four posts. While the fabric covering the tester was often plain, in the sumptuous beds of medieval England and later it was considered part of the *bed furniture, and as such was embroidered.

textile Generic term applied to any fabric produced by weaving animal, vegetable, mineral, or man-made fibres on a loom.

Textile Museum (Washington DC) Comprehensive collection of textiles and carpets from the Americas, Near and Far East, Spain, Portugal, Africa, and Oceania. The Museum's *Catalogues Raisonnés* give complete illustrated lists and thorough historical and technical analysis about specific items in the museum.

texture Originally the product of any form of weaving, but now generally taken to mean the characteristics of weaving, such as the smoothness, thickness, or type of pattern. In embroidery this definition is enlarged to include the qualities with relation to the thickness or fineness of the thread used, its suppleness or stiffness, and whether it is smooth or knobbly. In modern work the use of texture plays a very important part.

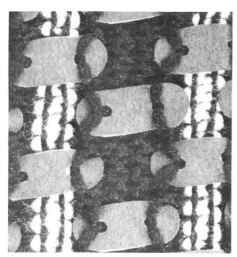

texture: French cloth, wool, suede and linen.

thimble Rigid cap for the second finger of either hand, used to protect the finger when pressing the needle through fabric. They can be made in any metal or combination of metals, with tops either matching the sides or of semi-precious stones, or they can be made of bone, ivory, mother-of-pearl, porcelain, wood, leather, plastic, or glass. Some thimbles, notably those used by tailors and the Chinese, have no tops and the side presses the needle. In fact it is a matter of opinion as to whether the top of the finger or the side does the work, and needleworkers have differing ideas on this. Usually both the sides and top are pitted with small indentations to stop the needle from slipping, but in porcelain and some other types only the top has them. Today it is possible to find very small thimbles in antique shops, and also series of them where one fits into another. These were not for dolls but for very small children, for sewing was a craft girls learnt very young, and before the present day everyone used a thimble and it was often a prized possession. See also sailor's palm.

thimble: a collection from the 19th and 20th century.

Thomas, Mary (1889–1948) Born Mary Hedger in Cheltenham, Gloucestershire, she went to New York in 1911 to work as a fashion journalist, but was also a gold medal pianist. During the First World War she served with the Women's Nursing Corps in France and married W. A. Thomas, and after the war they started an unsuccessful school in Nantes, France. In 1922 she joined the *Gentlewoman* magazine and went on to edit its successor, *Needlewoman*, a popular English journal of the 1920s and 30s. It was not until 1933 that she began to write her well-known books, *Mary Thomas's Dictionary of Embroidery Stitches* (1934), *Mary Thomas's Embroidery Book* (1936), and *Mary Thomas's Knitting Book* (1938).

thread Fine cord made from the fibres or filaments of any vegetable, animal, or synthetic material, spun to a considerable length; it is especially such a cord made from two or more of these fibres or filaments twisted together. In needlework this definition is extended to all material with which it is possible to sew, including animal sinew and intestines, metal wire, and metal beaten thin and wrapped round a vegetable core. See also embroidery threads.

thread canvas Hempen canvas used for the ground of carpets and rugs in the 19th century.

thread holders Cases of varying sizes, shapes, and designs in which threads, especially silk, were kept clean and untangled. They could be in the form of a book with separate leaves for each skein, or flat pieces of fabric with tape stitched across at intervals allowing the skeins to be put in singly, and the case to be rolled up and tied. Most of these were homemade, but one commercial type was Schroeder's Practical Thread Holder for Art Needleworkers.

thread winders: an assortment illustrating the various shapes, sizes and materials.

thread winders Small objects of bone, ivory, mother-of-pearl, wood, or glass cut into shapes which would hold a thread when wound round them. These varied from a rectangle with indentations to a shape resembling a snowflake. Some thread winders fitted into 18th and 19th century workboxes. See also skein holder.

three-sided stitch see point turc.

throat plate see cover plate.

thrum Warp ends and waste thread left after weaving, generally applying to the waste from carpet-making which is nowadays sold for domestic rug-making. In his *Voyages* Hakluyt describes Persian rugs made from coarse 'thrummed wool so well dyed that neither rain, wine nor vinegar will stain them', and in the inventory of John Skelton of Norwich (1611) is '5 ould thrum cushions'.

thummel see sailor's palm.

Thurstone, Mary and Sarah The names on two coverlets, one in the Fitzwilliam Museum, Cambridge (Mary Thurstone), and one in the Victoria and Albert Museum, London (Sarah Thurstone). These coverlets, both dated 1694, are nearly identical, but their origin is uncertain. They each contain a Shield of Arms of Thurston of Challock, quartering Woodward, and they are particularly interesting in that the design is of a very definite chinoiserie type which was much more usual about thirty years later. (Colour illustration p 251)

Tiahuanaco embroidery Worked in the highlands of Peru about AD 600, it consisted of cotton embroidered with wool in darning stitch, showing figures on chequered ground similar to those found on th monolithic Gateway of the Sun at the ceremonial centre at Tiahuanaco near Lake Titicaca. Tiahuanaco, better known for tapestries than embroideries, held religious domination of Peru at this period, with an auxiliary centre at warmer Huari. An example of this work is in the Metropolitan Museum of Art, New York. (Means 1930)

Tibetan appliqué The most widespread needlework art in Tibet. It is used to decorate clothing, house furnishings, tents, banners, and hangings worked on felt or leather with applied silk. Many details are couched with coloured silks. See also t'angka.

ticking Very closely-woven twill-weave fabric used as a covering for pillows, bolsters, and mattresses. It was originally linen but is now generally cotton, is usually striped, and is very strong. When soaped inside it becomes downproof.

ticking work The stripes on *ticking make it a fabric suitable for very decorative, gay, and bold embroidery, and it has been used in this way at least since the 18th century when it was sometimes embroidered and then made up into shoes. In the late 19th century, ticking was considered suitable for 'a modern embroidery worked in imitation of the

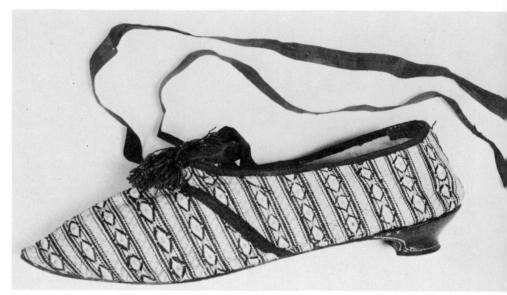

ticking work: late 18th century English shoe.

bright and elaborate embroideries executed in Arabia, Persia, and Turkey, and one which reproduces the gorgeous colouring for which they are celebrated, without the same amount of labour being expended' (Caulfeild and Saward 1882). These were then made up into articles such as summer carriage rugs, garden chairs, parasol covers, bags, and cushions, and as well as the stitching, velvet and china ribbons were used. In the mid 20th century, the work is generally used for chair seats, the strength of the fabric making it very suitable.

tidy 1. In America, a length of fabric, often highly decorated, used to cover the backs of chairs or sofas; also an *antimacassar. 2. In England, a small bag, either floppy or stiff and decorated with embroidery or beadwork, which is hung on a dressingtable mirror for collecting hair combings; also a hair tidy.

tie see bar.

tinsel Originally ornamentation on fabric in gold and silver in the form of threads, spangles, or strips which made the fabric sparkle. Later the word became more applicable to the sparkle than to the precious metal. And now tinsel means a flattened copper wire of various widths and thicknesses electroplated to give it a silver, gold, or other coloured surface. It is also anything which glitters.

tinsel embroidery Popular late 19th century embroidery on net, tulle, or thin muslin in gold or *tinsel thread. It was an imitation of Turkish embroideries on fine fabrics, and consisted of simple designs darned in outline with a few filling stitches.

tissue Word meaning any fabric or woven textile, but it is usually employed in a more specific sense, applying originally to a rich fabric woven with metal threads, and now to a thin, gauzy, delicate fabric sometimes interwoven with metal threads.

tissue basting See transferring designs (number 2).

tobacco pouch Bag often made of skin decorated with beads, reindeer hair, moosehair, or quillwork, which contains tobacco for smoking or chewing and keeping it dry. These pouches are used by many tribes in the northern hemisphere, from the American Indians to the Nurmichan group of peoples in Arctic Asia. In late Victorian England, tobacco pouches which rolled up were embroidered by ladies as presents for their friends and relations.

toile 1. Linen cloth; also, in the late 19th century, a dress fabric made of silk and linen. 2. The basic design of a dress made up in muslin from which the dress itself will be cut; also the shape of a person cut out in muslin and used as the basis for any garment made for that person. In America this is known as a sloper. 3. The pattern of a piece of bobbin lace as distinct from the ground.

toile cirée (American cloth, wax cloth) Oiled cloth made to look like leather and used in upholstery, but it can also be used in place of parchment in some forms of cutwork. It is tacked under the work, keeps the shape of the squares perfect and, as it is smooth and shiny, the needle slides along its surface instead of going through.

toilet case Case, usually for travelling, made to hold toilet necessities such as comb, mirror, clothes-brush etc. These have been made at most dates in the style of the time, and some of the most charming are those of the 17th century which are often embroidered in metal threads or silk damask.

tomb cover Cloth, sometimes embroidered with a portrait of the deceased, used mostly in Romania and Russia during the middle ages up till about 1700 to cover a tomb as an act of reverence. They differ from the Western *pall in that way are made for one specific tomb, and are put on it after burial, not on the coffin before burial. (Johnstone 1967)

top The completed patchwork part of a quilt—the blocks, set, and border if pieced, or the whole design if applied—ready to be quilted to the wadding and lining.

top sewing (oversewing, overhanding) Used to join selvage and folded edges, for *print patches, to attach tapes etc. It consists of holding the two edges together and working a small even stitch over and through both edges on the right side. See also seaming and oversewn seam.

top sewn seam see oversewn seam.

top stitch In plain sewing and dressmaking the stitching of a seam on the top of the work so that the stitches show and become a decoration.

Torah ark curtain (parokheth) Curtain which hangs in front of or behind the doors of the Holy Ark (the place in a synagogue where the Torah is kept).

Torah ark curtain: in violet silk with appliqué and embroidery, Italian, 1681.

They are often elaborately embroidered and are drawn closed when the Torah is not in use.

Torah mantle Protective, decorative sleeve-like covering for the Torah, often made of brocade or embroidered velvet.

toran Embroidered *frieze with a row of pointed pendants at its lower edge, hung over the lintel of a door or a window on festive occasions in Kathiawar, India. These were richly embroidered in strong colours in silk on silk, and sometimes had discs of mirror glass added. (Irwin and Hall 1973) (Colour illustration p 252)

toscas see rocailles.

tow 1. Short irregular fibres of flax, hemp, or jute, left after the long fibres have been spun. When packed together they make useful padding for various purposes. 2. Short fibres, spun and woven into a coarse, tabby-weave fabric, used in America in the 18th and early 19th centuries as a base for *yarn sewn rugs.

towel Cloth usually made from linen, hemp, or cotton, and used for drying either the body or some object. They have always been an indispensable item in any home, and while generally plain, some countries have a tradition of embroidered towels, especially in eastern Europe. In the Greek Islands and Turkey particularly, towels are embroidered in stitches worked by the counted thread as well as freehand stitchery, and in a number of countries *show towels are common. In parts of North Africa embroidered towel-scarfs (*tenchîfa) are used to wind round the head after a bath.

towel: with embroidered ends, Greek Islands.

toys: made of felt, c. 1950.

toys The craft of making embroidered toys, some so charming as to be ornaments rather than toys, has received an enormous impetus in the last fifty years. There have always been decorated toys for children, but from the needlework point of view these seem to have been confined to dolls and their clothes. Unfortunately, few examples from before the 17th century remain and there is no record of what loving parents and nurses have made for their children. From the 18th century, however, more is known as there are many dolls in existence from this time with exquisitely made clothes, as well as doll's houses with the hangings, carpets, and clothes all embroidered. In the 19th century the emphasis was still on dolls, sometimes with elaborate trousseaux, but with the 20th century more people turned to toy-making as a relaxation, and today there are many beautiful and ornamental toys made from felt and other fabrics.

tracing paper Thin paper, sufficiently transparent for a design underneath to be traced through. In America, tracing paper (or copying paper) means coloured waxed paper used mainly in dressmaking. In *1857* *Godey's Lady Book* advertised 'The patterns in this number can all be readily copied by using our copying paper. Price 25 cents a package, containing several colors.'

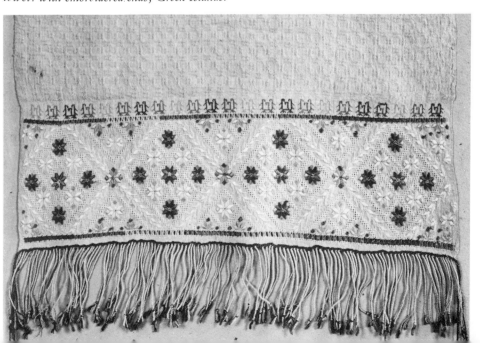

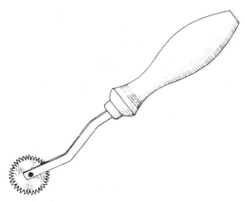

tracing wheel Tool consisting of a rowel set into a shaped piece of steel and fitted to a wooden handle, which can be used to transfer designs or marks onto some fabrics. The tracing wheel is run over the outline of the design, which is drawn on fairly thin or tissue paper, to make a series of small pricks in the fabric below; these are then painted or otherwise consolidated.

trade cards The study of the cards prepared as advertisements for individual shops and craftsmen can be a source of interest and enlightenment, and those of embroiderers to be found in the Heal collection in the print room at the British Museum (London) are no exception. They are very decorative, often show tools or dress and tell of such interesting matters as that C. Clark is not only a tambour worker but also teaches 'Lady's the Tambour at half a Guinea Each' and does drawings for needlework; that Andrew Hercloms of Drury Lane who is a tailor and habit maker also does 'embroidery in the newest taste'; and that Goodwin and Hazelhurst, embroiderers of Leicester Square do 'Court Dresses, Epaulettes, Waistcoats, all sorts of Ornamental Embroidery and Tambour', with 'Foreign Orders duly attended to'. Trade cards can also be found in a number of provincial record offices and libraries.

trade goods Items, usually cheap and of European manufacture, used by white traders as barter with primitive peoples in exchange for valuable raw materials such as furs, ivory, and land. Trinkets and cloth were especially popular, as were needles, ribbons, and beads, which radically changed the embroidery forms of the North American Indians. The 1748 trade list for the *Hudson's Bay Company lists large Milk Beads valued at 1 Beaver skin for $\frac{1}{2}$ pound of beads; Beads of Colours—$\frac{3}{4}$ pound per beaver skin; and Beads of All Sorts—1 pound for two beaver skins. A reverse trade of souvenirs 'in the native taste' was established by popular demand from Europe, and included Indian mocassins, birch bark

boxes decorated with quills or moosehair, and other small curios. The *Ursuline nuns in Canada worked many of these Indian souvenirs themselves to support their convents. (Ewers 1945, Turner 1955)

Intertribal bartering of goods in North America was prevalent before the arrival of the white man, and included utilitarian objects like baskets and pottery, and especially items which could be strung as beads or used for decoration: walrus ivory from the north; clam, oyster, and periwinkle shells from the east; odd-shaped, highly-coloured shells from the south; freshwater pearls from the midwest; dentalium, abalone, and olwella shells from the Pacific; animal teeth, especially elk, from the Great Plains and the Rockies; turquoise from the Pueblo country; and bear claws from several regions. By the time the first white explorers arrived, the Dakotas (*Sioux) possessed wampum from the Atlantic and dentalium from the Pacific. (Terrell and Terrell 1974)

tram The *weft of a fabric, especially applied to silk tram which is two or more single threads loosely twisted together and used for the weft of good quality silk fabrics. The meaning is extended to include the tramming of canvases, which is the laying of a thread of wool across the weft of the canvas in the correct colour to be used in the design. This serves two purposes: it fills out the stitch which will be worked over it and helps to hide any thread of canvas, and it serves as a reminder of the design and colours to be used. In America the word is sometimes spelt trame.

transfer ink Medium used to consolidate the design on a piece of fabric after pricking and pouncing or using a *tracing wheel. It is also used to draw a design on tissue paper which can then be ironed directly onto the fabric. Miss Lambert (1843) suggests a tablespoonful of spirits of wine coloured with indigo in which are dissolved small quantities of gum Arabic and sugar in equal parts, but the more usual recipe today is equal parts of Reckitts blue and caster sugar dissolved in enough water to make a thick cream. See also prick, pounce.

transfer pencil Heat-sensitive indelible pencil used to transfer designs from the wrong side of tracing paper onto fabric. The paper is put over the fabric and the design is ironed off.

transferring designs The transferring of designs onto the fabric to be worked has taxed the ingenuity of embroiderers all through the ages, and half-finished

transferring designs: detail of coarse linen sampler with outline designs, c.1600.

pieces of work from the 17th and 18th centuries show that this was probably undertaken by professional *pattern drawers, as the line is usually fine and without any form of smudge. For the average worker, many methods have been tried with varying degrees of success, often depending on the type of fabric to be embroidered, and are as follows. 1. Iron-on transfers, first invented by three employees of the firm of William Briggs in 1875. 2. For velvet or other fabrics which will not take an inked line, drawing the design on tissue paper which is tacked onto the velvet; the design is outlined with running stitches through the fabric and the paper pulled away. 3. Dressmaker's carbon paper, which is waxed and can be used with a *tracing wheel. 4. Pricking and pouncing: see prick, pounce. 5. *Transfer pencil or *transfer inks. 6. Ironing or drawing the design onto a piece of tarlatan (a stiff openweave muslin) which is laid over the fabric and the design painted over; just enough paint will go through the tarlatan to make a clear but not heavy outline. 7. From *Cranford* by Mrs Gaskell (1851) it is learnt that '. . . she had also once been able to trace out patterns very nicely for muslin embroidery, by dint of placing a piece of silver paper over the design to be copied, and holding both against the window-pane while she marked the scallop and eyelet holes.'

trapunto (stuffed quilting) Form of *quilting which consists of a main fabric, often silk but sometimes linen, and (as in italian quilting) a lining of muslin or scrim. The design is worked through both layers in running or back stitch, and then, to bring the design up into relief where required, the threads of the backing are pulled apart and small pieces of soft wool or cotton wool are inserted. This is a very old form of quilting and the well-known Sicilian quilt dating from about 1395 which shows the Legend of Tristram, is worked by this method. It is often combined with false and cord quilting, and there is much scope for modern designs to be tried out using all these methods together.

Traquair, Mrs Phoebe (1852–1936) Irishwoman who spent her married life in Edinburgh and became one of the foremost artist/craftswomen of Scotland. She was a considerable mural painter, an enameller, jeweller, illuminator, and also an excellent embroiderer. She worked largely within the conventions of her time, but her drawings of flowers, beasts, and insects are meticulous and translate beautifully into embroidery. (Morris 1966)

Traquair: linen table cover embroidered in crewel wools, 19th century.

tray cloth Being small, flat, and able to show off work well, tray cloths are favourite articles for beginners to embroider. They may be any size according to the tray and worked in any technique, so long as they are washable and stand up to ironing.

Tree of Jesse Design used in ecclesiastical embroideries of the middle ages in which a tree springs from the body of Jesse, and on each branch is one of his descendents, including David and Solomon, culminating in Jesus Christ on the topmost branch. Sometimes each figure is in a *roundel on its particular branch.

Tree of Life Oriental design based on the age-old conception of the Tree of Knowledge of Good and Evil in Paradise. This conception was known in Hebrew and in Hindu mythology and the Tree of Life in various forms has been widespread in art, especially that deriving from the East. The design appears under various names in American patchwork, where it was probably adapted from oriental rugs—willow tree, tree everlasting, and pine tree are some of the forms it took. In England, 17th century hangings were said to have been based on the Indian Tree of Life design, but it is now considered that they are more likely to have come from the earlier Flemish and French verdure tapestries.

Tree of Life: detail of a Turkish embroidered hanging, late 17th century.

trellis work Embroidery dating from the 1870s which was intended to represent plants climbing over a trellis. Material such as toile cirée represented the trellis, with sateen and cretonne for leaves and flowers. They were all pasted onto a linen backing, buttonholed to it, and the spare linen was cut away. See also Roman cutwork.

Trevelyon: from one of his embroidery designs.

Trevelyon, Thomas English author of a miscellany dated 1608 and another completed in 1616, both of which contain, among other things, patterns suitable for embroidery. Very little is known about Trevelyon but Nevinson (1968) deduces that he was a writing-master who probably worked in Blackfriars or the Strand in London. The most notable point about his drawings is that they are not obviously related to either the contemporary English samplers or to the Italian lace and embroidery pattern books of that date.

triangle Shape frequently used in patchwork. It is often half a square, but may also be equilateral or of other proportions.

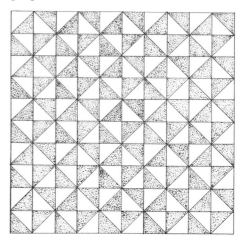

Trinity Christian symbol of the Father, Son, and Holy Ghost, separate but indivisible, and interpreted in various ways: as two linked equilateral triangles; the triple leaves of an anemone plant; the clover leaf or trefoil; or as a device consisting of a central circle linked by three arms to three circles which are joined in a shield shape, proclaiming both the separateness and the oneness.

trompe-l'oeil Picture which deceives the onlooker into thinking it is real. In embroidery such designs are rare, but they sometimes occur on worked upholstery or on card tables where the objects associated with gaming may be portrayed on the table as if they had just been thrown there. See also Conyers, Sophia.

trompe-l'oeil: detail of a card-table, possibly French, mid 18th century.

trou-trou Term used in the *Ladies' Home Journal* of 1895 to describe stamping or cutting out a pattern of flowers, arabesques, or other designs in a type of perforated or eyelet work. It added that whenever possible this work was to be done on a tightly woven fabric which would not need hemming.

true marking see brave bred stitch.

trunk covers see suitcase covers.

tuck Fold running straight with the grain of fabric, which is stitched in a variety of ways. There may be one tuck, or a series of tucks all of one width or of graduated widths, which may be purely ornamental or, when vertical, a means of controlling fullness. Horizontal tucks in children's clothes allow for extra fabric to be let out as the child grows. Tucks can be machined, run by hand, hemstitched, or worked with a shell edge, and it is possible to make narrow ones which are not straight with the grain, but this usage is rare. In the US tucks put in to allow for fabric shrinkage are called wash tucks.

tucker see attachments.

tufting 1. Alternative word for *candlewick. This is thought of as a craft known no earlier than the 18th century, but in the Hardwick Hall inventories of 1601 is 'fowre Curtains for the windowes of grene and yellowe tufted sacking' (Boynton 1971), which does not sound like a pile-woven fabric (often known as 'tufted') but more like a hand-decorated fabric. 2. Method of holding all the layers of a cover together without quilting. A thread is taken through all layers leaving an end about 2 inches (5 centimetres) long and a back stitch is made and drawn up firmly. A reef knot

tufting: detail of a bedspread dated 1819 from the Index of American Design.

is then tied and the ends cut off to about $\frac{1}{3}$ inch (1 centimetre). It is often found on crazy quilts and the quilts of The *Mountain Artisans in America, while in England, where the quilting of patchwork is not so general, it is a common method of finishing off patchwork and is more usually known as tying or knotting. It is also used with leather buttons to secure hair mattresses and upholstery.

tulle embroidery Type of embroidery worked on the light ball dresses of the young in the 19th century, and now generally confined to wedding veils. Tulle, a fine silk bobbin net, is worked with self-coloured floss silk in darning or satin stitches in a very simple design, using the holes in the net as a guide. See also net embroidery.

tunic Garment derived from the tunica of the Greeks and Romans, differing in shape at different periods. 1. Body garment or coat worn by men and women in medieval times, usually under a cloak or mantle. 2. Vestment worn by subdeacons and clerks assisting at the service of the Eucharist. In cut it resembles the dalmatic but has narrower sleeves, and being worn by less important people it is generally plainer. It may have borders and apparels of embroidery, and also orphreys and fringes. 3. Military surcoat of the middle ages. 4. Close-fitting jacket with a tight standing collar worn by the military in the 18th, 19th, and 20th centuries, and by other bodies such as policemen and firemen in the 19th and 20th centuries. 5. Women's overdress worn in the 19th and 20th centuries over a longer skirt, and often highly decorated and embroidered. 6. Schoolgirl's uniform.

Turcoman tribes Nomads who before the end of the 19th century wandered over parts of the Central Asian steppes, westward and south from the Caspian Sea. In the 20th century they have been partly domiciled in Turkmenistan, Persia (Iran), and Afghanistan, and now their

Turcoman tribes: woman's silk paranji, *early 20th century.*

old tribal life and their indigenous crafts are disappearing before the onslaught of the tourist trade. Originally they had very little contact with outside cultures and their crafts (mainly weaving, carpetmaking, and embroidery) and the designs they used followed their own lines. The men felt that decoration on costume was not for them, and embroidery was concentrated on the tents, horse and camel furniture, tent and other smaller bags, and the clothing of the women. They used patchwork combined with stitchery, and also many flat stitches, originally worked in silk but now in mercerised cotton. Hooked stems and symmetrically paired hooks are prominent among the designs they use. 'Allgrove 1973)

Turkey For many centuries Turkey was at the centre of the powerful Ottoman Empire, and is equally poised between East and West on some of the oldest trade routes in the world. So the Turks have had access to the best silks, both threads and fabrics, from Persia and India as well as those produced at Constantinople from the 7th century, and also to metal threads, Indian cotton, and Egyptian linen. Being a mainly Moslem country, the designs show stylised plants and foliage and swirling curves, with a minimum of human and animal figures. Embroidery is worked on many domestic articles—towels, hangings, cushion

Turkey: a 19th century cushion cover.

covers, and on women's costume, especially mantles. Nowadays Turkish needlecraft is generally thought of in connection with turkey work, turkey red, Turkey carpets, and point turc or turkish stitch.

turkey red Term referring to a brilliant scarlet colour, or to cotton cloth, generally twill-woven, dyed that colour. The technique of producing this dye (a blend of madder red and fat with nutgalls and a red mordant) was evolved in Turkey but its use became general. In the second half of the 19th century it was used a great deal in patchwork, many bedcovers being made in red and white, and it was also combined with holland to enliven rather prosaic children's dresses.

turkey wool Six-ply wool used in commercial carpet-making and by the domestic rugmaker for a thick-pile rug, generally hooked.

turkey work In the 16th and 17th centuries, carpet knotting practised in England by both professionals and amateurs, copied from the carpets imported from Turkey and the Levant. From the amount still to be seen (at Aston Hall, Hardwick Hall, and Norwich Cathedral among other places), it must have been a craft which enjoyed great popularity, and it was used for upholstery on farthingale chairs as well as on bigger chairs and cushions. The wool was knotted into a heavy-weave linen canvas, and was sometimes combined with cross stitch. Designs clearly

show the difference between home-produced turkey work, with its rather stiff, angular Stuart flowers, and that which was imported. The set of twelve cushions, of which ten are now in Norwich Cathedral, was made for the use of the aldermen when using Blackfriars Hall in Norwich as a council chamber, and was given by the then mayor in 1651.

Turkish embroidery 1. Type of embroidery popular in the 1880s in both America and England and based on Turkish designs. It was worked on toile colbert, a thin open canvas, with silks, gold thread, and tinsel, and the patterns were outlined and then filled in with various stitches. After working, the design was cut from the canvas and applied to velvet or plush. Turkish embroidery was considered suitable decoration for furniture covers, sheets, picture frames, tidies, and piano furniture. 2. See Turkey.

turkish stitch see point turc.

turning 1. The amount of fabric allowed on an unfinished edge for folding under. 2. The amount of fabric beyond the seam line allowed when cutting out, in other words, the seam allowance. 3. In knitting, making the heel of a sock or stocking. 4. Thrifty method of prolonging the life of a garment by unpicking the seams and remaking after reversing the fabric.

tweezers see burling irons.

twill weave Form of *weave in which a diagonal line is produced in the fabric. In each line of weft a different series of warp threads is covered, though always in the same relation: for example 2×1 means that in the first row the shuttle goes over two warp threads and under one, and the second row repeats the pattern one thread further along. There can be several varieties of twill, 2×2, 3×1, 4×2, and so on. Twill-woven fabrics are stronger than *tabby-woven ones.

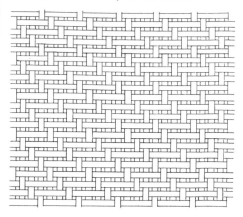

twist 1. Shape used in quilting resembling the twist in rope. 2. Thread formed of two or more strands spun hard together, as in buttonhole twist. This is an old as well as modern use of the word, and in the Hardwick Hall inventories (1601) is 'a tester of oring and murry coloured velvet imbrodered with gold and silver twist', and another reference from the same inventory implies a fine cord couched on: 'of red cloth layde on with twyst of white thread' (Boynton 1971). 3. Measure consisting of a number of twists in one inch of cotton.

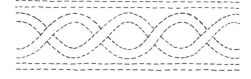

twisted gold see skanny.

twisted knot stitch see french knot.

two-sided cross stitch see brave bred stitch.

two-sided line stitch (two-sided stroke stitch) see double running stitch.

tzut Square cotton textile embroidered with stylised symbols and animals and used as the ceremonial head-dress of men in Guatemala. They are available in various sizes for use as handkerchiefs, hatbands, and baby slings. (Kelsey and Osborne 1952)

ubrús Russian name for an icon cover, a towel or scarf embroidered at both ends with a powdering in the centre, which was hung over the icon. More elaborate ones, made of as many as five different pieces resembling a frame, were embroidered in gold and silver thread, silks, tassels of gold and silver, and strings of pearls. (Tolmachoff 1947)

underbraider see attachments.

underside couching Method of *couching metal threads, generally used in the opus anglicanum of the middle ages, in which no tying-down thread is visible. The couching thread, of well-waxed linen, is underneath the work and is brought to the surface at regular intervals to encircle the metal thread, and is put back through the same hole as it came up. With a sharp tug a tiny loop of metal thread is pulled down to the back and held there. The secret of this technique had been lost until, at the beginning of this century, it was rediscovered by Louis de Farcy who called it point couché rentré ou retiré. This method makes for much longer wear than surface couching, as in gold work it is usually the couching threads which give way, leaving the strands of metal threads loose. (Christie 1906)

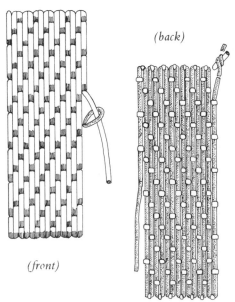

(back)

(front)

uniform The dress of a particular group of people, which is similar in most respects. Often the differences are shown by embroidery, as in the motifs on blazer pockets or the epaulettes or arm badges on military uniform.

union Fabric made with the warp of one fibre and the weft of another, as for example a silk warp and woollen weft, or a linen warp and cotton weft.

United States of America Native Indian embroidery, worked in available materials, was established long before the first European settlers came to America in the early 17th century, bringing with them household objects decorated with current forms and patterns of traditional European needle arts. Crewel embroidery, canvas work, quilting, and samplers, as well as plain sewing, were familiar to most colonists and later immigrants, and they adapted local materials—flax, indigo, native dyes, and wool—to their traditional forms to decorate useful objects such as bed furnishings, yarn sewn rugs, pockets, wallets, and petticoats. Economical surface stitches were used to conserve thread and patterns tended to be open.

By the mid 18th century, living had become easier and money more plentiful. Crewels, dress and embroidery silks, fine linens and canvas, wallpapers, and patterned textiles were imported. Dame schools taught basic sewing and embroidery, as well as the 'three Rs'. Finishing schools in the East Coast cities offered classes in tambour, sprigging, darning, catgut, French quilting, lace work, painting, and drawing. The Moravian School in Bethlehem, Pennsylvania, was founded in 1749 and rapidly established a reputation for exquisite floral and picture embroideries. Mourning and portrait embroideries as well as print work were fashionable, and also needle laces, mulls embroidered in tambour and various embroidery stitches, quilting (often stuffed), and candlewicking. However most of this American needlework continued to be influenced by European modes. Berlin woolwork, with patterns and wools imported from Germany, was fashionable in the 1830s. Encouraged by

the ladies' magazines, by the third quarter of the 19th century it had become the most popular form of embroidery. During this time various other embroideries reflecting foreign origins were also worked, such as embroidered morocco leather, Ayrshire and Mountmellick whitework, and pieced and appliqué quilts. The quilts were a household necessity and were evolved as an American form from the economy of the scrap box to the luxury of calculated patterns in new materials.

In 1872 the *Royal School of Needlework in England reintroduced and taught Georgian and Stuart forms of embroidery (as a reaction against Berlin woolwork), and these were exhibited at the Centennial Exposition in Philadelphia in 1876. The great interest generated by this exhibition revived concern for producing high quality needlework in America. Various societies were created as part of this revival, including the Deerfield Society of Blue and White Needlework, Society of Decorative Arts, and exchanges for women's work, which have continued to this day. Needleworked pictures, decorative household articles, and costume accessories continued to be worked in various types of embroidery, many of which were introduced through the *Modern Priscilla* and other women's magazines.

Needlework has again gained popularity during the third quarter of the 20th century, including crewel and canvas work (needlepoint), and quilting, some retaining the old patterns and stitches, some using new materials in traditional methods, and some using old methods and stitches in new patterns and combinations.

universal foot see attachments.

University Museum of the University of Pennsylvania Archaeological museum founded in 1887, containing one of the largest collections of artefacts of primitive cultures from all areas of the world, but especially strong on North, South, and Central America. Many items were gathered on university-sponsored archaeological expeditions, including the significant one by Max Uhle in 1901 which discovered the *Nazca culture. This expedition determined the distinguishing characteristics of various pre-Colombian periods. (Mason 1957, Marion 1974)

Untermeyer collection see Irwin Untermeyer collection.

upholstery 'Fabrics and materials used in the covering and stuffing of furniture' (OED). From the 16th century, chairs began to be generally used, and a number of them as well as stools and later sofas have been covered in needlework, usually in the form of canvas work (needlepoint), but also in applied and crewel work. The two essentials are that the embroidery is flat on the fabric with nothing loose to be caught and torn, and that it is hard

upholstery: an 18th century French armchair.

wearing, and so the most suitable medium is wool on cotton or linen. That these rules were generally kept can be seen by the large number of pieces of furniture which have survived with their coverings still in excellent condition.

urn rugs Small circular mats with an embroidered surface and a hard base surrounded with a raised woollen fringe. They were for standing first the tea urn and later the teapot on, to protect the table from heat. Frequently they were worked in Berlin wools, but Miss Lambert (1843) considers that the raised fringe should be made from worsted. In 1819 a shop in Norwich (England) sold 'worsteds, Canvas and Patterns worked and drawn for Urn and Tea-pot rugs etc'.

Ursuline nuns Roman Catholic order which was founded in Italy in 1535 by Angela da Brescia, spread to France in 1574, and then to America. In 1639 in Quebec, two French Ursuline nuns, one of whom was Marie de l'Incarnation, a skilled embroideress, started to teach needlework to Indian and white girls using European floral patterns in native materials—quill, moosehair, and buckskin. The order also taught embroidery in silk and cotton, beads and ribbonwork to the *Iroquois and Algonquin tribes, which

Ursuline nuns: detail from a tablecloth embroidered in dyed moosehair.

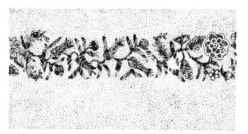

then spread from Maine to the Northwest Territory. In addition they were responsible for the embroidery of many beautiful vestments. See also Huron.

USSR It is impossible to talk about the embroidery of a country so vast as Russia in general terms, but there are a few main characteristics which seem to have been constant over the whole area through many generations. The first is a great love of brilliant colour. This is particularly noticeable in the states round the Black Sea bordering on Turkey and Persia (Iran) on one side and the Slav countries (Romania, Moldavia, and Czechoslavakia) on the other. It cannot be repeated too many times that art, in whatever form, does not stop at frontiers and strong influences from one country will always spill over into its near neighbours. Another characteristic is the barbaric splendour of much of the early work. The court of St Petersburg was never noted for restraint and many of the embroideries reflect this, being loaded with metal threads and jewels, especially pearls. Russia has produced great quantities of freshwater pearls and these have been liberally used in ecclesiastical as well as court embroideries and even on peasant costume, where head-dresses in particular have been festooned with them. The other type of embroidery prevalent in Russia is counted thread work on homespun linen or cotton. This resembles the embroidery found in most of eastern Europe and is worked on domestic articles such as sheets, pillow cases, towels etc, as well as on dresses. Examples of the headdresses can be seen in the Brooklyn Museum and the Cleveland Museum of Art.

USSR: embroidered net panel, 18th century.

valance: American, dated 1714.

valance Hanging drapery attached to a canopy, altar, top of a window frame, or bed (both from the tester and the frame). Generally they are gathered, pleated, formed into swags, or otherwise decorated with tassels or braid.

Valentine Museum (Richmond) One of the important research centres of the United States, it includes an extensive collection of costume materials, a manuscript collection containing a rare volume of embroidery patterns, textiles, and embroideries. Courses are held yearly as well as exhibitions of modern and historical needlework. See also embroidery design (number 2).

vandyke Notched, deeply-indented or zigzag border or edge, named after the shapes edging the collars portrayed by the painter Anthony Van Dyck or Vandyke (1599-1641).

vanishing muslin Stiffened, treated muslin which can be used as a backing for some kinds of hand and machine embroidery. The work is done through the main fabric and the muslin, and the surplus muslin vanishes when pressed with a warm iron.

vegetable parchment see parchment paper.

veil Fine muslin, crape, net, tulle, or silk, used in various ways to shade the face from sun, or to protect it from dust or the gaze of the curious; also a covering for a sacred object. 1. Bonnet veils: in the early 19th century these were tied round the brim of the bonnet and either hung down in front of the face or were thrown back. They varied in length from about 12 inches to as much as 36 inches (30 to 90 centimetres), and were embroidered in many different techniques, especially those of the net laces. 2. Bridal veils: cover for the head fastened with a wreath of fresh or artificial flowers, a tiara, or a coronet, usually worn over the face before marriage and thrown back after the ceremony. They may be of lace but sometimes tulle embroidery is used, as well as the net laces. At different times they have been several yards (metres) in length or quite short. 3. Eye veils: small veils which in the mid 20th century were frequently attached to the brims of small hats and reached to the nose. Often they were machine embroidered. 4. In churches, various sacred objects are usually kept veiled and only exposed on special occasions, while in some churches a *humeral veil is worn in the folds of which the priest lifts the monstrance or paten. See aumbry veil, chalice veil, monstrance veil.

veining 1. The making of any patterns resembling the veins on leaves, especially on muslin. 2. The joining of two pieces of fabric by embroidery stitches instead of a seam: in Ireland between 1830 and 1850 thousands of children between the ages of five and twelve received 1s 6d a week for this type of work. 3. The small ladder-like stitches used in whitework, especially Ayrshire embroidery, more generally known as *beading.

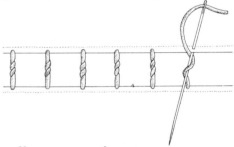

vellum see parchment.

velvet Fabric made from silk or nylon with a woven-in, short, dense pile. It was first made in the East, and was known in England in the 14th century, where it quickly became used for the richest garments and vestments. It can be plain or raised, in which case parts of the pile were left higher than others in pattern, giving a particularly sumptuous appearance. The best raised velvets come from Genoa (Italy) and Lyons (France). Using cotton or rayon thread the same weave gives velveteen, velours, or corduroy.

velvet: detail of boy's suit, American, c.1855.

velvet stitch   see plush stitch.

velvet woolwork   see french raised work.

velvet work   Embroidery on velvet is difficult because of the pile, and when the fabric has been enriched as for church vestments, it has been usual to work suitable motifs on linen and apply them to the velvet, only putting a few connecting stitches or tendrils onto the fabric itself. However in the late 19th century two other types of velvet embroidery are suggested by Caulfeild and Saward (1882): 1. outlining the pattern on raised or embossed velvet in silk or gold thread, and marking in any veins or flower centres of the design in silk with crewel or long satin stitches; 2. applying velvet to silk by pasting linen or holland to the back of the velvet, cutting out shapes and sewing them onto the silk, adding gold or silk outlines.

Venetian cutwork   see Roman cutwork.

Venezuelan drawn work   Type of 19th century embroidery from Venezuela which resembled ordinary *drawn threadwork except that instead of the bars and edges being overcast or buttonholed in linen thread, coloured purse silks were used.

Venice gold   Gold thread imported into England by the Venetian traders in the 16th and 17th centuries. It superseded the earlier *Cyprus or sipers gold, and in the 1582 *Book of Rates* is 'venice golde or silver the pound containing XII unces', rated at 54s 4d (Willan 1962). In the wardrobe account of Henry VIII (1533) is 'It'm for making a jacquette of blacke velvette, embrowdered with Venyse golde of our store, lyned with satten and cotton of oure greate wardrobe . . .' (Caley 1789).

vermicular   see meander.

vest   see waistcoat.

vestments   Word which nowadays generally refers to a set of ritual garments worn by clergy at the Eucharist service. It sometimes also refers to a complete set of furnishings for priest, assistants, and place of worship. A few of these garments are worn by sovereigns at their coronation, with the addition of mantles, gloves etc. There are some medieval sets of vestments, both ecclesiastical and lay, still extant, the most important being the following. 1. A set of *opus anglicanum from the shrine at Pontogny of St Edmund Rich, Archbishop of Canterbury

vestments: detail of the dalmatic from the Goss vestments, mid 15th century.

(1234-1240), now in Sens Cathedral (France). 2. A set in the Österreichisches Museum für Angewandte Kunst in Vienna, made by the nuns and used in the Benedictine nunnery of Goss in Styria. Its woven inscriptions date between 1239 and 1269. 3. The vestments of the Golden Fleece in the Weltliche und Geistliche Schatzkammer in Vienna. This is a tremendous set, large in number, technique and scope. The articles are in excellent condition and show the technique known as or nué at its best. 4. See coronation.

Victoria and Albert Museum (London) Museum with a superb textile section which includes lace, ecclesiastical embroidery, foreign and English embroideries and a very large collection of costume. It also has a big textile study room where students can look at examples of embroideries and fabrics from several centuries and from many countries.

Victoria and Albert Museum: German table cover.

Victorian: a long sampler.

Victorian Period in British history which spanned the long reign of Queen Victoria from 1837 to 1901. In needlework it saw far reaching changes, the greatest of which was the common use of the sewing machine which revolutionised both domestic and commercial sewing. In embroidery the period is generally thought of in connection with Berlin woolwork, broderie anglaise or eyelet embroidery, and William *Morris and his associates who influenced all matters of taste in craft work. The term often denotes the same period in America.

Vinciolo, Federic di Venetian designer of cutwork and lace who published in 1587 *Les singuliers et nouveaux pourtraicts et ouvrages de Lingerie. Servans de patrons a faire toutes sortes de poincts couppe, Lacis & autres.* This book, produced at the French court of Catherine de' Medici, ran through many editions until 1623 and the designs were used by numbers of needleworkers.

vine The symbol of the Blood of Christ, and as such used in many church embroideries, especially those to do with the service of Holy Communion.

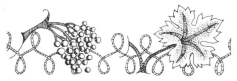

viteika Implement resembling a lace bobbin (without the beads) which was used in pearl embroidery in Russia. The pearls were threaded and wound round the viteika, so that the worker was able to pull the thread tight while sewing without handling the pearls. (Edwards 1966)

voided Word describing part of a design where the pattern is defined by what is left unworked rather than by what is put in, as in stencilling. Many oriental embroideries make use of this technique, and Assisi embroidery is another example where the design is voided, with only the background being worked.

voile Semi-transparent, tabby-woven fabric, plain or with self stripes and checks in the weave, or machine embroidered with spots or little motifs, used in the late 19th and 20th centuries mainly for blouses, children's dresses, and light curtaining. Voile with a tiny, evenly-spaced spot was much used for smocking in the 1930s on nightgowns and children's dresses, as the spot could be used as a guide for the gathering thread.

Voysey Charles Annesley (1857-1941) Influential English figure in the field of *art nouveau at the turn of the century. He was an architect who also designed textiles, needlework, metalwork, and furniture, and his work (more simplified in line than that of some of the other designers of his time) carried on from art nouveau to the *arts and crafts movement. Sadly there are no known embroideries from his designs to be seen anywhere, but a few of his designs are still extant, which clearly show his style.

Voÿsey: design for embroidery, 1903.

Ww

wadded quilting (Durham quilting) Best known and also the most basic, utilitarian, and possibly the most beautiful type of quilting, used extensively for bedcovers in Britain (particularly the north of England and Wales) and North America. It consists of a top of plain or pieced fabric, and interlining of sheep's wool, cotton batt, polyester, or old blanket, and a lining, all of which are held together by close running stitches in a series of patterns. It is the patterns and their arrangement which give this quilting its beauty; over the years certain shapes have been found to hold the layers well together, so they have been perpetuated, though different areas have had their favourites which now appear to belong to that district. The lining is put into a quilting frame and the interlining is laid over, with the top, on which the design has been marked, over all. Some quilters have been able to mark out their own designs, with the help of templates, but numbers have used the knowledge and skill of professional and semi-professional pattern drawers like George *Gardiner and Elizabeth *Sanderson.

wadded quilting: detail of an American coverlet in deep red cotton twill, 19th century.

wadding Fibrous carded wool, cotton, kapok, or synthetic filling, used as an interlining to conserve heat for articles such as quilts, comforters, tea and coffee cosies, etc. See also batting, padding.

waistcoat Garment normally associated with men but also worn by women, covering the body from neck to waist and usually worn, partly showing, under an outer garment. Those for men appeared in the 16th century and were originally underjackets of a contrasting colour which showed through the slashes and pinking of the top garment or doublet. By the mid 17th century they had become long vests (by which name they are still known in America) worn under coats, and during the early part of the 18th century they might or might not have sleeves, and were lavishly embroidered. Their length kept pace with the length of the coat, getting shorter as the century progressed, and they were often worn as a decorative contrast to the coat and breeches. As men's garments got more and more sober in the 19th century it was only in the waistcoat that a touch of

waistcoat: made for a wedding, c.1840.

flamboyance was allowed, and generally speaking that rule has held good until recently. Many suits for formal occasions are made with a waistcoat to match.

For the 16th century woman, waistcoat was synonymous with jacket or bodice and referred to those short garments, with sleeves or detachable sleeves, which were usually of white linen and embroidered all over. They were often given to Elizabeth I, as in 1588-1589: 'By the Baroness Lumley, a wastecoate of white taffety, imbrodered all over with a twist of flowers of Venis gold, silver and some black silke' (Nichols 1823). They remained short bodices during the early part of the 18th century after which they became part of a riding habit, and they did not become garments in their own right until the late 19th century when they were worn with the mannish tailor-made suit. Today they have come back into fashion, often knitted or crocheted, but sometimes worked in a very eye-catching style.

Waldstein vestments see Walston vestments.

Wallington Hall (Northumberland) House built in 1688, now owned by the National Trust. Needleworkers will be interested in the tent stitch panels and screens worked by Lady Julia *Calverley in the early 18th century, and in the modern panel worked by Mrs Dower, daughter of the late Sir Charles Trevelyan, the last owner of Wallington. It shows the history of the house and is worked in the same style as the screens.

wall pockets (comb pockets) Hanging wall pockets with three or four sections made in Europe during the 17th and 18th centuries. Usually of dark material, linen, leather, wool, or silk, they are gaily decorated with flowers and figures (often allegorical) in polychrome silks, and sometimes they are further embellished with ribbon bindings and metallic laces. (Schneider 1968) See also semainier.

yarn sewn rug: detail of an American needle-embroidered rug worked in wool on linen, early 19th century.

Walston vestments (Waldstein vestments) Splendid set of vestments consisting of a cope, now at the Victoria and Albert Museum (London), and two dalmatics, one at the Metropolitan Museum of Art (New York) and one at the Fitzwilliam Museum (Cambridge, England). They are thought to be Spanish, worked between 1500 and 1520.

Walston vestments: dalmatic, probably Spanish, 1500-20, above complete, below detail.

Yugoslavia: velvet waistcoat embroidered in gold twist, sequins, rough purl and gold braids, 19th century.

wampum Cylindrical white, purple, or black shell beads made from the inside of the quahog clam found along the New England coast. Manufacture of the beads was extremely difficult, which made them valuable both as ornament and as legal tender. The *Iroquois and other eastern tribes used wampum as money until the early 20th century.

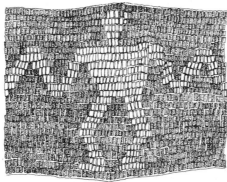

wampum: detail of a belt.

wangles Small inaccuracies in regular stitching needed to turn a corner or keep a pattern correct. It is necessary to wangle in many techniques, for example in canvas work (needlepoint) when changing from one stitch to another, or in lacis work when changing direction.

warp The strong hard-twisted threads which are fastened lengthwise in the loom. They are then interwoven by the weft threads to make the complete web or piece.

Warren, Mercy Otis (1728-1814) Skilled American needlewoman who lived at Barnstable, Massachusetts. She was the wife of James Warren and author of political dramas, poems, satires, and a history of the American Revolution. A canvas work (needlepoint) cardtable top, complete with cards and dice which she worked c 1754, is in the collection of the Pilgrim Society, Plymouth, Massachusetts.

wash blond Name frequently used in America for light-coloured, fine mesh *bobbin net used for ruffles and quilling, and as a background for darned net.

watch backs see watch papers.

watch bottoms see watch papers.

watch papers (watch backs, watch bottoms) Circles of paper or embroidery used as padding between the inner and outer cases of a verge watch in the 18th and 19th centuries. *The *Lady's Magazine* devoted several sheets to patterns for the embroideress, which were often plagia-

rised and sold for a shilling a sheet. Although intended for embroidery on fabric these were called 'papers' in the magazine but genuine papers are often of a later date and, while extremely decorative, they also give the name and address of the retailer or repairer, and act as a small trade card. In collections, care needs to be taken to distinguish between watch bottoms and bonnet crowns for babies, as these are of approximately the same size and shape and are in the same styles of embroidery.

watch pockets Elaborately beaded or embroidered pockets which usually hung on either side of the bed in the mid 19th century. They held the owners' watches during the night so that they were visible and accessible.

Water Poet see Taylor, John.

Watts, Isaac (1674-1748) English theologian and writer, who in 1715 wrote *Divine Songs for Children*. These are the source for many of the verses found on samplers.

wave Shape often used in embroidery, especially quilting. It may be a very stylised or a naturally-shaped wave.

wax cloth   see toile cirée.

weave   Method of interlacing the *warp and *weft of a web to form a distinctive pattern. The variation between fabrics lies in the relationship between the warp and weft threads, and in the numerical progression of the weft across the warp. See basket weave, chevron, gauze, nap (number 2), satin, tabby weave, twill weave.

web   Length of finished fabric taken from the loom.

Webb, Philip (1831–1915) English architect and designer who after his training became principal assistant to G. E. *Street. He met William *Morris in 1856, and in 1859 he left Street and set up in private practice, designing furniture as well as houses, one of which was Morris's The Red House, at Bexleyheath, Kent. In 1861 he became one of the founder members of Morris, Marshall Faulkner & Co for whom he designed furniture, metalwork, glass etc. He was also interested in textiles and designed several pieces of embroidery for churches, including one for Deaconess House at Clapham. (*Catalogue of Morris Collection* 1969)

Webb: detail of a design for a superfrontal for Deaconess House, Clapham.

weft (woof)   The threads which cross from side to side of a web at right angles to the warp threads with which they are interlaced.

weight (weighted pillow)   see lead cushion.

welting   see piping.

Wessex stitchery   Method of stitchery evolved by Mrs Foster of Bath (England) in the early 20th century. She believed in creating pattern directly with the needle and in letting simple stitches, combined in many ways, form designs. She worked on handwoven linen with cotton, linen, or silk thread and said 'A Wessex needle . . . asks for no suggestion for pattern or design on paper or material; it can even produce good effects without any previous planning of the worker's thought and brain for it has stitches of its own by the use of which patterns will, as it were, evolve themselves . . .' (SNE 1934)

wheat   Symbol in ecclesiastical embroidery representing the Body of Christ and frequently used in designs on vestments and church furnishings, especially those to do with the service of Holy Communion.

Wheeler, Candace Thurber (1828–1923) American author, educator, and influential embroidery and textile designer. She was the founder in 1877 of the *Society of Decorative Art, and was a partner from 1879–1883 and president from 1883–1907 of the *Associated Artists. Her books, which reached a wide public, include *The development of embroidery in America, How to make rugs,* and *Principles of Home Decoration.*

Wheeler: detail, Consider the Lilies of the Field, *one of a pair of portières, 1883–1907.*

whip   To oversew a rolled edge. This can be used as a neatening stitch, or for making frilling—here the thread is drawn tight so that the edge is pulled into fine gathers which can then be sewn to a cuff, neck, collar, or wherever required.

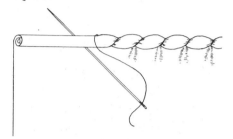

whitework   Term referring to any embroidery worked in white thread on a white ground, but especially to muslin embroidery, Ayrshire embroidery, broderie anglaise (eyelet embroidery), Madeira work, Renaissance embroidery, and Richelieu embroidery. It can also refer to plain sewing.

whitework: man's wedding shirt, c.1840.

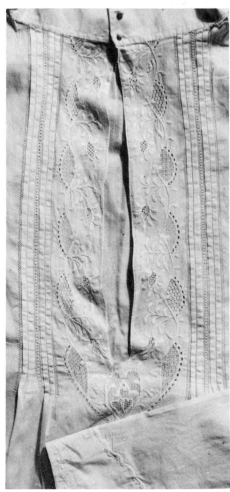

Whiting Collection   see Museum of International Folk Art, Santa Fé.

Whitman samplers: an example from the collection, worked by Mark Wiggin, 1797.

Whitman samplers Trade-name for a box of chocolates containing a 'sample' of each kind that the company made. The idea, devised in 1911, came from a stitchery sampler owned by the Whitman family, the name was suggested by an employee, and the top of the box, which has varied slightly over the years, is in an old sampler design. During the First World War when business was slack, instead of being laid off, the candy factory employees were sent to search out additional stitchery samplers, which were used as a changing display on the walls of the Whitman candy and ice cream shop in Philadelphia, and resulted in a large representative collection which is now in the Philadelphia Museum of Art (Pennsylvania).

Whitney Geoffrey English compiler and part author of a *pattern book published in Leydon in 1586 called *A Choice of Emblemes and other Devises for the most parte gathered out of sundrie writers, Englished and Moralized. And divers newly devised.* See also emblems.

Williamsburg (Virginia) The reconstructed capital of Virginia where 88 buildings dating from 1693 have been repaired and restored, 300 rebuilt on their original site, and 50 18th century gardens laid out—all creating a living museum, with craftsmen working and shops in operation. Collections include the Abbey Aldrich Rockfeller Collection of American Folk Art, decorative arts, and an extensive collection of sewing implements, textiles, and embroideries dating from before 1830.

wimpel Literally a binder, which in the Jewish faith referred to the swaddling bands worn by male babies at their circumcision. After the ceremony, the mother, if a good needlewoman, would embroider the name of the child with the date of birth and a prayer onto the binder, which might then then be used to bind the Scroll or Torah when this was not in use. See also Jewish ritual embroidery. (Cohen 1966)

wimpel: linen embroidered in silk, Germany, 1738.

Winchester Broderers see Pesel, Louisa Frances.

Winchester canvas Evenweave single-thread canvas with an attractive irregularity in the fibre. It was called this because it was produced as the ground fabric for all the canvas work (needlepoint) done for Winchester Cathedral in the 1930s under Louisa *Pesel, and it was found so suitable that it has been used for many other large projects since.

winding clamps see skein holder.

window carpets Length of fabric, often pile knotted or embroidered, hung against windows in Elizabethan England. They were considered of little importance in the furnishings of a room and would be indistinguishable from a table carpet or bedcover. (Digby 1963)

window curtains Coming later in time than bed curtains, window curtains were probably not much used before the 16th century, but once they were seen to be both useful and decorative they were quickly accepted as a necessary part of the furnishing of practically every room. They have often been made of fabric unornamented except by the weave or by printing, staining, or painting, but sometimes they were embroidered in the idiom of the period, either with an all-over design or with a decorated border and hem. It is interesting to note in the Hardwick Hall inventories (1601) that while the Pearl bed chamber had bed curtains of a rich heavily-embroidered fabric, there are only 'too Curtins for the windowes of darnix', a very poor, ordinary fabric (Boynton 1971). Not so many good examples of embroidered window curtains have lasted as well as other embroideries, largely due to the rotting effect light has on fabrics and to the fact that curtains are often pulled by hand, using just the part that has been weakened by the effect of light—the inside border.

window drapery   see drapery.

wine glass   Shape consisting of a circle (or base of a wine glass) overlapping other circles to form patterns, a much used quilting design.

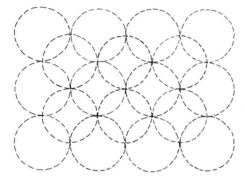

Winterthur (near Wilmington, Delaware)   Winterthur Museum and School of Decorative Arts is in an 1827 country residence inherited by Henry Francis Du Pont in 1929. It was converted into a museum in 1951 and now contains one of the most comprehensive collections of American Decorative Arts from 1640–1840, including 125 period rooms, furnishing fabrics, embroideries and sewing/work tables.

Winterthur: detail of an 18th century crewel work bedspread.

wire canvas   Fine wire mesh used in the second quarter of the 19th century as a ground for Berlin woolwork on hand firescreens. It had the advantage of being rigid so the background could be left unworked, the embroidery in the centre could be tidily backed, and the rest of the canvas left plain. This made a very light and attractive handscreen.

wire canvas: detail of an English handscreen c.1840.

witch stitch   see herringbone stitch.

Wittich, L. W.   Berlin printseller who, in 1810, was encouraged by his wife (an enthusiastic needlewoman who drew her own designs) to enter the new field of charts for Berlin woolwork. They made such a success of selling these hand-coloured cross stitch charts based on her designs as well as others, that for many years they led the field in producing the countless patterns which flooded Europe and America in the 19th century. (Colour illustration p 262)

women's organisations   Some women's organisations, particularly those devoted to the betterment of life in villages and small towns, have had a great influence on 20th century needlework. In most European countries as well as in North America and other parts of the world, confederations or groups meet together to discuss all the different facets which make up a good life, and needlework is one of their main subjects. Demonstrations are given and classes formed for many different handcrafts and the general standards of technique and quality of work are immeasurably improved.

Wood, Mrs St Osyth (1888–1972)   One of the finest amateur needlewomen in England in the 20th century. She lived at Bures in Suffolk and never taught but always inspired others by her meticulous

Wood: detail of a blackwork sampler typical of the 1930s.

craftsmanship. Her book of samplers worked during the Second World War and her embroidered casket are objects of great beauty, though like all her work completely traditional in style. She is also remembered for her work on the miniature Essex Model Home which was to show future generations what an English country house was like.

wool   Hair from the fleece of sheep and other similar animals, especially when cleaned, combed, or carded, and spun into lengths ready for use in weaving, knitting, crochet, sewing, or other crafts. The short fibres are carded, that is they are passed over wooden rollers covered with fine wires which remove impurities and produce a fine film of wool with the fibres lying at all angles. This makes a hairy cloth and one which will felt, that is, absorb moisture and thicken. The long fibres are combed before spinning which makes them lie parallel with each other, and produces a smooth cloth called *worsted. Wool is extremely versatile and can be woven into a felted cloth which is impervious to rain and an admirable protection against cold winds, or into a gossamer fine web such as the mousseline-de-laine so popular in the first half of the 19th century. In embroidery the most popular threads have been *crewel wools, used in crewel work from the 17th century onwards and also for so many tent stitch embroideries and chair and sofa covers; *tapestry wool, a thicker wool also used for upholstery; and in the 19th century, *Berlin wool, used for the innumerable articles and furniture covers worked in Berlin woolwork.

woollen canvas   German product used in the 1840s for Berlin woolwork where the background was not to be covered. It was made in claret, black, white, and primrose. (Lambert 1843)

wool needle   see tapestry needle.

wool-on-wool coverlet   Type of bed-cover made in the eastern states of America, consisting of large scrolled motifs worked with heavy wool yarn on a ground of wool blanketing, either by hooking or a combination of hooking and coarse needlework. It is also known as a 'bed rugg'. (Peto 1949)

woolwork Any embroidery worked in wool but more specifically canvas work (needlepoint) in wool.

woolwork: detail, flame stitch chair seat, American, 1740-50.

woolwork flowers Handmade flowers made into bouquets and other arrangements and usually put under a glass dome or shade in the mid 19th century. They were made by winding Berlin wool round a crinkled wire shaped like the petals and leaves of the chosen flower.

work 1. Piece of needlework or sewing on which a person is engaged. 2. Any form of needlework. 3. The art of embroidery or sewing, as in 'to work a buttonhole'.

workbox (work bag, work basket) Container for needlework and the tools used in needlework. Bags and baskets have been made in any and every style and material, some with compartments for tools, but some only suitable for carrying work from place to place. Boxes, on the other hand, have often been very beautiful and elaborate objects in their own right, especially those made between about 1770 and 1900. Generally they were of wood or papier-mâché, possibly veneered or inset with ivory or mother-of-pearl, or studded with cut steel. The interior might have a space at the bottom to hold small pieces of work and threads, while the tray would be fitted with scissors, thimbles, needlecase, threadwinders, wax, pincushion, and often other tools needed by the housewife, such as buttonhook, pencil, nut pick, vinaigrette etc. This tray, covered with velvet or satin, would have impressions so that each tool fitted exactly into its own compartment. Unfortunately many of the old boxes found

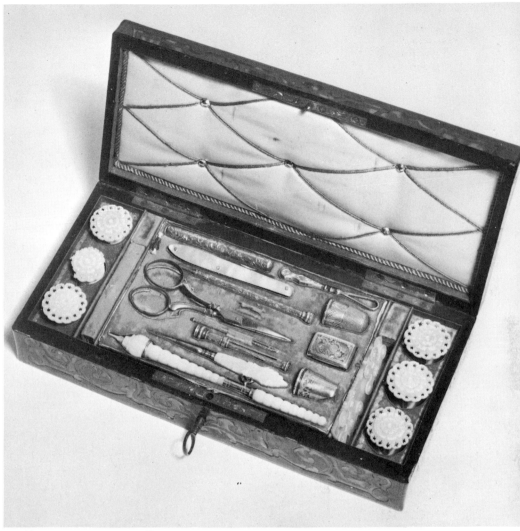

workbox: an English boulle box c.1823, complete with all its fitments.

today have one or more objects missing, generally the scissors and thimble. An interesting box at the American Museum in Bath belonged to Peggy Arnold, the wife of Benedict Arnold. It was given to her by a member of the Micmac tribe of North American Indians when she left for England in 1791, and it consists of a maple box containing nine small birch bark boxes, each having a silk covered medallion embroidered with silk flowers.

work tables Tables of varying sizes with lifting or sliding lids and a drawer or pouch at the bottom to hold work and equipment. Those of the late 18th and early 19th centuries generally had a tray under the lid which contained all necessary tools, not only for needlework, but for allied crafts such as netting, tatting etc. Another type is round with a series of nests on the outer circle and a deep hole in the centre for work. Whatever the shape they made a charming addition to the drawing room or boudoir furniture.

worsted Fabric or yarn made from the long-stapled fibres of a sheep's fleece. These fibres are combed parallel so do not felt (absorb moisture and thicken) and are woven into smooth-faced fabrics. Properly speaking all 'stuffs' are worsted, though nowadays the word stuff is used in a wider sense. See also wool.

worsted work on canvas see french raised work.

wound stitch see french knot.

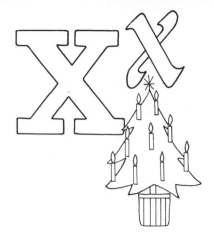

xocbichuy Mayan word meaning to count with the needle, or counted thread embroidery. According to a legend in the Yucatan, it is believed to be necessary to pass the hand over a rattlesnake in order to learn how to do xocbichuy. The legend probably originated in ancient Mayan civilization when the serpent was the genius which both possessed and inspired art. (Mozzi 1968)

yard Measure of length equal to 3 feet or 36 inches, which is the standard American measure and was standard in Britain until 1974 when the metric system was adopted. In old writings the term 'cloth yard' is sometimes used—this was the standard length for arrows, and also for measuring cloth, and according to an Act of Edward VI (1537-1558) 'Cloth was to be meten and measured by the yarde, adding to every yard one inch of the rule' that is, 37 inches. Its metric equivalent is 0.914 metres. See also inch.

yard goods Any materials sold by the yard, which can include fabrics, ribbons, tapes, elastic etc.

yard rule (yard stick) Originally, any piece of wood which exactly measured one yard. Later these yard sticks were specially made, often with a metal edge or entirely of metal. Before *tape measures were standardised and manufactured, most housewives made their own by cutting off a length of ribbon or tape by the household yard rule or stick and marking it off in inches or nails. When it wore out another could be prepared in the same way.

yarn Thread spun from any fibre such as silk, wool, cotton, hemp, jute, flax, rayon, or man made.

yarn sewn rugs Needle embroidered rugs made in America during the 18th and early 19th centuries. They were worked in wool with a looped running stitch in a close, solid pattern on home-spun linen or tow grain bags, and were used as bed, table, and chest coverings as well as hearth rugs. See also bed rugs, Acadian rug. (Colour illustration p 279)

Yew Tree Linen Industry Co-operative venture by a group of women living in Twyford (Hampshire) under the direction of Louisa *Pesel, in the early 1930s. Their aim was to become expert in a type of linen embroidery using some of the pulled and surface stitches found in English 17th century white samplers, and only secondly to make money in a part-time occupation. Unfortunately the venture was stopped by the Second World War.

yo-yo quilt see Suffolk puffs.

Yugoslavia (Jugoslavia) For a long time this area was part of the Ottoman Empire, but there is, perhaps surprisingly, less Turkish influence in the embroidery designs than there is pure Slav. It is now a modern state which includes parts of Macedonia, Serbia, Croatia, Slavonia, and Slovenia as well as other provinces. In the south, heavy embroidery on sleeves and hems of dresses often has patterns worked in chain stitch or couched braid in the favourite deep red, with the spaces between filled in with diagonal rows of gobelin stitch. In Montenegro some very fine all-black work is done, covering the ground to give a damasked effect. The chief Moslem districts are in Bosnia and Herzegovina and here Turkish designs are more apparent. Over the whole country there are two distinct types of design and work: that done by counted stitches, and that done by traced and memorised pattern, where generally blocks of strong colour with only one or two other colours are preferred. (Raffé 1934, Johnstone 1952) See also Bosnia-Herzegovina embroidery, Slavonic embroidery. (Colour illustration p 280)

Yugoslavia: embroidered cover.

zari embroidery Type of north Indian work which covers the ground fabric almost entirely with metal thread, spangles, and jewels. Now it is done only for the tourist trade, and sold on small articles such as caps, belts, and evening bags. It is said that the most exquisite example of zari work ever to be prepared was a carpet made for the Maharaja of Baroda and exhibited at the Delhi Art Exhibition of 1902. This was worked entirely with seed pearls, large-sized pearls, diamonds, and rubies, and was stitched together with gold wires. (Dhamija 1964)

zephyr merino   see Berlin wool.

zip (zipper) foot   see attachments.

Bibliography

Adburgham, A. (1975). *Liberty's: A Biography of a Shop.* London: George Allen & Unwin.

Allgrove, J. (1973). Turcoman embroideries. *Embroidery,* vol. 24, no. 2.

A Magyar Hazi ipar Diszitmenyei (n.d.). Budapest: Magyar Nemzeti Museum.

Amyot, T. (ed.) (1825). Transcript to two Rolls, containing an inventory of Effects formely belonging to Sir John Fastolf. *Archaeologia,* vol. 21.

Anon (1965). A military skirt. *Embroidery,* vol 16, no. 4.

Anon (1969). Embroideries from the East. *Embroidery,* vol. 20, no. 1.

Anon (1960). Linen hanging—German 1623. *Embroidery,* vol. 11, no. 1.

Anson, P. F. (1960). *Fashions in Church Furnishings 1840–1940.* London: The Faith Press.

Armes, A. (1939). *Ideas for Plain Sewing.* London: National Federation of Womens' Institutes.

Art of the Great Lakes Indians, The (1973). Flint, Michigan: Flint Institute of Arts.

Ashton, L. (1928). Martha Edlin; a Stuart embroidress. *Connoisseur,* August, 1928.

Baildon, W. P. (1911). A Wardrobe account of 16–17 Richard II, 1393–4. *Archaeologia,* vol. 62, part 2.

Baker, M. L. (1966). *A Handbook of American Crewel Embroidery.* Rutland, Vt.: Charles E. Tuttle.

Baker, M. L. (1968). *The ABCs of Canvas Embroidery.* Sturbridge, Mass.: Old Sturbridge Inc.

Baker, M. L. (1971). *The XYZs of Canvas Embroidery* (Reprinted 1972). Meriden: The Meriden Gravure Co.

Ball, A. H. R. (ed.) (1949). *Selections from the Paston Letters.* London: Harrap.

Bazielichowna, B. (1959). Slavonic folk embroidery, from *Art Populaire Slovaque,* 1953, XXI, quoted in *Embroidery,* vol. 10, no. 3.

Beck, S. W. (1882). *The Drapers' Dictionary.* London: The Warehouseman and Drapers' Journal Office.

Bed Ruggs (1972). Exhibition Catalogue. Hartford, Conn.: Wadsworth Atheneum.

Bennett, W. C. and Bird, J. B. (1960). *Andean Cultural History.* American Museum of Natural History Handbook Series, no. 15, 2nd rev. ed., New York.

Bhushan, J. B. (1958). *The Costumes and Textiles of India.* Bombay: D. B. Taraporevala Sons and Co.

Bird, E. (1974). *Popular Arts of Spanish New Mexico.* Santa Fe: Museum of New Mexico Press.

Bird, J. and Billinger, L. (1954). *Paracas Fabrics and Nazca Needlework, 3rd Century B.C.—3rd Century A.D.* (The Textile Museum Catalogue Raisonné). Washington DC: National Publishing Co.

Birket-Smith, K. (1935). *The Eskimos* (trans. by W. E. Calvert, rev. by C. D. Forde). New York: E. P. Dutton.

Blencowe, R. W. (ed.) (1857). Extracts from the journal of Walter Gale, schoolmaster at Mayfield, 1750. *Sussex Archaeological Collection,* vol. 9.

Blum, S. (ed.) (1974). *Victorian Fashions and Costumes from Harper's Bazaar: 1867–1898.* New York: Dover publications.

Blunt, W. (1950). *The Art of Botanical Illustration.* London: Collins.

Bolingbroke, L. G. (1904). Two Elizabethan inventories (John West and Sir Roger Wodehouse). *Norfolk Archaeology,* vol. 15.

Bond, S. (1963). The history of sewing tools (Part 6). *Embroidery,* vol. 14, no. 4.

Boyle, E. (1971). *The Irish Flowerers.* Holywood, Co. Down: Ulster Folk Museum; Belfast: Institute of Irish Studies.

Boynton, L. (ed.) (1971). *The Hardwick Hall Inventories of 1601.* London: The Furniture History Society.

Bray, W. (ed.) (1793). Extract from the Wardrobe Account of Prince Henry, eldest son of King James, 1607. *Archaeologia,* vol. 11.

Broderies russes, tartares, arméniennes 1925 published at Paris international exhibition of decorative arts by Ernst.

Buck, A. (1963). The countryman's smock. *Folk Life Journal,* vol. 1.

Bushnell, G. H. S. (1965). *Ancient Arts of the Americas* (World of Art Series). London: Thames & Hudson; New York: Praeger.

Calendar of the Prayer Book, The (1870). London and Oxford: James Parker & Co.

Caley, J. (ed.) (1789). Wardrobe account of Henry VIII. *Archaeologia,* vol. 9.

Campbell (1747). *The London Tradesman* (reprinted 1969). Newton Abbott: David & Charles.

Carlisle, L. B. (1969). Pennsylvania German pillowcases. *Antiques,* vol. 95, p.4.

Catalogue of Algerian Embroideries (1915). London: Victoria & Albert Museum.

Catalogue of Folk Embroidery and Jewellery of Bosnia-Herzegovina (1975). London: Horniman Museum.

Catalogue of the Morris Collection. (1969). Walthamstow: William Morris Gallery.

Catlin, G. (1841). *Letters and Notes on the Manners, Customs and Conditions of the North American Indians* (2 vols.). London.

Caulfeild, S. F. A. and Saward, B. C. (1882). *The Dictionary of Needlework* (2nd ed.). London: L. Upcott Gill.

Cave, O. (1965). *English Folk Embroidery.* London: Mills & Boon.

Champlin, J. D. and Perkins, C. C. (eds.) (1887). *Cyclopedia of Painters and Paintings* (reprinted 1969). New York: Charles Scribner's Sons; Kennikar: Folkestone.

Chaucer, G. (1960). *The Canterbury Tales* (translated into modern English by Nevill Coghill). London: Penguin Books.

Chaves, M. D. and Angermuller, L. (1969). *About Molas.* Florida: Florida State University Publications.

Christie, Grace (Mrs A. H.) (ed.) (1909). *Embroidery*—a collection of articles on subjects connected with the study of fine needlework. London (?): James Pearsall.

Christie, Grace (Mrs A. H.) (1906). *Embroidery and Tapestry Weaving.* In The Artistic Crafts Series of Technical Handbooks. London (?): John Hogg.

Christie, Grace (Mrs A. H.) (1920). *Samplers and Stitches.* London: Batsford.

Christie, Grace (Mrs A. H.) (1938). *English Medieval Embroidery.* Oxford: Clarendon Press.

Cohen, S. (1966). Jewish ritual textiles. *Embroidery,* vol. 17, no. 1.

Colby, A. (1958). *Patchwork.* London: Batsford; Newton Centre, Mass.: Branford.

Colby, A. (1972). *Quilting.* London: Batsford; New York: Charles Scribner's Sons (1971).

Cooper, G. R. (1968). *The Invention of the Sewing Machine.* Washington DC: Smithsonian Institution Press

Cooper, G. R. (1971). *Thirteen Star Flags, Keys to Identification,* Smithsonian Studies in History and Technology, No. 21. Washington DC: Smithsonian Institution Press.

Crawford, M. D. C. (1916). Peruvian textiles. *Anthropological Papers of American Museum of Natural History,* Part 3-1915, Part 4-1916, XII.

Crowfoot, G. (1950). The Embroidery of the Northern Sudan. *Embroidery*, vol. 1, no. 1.

Cunnington, C. W., and Cunnington, P. (1951). *The History of Underclothes*. London: Michael Joseph.

Currey, C. M. (1951). Chevening. *Embroidery*, vol. 2, no. 3.

Davenport, C. (1899). *English Embroidered Bookbindings*. London: Kegan Paul; Houston, Texas: Trench, Trübner & Co.

Davis, M. J. (1969). *The Art of Crewel Embroidery*. New York: Crown; London: Studio Vista.

Davis, M. J. (1971). *Embroidery Designs*. New York: Crown.

Day, L. F. and Buckle, M. (1900). *Art in Needlework*. London: Batsford.

Dean, B. (1958). *Ecclesiastical Embroidery*. London: Batsford.

Dean, B. (1961). *Church Needlework*. London: Batsford.

Dean, B. (1968). *Ideas for Church Embroidery*. London: Batsford.

Dearmer, P. (1920). *The Ornaments of the Ministers*. London, Oxford and Milwaukee: A. R. Mowbray.

de Dillmont, T. (n.d.) *Encyclopedia of Needlework*. Mulhouse, France: D.M.C. Library; Philadelphia: Running Press (1972).

de Farcy, L. (1914). Colifichets. *Needle and Thread*, July, 1914.

de Farcy, L. (1919). *La broderie du XIe siècle jusqu'à nos jours*. Angers: published by the author.

de Zulueta, F. (1923). *Embroideries by Mary Stuart and Elizabeth Talbot at Oxburgh Hall, Norfolk*. Oxford: University Press.

Dhamija, J. (1964). The survey of embroidery traditions. *Marg* (Bombay), March 1964.

D'Harcourt, R. (1962). *Textiles of Ancient Peru and Their Techniques* (ed. G. Denny and C. Osbourne, trans. S. Brown). Seattle and London: University of Washington Press.

Dictionary of National Biography (1885), ed. Stephen L. London: Smith Elder & Co.

Digby, G. W. (1963). *Elizabethan Embroidery*. London: Faber & Faber.

Dillmont, Thérèse de, (1924). *Encyclopedia of Needlework* (published also in French, Italian and German). Mulhouse, France: T. de Dillmont.

Dillon, Viscount, and Hope, W. H. St. J. (1897). Inventory of the goods and chattels belonging to Thomas, Duke of Gloucester . . . (1397) . . . *Archaeological Journal*, 54.

Dockstader, F. J. (1961). *Indian Art in America*. Greenwich, New York: New York Graphic Society.

Dockstader, F. J. (1964). *Indian Art in Middle America*. Greenwich, New York: New York Graphic Society.

Donaldson, N. (1941). Norwegian embroidery. *Embroidery*, vol. 9, no. 2.

Dowling, M. (1933). Some 16th-century pattern books. *Embroidery*, vol. 1, no. 3.

Drobna, Z. (1950). *Les trésors de la broderie religieuse en Tchécoslovaquie*. Prague: Sfinx.

Eastlake, C. L. (1878). *Hints on Household Taste*, 4th ed. New York (?). Longman Green; reprinted (1970) New York and London: Dover Publications.

Edwards, J. (1966). *Bead embroidery*. London: Batsford; New York (1972): Taplinger.

Edwards, Joan (1975). *Crewel Embroidery in England*. London: Batsford; New York: Morrow.

Elsey, R. (1972). Schiffli machine embroidery. *Embroidery*, vol. 23, no. 2.

Emery, I. (1949). Wool embroidery of New Mexico. *El Palacio*, Nov. 1949.

Emery, S. A. (1974). Reminiscences of a nonagenarian. *Antiques*, Feb. 1974.

Engelstad, H. (1960). Norwegian peasant embroidery. *Embroidery*, vol. 11, no. 3.

Erskine, Mrs S. (1925). Some Bethlehem embroideries. *The Embroideress*, no. 15.

Ewers, J. C. (1945) *Blackfeet Crafts*. Lawrence, Kansas: US Indian Service.

Ewing, E. (1974). *History of 20th Century Fashion*. London: Batsford.

Fairholt, F. W. (1846). *Costume in England*. London: Chapman & Hall.

Fanelli, R. B. (1970). An Indo-Portuguese embroidery in the Bargello. *Bulletin of the Needle and Bobbin Club*, vol. 53, nos. 1 and 2.

Faude, W. (1975). *Associated Artists and the American Renaissance in the Decorative Arts*. Winterthur Portfolio 10.

Feder, N. (1971). *Art of the Eastern Plains Indians*, The Nathan Sturgis Jarvis Collection. Brooklyn, New York: Brooklyn Museum (Catalog).

Fél, E. (1961). *Hungarian Peasant Embroidery*. London: Batsford.

Fennelly, C. (1966). *The Garb of Country New Englanders 1790–1840: Costumes at Old Sturbridge Village*. Sturbridge, Mass: Old Sturbridge Village.

Finley, R. E. (1929). *Old Patchwork Quilts and the Women who made them*. New York: Grosset & Dunlap.

Finley, R. E. (1931). *The Lady of Godey's: Sarah Josepha Hale*. Philadelphia and London: J. B. Lippincott.

Fitzrandolph, M. (1954). *Traditional Quilting*. London: Batsford.

Forbes, M. (1966). Laidwork. *Embroidery*, vol. 17, no. 2.

Freeman, M. B. (1968). *The St. Martin Embroideries*. New York: Metropolitan Museum of Art.

Freeman, R. (1948). *English Emblem Books*. London: Chatto & Windus.

Fry, G. W. (1935). *Embroidery and Needlework* (5th ed. 1959). London: Pitman.

Garrett, E. D. (1974). American samplers and needlework pictures in the D.A.R. Museum 1739–1806. *Antiques*, vol. 55, no. 2.

Giffen, J. C. (1970). Susanna Rowson and her academy. *Antiques*, vol. 98, no. 3.

Gillespie, C. C. (1959). *A Diderot Pictorial Encyclopedia of Trades and Industries*, from *L'Encyclopédie, ou Dictionaire Raisonné des Sciences, des Arts, et des Métiers*. New York: Dover Publications.

Gloag, J. (ed.) (1969). *Hints on Household Taste*, by C. L. Eastlake. New York and London: Dover Publications.

Gostelow, M. (1975). *A World of Embroidery*. London: Mills & Boon.

Grout & Company. *Account Books*. Norfolk and Norwich Record Office.

Groves, S. (1966). *The History of Needlework Tools*. Country Life.

Groves, S. (1969). The bloom on the woollen peach: French raised work. *Country Life*, March, 1969.

Gudjonssen, E. (n.d.) *Icelandic Embroidery*. (n.p.).

Gudjonssen, E. (1970). *The National Costume of Women in Iceland*. (n.p.).

Gunther, E. (1966). *Art in the life of the Northwest Coast Indians*, with catalog of the Rasmussen Collection of NW Indian art at the Portland Art Museum, Seattle: Superior Publishing Co.

Hackenbrock, Y. (1960). *English and Other Needlework, Tapestries and Textiles in the Irwin Untermeyer Collection*. London: Thames & Hudson; New York (1962): Metropolitan Museum of Art.

Hake, E. (1936). *English Quilting Old and New*. London: Batsford.

Hakluyt, R. (1958). *Voyages and Discoveries*. Reprinted (2nd ed. 1972). London: Penguin Books; Santa Fe: Gannon.

Hall, M. R. (1901). *English Church Needlework*. London: Grant Richards; New York: Dutton.

Halls, Z. (1973). *Machine-made Lace in Nottingham* (2nd ed.). Nottingham: City of Nottingham Museums and Libraries Committee.

Halls, Z. (1973). *Coronation Costume 1685–1953*. London: H.M.S.O.

289

Hands, H. (1920). *Church Needlework.* London: Faith Press.

Hanley, H. (1966). *Needlepoint.* London: Faber & Faber; New York: Charles Scribner's Sons.

Harbeson, G. B. (1938). *American Needlework.* New York: Coward-McCann.

Harkness, D. N. (1959). Romanian embroidery; a dying folk-art. *Needle and Bobbin Club Bulletin,* vol. 43, nos. 1 and 2.

Harris, K. (n.d.). *Altar Linen.* London: The Embroiderers' Guild.

Hartley, F. (1859). *Lady's Handbook.* Philadelphia.

Hartshorne, C. H. (1848). Mediaeval English embroidery. *Archeaological Journal,* vol. 4.

Hawthorn, A. (1967). *Art of the Kwakiutl Indians and other northwest coast Tribes.* Vancouver: University of British Columbia; Seattle (and London, 1968): University of Washington Press.

Heal, Sir A. (1933). Samuel Pepys his Trade-cards. *Connoisseur,* vol. 91.

Hicks, A. M. (1938). *The Craft of Handmade Rugs.* New York: Empire State Book Co.

Higgin, L. (1880). *Handbook of Embroidery.* London: Sampson Low, Marston, Searle & Rivington.

Hillier, B. (1968). *Art Deco of the 20s and 30s.* London: Studio Vista; New York: Dutton.

Hind, A. L. (1934). *Needlework and Dressmaking* (4th ed. enlarged and revised by N. Bray 1949). Anglo-Scottish Press.

Hind, A. M. (1933). Studies in English engraving. *Connoisseur,* vol. 91.

Hird, A. L. (1934). *Principles and Practice of Needlework and Dressmaking.* Anglo-Scottish Press. 4th ed. (1949) revised by Natalie Bray.

Holford, C. (1910). *A Chat about the Broderers' Company.* London: George Allen.

Holme, Randle. (1688). *The Academy of Armory, or, a Storehouse of Armory and Blazon.* Chester.

Home (ed.) (1889). *The Letters and Journals of Lady Mary Coke 1756-1774.* Privately printed. Reprinted (1970) Bath: Kingsmead Reprints.

Hornor, M. M. (1971). *The Story of Samplers.* Philadelphia: Philadelphia Museum of Art.

Hornung, C. P. (1972). *Treasury of American Design* (2 vols.). New York: Abrams.

Howe, B. (1973). *Antiques from the Victorian Home.* London: Batsford; New York; Scribner.

Howe, M. B. (1963). *Early American Embroideries in Deerfield Massachusetts.* Chicago: Heritage Foundation.

Hughes, T. (1961). *English Domestic Needlework 1660-1860.* London: Lutterworth Press; New York: Macmillan.

Hunt, W. B. and Burshears, J. F. (1951). *American Indian Beadwork.* New York: Bruce Publishing Co.

Ickis, M. (1949). *The Standard Book of Quilt-Making and Collecting.* Reprinted 1959. New York: Dover.

Irwin, J. (1951). *Indian Embroidery.* London: Victoria and Albert Museum, catalogue.

Irwin, J. (1959). Indo-European embroidery. *Embroidery,* vol. 10, no. 1.

Irwin, J. and Schwartz, P. R. (1966). *Studies in Indo-European Textile History.* India, Ahmedabad: Calico Museum of Textiles.

Irwin, J. (1973). *The Kashmir Shawl.* London: H.M.S.O.

Irwin, J. and Hall, J. (1973). *Indian Embroideries.* Ahmedabad, India: Calico Museum of Textiles.

Irwin, J. and Hanish, B. (1970). Notes on the use of the hook in Indian embroidery. *Needle and Bobbin Club Bulletin,* vol. 53, nos. 1 and 2.

Jessup, A. L. (1913). *The Sewing Book.* New York: Butterick Publishing Co.

Johnsen, E. (1955). *Gamla Danska Korsstingsmotiver fra Amager.* Copenhagen: Host & Sons.

Johnstone, P. (1952). Embroidery in Yugoslavia. *Embroidery,* vol. 3, no. 2.

Johnstone, P. (1957). Some notes on a visit to Japan. *Embroidery,* vol. 8, no. 2.

Johnstone, P. (1967). *Byzantine Traditions in Church Embroidery,* London: Tiranti.

Johnstone, P. (1972). *A Guide to Greek Island Embroidery.* London: H.M.S.O.

Jones, M. (1954). A cure for untidiness? *Country Life.*

Jones, N. (1965). Choosing a sewing machine. *Embroidery,* vol. 12, no. 3.

Jones, N. (1968). Albanian costume. *Embroidery,* vol. 19, no. 2.

Jourdain, M. A. (1910). *English Secular Embroidery.* London: Kegan Paul; Houston, Texas: Trench, Trübner & Co.

Kapp, K. S. (1972). *Mola Art from the San Blas Islands.* New York: K. S. Kapp publications.

Kelemen, P. (1943). *Medieval American Art: Masterpieces of the New World before Columbus.* 3rd rev. ed., New York: Macmillan; reprinted (1969) New York and London: Dover Publications.

Kelsey, V. and Osborne, L. (1952). *Four Keys to Guatemala.* New York: Funk & Wagnalls.

Kendrick, A. F. (1928). An English coverlet of 1694. *Connoisseur,* Sept.Dec., 1928.

Kendrick, A. F. (1933). *English Needlework.* London: A. & C. Black.

Kendrick, A. F. (1934). *English Decorative Fabrics of the 16th to 18th Century.* London: F. Lewis.

King, D. (1960). *Samplers.* London: H.M.S.O.

King, D. (1961). Boxers. *Embroidery,* vol. 12, no. 4.

King, D. (1962). The earliest dated sampler. *Connoisseur,* April 1962.

King, D. (1963). *Opus Anglicanum.* London: Victoria & Albert Museum, catalogue.

Koch, R. (1930). *The Books of Signs.* New York: Dover Publications.

Kockum-Overengen, U. (1951). The living tradition of Swedish needlework. *Embroidery,* vol. 2, no. 2.

Krishna, M. (1962). Burmese appliqué hangings. *Embroidery,* vol. 13, no. 2.

Krishna, M. (1963). Designs from Burmese Kalangas. *Embroidery,* vol. 14, no. 3.

La broderie nationale de Bulgare (1913). Sofia, Bulgaria: La Ministère du commerce, de l'industrie et du travail.

Ladies' Memorial, The (1849). H. B. Skinner and J. B. Hall, Boston, Mass.

Ladies' Work-table Book, The (1858). T. B. Peterson, Philadelphia.

Lambert, Miss (1843). *The Handbook of Needlework* (3rd ed.) London: John Murray; Philadelphia: Willis P. Hazard.

Lambert, Miss (1844). *Church Needlework.* London: John Murray.

Lefebvre, E. (1888). *Embroidery and Lace.* H. Grevel & Co.

Leonard, J. N., and editors of Time/Life Books (1967). *Ancient America.* New York: Time Inc.; London: Time Life Int. (1968).

Levey, S. (1971). *Discovering Embroidery of the 19th Century.* Tring, Herts.: Shire Publications.

Lewis, A. A. (1973). *The Mountain Artisan Quilting Book.* New York: Macmillan.

Llanover, Lady (ed.) (1861). *The Autobiography and Correspondence of Mary Granville, Mrs Delaney.* London: Richard Bentley.

Lothrop, S. K. (1929). . . . . Polychrome Guanaco Cloaks of Patagonia'. Series contributions from the Museum of the American Indian. New York: Museum of the American Indian, Heye Foundation.

Lovelock, B. (1952). Embroidery of Tsu Hsi. *Embroidery,* vol. 3, no. 1.

Macmillan, S. L. (n.d.). *Greek Islands Embroideries.* Boston, Mass.: Museum of Fine Arts.

Madden, Sir F. (1835). Warrant to the Great Wardrobe on the Princess Elizabeth's Marriage 1612-13. *Archaeologia*, vol. 26.

Marg, vol. 17, no. 2. (1964). Bombay: Marg Publications.

Marion, J. F. (1974). *Bicentennial City: Walking Tours of Philadelphia*. Princeton, New Jersey: Pyne Press.

Martin, E. (1962). Traditional Swedish embroidery. *Embroidery*, vol. 13, no. 2.

Mason, J. A. (1957). *The Ancient Civilisations of Peru*. Harmondsworth: Penguin Books, rev. ed. 1968; reprinted Baltimore, Penguin Books, 1973.

Mason, F. N. (ed.) (1968). *John Norton & Sons, Merchants of London and Virginia*. Newton Abbott: David & Charles.

Mathews, S. I. (1960). *Needlemade Rugs*. London: Mills & Boon; New York: Hearthside Press Inc.

McCalls Needlework in Colour (1964). London: Hamlyn (4th ed. 1972).

McCracken, H. (1959). *George Catlin and the old Frontier*. New York: Dial Press.

McRoberts, D. (n.d.). *The Fetternear Banner*. Glasgow: John S. Burns & Sons.

Means, P. A. (1930). *A Study of Peruvian Textiles*. Boston, Mass.; Museum of Fine Arts.

Mera, H. P. (1943). Pueblo Indian embroidery. *Memoirs of the Laboratory of Anthropology*, vol. 4. New Mexico: University Press.

Millar, O. (ed.) (1970-2). The Inventories and Valuations of King's Goods, 1649-1651. *Walpole Society*, vol. 43.

Molas: art of the Cuna Indians (1973). Washington DC: The Textile Museum.

Moore, D. L. (1971). *Fashion through fashion plates 1771-1970*. London: Ward Lock; New York: Intl. Pubns. Serv. 1972.

Moore, M. (1956). Coggleshall embroidery. *Embroidery*, vol. 7, no. 2.

Morgan, F. C. (ed.) (1945). Private purse accounts of the Marquis of Hertford Michaelmas 1641-2. *Antiquaries' Journal*, vol. 25.

Morris Collection (1969). Walthamstow: Catalogue of the William Morris Gallery (2nd rev. ed.).

Morris, B. (1962). *Victorian Embroidery*. London: Herbert Jenkins; New York: Thomas Nelson and Sons.

Morris, B. (1966). Some early embroideries by Mrs Phoebe Traquair. *Embroidery*, Diamond Jubilee Number.

Mozzi, C. M. (1968). *Indian dress in Mexico*. vol. 2. Mexico: Instituto Nacional de Antropologia e Historia.

Munro, N. G. (ed.) (1963). *Ainu Creed and Cult*. New York: Columbia University Press.

Murphy, W. S. (n.d.). *Modern Drapery and Allied Trades (vol. 4)*. London: Gresham.

National Federation of Womens' Institutes (1951). *Introduction to the Making of Surrey Stitch Rugs*.

Naylor, G. (1971). *Arts and Crafts Movement*. London: Studio Vista; Cambridge, Mass.; Massachusetts Institute of Technology Press.

Needlecraft—Artistic and Practical (1890). New York: The Butterick Publishing Corp.

Nevinson, J. L. (1938). *Catalogue of English Domestic Embroidery*. London: Victoria and Albert Museum.

Nevinson, J. L. (1968). The embroidery patterns of Thomas Trevelyon. *The Walpole Society*, vol. 41.

Newberry, E. W. (1940). Embroideries from Egypt. *Embroidery*, vol. 8, no. 2.

Nichols, J. (1780). *A collection of all the Wills now known to be extant of the Kings and Queens of England . . .* Printed by and for J. B. Nichols, Printer to the Society of Antiquaries, London.

Nichols, J. (1823). *The Progresses and Public Processions of Queen Elizabeth* (3 vols.) London.

Nichols, J. G. (ed.) (1855). View of the Wardrobe Stuff of Katharine of Arragon. *Camden Miscellany*, vol. 3.

Nichols, J. G. (ed.) (1859). Inventory of the goods of Dame Agnes Hungerford attainted of murder 14 Hen. VIII. *Archaeologia*, vol. 38.

Nichols, M. (1973). *Encyclopaedia of Embroidery Stitches, including Crewel*. New York: Dover.

Oajes, A. and Hill, M. (1970). *Rural Costume*. London: Batsford; New York: Van Nostrand Reinhold.

Olson, E. (1950). Tibetan appliqué work. *Bulletin of the Needle and Bobbin Club*, vol. 34, nos. 1 and 2.

Oxford English Dictionary (1971) (complete ed.). Oxford: Clarendon Press.

Palliser, Mrs B. (1869). *History of Lace* (2nd ed.). London: Sampson Low, Son & Marston.

Pass, O. (1957). *Dorset Feather Stitchery*. London: Mills & Boon.

Parker, K. (1893). *Leek Embroidery Society*. Studio vol. 1.

Pesel, L. F. (1913). *Stitches from Eastern Embroideries* (2nd ed. 1921). Bradford: Percy Lund, Humphries & Co.

Pesel, L. F., Newberry, E. W. (1921). *A book of Old Embroidery*. The Studio.

Peto, F. (1949). *American Quilts and Coverlets*. London: Max Parrish & Co.

Picken, M. B. (1939). *The Language of Fashion*. New York: Funk & Wagnalls.

Pickup, J. and Field, P. (1974). Ideas in Suffolk Puffs. *Embroidery*, vol. 25, no. 1.

Pilcher, A. M. (1965). Cretan designs. *Embroidery*, vol. 16, no. 4.

Plain Needlework (1860). Finchley Manuals of Industry No. 4, (3rd ed.). London: Joseph Masters.

Planché, J. R. (1847). *History of British Costume*. London: C. Cox.

Pollard, A. W. (ed.) (1965). *Works* (Chaucer). London: Macmillan.

Raby, W. L. (1958). Greek lace—Ruskin linen work. *Embroidery*, vol. 9, no. 3.

Radin, P. (1923). *The Winnebago tribe*. Washington DC: Smithsonian Institution Press. (Reprinted by University of Nebraska Press, Lincoln, 1970.)

Raffé, W. G. (1934). The embroideries of Yugoslavia. *The Embroideress*, no. 49.

Rice, D. S. (1959). Fermo chasuble of St Thomas à Becket. *Illustrated London News*, Oct. 3, 1959.

Risley, C. (1961). *Machine Embroidery*. London: Studio Vista.

Roediger, V. M. (1941). *Ceremonial Costumes of the Pueblo Indians*. Berkeley, Calif.: University of California Press.

Rollins, J. G. (1969). *The Early Victorian Needlemakers 1830-1860*. Early Victorian Costume Society.

Roseaman, I. P. (1949). *Rug making*. Leicester: Dryad Press.

S.N.E. (1934). Wessex stitchery. *Embroidery*, vol. 2, no. 3.

Safford, C. L. and Bishop, R. (1972). *America's Quilts and Coverlets*. New York: Dutton; London: Studio Vista, 1973.

Saint-Aubin, M. de (1770). *L'art du brodeur*. Paris: Académie des Sciences, Arts et Métiers.

Salmony, A. (1942). Archaeological background of textile production in Soviet Russian territory. *Bulletin of the Needle and Bobbin Club*, vol. 26, no. 2.

Scanno (1914). Pattern shirring. *Needle and Thread*, no. 2.

Schiffer, M. B. (1968). *Historical Needlework of Pennsylvania*. New York: Charles Scribner's Sons.

Schneider, J. (1968). Wall pockets from the Engadine and some remarks about Swiss embroidery in the 18th century. *Bulletin of the Needle and Bobbin Club*, vol. 51, nos. 1 and 2.

Schuette, M. and Müller Christensen, S. (1964). *The Art of Embroidery*. London: Thames & Hudson.

Schuster, C. (1935). Some peasant embroideries from western China. *Embroidery*, vol. 3, no. 4.

Seligman, G. S. and Hughes, T. (? 1928). Domestic needlework—its origins and customs throughout the centuries. *Country Life*.

Serjeantson (1939). Mabilia of St Edmunds Bury. *Embroidery*, vol. 7, no. 3.

Shepherd, D. (1960). A Romanesque Lenten cloth from Germany. *Embroidery*, vol. 11, no. 1.

Shirley, E. P. (ed.) (1869). An Inventory of the Effects of Henry Howard, K.G. Earl of Northampton taken on his death in 1614 together with a transcript of his will. *Archaeologia*, vol. 42.

Sieber, R. (1972). *African textiles and decorative arts*. New York: The Museum of Modern Art, catalogue.

Inventory of John Skelton of Norwich (1611). Norfolk and Norwich Record Office.

Snook, B. (1960). *English Historical Embroidery*. London: Batsford.

Snook, B. (1971). *The Craft of Florentine Embroidery*. New York: Charles Scribner's Sons.

Speck, E. G. (1940). Eskimo jacket ornaments. *American Antiquity*, vol. 3.

Speltz, A. (1959). *The Styles of Ornament*. New York: Dover Publications.

Start, L. E. (1939). *The Durham Collection of Garments and Embroideries from Albania and Yugoslavia*. Bankfield Museum Notes, no. 4.

Start, L. E. (1963). *The McDougall Collection of Indian Textiles from Guatemala and Mexico*. Oxford: Pitt Rivers Museum.

Steer, F. W. (ed.) (1950). *Farm and Cottage Inventories of Mid-Essex, 1635-1749*. Chichester: Phillimore.

Steinman, A. (1946). The ship of the dead in the textile art of Indonesia. *Ciba Review*, vol. 52.

Strong, R. (1969). *The English Icon*. London: Routledge and Kegan Paul; New York: Pantheon Books.

Strutt, J. (1842). *The Dress and Habits of the People of England*. Reprinted London (1970): Tabard Press.

Sturge, A. (1934). Swedish royal dress in the 16th and early 17th centuries. *The Embroideress*, no. 51.

Will of Joan Sutton of Grimston (1633). Norfolk and Norwich Record Office.

Swain, M. H. (1955). *The Flowerers—Ayrshire Needlework*. Edinburgh: W. R. Chambers Ltd.

Swain, M. H. (1965). Colifichets. *The American Connoisseur*, August, 1965.

Swain, M. H. (1966). Block printing and embroidery. *Embroidery*, vol. 17, no. 3.

Swain, M. H. (1973). *The Needlework of Mary Queen of Scots*. New York: Van Nostrand Reinhold Co.

Swain, M. H. (1973). Mrs J. R. Newbury 1864-1948. *Embroidery*, vol. 24, no. 4.

Swain, M. H. (1974). Ann Macbeth. *Embroidery*, vol. 25, no. 1.

Symonds, M. and Preece, L. (1924). *Needlework in Religion*. London: Pitman and Sons.

Symonds, M. and Preece, L. (1928). *Needlework through the Ages*. London: Hodder & Stoughton.

Terrace, L. C. (1964). Notes on a pattern for needlework. *Bulletin of the Needle and Bobbin Club*, vol. 48, nos. 1 and 2.

Terrell, J. U. and Terrell, D. M. (1974). *Indian Women of the Western Morning*. New York: Dial.

Thomas, B. and Gamber, O. and Schedelmann, H. (1964). *Arms and Armour*. London: Thames & Hudson.

Thomas, M. (1934). *Mary Thomas's Dictionary of Embroidery Stitches*. London: Hodder & Stoughton.

Thomas, M. (1936). *Mary Thomas's Dictionary of Embroidery*. London: Hodder & Stoughton.

Thompson, E. M. (ed.) (1878). The Will and inventory of Robert Morton, A.D. 1486-1488. *Journal of the British Archaeological Association*, vol. 33.

Tolmachoff, E. (1947). Some Ancient Greek textiles found in South Russia; adapted from the German text of Ludolf Stephani with additional notes. *Bulletin of the Needle and Bobbin Club*, vol. 26, no. 2.

Townsend, G. (1944). Flowers in English Needlework. *Antiques*, vol. 45, no. 4., April.

Townsend, W. G. P. (1899). *Embroidery or the Craft of the Needle*. London and New York: Truslove Hanson & Comba.

Trendall, P. G. (1926). Miss Linwood and her needlework pictures. *Embroideress*, no. 16.

Tucker, S. I. (ed.) (1875). Descent of the manor of Sheffield—appendix II. An inventory of all the household goods and furniture belonging to George Earl of Shrewsbury at Sheffield Castle and the Lodge 1582. *Journal of the British Archaeological Association*, vol. 30.

Turner, G. (1955). *Hair Embroidery in Siberia and North America*. Occasional Papers on Technology no. 7. Oxford: Pitt Rivers Museum.

Uzanne, O. (1884). *The Fan*. London: J. C. Nimmo and Bain.

Wade, N. V. (1960). *The Basic Stitches of Embroidery*. London: Victoria and Albert Museum.

Walker, C. (n.d.). *The Ritual Reason Why*. J. T. Hayes.

Ward, A. (1966). Quilting in the north of England. *Folk Life*, vol. 4.

Wardle, G. C. (1909). Memoir of Sir Thomas Wardle. *Journal of Indian Art and Industry*, vol. 13. London: W. Griggs and Sons.

Wardle, P. (1968). *Victorian Lace*. London: Barrie & Jenkins; New York: Praeger (1969).

Wardle, P. (1970). *Guide to English Embroidery*. London: Victoria and Albert Museum.

Waring, M. E. (n.d.). *An Embroidery Pattern Book*. London: Pitman.

Warren, Mrs and Pullan, Mrs (1855). *Treasures in Needlework*. London: Ward Lock.

Wascher, H. (1947). Moldavian Wallachian embroidery. *Ciba Review*, Sept.

Webster, M. D. (1915). *Quilts, their Story and how to make them*. New York: Doubleday Page & Co.; Tudor Pub. Co. (1948).

Weir, S. (1969). Traditional costumes of the Arab women of Palestine. *Costume*, no. 3. (Journal of the Costume Society, London).

Whitcomb, N. R. (n.d.). *Mary Linwood*. Leicester: City of Leicester Museum and Art Gallery.

Whiting, G. (1928). *Tools and Toys of Stitchery*. New York: Columbia University Press. (Reprinted 1971, entitled 'Old-time Tools and Toys of Needlework', Dover).

Whymant, N. (1935). Traditional Chinese embroidery. *Embroidery*, vol. 3, no. 4.

Willan, T. S. (ed.) (1962). *A Tudor Book of Rates*. Manchester: University Press.

Wilson, E. (1964). *Crewel Embroidery*. London: Faber & Faber.

Wilson, E. (1973). *Erica Wilson's Embroidery Book*. New York: Charles Scribner's Sons.

Wilton, Countess of, (1840). *The Art of Needlework*. London: Henry Colburn.

Wingate, Dr I. B. (ed.) (1967). *Fairchild's Dictionary of Textiles*. New York: Fairchild Publications Inc.

Winters, D. (1954). *Plain Sewing*. Leicester: Dryad Press.

Woodfords, D. H. (ed.) (1932). *Woodforde Papers and Diaries*.

The Workwomen's Guide (2nd ed.) (1840). Reprinted in facsimile (1975), Bloomfield Brooke Publications.

Yule, H. and Burnell, A. C. (1903). *Hobson-Jobson—A Glossary of Anglo-Indian Colloquial Words and Phrases and Kindred Terms*. (New ed.) London: John Murray.

Museums and Collections

A select list of museums and collections where
textiles can be seen

Bath: American Museum in Britain, *Claverton Manor;
Museum of Costume; Holburne of Menstrie Museum.
Bedford: Cecil Higgins Art Gallery.
Birmingham: *Aston Hall; City of Birmingham Museum
and Art Gallery.
Bury St Edmunds: *Moyses Hall.
Calstock, Cornwall: *Cotehele House.
Cambo, Northumberland: *Wallington Hall.
Cambridge: *Anglesey Abbey; *Fitzwilliam Museum; University Museum of Archaeology and Ethnology.
Chesterfield, Derbyshire: *Hardwick Hall.
Dorking, Surrey: *Polesdon Lacey.
Edinburgh: National Museum of Antiquities of Scotland;
Royal Scottish Museum.
Exeter: Royal Albert Memorial Museum.
Glasgow: Art Gallery and Museum, Kelvingrove; *Burrell
Collection.
Guildford: *Clandon Park; *Gubbay Collection.
Halifax: Bankfield Museum.
London: British Museum; *National Army Museum; William
Morris Gallery, Walthamstow; *Victoria and Albert
Museum.
Maidstone, Kent: Maidstone Museum and Art Gallery.
Manchester: Gallery of English Costume, Platt Hall; Whitworth Art Gallery.
Norwich: *Strangers Hall Museum.
Nottingham: Castlegate Museum; *Lord Middleton Collection.
Nuneaton, Warwickshire: *Arbury Hall.
Oxford: The Ashmolean Museum; Pitt-Rivers Museum.
Padiham, Lancs: *Gawthorpe Hall; Kay-Shuttleworth Collection.
Pulborough, Sussex: *Parham Park.
Saffron Waldon, Essex: The Museum.
Sevenoaks, Kent: *Knole House.
Sudbury, Suffolk: Melford Hall.
Yeovil, Somerset: *Montacute House.

Baltimore, Maryland: Walker's Art Gallery.
Bethlehem, Pennsylvania: Moravian Museum of Bethlehem.
Boston, Massachusetts: Bostonian Society, Old State House;
*Museum of Fine Arts.
Browning, Montana: *Museum of the Plains Indian.
Chicago, Illinois: *Art Institute of Chicago.
Cincinnati, Ohio: Cincinnati Art Museum.
Cleveland, Ohio: Cleveland Museum of Art.
Darien, Massachusetts: Historic Deerfield Inc.; Pocumtuck
Valley Memorial Association.
Denver, Colorado: Denver Art Museum.
Hartford, Connecticut: Mark Twain Memorial; Wadsworth
Atheneum.
Houston, Texas: Museum of Fine Arts.
Lawrence, Kansas: Museum of Art, University of Kansas.
Los Angeles, California: Los Angeles County Museum of Art.
Minneapolis, Minnesota: Institute of Arts.
Montreal, Quebec: McCord Museum.

Mt. Vernon, Virginia: Mt. Vernon Ladies Association.
Newark, New Jersey: Newark Museum.
New York: *Brooklyn Museum; Carnegie Museum;
*Cooper-Hewitt Museum of Design, Smithsonian Institution; Jewish Museum; *Metropolitan Museum of Art;
*Museum of the American Indian – Heye Foundation
Institution; Museum of Modern Art; Museum of Primitive Art.
Oberlin, Ohio: Allen Art Museum, Oberlin College.
Ottawa, Quebec: National Museum of Canada.
Philadelphia, Pennsylvania: Museum of Art; *University
Museum of Pennsylvania.
Richmond, Virginia: *Valentine Museum.
Rochester, New York: Strong Museum.
St Louis, Missouri: St. Louis Art Museum.
Salem, Massachusetts: Essex Institute; Peabody Museum of
Salem.
Santa Fe, New Mexico: *Museum of New Mexico, International Folk Art Foundation Collection; Spanish Colonial
Arts Society.
Shelburne, Vermont: *Shelburne Museum.
Sturbridge, Massachusetts: Old Sturbridge Village.
Toronto, Ontario: *Royal Ontario Museum.
Vancouver, British Columbia: Museum of Ethnography,
University of British Columbia.
Washington, DC: *Daughters of the American Revolution
Museum; National Gallery of Art; *Index of American
Design, National Gallery of Art; *Smithsonian Institution; *Textile Museum.
Wenham, Massachusetts: Historical Association and Museum.
Williamsburg, Virginia: Abby Aldrich Rockefeller Folk Art
Collection, *Colonial Williamsburg.
Winnipeg, Manitoba: *Hudson's Bay Company Museum.
Winterthur, Delaware: *Henry Francis du Pont Winterthur
Museum.
York, Maine: Old Gaol Museum.

Amsterdam, Holland: Rijksmuseum.
Athens, Greece: Benaki Museum.
Basel, Switzerland: Historisches Museum.
Bayeux, France: Musée de la Reine Mathilde.
Belgrade, Yugoslavia: Musée des Arts Decoratifs.
Berlin, West: Kunstgewerbemuseum.
Berne, Switzerland: Abegg-Stiftung; Bernisches Historisches
Museum.
Bologna, Italy: Museo Civico.
Brussels, Belgium: Musées Royaux.
Bucharest, Romania: Museum of Arts.
Budapest, Hungary: Magyar Nemzeti Muzeum.
Cairo, Egypt: Boulak Museum.
Cleb, Czechoslovakia: Musée Municipal.
Copenhagen, Denmark: Museum of Decorative Art;
Nationalmuseet.
Florence, Italy: Museo Nazionale del Bargello.
Freiburg-im-Breisgau, Germany: Augustiniermuseum; Bilderverlag.

* = entry in Dictionary

Hamburg, Germany: Museum für Kunst und Gewerbe.
Helsinki, Finland: Suomen Kansallismuseo.
Istanbul, Turkey: Topkapi Palace Museum.
Leningrad, USSR: Hermitage Museum.
Lima, Peru: National Museum of Anthropology and Archaeology.
Lisbon, Portugal: Gulbenkian Museum.
Lyons, France: Musée Historique des Tissus.
Marburg, W. Germany: Museum für Kunst und Kulturgeschichte.
Melbourne, Australia: National Gallery of Victoria.
Moscow, USSR: Museum of the Moscow Kremlin.
Munich, W. Germany: Bayerisches Nationalmuseum; Münchner Stadtmuseum.
Oslo, Norway: Norsk Folkemuseum.
Paris, France: Musée Cognacq-Jay; Musée de Cluny; Musée du Louvre.

Regensburg, W. Germany: Kunstsammlungen du Bistums Regensburg Diozesanmuseum.
Rome, Italy: Vatican Museums.
Sarajevo, Yugoslavia: National Museum.
Sens, France: Cathedral Treasury.
Stockholm, Sweden: Kungl Livrustkammaren; Nordiska Museet.
Taipei, Taiwan (Formosa): National Palace Museum.
Tokyo, Japan: National Museum of Tokyo.
Venice, Italy: Museo Correr.
Vienna, Austria: Kursthistorisches Museum; Oesterreichisches Museum für Angewandte Kunst; Völkerkunde Museum; Waffensammlung.
Weimar, DDR: Kunstsammlungen zu Weimar.
Wurzburg, W. Germany: Mainfränkisches Museum.

* = entry in Dictionary

Picture Acknowledgements

Page numbers of colour illustrations are given in **bold.** Where more than one black-and-white photograph or line drawing appear on a page, they are identified by the letters *a, b, c* etc., running down each column on the page in turn, starting on the left. Where the basis of a line drawing is in a work listed in the Bibliography, we have listed here only the entry name and date. The entry in the Bibliography will give further details.

Photographs in Colour and Black-and-White

Abby Aldrich Rockefeller Folk Art Collection, Williamsburg, Virginia: 220*c*. Abegg Stiftung, Berne: 71*b*. Allen Memorial Art Museum, Oberlin College, Ohio: 42*e*. Reproduced by permission of the American Museum in Britain, Claverton Manor, Bath: **17**, 73*a*, 131*b*, **199**, 219*c*, 278*a*, 285*a*; photos by R. Shone: 32*a*, **45**, 248*d*. Courtesy of the Art Institute of Chicago, Illinois: 20*b*. Ashmolean Museum, Oxford: **209**. Augustinermuseum, photo supplied by Bildverlag, Freiburg-im-Breisgau: 163*b*, 195*b*. Author's Collection: 132*d*, 263*b*, 265*b*, 285*b*; photo by A. E. Coe & Sons Limited, Norwich: **128**. Bankfield Museum, Halifax, photos by Pennine Graphic Studios Limited: 119*a*, 146*b*, 146*c*. Bayerisches Nationalmuseum, Munich: 191*a*. Bayou Bend Collection, Museum of Fine Arts, Houston, Texas: 51*c*, 208*e*. City of Birmingham Museums and Art Gallery: 134*b*. Courtesy of the Bostonian Society, Old State House, Boston, Massachusetts: 165*a*. By permission of the British Library Board, London: 34*a*. Brooklyn Museum, New York: 28*a*, 120*c*, 154*e*, 233*a*; gift of Miss Mary Louise Denning: 64*a*; gift of Edward S. Harkness: 274*b*; Nathan Sturgis Jarvis Collection: 178*d*; Alfred W. Jenkins Fund: 196*b*; gift of Miss Nancy McLeod: 228*b*; John T. Underwood Memorial Fund: 40*c*; gift of Helen Garner Williams: 70*a*. Caisse Nationale des Monuments Historiques, Archives Photographiques, Paris: 26*b*. Cambridge University Museum of Archaeology and Ethnology: 24*b*, 25*c*, 31*a*, 149*c*, 173*d*, 174*a*, 206*f*, **221**, 223*a*, 233*b*. Camera and Pen/J. Allan Cash Limited, London: 73*e*, 257*a*. By kind permission of the Dean and Chapter of Canterbury Cathedral, photo by Entwhistle: 31*b*.

Castle Museum, Nottingham, Thompson Collection: 27*b*. Courtesy Castlegate Museum, Nottingham: 10*a*, 11*b*, 124*b*, 238*b*; Lord Middleton Collection (by kind permission of Lord Middleton and Colonel Wharton): 92*b*, 100*b*, 152*c*, 172*c*, 244*c*, 254*b*, 268*b*. Chester County Historical Society, Pennsylvania, photo by Dan Coxe: 119*c*. Courtesy Chicago Historical Society, Illinois: **35**. Cincinnati Art Museum, Ohio: 66*c*, 160*c*. Cleveland Museum of Art, Ohio: 159*b*; the Norweb Collection: 213*b*; the Ellen Garretson Wade Memorial Collection: 77*a*; gift of J. H. Wade: 42*b*; purchase from the J. H. Wade Fund: 61*b*. Cliché des Musées Nationaux, Paris: 41*a*. Courtesy of the Cooper-Hewitt Museum of Decorative Arts and Design, Smithsonian Institution, New York: 65*c*, 226*c*. Copyright reserved: 151*b*. Copyright Country Life, London, from the Leonard Messell Collection, by kind permission of the Countess of Rosse: **87**. By permission of the Provost and Council, Coventry Cathedral, photo by P. W. and L. Thompson Limited, Coventry: **75**. Courtesy of the DAR Museum, Washington D.C.: 44*b*, 227*d*; photo by Helga Photo Studio: 80*d*. Denver Art Museum, Colorado, gift of Mrs Thelma Johns: 204*b*; gift of Dr Arnold L. Tannis: 82*c*. Dean and Chapter of Durham Cathedral: 164*b*. The Embroiderers' Guild Collection, London: **155**, **181**, **280**. The Essex Institute, Salem, Massachusetts, photo by Richard Merrill: 198*a*. Exeter Museum: 51*b*. The Fine Arts Museums of San Francisco, California, M. H. de Young Memorial Museum: 201*a*. By permission of the Syndics of the Fitzwilliam Museum, Cambridge: 12*c*, 29*b*, 33*a*, 49*a*. 53*a*, 69*a*, 71*a*, 81*a*, 82*b*, **97**, 101*c*,

107d, 113a, **115**, 117e, 121c, 123e, **126**, 147b, 171e, 196a, 203b, 205a, 214a, 215c, 220b, 232b, **251**, 253c, 267b, 272a, 281a, 281b, 287a. Werner Forman Archive, London/Private Collection: **58**. Gerona Cathedral, photo supplied by Ampliaciones y Reproducciones, MAS Barcelona: 84d. Glasgow Art Gallery and Museum, the Burrell Collection: 29a, 41c, 43b, 78b, 103d, 235d, 270e. Collections of Greenfield Village and the Henry Ford Museum, Dearborn, Michigan: 238a. By kind permission of Mrs C. Van Helfteren, photo A. C. Cooper Limited, London: **157**. Reproduced by courtesy of the Cecil Higgins Art Gallery, Bedford, photo Hawkley Studio Associates Limited, London: 54a. Historic Deerfield Inc., Massachusetts: 90b. Historische Museum, Basel: 133b. Holy Trinity, Sloane Street, London, photo by A. C. Cooper Limited, London: **239**. By kind permission of the Court of Assistants of the Honourable Artillery Company, London: **98**. Institute for History and Arts, Bucharest: **211**. International Folk Art Foundation. Collection in the Museum of New Mexico, Santa Fe, photos by David Stein: 83a, 136b, 149a, 189a. Collection the Jewish Museum, New York: 267a, 283b. *Journal of Indian Art and Industry*, Volume XIII, 1909: 159a. Kunsthistorisches Museum, Vienna: 140c, **180**. Kunstsammlungen des Bistums (Diözesanmuseum) Regensburg, photo by Wilkin Spitta: 224b. Kunstsammlungen zu Weimar, DDR, Schlossmuseum: 94b. Levi's Denim Art Contest, San Francisco, California: 82a, **137**, 146d. Lincoln City and County Museum, photo G. K. and J. Benton: 234c. Lord Dulverton: 193a. McCord Museum, Montreal: 106a. The Maidstone Museum and Art Gallery: 225b. Manchester Town Hall, photo Guttenberg Limited: 213c. Metropolitan Museum of Art, New York, Harris Brisbane Dick Fund, 1944: 37c; Fletcher Fund, 1927: 171c; Rogers Fund, 1922: 38b, Rogers Fund, 1936: 130d; gift of R. Thornton Wilson, 1943, in memory of Florence Ellsworth Wilson: 185d; collection of Mr and Mrs Charles B. Wrightsman: 274a. Moravian Museum of Bethlehem, Pennsylvania: 110a. William Morris Gallery, Walthamstow: 20a, 175a, 204a. Tony Morrison: **169**, **182**. Courtesy of the Mount Vernon Ladies' Association, Virginia: 72c. Moyse's Hall Museum, Bury St. Edmunds, photos by E. Leigh: 133c, 159c. Münchner Stadtmuseum, Munich: 21a. Lent by Miss Veronica Murphy, photos by A. C. Cooper Limited, London: **125**, **252**. Musée Cognacq-Jay, photo supplied by Photographie Bulloz, Paris: 95b. Musée Historique des Tissus, Lyon: 177a. Museum of the American Indian, Heye Foundation New York: 23a, 91a, 139b, **200**, 207c, 233c, 242b. Museum of Costume, Bath, photos by Desmond Tripp Studios Limited, Bristol: 26c, 62c, **138**. Museum of Cultural History, University of California, Los Angeles: 16a. By Courtesy of the Museum of Decorative Art, Copenhagen: 13b, 131c. Courtesy Museum of Fine Arts, Boston, Massachusetts, Helen and Alice Colburn Fund: 275a; The Elizabeth Day McCormick Collection: 84c, 93a, 142a. Museum Heimathaus Münsterland, Telgte: 139a. Museum für Kunst und Gewerbe, Hamburg: 13a, 60d. The Museum of Modern Art, New York, acquired through the Lillie P. Bliss Bequest: 55c. Museum of the Suffolk Regiment Association, Bury St Edmunds: 231a. National Army Museum, London: 64b, 132b, 135b, 171b, 183a. National Gallery of Art, Washington D.C.: 176b, 271a, 275d. National Museum of Canada: 183b. National Museum, Copenhagen: 166c. National Museum, Stockholm: 257c. National Portrait Gallery, London: 19a. The National Trust, Anglesey Abbey: 15a, 41b, 114b; Clandon Park, photo Hawkley Studio Associates, London: 122b; Cotehele House, photo by Robert Chapman: 68a; Gawthorpe Hall, Rachel Kay-Shuttleworth Collection: 117c; Hardwick Hall, photos by J. Whitaker: **85**, **158**; Knole, photo by J. Whitaker: 150c; Montacute House, photo by J. Bethell: **250**; Polesden Lacey, photo by J. Bethell: 213a; Wallington, photo by J. Bethell: **48**. Collection of the Newark Museum, New Jersey, photos by Armen: 21b, 263a;

gift of Miss Clara E. Ball, 1929: 225a; gift of J. Ackerman Coles, 1920, Coles Collection: 29c; Belinda Hearn Jouet Bequest, 1938: 205b; gift of Miss Myra H. Maxwell, in memory of Miss Grace Nicholson, 1952: **179**; gift of Miss Marie Porsch, 1946: 77b; gift of Miss C. Wood, 1933: 52a. Dorothea Nield: 229b. Norfolk Museums Service (Norwich Castle Museum): 244b; (Strangers Hall, Norwich): 16b, **18**, 20c, 22b, 23d, 25a, 27a, 28c, 30a, 33b, 37b, 37e, 39b, 39d, 40a, 40b, 50b, 50c, 51a, 52c, 54c, 56a, 56b, **57**, 59d, 60b, 63b, 65b, 67c, 73b, **76**, 79c, 80a, 80b, 89c, 89d, 90a, 90c, 94a, 104b, 107b, 109b, 110b, 112c, 117c, 118b, 120a, 122a, 123b, 124c, 129c, 129d, 143a, 153b, 153c, 160a, 160b, 163a, 166b, **167**, 174c, 178a, 184a, 184b, 185g, 187a, 188b, 191c, 194a, 197a, 197b, 208c, **210**, 215a, 216b, 217a, 218b, 218c, 224a, 226a, 232a, 242a, 243b, 245b, 245c, 245e, 246a, **249**, 254d, 255b, 256b, 260b, **262**, 263b, 263c, 265c, 266a, 277a, 278b, 282e, 284c; on loan from Canon Gilchrist: 264a; on loan from Shadingfield P.C.C.: 103c. Norsk Folkemuseum, Oslo: 189b, 207b. Norwich Cathedral: 24e. Old Gaol Museum, York, Maine: 14a. Old Sturbridge Village, Massachusetts: 43c, 108c, 228e; photo Donald F. Eaton: **279**. Österreichisches Museum für Angewandte Kunst, Vienna: 276a; photo supplied by Bundesdenkmalamt: 162a. From the Collection at Parham Park, Sussex: 172a, 196c. Peabody Museum, Salem, Massachusetts: 171d. Philadelphia Museum of Art, the Whitman Sampler Collection, given by Pet Incorporated, photo A. J. Wyatt: 283a. Mrs Phoebe Phillips: 118c, **127**, 130c, 134c, 247a, 265a. Photo Researchers Inc., New York, photo by Tomas D. W. Friedman: **36**; photo by Russ Kinne: 236d. The Pocumtuck Valley Memorial Association, Deerfield, Massachusetts: 81c. The Press Association Limited, London: 201d. By kind permission of Mr and Mrs Theodore Roosevelt IV, photo by Mary Lawrence Wathen: **212**. Royal Ontario Museum, Toronto: 105b. Mrs P. Russell, photo by Michael Dudley: **156**. The St Louis Art Museum, Missouri: 133f. St Martin's Episcopal Church, New Canaan, Connecticut, photo by Scutti Photography, Stamford: 61a. Saffron Walden Museum, Essex, photos by David Campbell: 30c, 63e, **116**, 120d. Reprinted by permission of Charles Scribner's Sons, from *4-Way Bargello* by Dorothy Kaestner, photo by George F. Kaestner: 111b. Shelburne Museum Inc., Vermont: 40d, 238c. Smithsonian Institution, Washington D.C.: 108b. Messrs Sotheby & Co., London: 188a. Spanish Colonial Arts Society, Inc., Collection in the Museum of New Mexico, Santa Fe: 63c. Staatliche Museen Preussischer Kulturbesitz, Kunstgewerbermuseum, Berlin: 118a. Strong Museum, Rochester, New York, photo Gary Calderwood: **240**. The Tate Gallery, London, photo A. C. Cooper Limited: **46**. Mr and Mrs A. C. Tuke, photo A. C. Cooper Limited, London: **222**. Mark Twain Memorial, Hartford, Connecticut: 148b, 282c. Victoria and Albert Museum, London, Crown copyright: 31c, 34b, 52b, 55b, 69b, 74a, 74b, 92a, 101b, 101d, 107c, 113b, 123d, 130a, 130b, 141a, 143c, 144a, 145b, 148a, 150b, 164c, 165b, 176d, 186a, 191b, 192a, 193c, 202f, 214b, 226b, 230a, 243a, 246b, 254c, 258b, 258c, 259c, 269a, 270a, 276b, 277b, 282a; photo C. Cannings: 25b, 131a, 161a, **168**; photo A. C. Cooper Limited: 55a, **261**. Courtesy Wadsworth Athenaeum, Hartford, Connecticut: 8-9. Weltiche Schatzkammer, Vienna, photo supplied by Kunsthistorisches Museum: 67b, 83b, 147a, 201c. Courtesy of the Wenham Historical Association and Museum, Inc., Massachusetts, photo by Markham Sexton, Salem: 32b, 96c. Western Americana Picture Library, Brentwood, Essex: 53c, 216a. Whitworth Art Gallery, University of Manchester: 271c. Mr and Mrs J. R. Williams: **86**. Courtesy, The Henry Francis du Pont Winterthur Museum, Delaware: contents page, **47**, **88**, 284b. Worshipful Company of Broderers, London: 39c; photo supplied by Victoria and Albert Museum, London: 65a. Mr and Mrs William Zorach, New York, photo by Mary Lawrence Wathen: **170**.

A Magyar Hazi ipar Diszitmenyei (n.d.): 72*b*, 175*c*. American Museum of Natural History. New York: 149*b*. Anson, 1960: 202*a*, 259*b*. Armes, 1939: 24*c*, 83*c*, 144*b*, 214*c*. *Art of the Great Lakes Indians*, 1973: 219*b*. Author's Collection: 28*b*, 43*a*, 80*c*, 90*d*, 107*a*, 152*a*, 235*a*, 235*b*, 236*b*, 237*a*, 248*a*, 253*b*, 260*c*, 267*c*, 268*a*. Norfolk Museums Service (Bridewell Museum of Local Industries and Rural Crafts, Norwich): 237*b*. *Broderies russes, tartares, arméniennes*, 1925: 19*b*. *The Calendar of the Prayer Book*, 1870: 143*b*. Carnegie Museum, Pittsburg: 228*c*. Caulfeild and Saward, 1882: 53*b*, 66*e*, 117*d*, 152*b*, 247*b*. Rt. Hon. J. Chichester-Clark: 206*a*. G. Christie, 1906: 66*b*, 105*c*, 273*a*. Colby, 1972: 67*a*, 105*a*, 124*a*, 247*c*, 281*e*, 284*a*. *Costume*, No. 5, 1971: 146*e*. Couvent des Bénédictins, Broumov, Czechoslovakia: 164*a*. Crawford, 1961: 140*a*. Currey, 1951: 59*b*. Dearner, 1920: 173*b*. De Farcy, 1919: 129*a*, 188*c*. Denver Art Museum, Colorado: 135*a*. Dhamija, 1964: 11*a*. Eastlake, 1969: 39*a*. *The Edinburgh Book of Plain Sewing*: 49*b*. *The Embroideress* (undated bound volume): 32*c*. *Embroidery*, Vol. XII, 4, 1961, P. King: 37*a*; Vol. XX, 1, 1969: 241*c*; Winter 1972, Mrs St Osyth: 284*d*. Emery, 1949: 63*d*. Ewing, 1974: 19*d*. Fairholt, 1846: 78*a*. Feder, 1971: 140*b*. Fél, 1961: 190*c*, 256*a*. Fry, 1935: 227*b*. Groves, 1966: 102*a*, 166*a*. Hall, 1901: 11*c*, 257*b*. Harris (n.d.): 277*b*. Hird, 1934: 78*c*, 110*c*, 132*a*, 254*a*. Hunt and Burshears, 1951: 154*d*, 228*d*. Irwin and Hall, 1973: 42*a*. Irwin and Hanish, 1970: 178*b*. Jessup, 1913: 255*d*. Johnstone, 1972: 119*b*. The Ladies' Treasury, 1887: 166*e*. *Ladies' Work Table Book*, 1858: 120*b*. Lambert, 1843: 89*a*, 171*a*. McCall's Book of Quilts: 220*a*. Mathews, 1960: 185*c*. Metropolitan Museum of Art, New York: 96*a*, 172*b*. Moyse's Hall, Bury St Edmunds: dedication page. Museum of Anthropology, University of British Columbia, Vancouver B.C.: 79*b*, 151*c*. National Museums of Canada, Ottawa: 183*b*. National Museum, Copenhagen: 185*e*. *Needlecraft*, 1890: 89*b*, 165*c*, 218*a*, 259*d*. Nevinson, 1968: 270*c*. Norfolk Museums Service (Strangers Hall), Norwich: 26*a*, 44*c*, 62*a*, 63*a*, 73*d*, 81*b*, 99*a*, 99*b*, 106*b*, 106*c*, 151*a*, 153*d*, 154*b*, 176*a*, 176*c*, 203*a*, 206*b*, 206*c*, 206*d*, 215*b*, 235*c*, 236*a*, 244*a*, 247*d*, 271*b*, 275*b*, 281*d*. Oakes and Hill, 1970: 38*c*. Pass, 1957: 83*d*. Pesel, 1913 and 1921: 23*b*, 54*b*, 56*c*, 84*a*, 84*b*, 133*e*, 145*a*, 153*a*, 161*e*, 234*a*, 247*e*. *The Queen Lady's Newspaper and Court Chronicle*, March 10th 1877: 93*b*; March 11th 1878: 226*d*; July 13th 1878: 44*d*; October 1881: 23*c*; supplement to 1881: 175*b*; March 25th 1882: 270*b*. Roediger, 1941: 216*d*. Roseaman, 1949: 185*a*, 185*b*. Royal Ontario Museum, University of Toronto: 229*a*, 281*c*. St Peter Mancroft, Norwich: 154*c*. Scanno, 1914: 198*b*. Speltz, 1959: 148*c*. Start, 1939: 136*a*, 190*b*, 192*b*. Strong, 1969: 129*b*. Swain, 1973: 166*a*. Tate Gallery, London: 255*a*, Thomas, 1934: 227*c*. Turner, 1955: 42*c*, 104*a*. Victoria and Albert Museum, London: title page, from photograph of detail of an English sampler dated 1661; 69*c*, 111*a*, 229*c*, 231*b*, 258*a*, 274*c*. Waring (n.d.): 236*c*. Wilson, 1964: 96*b*. The drawings for the alphabetical headings are based on the alphabet panel by Pat Russell, illustrated in colour on page 156.

The Prayse of the Needle

To all dispersed sorts of ARTS and TRADES,
I writ the needles prayse (that never fades)
So long as children shall be got or borne,
So long as garments shall be made or worne,
So long as Hemp or Flax or Sheep shall bear
Their linnen woollen fleeces yeare by yeare:
So long as Silk-wormes, with exhausted spoile,
Of their own Entrailes for mans gaine shall toyle.
Yea till the world be quite dissolv'd and past;
So long at least, the Needles use shall last:
And though from earth his being did begin,
Yet through the fire he did his honour win:
And unto those that doe his service lacke,
Hee's true as steele and mettle to the backe.
He hath I per se cye, small single sight,
Yet like a Pigmy, *Polipheme* in fight:
As a stout Captaine, bravely he leades on,
(Not fearing colours) till the worke be done,
Through thicke and thinne he is most sharpely
   set,
With speed through stitch, he will the conquest
   get.
And as a souldier Frenchefyde with heat,
Maim'd from the warres is forc'd to make
   retreat;
So when a Needles point is broke, and gone,
No point Mounsieur, he's maim'd, his worke is
   done.
And more the Needles honour to advance,
It is a Taylors Javelin, or his Launce;
And for my Countries quiet, I should like,
That women-kinde shoulde use no other Pike.
It will increase their peace, enlarge their store,
To use their tongues lesse, and their Needles
   more.
The Needles sharpnesse, profit yeelds, and
   pleasure,
But sharpnesse of the tongue, bites out of
   measure.
A Needle (though it be but small and slender)
Yet it is both a maker and a mender:
A grave Reformer of old Rents decayd,

Stops holes and seames and desperate cuts
   displayd,
And thus without the Needle we may see
We should without our Bibs and Biggins bee;
No shirts or Smockes, our nakednesse to hide,
No garments gay, to make us magnifide:
No shadowes, Shapparoones, Caules, Bands,
   Ruffs, Kuffs,
No Kerchiefes, Quoyfes, Chin-clouts, or
   Marry-Muffes,
No cros-cloathes, Aprons, Hand-kerchiefes, or
   Falls,
No Table-cloathes, for Parlours or for Halls,
No Sheetes, no Towels, Napkins, Pillow-beares,
Nor any Garment man or woman weares.
Thus is a needle prov'd and instrument
Of profit, pleasure, and of ornament.
Which mighty Queenes have grac'd in hand to
   take,
And high borne Ladies such esteeme did make,
That as their Daughters Daughters up did grow
The Needles Art, they to their children show.
And as 'twas then an exercise of praise,
So what deserves more honour in these dayes,
Than this? which daily doth itselfe expresse,
A mortall enemy to idlenesse.
The use of Sewing is exceeding old,
As in the sacred Text it is enrold:
Our Parents first in Paradise began,
Who hath descended since from man to man:
The mothers taught their Daughters, Sires their
   sons,
Thus in a line successively it runs
For generall profit, and for recreation,
From generation unto generation.
With work like Cherubims Embroidered rare,
The Covers of the Tabernacle were.
And by the Almighti's great command, we see,
That *Aarons* Garments broydered worke should
   be;
And further, God did bid his Vestments should
Be made most gay, and glorious to behold.